CliffsNotes®

ACT®

CRAM PLAN™

2nd Edition

William Ma, Jane R. Burstein, and Nichole Vivion

Houghton Mifflin Harcourt
Boston • New York

About the Authors

William Ma was chairman of the Math Department at the Herricks School District on Long Island for many years before retiring. He also taught as an adjunct math instructor at Baruch College, Columbia University, and Fordham University. He is the author of several books including two calculus review books, an SAT prep book, and was the author of an online review course for the New York State's Math A Regents Exam. He is currently a math consultant.

Jane Burstein taught English at Herricks High School in New Hyde Park, New York, for 36 years. She is the author of SAT, GMAT, and GRE prep books and has been an ACT and SAT tutor for 25 years, an instructor at Hofstra University, and a reader for AP exams.

Nichole Vivion is the author of several biology and test-prep publications including *CliffsNotes AP Biology Flashcards*, and is a contributor to *CliffsNotes Test Success for AP Biology*. She currently teaches upper school science courses in biology, biotechnology, environmental science, and public health at The Nightingale-Bamford School in New York City, where she also acts as chair of the science department.

Acknowledgments

My wife, Mary, and my daughters, Janet and Karen, who gave me much help in putting the book together. Copy editor Donna Wright, tech editors Mary Jane Sterling and Tom Page, and especially Christina Stambaugh, the developmental editor, for their patience and assistance.
—William Ma

I would like to thank my husband, David, and children, Jessica, Jonathan, Beth, and Seth, for their encouragement and helpful suggestions.
—Jane Burstein

Thanks to my husband Aleks for his ongoing support and humor throughout the writing process, and to my incredible colleagues for their constant inspiration and boundless knowledge.
—Nichole Vivion

Editorial

Executive Editor: Greg Tubach
Senior Developmental Editor: Christina Stambaugh
Copy Editor: Donna Wright
Technical Editors: Barbara Swovelin, Mary Jane Sterling, Scott Ryan, Tom Page, and Scott McDougall

Composition

Proofreader: Lynn Northrup

CliffsNotes® ACT® Cram Plan™, 2nd Edition

Copyright © 2014 by Houghton Mifflin Harcourt Publishing Company
All rights reserved.

Library of Congress Control Number: 2014931286
ISBN: 978-0-544-22726-2 (pbk)

Printed in the United States of America
DOC 10 9 8 7 6 5 4   4500568929

For information about permission to reproduce selections from this book, write to Permissions, Houghton Mifflin Harcourt Publishing Company, 215 Park Avenue South, New York, New York 10003.

www.hmhco.com

Table of Contents

Introduction xi
    An Overview of the Cram Plan for the ACT xi
    General Test-taking Strategies xi
    Using a Graphing Calculator xii
    Format of the ACT xii
    Security xiii

I. Two-Month Cram Plan for the ACT 1

II. One-Month Cram Plan for the ACT 5

III. One-Week Cram Plan for the ACT 9

IV. Diagnostic Test 11
    Answer Sheet 13
    Section 1: English Test 17
    Section 2: Mathematics Test 26
    Section 3: Reading Test 31
    Section 4: Science Test 38
    Section 5: Writing Test 50
    Scoring the Diagnostic Test 51
        Answer Key 51
            Section 1: English Test *51*
            Section 2: Mathematics Test *51*
            Section 3: Reading Test *52*
            Section 4: Science Test *52*
    Answer Explanations 53
        Section 1: English Test 53
            Passage I *53*
            Passage II *54*
            Passage III *55*
        Section 2: Mathematics Test 55
        Section 3: Reading Test 58
            Passage I *58*
            Passage II *59*
            Passage III *59*
            Passage IV *60*
        Section 4: Science Test 60
            Passage I *60*
            Passage II *61*
            Passage III *61*

     Passage IV 62
     Passage V 62
   Section 5: Writing Test 63
     Sample Scored Essays 63
 Scoring Worksheets 65
   Sections 1–4 65
     English Test 65
     Mathematics Test 66
     Reading Test 66
     Science Test 66
   Section 5: Writing Test 67
     The Rubric 67

V. English Test 69

 Format 69
 Content 69
 A. Usage and Mechanics 69
 B. Important Terms to Know 70
 C. Understanding Mechanics 70
   1. The Apostrophe 70
     a. To Indicate Possession 70
     b. In Contractions 71
     Examples 72
   2. Colons 72
     a. Before a List 72
     b. Before a Long, Formal Statement 73
     c. Before an Explanatory Statement 73
     Examples 73
   3. Semicolons 74
     a. Join Main Clauses 74
     b. Connection between Main Clauses 74
     c. Separate Main Clauses 74
     Examples 75
   4. Commas 75
     a. Separate Items in a Series 76
     b. Join Main Clauses 76
     c. Set off Expressions 76
     d. Direct Quotation 76
     e. Set Off an Appositive 77
     f. Non-restrictive Clause or Phrase 77
     g. Geographical Names, Addresses, and Dates 77
     h. Separate Two Adjectives 78
     i. Separate Contrasting Parts of a Sentence 78
     j. Introductory Phrase or Clause 78
     k. Avoid the Comma Splice Error 78
     Examples 79

5. The Dash...80
   a. Abrupt Break in Thought.......................................*80*
   b. Before a Summary...*80*
6. The Parentheses..80
   Examples..*81*
7. Question Marks and Exclamation Marks.................................81
   a. Question Marks...*81*
   b. Exclamation Marks..*82*
   Examples..*82*
D. Grammar and Usage...82
1. Pronoun Errors..83
   a. Pronoun Antecedent Agreement Errors..........................*83*
   b. Indefinite Pronouns..*83*
   c. Singular Antecedents and Singular Pronouns...................*84*
   d. Clear Antecedents..*84*
   e. Pronoun Case Errors..*85*
   Examples..*86*
2. Redundancy..87
   Examples..*88*
3. Idioms..88
   Examples..*89*
4. Modification..90
   a. Misplaced Modifiers..*90*
   b. Dangling Modifiers...*91*
   Examples..*91*
5. Parallelism...92
   Examples..*92*
6. Errors with Adjectives/Adverbs......................................93
   a. Comparisons..*93*
   b. Adjective/Adverb Confusion...................................*94*
   Examples..*94*
7. Diction...95
   Examples..*95*
8. Comparisons...96
   a. Illogical Comparisons..*96*
   b. Unbalanced Comparisons.......................................*96*
   c. Faulty Comparisons...*97*
   Examples..*97*
9. Agreement...97
   a. Agreement of Subject and Verb................................*98*
   b. Noun Agreement..*100*
   Examples...*100*
10. Tense...100
   Examples...*102*
11. Sentence Structure..103
   a. Run-on Sentences..*103*

        b. Sentence Fragments *103*

        Examples *104*

   E. Rhetoric 104

     1. Style 104

     2. Writing Strategy 105

     3. Organization 107

        a. Order and Coherence *107*

        b. Transitional Words and Phrases *108*

        Examples *109*

VI. Reading Test 111

   A. Overview of the ACT Reading Test 111

   B. General Strategies for the Reading Test 111

   C. Types of Reading Questions 112

     1. Main Idea 112

     2. Main Conflict Questions 112

     3. Passage-as-a-Whole Questions 112

     4. Main Point of a Paragraph 112

     5. Detail Questions 114

        a. Directly Stated Details *114*

        b. Implied Details *114*

     6. Relationships 115

        a. Comparison/Contrast *115*

        b. Cause and Effect *115*

        c. Sequence of Events *115*

     7. Generalizations 115

     8. Author's Voice and Method 117

     9. Vocabulary in Context 117

   D. Practice Questions 120

     Answer Explanations 123

VII. Strategies for Solving ACT Math Problems 125

VIII. Applying Pre-Algebra Skills 127

   A. Real Numbers 127

   B. Integers 128

   C. Fractions and Decimals 129

   D. Absolute Value 131

   E. Scientific Notation 132

   F. Exponents and Radicals 133

   G. Percents 134

   H. Ratios and Proportions 135

   I. Linear Equations 136

   J. Counting Problems 137

   K. Probability 139

   L. Mean, Median, and Mode 141

M. Data Interpretation 143
N. Sets 146

IX. Solving Elementary Algebra Problems 149
A. Rational Expressions 149
B. Properties of Exponents 150
C. Factoring Polynomials 151
D. Adding and Subtracting Polynomials 152
E. Multiplying and Dividing Polynomials 153
F. Quadratic Equations 153
G. Word Problems 154

X. Studying Intermediate Algebra 157
A. Algebraic Expressions 157
B. Algebraic Expressions Involving Absolute Value 158
C. Algebraic Expressions Involving Exponents and Radicals 159
D. Equations 161
E. Inequalities 162
F. Systems of Equations 163
G. Functions 164
H. Logarithmic and Exponential Functions 166
I. Modeling 167
J. Complex Numbers 169
K. Patterns and Sequences 170
L. Matrices 171

XI. Answering Coordinate Geometry Questions 173
A. Points, Lines, and Planes 173
B. Conic Sections and Other Curves 175
C. Odd and Even Functions 180
D. Graphing Inequalities 183
E. Slopes 186
F. Parallel and Perpendicular Lines 188
G. Midpoints 189
H. Distance Formula 190

XII. Working with Plane Geometry 191
A. Measurement of Angles and Line Segments 191
B. Properties of Triangles 193
C. Properties of Quadrilaterals 195
D. Similarity 197
E. Areas and Perimeters 200
F. Solids, Volumes, and Surface Areas 202
G. Properties of Circles 204
H. Concept of Proof 207
I. Transformations 209

XIII. Tackling Trigonometry 215
A. Trigonometry of the Right Triangle 215
B. Trigonometric Functions of Non-Acute Angles. 218
C. Laws of Sine and Cosine. 220
D. Graphs of Trigonometric Functions. 223
E. Trigonometric Identities 225
F. Solving Trigonometric Equations. 226

XIV. Science Test 227
A. Overview 227
B. General Strategies. 227
C. Visual Representations of Data. 229
   1. Understanding Data Tables. 229
   2. Understanding Graphs 230
D. Types of Science Questions 232

XV. Writing Test 243
A. Approach to the Essay: Thinking (2–3 minutes) 243
B. Approach to the Essay: Planning (2–3 minutes) 243
C. Approach to the Essay: Writing (18–22 minutes). 244
   1. State Thesis Clearly in Introductory Paragraph 244
   2. Develop Your Examples 244
   3. Organize Coherently 244
   4. State the Counterargument 245
   5. Use Active Verbs 246
   6. Vary Sentence Structure 246
D. Proofread (2–3 minutes). 246

XVI. Full-Length Practice Test with Answer Explanations 247
Format of the ACT Practice Test. 247
Answer Sheet. 249
Section 1: English Test 253
Section 2: Mathematics Test 271
Section 3: Reading Test 281
Section 4: Science Test. 292
Section 5: Writing Test 313
Scoring the Practice Test. 314
   Answer Key. 314
      Section 1: English Test. 314
      Section 2: Mathematics Test. 314
      Section 3: Reading Test. 315
      Section 4: Science Test. 315
   Answer Explanations 316
      Section 1: English Test 316
      Passage I. 316
      Passage II 316
      Passage III. 317

Passage IV..318
Passage V..318
Section 2: Mathematics Test.................................319
Section 3: Reading Test......................................325
Passage I...325
Passage II..326
Passage III...326
Passage IV...327
Section 4: Science Test......................................328
Passage I...328
Passage II..328
Passage III...329
Passage IV...330
Passage V..330
Passage VI...331
Passage VII..331
Section 5: Writing Test......................................332
Sample Scored Essays......................................332
Scoring Worksheets..335
Sections 1–4...335
English Test...335
Mathematics Test..335
Reading Test..335
Science Test..336

Appendix A. Using a Graphing Calculator 339

Appendix B. Common Math Formulas and Theorems for the ACT 347

Real Numbers..347
Sequences...347
Absolute Values...347
Exponents...348
Direct and Inverse Variation................................348
Measurement of Angles......................................348
Properties of Triangles......................................349
Similarity...349
Solids, Volumes, and Surface Areas..........................350
Properties of Circles...350
Coordinate Geometry..350
Slopes and Lines..350
Counting Principle..351
Probability..351
Mean, Median, and Mode....................................351
Quadratic Formula...351
Equation of a Parabola.......................................351
Equation of a Circle...352
Trigonometric Functions.....................................352
Pythagorean Identities.......................................352

Quotient Identities 352
Reciprocal Identities 352
Functions of the Sum of Two Angles 352
Functions of the Double Angle 352
Law of Sines 353
Law of Cosines 353
Properties of Logarithms. 353
Graphs of Sine and Cosine 353

Introduction

Many juniors and seniors take the ACT as part of the college admissions process. By taking this test, students give the admissions officers an objective standard that can be used to compare one student to other students. Colleges use these scores, along with the high school transcripts, résumés of extracurricular activities, letters of recommendation, and application essays as a guide to predict how well each individual will do in college-level courses.

Now that you have decided to take this exam, you are ready to begin the preparation process. All you need for success is some time and determination. Whether you have two months, one month, or one week, you can achieve your goals if you are organized, hard-working, and willing to stick to the plan.

This guide introduces you to different sections of the test, provides you with three sample schedules to help you plan your preparation, and presents guided practice to help improve your English, mathematics, reading, and science skills. For those students who are taking the optional Writing Test, Chapter XV reviews writing strategies.

An Overview of the Cram Plan for the ACT

The ACT is not an intelligence test; it is an achievement test. This means that it tests your ability in four content areas: English, mathematics, reading, and science (and writing if you opt for the Writing Test). The best way to get ready for this test is to first determine exactly how much time you have to prepare and then follow the appropriate plan: the two-month plan, the one-month plan, or the one-week plan.

Each plan has a schedule for you to follow along with the approximate time you will need to allot to each task. In addition, subject review chapters give you strategies for that part of the test. Included in each subject-review chapter are practice exercises to assist you in the areas in which you are weakest and to help you continue to maximize your strengths.

Once you determine which cram plan to follow, the next step is to take the Diagnostic Test. The Diagnostic Test will help you diagnose your areas of weakness: those parts of the test on which you will need to focus your attention. The answer explanations will guide you to the specific chapters that cover the topics in which you need the most help. After the Diagnostic Test, you will find a scoring guide that will give you an indication of your baseline score on each section of the ACT. Then you can begin to focus on the subject review chapters. After you have completed the review, you can take the Practice Test, a full-length simulated ACT.

General Test-taking Strategies

- Become familiar with the format of the test. If you know what to expect, you will be less nervous and more confident on the day of the test.
- Use this book to familiarize yourself with the directions to each section of the test. Knowing the directions to each section ahead of time will save you precious minutes on the day of the test.

- Work at a steady pace. You do not have the time to get bogged down on any one question. If you are having difficulty with a question, take your best educated guess and move on. The Diagnostic Test and the Practice Test will help you learn to pace yourself properly.

- Read each question very carefully, and be sure you know exactly what it asks. Many questions require you to note very specific details. Watch for **signal words** like *most, seldom, highest*, and *lowest*.

- Always read all the answer choices carefully, and use **POE** (Process of Elimination) to narrow down the choices.

- Use the answer choices to help you when you are unsure. On any multiple-choice test, the answer is always right in front of you.

- If you take the Writing Test, read the prompt carefully, and be sure to address the issue as it is presented.

- Make sure you completely fill in the corresponding circle on your answer sheet. Check yourself every 5 questions.

- There is no guessing penalty on the ACT. Answer **EVERY** question. Confirm that you have filled in only one circle for each question. Carefully erase any changed answers.

- Bring everything you will need with you on the day of the test: sharpened no. 2 pencils with good erasers, calculator, and tissues. It is a good idea to bring your own watch; you cannot be sure you will have a visible clock in the testing room, and cell phones are prohibited. Don't forget to have your admission ticket and photo ID with you.

Using a Graphing Calculator

All questions in the math portion of the ACT can be solved without a calculator; however, using a calculator, particularly a graphing calculator, can help you solve a problem faster and avoid making careless errors. In this book, every question that can be solved with the help of a graphing calculator is indicated by a calculator icon. However, this icon does not appear on the actual ACT exam. A special section on how to use a graphing calculator to solve some of the ACT math questions is included in Appendix A.

Please note that some calculators are NOT permitted on the ACT Mathematics Test, for example: Texas Instruments' TI-89, TI-92, and TI-Nspire CAS; Hewlett-Packard's HP 48GII; and Casio's Algebra fx 2.0, ClassPad 300, and ClassPad 330. To see the most up-to-date list of calculators permitted on the ACT Mathematics Test, visit www.actstudent.org/faq/calculator.html or call 319-337-1510 for a recorded message.

Note: Use of a calculator is not permitted on the ACT Science Test.

Format of the ACT

The ACT is a multiple-choice test comprised of four sections and one optional Writing Test (the essay). Section 1, the English Test, contains questions on grammar, usage, and rhetoric. Section 2, the Mathematics Test, is comprised of questions on pre-algebra, elementary algebra, intermediate algebra, coordinate geometry, plane geometry, and trigonometry. Section 3, the Reading Test, is comprised of four passages taken from different content areas including fiction, the social sciences, the humanities, and the natural sciences. Section 4, the Science Test, covers the application of science reasoning in biology, chemistry, earth/space sciences, and physics. The optional Writing Test, a persuasive essay in response to a specific prompt, is given after the first four sections. The multiple-choice test alone takes 2 hours and 55 minutes; the essay takes an additional 30 minutes.

Test	# of Questions	# of Minutes
English	75	45
Mathematics	60	60
Reading	40	35
Science	40	35
Optional Writing Assessment	1	30

Security

To ensure that all students have equal opportunity to demonstrate their abilities, the ACT administrators have instituted updated security procedures. When registering for the test, test-takers must electronically submit a current photo (head and shoulders only). This photo will be printed on the roster so proctors will be able to match the test-taker's photo ID to the photo on the roster. The photo will also be printed on the score report.

I. Two-Month Cram Plan for the ACT

	English	Mathematics	Reading	Science
8 weeks before the test	**Study Time:** 3 hours ❏ Take **Diagnostic Test** and review answer explanations. ❏ Based on the questions you missed, identify difficult topics and their corresponding chapters. These topics are your targeted topics. ❏ Compare your Writing Test (essay) to the rubric and the samples and target areas to improve.			

7 weeks before the test	**Study Time:** 1½ hours
	❏ **English Test:** Chapter V
	  ❏ Read Sections A–B.
	  ❏ Read Sections C.1–C.3 and do half the practice questions at the end of each section. For targeted topics, do all practice questions.
		Study Time: 3 hours
		❏ **Using a Graphing Calculator:** Appendix A
		  ❏ Do all problems.
		❏ **Applying Pre-Algebra Skills:** Chapter VIII
		  ❏ Do all practice problems.
		❏ **Strategies for Solving ACT Math Problems:** Chapter VII
		  ❏ Study.
			Study Time: 15 minutes
			❏ **Reading Test:** Chapter VI
			  ❏ Read Sections A–B.
				Study Time: 15 minutes
				❏ **Science Test:** Chapter XIV
				  ❏ Read Section A.

6 weeks before the test	**Study Time:** 1½ hours
	❏ **English Test:** Chapter V
	  ❏ Read Sections C.4–C.7 and do half the practice questions at the end of each section. For targeted topics, do all practice questions.
		Study Time: 2 hours
		❏ **Common Math Formulas and Theorems for the ACT:** Appendix B
		  ❏ Read and review.
		❏ **Solving Elementary Algebra Problems:** Chapter IX
		  ❏ Do all practice problems.
			Study Time: 30 minutes
			❏ **Reading Test:** Chapter VI
			  ❏ Read Sections C.1–C.4.
			  ❏ Do Practices 1 and 2.
				Study Time: 15 minutes
				❏ **Science Test:** Chapter XIV
				  ❏ Read Section B.

continued

	English	Mathematics	Reading	Science

5 weeks before the test	**Study Time:** 1½ hours
	❑ **English Test:** Chapter V
	  ❑ Read Sections D.1–D.5 and do half the practice questions at the end of each section. For targeted topics, do all practice questions.
		Study Time: 3 hours
		❑ Review targeted areas.
		❑ **Studying Intermediate Algebra:** Chapter X
		  ❑ Do all practice problems.
		❑ **Answering Coordinate Geometry Questions:** Chapter XI
		  ❑ Do all practice problems.
			Study Time: 30 minutes
			❑ **Reading Test:** Chapter VI
			  ❑ Read Sections C.5.a.–C.5.b.
			  ❑ Do Practice 3.
				Study Time: 20 minutes
				❑ **Science Test:** Chapter XIV
				  ❑ Read Section C.
				  ❑ Practice reading charts and graphs.

4 weeks before the test	**Study Time:** 1½ hours
	❑ **English Test:** Chapter V
	  ❑ Read Sections D.6–D.11 and do half the practice questions at the end of each section. For targeted topics, do all practice questions.
		Study Time: 3 hours
		❑ Review targeted areas.
		❑ **Working with Plane Geometry:** Chapter XII
		  ❑ Do all practice problems.
			Study Time: 30 minutes
			❑ **Reading Test:** Chapter VI
			  ❑ Read Sections C.6.a–c. and C.7.
			  ❑ Do Practice 4.
				Study Time: 30 minutes
				❑ **Science Test:** Chapter XIV
				  ❑ Read the introduction to Section D.
				  ❑ Read Passage I and answer questions 1–5. Review answers.

3 weeks before the test	**Study Time:** 1½ hours
	❑ **English Test:** Chapter V
	  ❑ Read Sections E.1–E.3 and do half the practice questions at the end of each section. For targeted topics, do all practice questions.
		Study Time: 2 hours
		❑ Review targeted areas.
		❑ **Tackling Trigonometry:** Chapter XIII
		  ❑ Do all practice problems.
			Study Time: 30 minutes
			❑ **Reading Test:** Chapter VI
			  ❑ Read Sections C.8 and C.9.
			  ❑ Do Practice 5.
				Study Time: 30 minutes
				❑ **Science Test:** Chapter XIV
				  ❑ Read Passages II–III in Section D and answer questions 6–15. Review answers.

2 weeks before the test	**Study Time:** 4 hours ❑ If you plan to do the Writing Test (essay), review Chapter XV. ❑ Take the entire **Practice Test** (2 hours, 55 minutes) and review your answers. Note those topics that you still need to work on. These are your targeted topics.			

	English	Mathematics	Reading	Science
7 days before the test	**Study Time:** 30 minutes ❑ **English Test:** Chapter V ❑ Review targeted topics in Sections C.1–C.3. ❑ For targeted topics, review all practice questions. Do any questions you have not already done.	**Study Time:** 1½ hours ❑ **Using a Graphing Calculator:** Appendix A ❑ Review. ❑ **Applying Pre-Algebra Skills:** Chapter VIII ❑ Review. ❑ **Strategies for Solving ACT Math Problems:** Chapter VII ❑ Study.	**Study Time:** 30 minutes ❑ **Reading Test:** Chapter VI ❑ Review targeted topics. Look over practice exercises.	**Study Time:** 20 minutes ❑ **Science Test:** Chapter XIV ❑ Review targeted topics.
6 days before the test	**Study Time:** 30 minutes ❑ **English Test:** Chapter V ❑ Review targeted topics in Sections C.4–C.7. ❑ For targeted topics, review all practice questions. Do any questions you have not already done.	**Study Time:** 1 hour ❑ **Common Math Formulas and Theorems for the ACT:** Appendix B ❑ Review. ❑ **Solving Elementary Algebra Problems:** Chapter IX ❑ Review.	**Study Time:** 30 minutes ❑ **Reading Test:** Chapter VI ❑ Continue review of targeted topics. Do practice questions 1–3 in Section D.	**Study Time:** 20 minutes ❑ **Science Test:** Chapter XIV ❑ Continue review of targeted topics.
5 days before the test	**Study Time:** 30 minutes ❑ **English Test:** Chapter V ❑ Review targeted topics in Sections D.1–D.5. ❑ For targeted topics, review all practice questions. Do any questions you have not already done.	**Study Time:** 1½ hours ❑ **Studying Intermediate Algebra:** Chapter X ❑ Review.	**Study Time:** 30 minutes ❑ **Reading Test:** Chapter VI ❑ Continue review of targeted topics. Do practice questions 4–5 in Section D.	**Study Time:** 15 minutes ❑ **Science Test:** Chapter XIV ❑ Practice reading charts and graphs.
4 days before the test	**Study Time:** 30 minutes ❑ **English Test:** Chapter V ❑ Review targeted topics in Sections D.6–D.11. ❑ For targeted topics, review all practice questions. Do any questions you have not already done.	**Study Time:** 1½ hours ❑ **Answering Coordinate Geometry Questions:** Chapter XI ❑ Review.	**Study Time:** 30 minutes ❑ **Reading Test:** Chapter VI ❑ Continue review of targeted topics. Do practice questions 6–8 in Section D.	**Study Time:** 15 minutes ❑ **Science Test:** Chapter XIV ❑ Practice reading charts and graphs.

continued

	English	Mathematics	Reading	Science
3 days before the test	**Study Time:** 30 minutes ❑ **English Test:** Chapter V 　❑ Review targeted topics in Section E. 　❑ For targeted topics, review all practice questions. Do any questions you have not already done.	**Study Time:** 1½ hours ❑ **Working with Plane Geometry:** Chapter XII 　❑ Review.	**Study Time:** 30 minutes ❑ **Reading Test:** Chapter VI 　❑ Continue review of targeted topics. Do practice questions 9–10 in Section D.	**Study Time:** 20 minutes ❑ **Science Test:** Chapter XIV 　❑ Reread Sections A–B.
2 days before the test	**Study Time:** 15 minutes ❑ **English Test:** Chapter V 　❑ Reread Sections A–B.	**Study Time:** 1 hour ❑ **Tackling Trigonometry:** Chapter XIII 　❑ Review.	**Study Time:** 15 minutes ❑ **Reading Test:** Chapter VI 　❑ Reread Sections A–B.	**Study Time:** 15 minutes ❑ **Science Test:** Chapter XIV 　❑ Reread Section C.
Night before the test	❑ Relax! You are well prepared for the test. Be confident in your ability to do well. ❑ Exercise. It helps to relieve stress, improve sleep quality, and boost brain performance. ❑ Get a good night's sleep. Try to unplug from electronic devices at least 30 minutes before bedtime and remove any distractions that might wake you during the night.			
Morning of the test	**Reminders:** ❑ Eat a well-balanced, nutritious breakfast. ❑ Take the following items with you to the test: 　❑ Your admission ticket and photo ID 　❑ Several no. 2 pencils and erasers 　❑ A calculator with fresh batteries 　❑ A watch ❑ Try to go outside for a few minutes and walk around before the test to relieve stress. ❑ **Most important:** Stay calm and confident during the test. Take deep, slow breaths and think positive thoughts if you feel nervous. You can do it!			

II. One-Month Cram Plan for the ACT

	English	Mathematics	Reading	Science
4 weeks before the test	**Study Time:** 3 hours ❑ Take **Diagnostic Test** and review answer explanations. ❑ Based on the questions you missed, identify difficult topics and their corresponding chapters. These topics are your targeted topics. ❑ Compare your Writing Test (essay) to the rubric and the samples and target areas to improve.			
	Study Time: 3 hours ❑ **English Test:** Chapter V ❑ Read Sections A–B. ❑ Read Sections C.1–C.7 and do half the practice questions at the end of each section. For targeted topics, do all practice questions.	**Study Time:** 5 hours ❑ **Using a Graphing Calculator:** Appendix A ❑ Do all practice problems. ❑ **Common Math Formulas and Theorems for the ACT:** Appendix B ❑ Read and review. ❑ **Applying Pre-Algebra Skills:** Chapter VIII ❑ Do all practice problems. ❑ **Solving Elementary Algebra Problems:** Chapter IX ❑ Do all practice problems. ❑ **Strategies for Solving ACT Math Problems:** Chapter VII ❑ Study.	**Study Time:** 1 hour ❑ **Reading Test:** Chapter VI ❑ Read Sections A–C.4. ❑ Do Practices 1 and 2.	**Study Time:** 45 minutes ❑ **Science Test:** Chapter XIV ❑ Read Sections A–C.
3 weeks before the test	**Study Time:** 4½ hours ❑ **English Test:** Chapter V ❑ Read Sections D.1–D.11 and E.1–E.3. ❑ Do half the practice questions at the end of each section. For targeted topics, do all practice questions.	**Study Time:** 6 hours ❑ **Studying Intermediate Algebra:** Chapter X ❑ Do all practice problems. ❑ **Answering Coordinate Geometry Questions:** Chapter XI ❑ Do all practice problems. ❑ **Working with Plane Geometry:** Chapter XII ❑ Do all practice problems. ❑ **Tackling Trigonometry:** Chapter XIII ❑ Do all practice problems.	**Study Time:** 1½ hours ❑ **Reading Test:** Chapter VI ❑ Read Sections C.5–C.9. ❑ Do Practices 3–5.	**Study Time:** 1 hour ❑ **Science Test:** Chapter XIV ❑ Read Section D. ❑ Answer questions 1–15 and review answers.
2 weeks before the test	**Study Time:** 4 hours ❑ If you plan to do the Writing Test (essay), review Chapter XV. ❑ Take the entire **Practice Test** (2 hours, 55 minutes), and review your answers. Note those topics that you still need to work on. These are your targeted topics.			

continued

	English	Mathematics	Reading	Science

7 days before the test	**Study Time:** 30 minutes
	❏ **English Test:** Chapter V
	  ❏ Review targeted topics in Sections C.1–C.3.
	  ❏ For targeted topics, review all practice questions. Do any questions you have not already done.
		Study Time: 1½ hours
		❏ **Using a Graphing Calculator:** Appendix A
		  ❏ Review.
		❏ **Applying Pre-Algebra Skills:** Chapter VIII
		  ❏ Read and review.
		❏ **Strategies for Solving ACT Math Problems:** Chapter VII
		  ❏ Study.
			Study Time: 30 minutes
			❏ **Reading Test:** Chapter VI
			  ❏ Review targeted topics. Look over practice exercises.
				Study Time: 20 minutes
				❏ **Science Test:** Chapter XIV
				  ❏ Review targeted topics.

6 days before the test	**Study Time:** 30 minutes
	❏ **English Test:** Chapter V
	  ❏ Review targeted topics in Sections C.4–C.7.
	  ❏ For targeted topics, review all practice questions. Do any questions you have not already done.
		Study Time: 1 hour
		❏ **Common Math Formulas and Theorems for the ACT:** Appendix B
		  ❏ Review.
		❏ **Solving Elementary Algebra Problems:** Chapter IX
		  ❏ Review.
			Study Time: 30 minutes
			❏ **Reading Test:** Chapter VI
			  ❏ Continue review of targeted topics. Do practice questions 1–3 in Section D.
				Study Time: 20 minutes
				❏ **Science Test:** Chapter XIV
				  ❏ Continue review of targeted topics.

5 days before the test	**Study Time:** 30 minutes
	❏ **English Test:** Chapter V
	  ❏ Review targeted topics in Sections D.1–D.5.
	  ❏ For targeted topics, review all practice questions. Do any questions you have not already done.
		Study Time: 1½ hours
		❏ **Studying Intermediate Algebra:** Chapter X
		  ❏ Review.
			Study Time: 30 minutes
			❏ **Reading Test:** Chapter VI
			  ❏ Continue review of targeted topics. Do practice questions 4–5 in Section D.
				Study Time: 20 minutes
				❏ **Science Test:** Chapter XIV
				  ❏ Continue review of targeted topics.
				  ❏ Practice reading charts and graphs.

4 days before the test	**Study Time:** 30 minutes
	❏ **English Test:** Chapter V
	  ❏ Review targeted topics in Sections D.6–D.11.
	  ❏ For targeted topics, review all practice questions. Do any questions you have not already done.
		Study Time: 1½ hours
		❏ **Answering Coordinate Geometry Questions:** Chapter XI
		  ❏ Review.
			Study Time: 30 minutes
			❏ **Reading Test:** Chapter VI
			  ❏ Continue review of targeted topics. Do practice questions 6–8 in Section D.
				Study Time: 15 minutes
				❏ **Science Test:** Chapter XIV
				  ❏ Practice reading charts and graphs.

	English	Mathematics	Reading	Science
3 days before the test	**Study Time:** 30 minutes ❏ **English Test:** Chapter V ❏ Review targeted topics in Section E. ❏ For targeted topics, review all practice questions. Do any questions you have not already done.	**Study Time:** 1½ hours ❏ **Working with Plane Geometry:** Chapter XII ❏ Review.	**Study Time:** 30 minutes ❏ **Reading Test:** Chapter VI ❏ Continue review of targeted topics. Do practice questions 9–10 in Section D.	**Study Time:** 20 minutes ❏ **Science Test:** Chapter XIV ❏ Reread Sections A–B.
2 days before the test	**Study Time:** 15 minutes ❏ **English Test:** Chapter V ❏ Reread Sections A–B.	**Study Time:** 1 hour ❏ **Tackling Trigonometry:** Chapter XIII ❏ Review.	**Study Time:** 15 minutes ❏ **Reading Test:** Chapter VI ❏ Reread Sections A–B.	**Study Time:** 15 minutes ❏ **Science Test:** Chapter XIV ❏ Reread Section C.
Night before the test	❏ Relax! You are well prepared for the test. Be confident in your ability to do well. ❏ Exercise. It helps to relieve stress, improve sleep quality, and boost brain performance. ❏ Get a good night's sleep. Try to unplug from electronic devices at least 30 minutes before bedtime and remove any distractions that might wake you during the night.			
Morning of the test	**Reminders:** ❏ Eat a well-balanced, nutritious breakfast. ❏ Take the following items with you to the test: ❏ Your admission ticket and photo ID ❏ Several no. 2 pencils and erasers ❏ A calculator with fresh batteries ❏ A watch ❏ Try to go outside for a few minutes and walk around before the test to relieve stress. ❏ **Most important:** Stay calm and confident during the test. Take deep, slow breaths and think positive thoughts if you feel nervous. You can do it!			

III. One-Week Cram Plan for the ACT

	English	Mathematics	Reading	Science
7 days before the test	**Study Time:** 3 hours ❑ Take **Diagnostic Test** and review answer explanations. ❑ Based on the questions you missed, identify difficult topics and their corresponding chapters. These topics are your targeted topics. ❑ Compare your Writing Test (essay) to the rubric and the samples and target areas to improve.			
	Study Time: 15 minutes ❑ **English Test:** Chapter V 　❑ Read Sections A–B.	**Study Time:** 1½ hours ❑ **Using a Graphing Calculator:** Appendix A 　❑ Do all problems. ❑ **Common Math Formulas and Theorems for the ACT:** Appendix B 　❑ Read and review. ❑ **Strategies for Solving ACT Math Problems:** Chapter VII 　❑ Study.	**Study Time:** 1 hour ❑ **Reading Test:** Chapter VI 　❑ Read Sections A–C.4. 　❑ Do Practices 1 and 2.	**Study Time:** 30 minutes ❑ **Science Test:** Chapter XIV 　❑ Read Sections A–B.
6 days before the test	**Study Time:** 2 hours ❑ **English Test:** Chapter V 　❑ Read Sections C.1–C.7. 　❑ Do a few practice questions at the end of each section. 　❑ For targeted topics, do half the practice questions.	**Study Time:** 2½ hours ❑ **Applying Pre-Algebra Skills:** Chapter VIII 　❑ Do all practice problems. ❑ **Solving Elementary Algebra Problems:** Chapter IX 　❑ Do all practice problems.	**Study Time:** 1 hour ❑ **Reading Test:** Chapter VI 　❑ Read Sections C.5–C.7. 　❑ Do Practices 3 and 4.	**Study Time:** 15 minutes ❑ **Science Test:** Chapter XIV 　❑ Read Section C.
5 days before the test	**Study Time:** 2 hours ❑ **English Test:** Chapter V 　❑ Read Sections D.1–D.5. 　❑ Do a few practice questions at the end of each section. 　❑ For targeted topics, do half the practice questions.	**Study Time:** 2½ hours ❑ **Studying Intermediate Algebra:** Chapter X 　❑ Do all practice problems. ❑ **Answering Coordinate Geometry Questions:** Chapter XI 　❑ Do all practice problems.	**Study Time:** 30 minutes ❑ **Reading Test:** Chapter VI 　❑ Read Sections C.8–C.9. 　❑ Do Practice 5.	**Study Time:** 30 minutes ❑ **Science Test:** Chapter XIV 　❑ Read the introduction to Section D. 　❑ Read Passage I and answer questions 1–5. Review answers.

continued

	English	Mathematics	Reading	Science

4 days before the test	**Study Time:** 2 hours
	❏ **English Test:** Chapter V
	  ❏ Read Sections D.6–D.11 and do a few practice questions at the end of each section.
	  ❏ For targeted topics, do half the practice questions.
	  ❏ Read Sections E.1–E.3 and do practice questions in each section.
		Study Time: 2½ hours
		❏ **Working with Plane Geometry:** Chapter XII
		  ❏ Do all practice problems.
		❏ **Tackling Trigonometry:** Chapter XIII
		  ❏ Do all practice problems.
			Study Time: 45 minutes
			❏ **Reading Test:** Chapter VI
			  ❏ Do additional practice (Section D) at the end of the chapter.
				Study Time: 30 minutes
				❏ **Science Test:** Chapter XIV
				  ❏ Read Passages II–III in Section D and answer questions 6–15. Review answers.

3 days before the test	**Study Time:** 4 hours ❏ If you plan to do the Writing Test (essay), review Chapter XV. ❏ Take the entire **Practice Test** (2 hours, 55 minutes), and review your answers. Note those topics that you still need to work on. These are your targeted topics.			

2 days before the test	**Study Time:** 1 hour
	❏ **English Test:** Chapter V
	  ❏ Review the targeted areas. Do a few more practice questions in each section.
		Study Time: 1 hour
		  ❏ Review the targeted areas.
		❏ **Common Math Formulas and Theorems for the ACT:** Appendix B
		  ❏ Reread and review.
			Study Time: 1 hour
			❏ **Reading Test:** Chapter VI
			  ❏ Reread and review targeted topics.
			  ❏ Look over practice exercises.
				Study Time: 45 minutes
				❏ **Science Test:** Chapter XIV
				  ❏ Review the targeted topics.
				  ❏ Practice reading charts and graphs.

Night before the test	❏ Relax! You are well prepared for the test. Be confident in your ability to do well. ❏ Exercise. It helps to relieve stress, improve sleep quality, and boost brain performance. ❏ Get a good night's sleep. Try to unplug from electronic devices at least 30 minutes before bedtime and remove any distractions that might wake you during the night.			

Morning of the test	**Reminders:**
	❏ Eat a well-balanced, nutritious breakfast.
	❏ Take the following items with you to the test:
	  ❏ Your admission ticket and photo ID
	  ❏ Several no. 2 pencils and erasers
	  ❏ A calculator with fresh batteries
	  ❏ A watch
	❏ Try to go outside for a few minutes and walk around before the test to relieve stress.
	❏ **Most important:** Stay calm and confident during the test. Take deep, slow breaths and think positive thoughts if you feel nervous. You can do it!			

IV. Diagnostic Test

This Diagnostic Test (excluding the essay) is half the length of the actual ACT. You will have a full 30 minutes for the essay.

The Diagnostic Test covers four content areas: English, Mathematics, Reading, and Science. The tests are designed to measure your ability in these four areas and to predict your success in college. Each question on the test is numbered. Choose the best answer for each question and fill in the corresponding circle on the answer sheet provided.

For each question, be sure to fill in only one circle on your answer sheet. If you erase, do so completely as the scoring device will pick up any stray marks. (Although this Diagnostic Test is just for practice and is not being mechanically scored, you should practice the way you would like to perform on the actual test.)

Your score will be based on the number of questions you have answered correctly during the time allowed for each section, so answer **all** questions, even if you are unsure and have to guess. Since no points will be deducted for incorrect answers, it is to your advantage to answer every question on the test.

If you finish a section before the allotted time runs out, you may not work on any other section. You may not go back to a previous section or move ahead to work on the next section.

You may use any open spaces on your test booklet for scrap.

The Diagnostic Test also includes the optional Writing Test. The Writing Test is an essay in which you demonstrate your writing and thinking skills. It is administered after the four sections of the ACT are completed. For more on the Writing Test, see Chapter XV.

Timing: You will need 1 hour and 59 minutes to complete the Diagnostic Test.

Test	# of Questions	# of Minutes
English	38	23
Mathematics	30	30
Reading	20	18
Science	20	18
Writing	1	30

After you complete the test, use the Answer Key and the Scoring Worksheets to obtain your scaled scores.

To score the Writing Test (Essay), refer to the rubric on pages 67–68 and to the sample essays and their evaluations starting on page 63.

Answer Sheet

Section 1: English Test

#		
1	Ⓐ Ⓑ Ⓒ Ⓓ	
2	Ⓕ Ⓖ Ⓗ Ⓙ	
3	Ⓐ Ⓑ Ⓒ Ⓓ	
4	Ⓕ Ⓖ Ⓗ Ⓙ	
5	Ⓐ Ⓑ Ⓒ Ⓓ	
6	Ⓕ Ⓖ Ⓗ Ⓙ	
7	Ⓐ Ⓑ Ⓒ Ⓓ	
8	Ⓕ Ⓖ Ⓗ Ⓙ	
9	Ⓐ Ⓑ Ⓒ Ⓓ	
10	Ⓕ Ⓖ Ⓗ Ⓙ	
11	Ⓐ Ⓑ Ⓒ Ⓓ	
12	Ⓕ Ⓖ Ⓗ Ⓙ	
13	Ⓐ Ⓑ Ⓒ Ⓓ	
14	Ⓕ Ⓖ Ⓗ Ⓙ	
15	Ⓐ Ⓑ Ⓒ Ⓓ	
16	Ⓕ Ⓖ Ⓗ Ⓙ	
17	Ⓐ Ⓑ Ⓒ Ⓓ	
18	Ⓕ Ⓖ Ⓗ Ⓙ	
19	Ⓐ Ⓑ Ⓒ Ⓓ	
20	Ⓕ Ⓖ Ⓗ Ⓙ	
21	Ⓐ Ⓑ Ⓒ Ⓓ	
22	Ⓕ Ⓖ Ⓗ Ⓙ	
23	Ⓐ Ⓑ Ⓒ Ⓓ	
24	Ⓕ Ⓖ Ⓗ Ⓙ	
25	Ⓐ Ⓑ Ⓒ Ⓓ	

#	
26	Ⓕ Ⓖ Ⓗ Ⓙ
27	Ⓐ Ⓑ Ⓒ Ⓓ
28	Ⓕ Ⓖ Ⓗ Ⓙ
29	Ⓐ Ⓑ Ⓒ Ⓓ
30	Ⓕ Ⓖ Ⓗ Ⓙ
31	Ⓐ Ⓑ Ⓒ Ⓓ
32	Ⓕ Ⓖ Ⓗ Ⓙ
33	Ⓐ Ⓑ Ⓒ Ⓓ
34	Ⓕ Ⓖ Ⓗ Ⓙ
35	Ⓐ Ⓑ Ⓒ Ⓓ
36	Ⓕ Ⓖ Ⓗ Ⓙ
37	Ⓐ Ⓑ Ⓒ Ⓓ
38	Ⓕ Ⓖ Ⓗ Ⓙ

Section 2: Mathematics Test

#	
1	Ⓐ Ⓑ Ⓒ Ⓓ Ⓔ
2	Ⓕ Ⓖ Ⓗ Ⓙ Ⓚ
3	Ⓐ Ⓑ Ⓒ Ⓓ Ⓔ
4	Ⓕ Ⓖ Ⓗ Ⓙ Ⓚ
5	Ⓐ Ⓑ Ⓒ Ⓓ Ⓔ
6	Ⓕ Ⓖ Ⓗ Ⓙ Ⓚ
7	Ⓐ Ⓑ Ⓒ Ⓓ Ⓔ
8	Ⓕ Ⓖ Ⓗ Ⓙ Ⓚ
9	Ⓐ Ⓑ Ⓒ Ⓓ Ⓔ
10	Ⓕ Ⓖ Ⓗ Ⓙ Ⓚ
11	Ⓐ Ⓑ Ⓒ Ⓓ Ⓔ
12	Ⓕ Ⓖ Ⓗ Ⓙ Ⓚ
13	Ⓐ Ⓑ Ⓒ Ⓓ Ⓔ
14	Ⓕ Ⓖ Ⓗ Ⓙ Ⓚ
15	Ⓐ Ⓑ Ⓒ Ⓓ Ⓔ
16	Ⓕ Ⓖ Ⓗ Ⓙ Ⓚ
17	Ⓐ Ⓑ Ⓒ Ⓓ Ⓔ
18	Ⓕ Ⓖ Ⓗ Ⓙ Ⓚ
19	Ⓐ Ⓑ Ⓒ Ⓓ Ⓔ
20	Ⓕ Ⓖ Ⓗ Ⓙ Ⓚ
21	Ⓐ Ⓑ Ⓒ Ⓓ Ⓔ
22	Ⓕ Ⓖ Ⓗ Ⓙ Ⓚ
23	Ⓐ Ⓑ Ⓒ Ⓓ Ⓔ
24	Ⓕ Ⓖ Ⓗ Ⓙ Ⓚ
25	Ⓐ Ⓑ Ⓒ Ⓓ Ⓔ

#	
26	Ⓕ Ⓖ Ⓗ Ⓙ Ⓚ
27	Ⓐ Ⓑ Ⓒ Ⓓ Ⓔ
28	Ⓕ Ⓖ Ⓗ Ⓙ Ⓚ
29	Ⓐ Ⓑ Ⓒ Ⓓ Ⓔ
30	Ⓕ Ⓖ Ⓗ Ⓙ Ⓚ

Section 3: Reading Test

#	
1	Ⓐ Ⓑ Ⓒ Ⓓ
2	Ⓕ Ⓖ Ⓗ Ⓙ
3	Ⓐ Ⓑ Ⓒ Ⓓ
4	Ⓕ Ⓖ Ⓗ Ⓙ
5	Ⓐ Ⓑ Ⓒ Ⓓ
6	Ⓕ Ⓖ Ⓗ Ⓙ
7	Ⓐ Ⓑ Ⓒ Ⓓ
8	Ⓕ Ⓖ Ⓗ Ⓙ
9	Ⓐ Ⓑ Ⓒ Ⓓ
10	Ⓕ Ⓖ Ⓗ Ⓙ
11	Ⓐ Ⓑ Ⓒ Ⓓ
12	Ⓕ Ⓖ Ⓗ Ⓙ
13	Ⓐ Ⓑ Ⓒ Ⓓ
14	Ⓕ Ⓖ Ⓗ Ⓙ
15	Ⓐ Ⓑ Ⓒ Ⓓ
16	Ⓕ Ⓖ Ⓗ Ⓙ
17	Ⓐ Ⓑ Ⓒ Ⓓ
18	Ⓕ Ⓖ Ⓗ Ⓙ
19	Ⓐ Ⓑ Ⓒ Ⓓ
20	Ⓕ Ⓖ Ⓗ Ⓙ

Section 4: Science Test

#	
1	Ⓐ Ⓑ Ⓒ Ⓓ
2	Ⓕ Ⓖ Ⓗ Ⓙ
3	Ⓐ Ⓑ Ⓒ Ⓓ
4	Ⓕ Ⓖ Ⓗ Ⓙ
5	Ⓐ Ⓑ Ⓒ Ⓓ
6	Ⓕ Ⓖ Ⓗ Ⓙ
7	Ⓐ Ⓑ Ⓒ Ⓓ
8	Ⓕ Ⓖ Ⓗ Ⓙ
9	Ⓐ Ⓑ Ⓒ Ⓓ
10	Ⓕ Ⓖ Ⓗ Ⓙ
11	Ⓐ Ⓑ Ⓒ Ⓓ
12	Ⓕ Ⓖ Ⓗ Ⓙ
13	Ⓐ Ⓑ Ⓒ Ⓓ
14	Ⓕ Ⓖ Ⓗ Ⓙ
15	Ⓐ Ⓑ Ⓒ Ⓓ
16	Ⓕ Ⓖ Ⓗ Ⓙ
17	Ⓐ Ⓑ Ⓒ Ⓓ
18	Ⓕ Ⓖ Ⓗ Ⓙ
19	Ⓐ Ⓑ Ⓒ Ⓓ
20	Ⓕ Ⓖ Ⓗ Ⓙ

Section 5: Writing Test

Section 1: English Test

23 Minutes—38 Questions

Directions: The English Test consists of three passages. In each passage, words and phrases are underlined and numbered. Following each passage are corresponding questions (on the actual exam, passages appear in the left-hand column, with corresponding questions in the right-hand column). Each question offers four alternatives for the underlined part. Consider the choices and then select the one that best fits the requirements of standard written English. Be sure to take into account the style and tone of the whole passage. If you think the word or phrase is correct as written, choose "NO CHANGE." For some of the questions, you will see a number in a box, which corresponds to a similar number within the passage. These questions ask about a section of the passage or about the passage as a whole. It is a good idea to read through the entire passage before you begin to answer the questions.

Passage I

The Tale of the Tail

[1]

Famous the world over, the cats of the Isle of Man <u>are famous</u> for the distinct absence of an attri-
₁
bute—their tails. These Manx, as the breed is <u>known</u>
₂
<u>are solid, stocky cats</u>, with dense coats and a distinc-
₂
tive round shape. Sometimes referred to as "rump-

ies," these cats <u>are either completely tailless or have</u>
₃
small stumps in place of the long, graceful tails of

other breeds.

1.
   A. NO CHANGE
   B. is notable
   C. was known
   D. are known

2.
   F. NO CHANGE
   G. known, are solid stocky cats
   H. known, are solid, stocky cats
   J. known are solid stocky cats

3.
   A. NO CHANGE
   B. either are completely tailless or have
   C. are, either completely tailless, or they have
   D. either are completely tailless or having

[2]

Many theories <u>have arose</u> about the origin of the
                    4
Manx. There is a rather humorous story that explains the cat's tailless state. According to this tale, Noah <u>was about to closing</u> the door to the ark
                              5
when he realized a cat was missing. This particular <u>cat; an excellent mouser, was stalking its prey</u> when
                                                      6
the rains began to fall. <u>Persistently unwilling to</u> give
                          7
up the chase, the cat continued its hunt as the water began to rise. Noah, anxious to seal the ark, began to close the great doors. Suddenly, the door closed, accidentally severing the cat's tail. ⬚8 Thus, the breed was born.

4.
F. NO CHANGE
G. have arisen
H. arised
J. had arose

5.
A. NO CHANGE
B. has been closing
C. was about to close
D. closed

6.
F. NO CHANGE
G. cat, an excellent mouser, was stalking their prey
H. cat, an excellent mouser, was stalking its prey
J. cat, an excellent mouser was stalking its prey

7. Three of the choices indicate that the cat was intent on accomplishing its goal. Which choice does NOT do so?

A. NO CHANGE
B. Loath to
C. Reluctant to
D. Resigned to

8. The writer is considering adding the following sentence at this point in the paragraph:

Consequently, that is the story of Noah and the cat.

Would this addition be appropriate here?

F. Yes, because it is an appropriate transitional sentence.
G. Yes, because it effectively concludes the story.
H. No, because it fails to include any relevant information.
J. No, because the following sentence provides a more appropriate conclusion to the paragraph.

[3]

Another myth about the Manx attributes its tailless state to <u>the proclivity of ancient warriors to decorate</u> their helmets with furry tails. Aware that their offspring would face imprisonment and possible death at the hands of the soldiers, mother cats bit off <u>it's kittens' tails</u> so the kittens would not be taken captive.

[4]

<u>Still another</u> conjecture involves the so-called "cabbit." In this legend, long ago on the Isle of Man, a cat and a rabbit mated, producing a round, tailless offspring that combined their physical traits.

9. Which of the following would NOT be an appropriate replacement for the underlined part?
   - **A.** the habit of ancient warriors of decorating
   - **B.** the fact that there was a tendency of ancient warriors who wanted to decorate
   - **C.** the inclination of ancient warriors to decorate
   - **D.** the tendency of ancient warriors to decorate

10.
   - **F.** NO CHANGE
   - **G.** its kitten's tail
   - **H.** their kittens tail
   - **J.** their kittens' tails

11. For the sake of logic and coherence, which would be the best transitional phrase to use?
   - **A.** NO CHANGE
   - **B.** Nevertheless,
   - **C.** In contrast,
   - **D.** Moreover,

[5]

Today, animal biologists consider the Manx to be a genetic mutation <u>at this time</u>. Since the Isle of
12
Man is a rather geographically isolated location, once the dominant mutant tailless gene appeared in the animal population, <u>it became</u> concentrated in
13
the gene pool. Thus, the "typical" cat on the island became the tailless variety. [14] [15]

12.
   F.   NO CHANGE
   G.   presently
   H.   currently
   J.   Omit the underlined portion

13.
   A.   NO CHANGE
   B.   they became
   C.   it has become
   D.   it was becoming

14. Suppose after rereading this essay the writer wants to add the following detail:

The long hind legs of the Manx and its peculiar hopping gait reinforce this speculation.

The most logical and effective place would be after the last sentence in which paragraph?
   F.   2
   G.   3
   H.   4
   J.   5

15. Suppose the writer had intended to write a scholarly essay disproving current theories about the influx of cats in Europe. Would this essay successfully fulfill that goal?
   A.   Yes, because the essay is formal in tone and covers the topic thoroughly.
   B.   Yes, because the essay cites relevant historical and statistical evidence to disprove the theories.
   C.   No, because the essay is not scholarly in tone and does not disprove any theories.
   D.   No, because the essay conclusively proves a theory.

Passage II

The Great Wall

[1]

The Great Wall of China is one of the Seven Wonders of the World. <u>Built</u> over 2,000 years ago by
16
Emperor Qin Shi Huang of China during the Qin Dynasty, <u>they wind</u> up and down for 4,000 miles
17
over mountains and plateaus. It is the longest man-made structure in the world.

[2]

The wall was conceived as a <u>defensive fortification</u>
18
<u>to protect the ones inside against marauders coming</u>
18
<u>from outside.</u> Each of the geographical regions
18
along the route <u>was</u> charged with constructing a seg-
19
ment. Thousands of soldiers, prisoners, and local townspeople <u>hauled and packed thousands of tons</u>
20
<u>of stones</u> and <u>earth, some sections</u> are up to
20   21

16.
- **F.** NO CHANGE
- **G.** Having been built
- **H.** It was built
- **J.** It had been built

17.
- **A.** NO CHANGE
- **B.** it winds
- **C.** it is winding
- **D.** which winds

18.
- **F.** NO CHANGE
- **G.** defensive fortification
- **H.** defensive fortification to protect and defend
- **J.** way to be a defensive fortification to protect and defend

19.
- **A.** NO CHANGE
- **B.** were
- **C.** were being
- **D.** was being

20.
- **F.** NO CHANGE
- **G.** hauled, and packed thousands of tons of stones
- **H.** hauled, and packed, thousands of tons of stones
- **J.** hauled and packed; thousands of tons of stones

21.
- **A.** NO CHANGE
- **B.** earth, in some sections
- **C.** earth. Some sections
- **D.** earth; with some sections

21

twenty-five feet high. The wall <u>not only was wide</u>
[22]

<u>enough for troops but</u> also for horse-pulled wagons
[22]

to travel across. Set at regular intervals along the

wall, watch towers and guard stations provided

lookouts and living quarters for soldiers. 23

[3]

The Emperor <u>envisioned the wall as protecting</u>
[24]

the Chinese Empire from invading armies.

<u>In addition</u>, many segments of the wall were never
[25]

<u>connected together with each other</u>. Since the
[26]

22.
- **F.** NO CHANGE
- **G.** not was wide enough for only troops and
- **H.** was wide enough for not only troops as well as
- **J.** was wide enough not only for troops but

23. The writer is considering adding the following information to the end of the preceding sentence.

   , who were often on duty for months at a time

   If the writer made this addition, the sentence would:

   - **A.** gain an interesting detail.
   - **B.** gain a transition.
   - **C.** become anecdotal.
   - **D.** contrast with the preceding one.

24. Which of the following choices would be acceptable to replace the underlined words?
   - **F.** imagined the wall would be to protect
   - **G.** envisioned the wall to be protection of
   - **H.** imagined the wall for protecting
   - **J.** imagined the wall would protect

25.
- **A.** NO CHANGE
- **B.** For example
- **C.** However
- **D.** On the other hand

26.
- **F.** NO CHANGE
- **G.** connected
- **H.** able to have a connection with each other
- **J.** linked as a connection

sections of the wall <u>is not contiguous</u>, it never
27

achieved its original purpose. It is, however, one of

the most visited tourist sites in the world. <u>People
28</u>

<u>with a camera</u> come from all over the world to pho-
28

tograph this amazing sight. 29

27.
- **A.** NO CHANGE
- **B.** is not linked
- **C.** are not contiguous
- **D.** has not been connected

28.
- **F.** NO CHANGE
- **G.** People who have a camera
- **H.** People with cameras
- **J.** People who bring a camera

29. Which of the following sentences, if included here, would best conclude the essay?

- **A.** I was there last year, and it was a thrill to walk on the wall.
- **B.** If you go to China, don't miss the wall!
- **C.** A visit to the wall is a reminder of the great perseverance and determination of the Chinese people.
- **D.** In China there are also many other great places to visit.

Passage III

Those Popular Penguins

[1]

These tuxedo-clad flightless birds, always fascinating to human beings, have become pop culture icons. No <u>lesser</u> than five films in the past five years
₃₀
have featured the birds. It is not hard to understand the popularity of <u>penguins: They</u> are "well-dressed,"
₃₁
playful, and <u>they are</u> unafraid of people. <u>Indeed,</u>
₃₂   ₃₃
these striking <u>bird's with their</u> distinct waddle <u>have</u>
₃₄   ₃₅
<u>become</u> synonymous with winter fun. Clumsy on
₃₅

30.
- **F.** NO CHANGE
- **G.** less
- **H.** lower
- **J.** fewer

31.
- **A.** NO CHANGE
- **B.** penguins, they
- **C.** penguins being
- **D.** penguins; who

32.
- **F.** NO CHANGE
- **G.** Omit underlined part
- **H.** they have been
- **J.** being

33. The writer would like to use a transitional word for emphasis here. What would best accomplish this?
- **A.** NO CHANGE
- **B.** For instance
- **C.** Nevertheless
- **D.** Similarly

34.
- **F.** NO CHANGE
- **G.** birds with its
- **H.** birds' with their
- **J.** birds with their

35.
- **A.** NO CHANGE
- **B.** has become
- **C.** has became
- **D.** have became

land, yet graceful in the water, <u>scientists have found</u>
₃₆

penguins <u>are superbly adapted to</u> life in the arctic.
₃₇

They have no land predators and need only to be

protected <u>away from</u> eager tourists.
₃₈

36.
    F.   NO CHANGE
    G.   Omit underlined part
    H.   scientists are finding
    J.   as found by scientists,

37. Which of the following would NOT be an acceptable replacement for the underlined part?

    A.   are well equipped for
    B.   are perfectly suited to
    C.   are able to be adapted to
    D.   are well suited to

38.
    F.   NO CHANGE
    G.   by
    H.   from
    J.   with

IF YOU FINISH BEFORE TIME IS CALLED, CHECK YOUR WORK ON THIS SECTION ONLY. DO NOT WORK ON ANY OTHER SECTION IN THE TEST.

Section 2: Mathematics Test

30 Minutes—30 Questions

Directions: Solve each problem and fill in the corresponding circle on the answer sheet. Figures are not necessarily drawn to scale. You may use a permitted graphing calculator.

1. If m and n are integers, which of the following must be an even integer?

   A. $m + n$
   B. $2m + 3n$
   C. $3m + 2n$
   D. $2(m + n)$
   E. $3(m + n)$

2. If $2(2^2) = 2^k$, what is the value of k?

   F. 0
   G. 1
   H. 2
   J. 3
   K. 4

3. Six years ago, Mary was x years old and Bill was exactly twice as old as Mary. Which of the following represents the sum of their current ages?

   A. $3x - 12$
   B. $3x - 6$
   C. $3x$
   D. $3x + 6$
   E. $3x + 12$

4. If $\overline{DE} \parallel \overline{BC}$, $DE = 3$, $AD = x$, and $DB = 2x$, what is the length of $\overline{BC}$?

   F. 3
   G. 6
   H. 9
   J. 12
   K. 15

5. A furniture store carries dining room sets consisting of tables and chairs as described here:

Tables	Chairs
Teak	with arms
Walnut	without arms
Oak	

   How many different dining room sets, consisting of 1 type of table and 1 type of chair, does the store offer?

   A. 2
   B. 3
   C. 5
   D. 6
   E. 8

6. If x is a negative integer, and $xy = -2$ and $y + x = 1$, what is the value of x?

   F. -2
   G. -1
   H. 0
   J. 1
   K. 2

7. Points B, C, and D lie on a straight line, and $\triangle ABC$ is isosceles. The measure of vertex $\angle A$ is $2x$. If $m\angle ACD = 140$, what is the value of x?

   A. 25
   B. 30
   C. 50
   D. 60
   E. 80

8. In the accompanying diagram, two lines intersect. Which of the following must be true?

   I. $x = 50$
   II. $y = 40$
   III. $x + y = 90$

   F. I only
   G. II only
   H. I and II only
   J. II and III only
   K. I, II, and III

9. If a function f is defined as $f(x) = x^2 + 4$, what is the value of $3f(1) + 2$?

   A. 15
   B. 17
   C. 21
   D. 39
   E. 85

10. Which of the following could be an equation of the accompanying figure?

   F. $y = -(x - 3)^2$
   G. $y = -x^2 + 3$
   H. $y = -|x| - 3$
   J. $y = -|x + 3| + 1$
   K. $y = -|x - 3| - 1$

11. What is the slope of the line passing through the points $A(-2,4)$ and $B(-6,-8)$?

   A. -3
   B. $-\dfrac{1}{3}$
   C. $\dfrac{1}{2}$
   D. $\dfrac{1}{3}$
   E. 3

12. Given that k is an integer and if k is decreased by 25 percent of itself, the result is 24, what is the value of k?

   F. 18
   G. 28
   H. 32
   J. 36
   K. 40

13. In the accompanying semicircle with center O, $\overline{AC}$ is a diameter, $AC = 8\sqrt{2}$, and $AB = BC$. What is the sum of the areas of the two shaded regions?

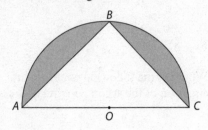

A. $16\pi + 16\pi$
B. $16\pi - 32$
C. $32 + 16\pi$
D. $16\pi + 32$
E. $32 + 32$

14. An equation of a circle is given as $x^2 + (y - 3)^2 = 1$. What is the area of this circle?

F. π
G. 2π
H. 3π
J. 9π
K. 10π

15. If n is a positive integer, and twice the square of n is the same as four times n, what is the value of n?

A. -4
B. -2
C. 0
D. 2
E. 4

16. If the midpoint of $A(2,4)$ and $B(h,k)$ is $(4,2)$, what is the value of k?

F. -2
G. 0
H. 2
J. 4
K. 6

17. At a bakery, the price of a doughnut is $0.80. After the first doughnut, each additional doughnut is $0.40. If Mary paid $4.00 for doughnuts, how many doughnuts did Mary buy?

A. 5
B. 6
C. 8
D. 9
E. 10

18. In the accompanying diagram, $CB = 12$, $AB = 13$, and $m\angle C = 90$. What is the value of $\cos A$?

F. $\dfrac{1}{13}$
G. $\dfrac{5}{13}$
H. $\dfrac{12}{13}$
J. $\dfrac{13}{12}$
K. 13

19. A square is inscribed in a circle with a radius of 10. What is the area of the square?

A. 100
B. $100\sqrt{2}$
C. 200
D. $200\sqrt{2}$
E. 400

20. What is the sum of the 5th and the 15th terms of the sequence 0, 5, 10, 15, …?

    F. 20
    G. 30
    H. 50
    J. 90
    K. 100

21. Which of the following points could represent the coordinate of $B + 2C$?

    A. A
    B. B
    C. F
    D. D
    E. E

22. Which of the following is an odd function?

    F. $h(x) = 3x - 5$
    G. $k(x) = x^2 - 7x + 9$
    H. $p(x) = x^3 - 3$
    J. $q(x) = x^3 + 1$
    K. $f(x) = x^5 - 2x^3$

23. If n is a positive integer and $\left(8^{\frac{2}{3}}\right)\left(n^{\frac{1}{4}}\right) = 16$, what is the value of n?

    A. 2
    B. 8
    C. 16
    D. 64
    E. 256

24. Let M be a set of real numbers that can be expressed as $2n^2 + 3$, where n is an integer. Which of the following could be a member of set M?

    F. −5
    G. 4
    H. 13
    J. 20
    K. 35

25. If 2 coins are tossed, what is the probability that you will have at least one head?

    A. $\dfrac{1}{8}$
    B. $\dfrac{1}{4}$
    C. $\dfrac{1}{3}$
    D. $\dfrac{1}{2}$
    E. $\dfrac{3}{4}$

26. Set $A = \{-2, -1, 0, 2, 3, 4\}$. If set B contains only members obtained by multiplying each member of set A by −1, what is the median of set B?

    F. −2
    G. −1
    H. 0
    J. 1
    K. 2

27. In the accompanying diagram, the figure is a rectangular solid. Line segment $\overline{AG}$ is not shown. If $HG = 6$, $GF = 4$, and $CG = 2$, what is the length of $\overline{AG}$?

    Not drawn to scale

    A. $\sqrt{40}$
    B. $\sqrt{54}$
    C. $\sqrt{56}$
    D. 8
    E. 12

29

28. If $\log_2 8 + \log_5 25 = \log_3 x$, what is the value of x?

    F. 15
    G. 34
    H. 81
    J. 125
    K. 243

29. If $0 < \theta < \dfrac{\pi}{2}$, which of the following is equivalent to $\dfrac{\cos\theta}{\sqrt{1-\sin^2\theta}}$?

    A. -1
    B. $-2 - \cos 2x$
    C. $2 - \sin x$
    D. $1 + \cos\theta$
    E. 1

30. Given $i = \sqrt{-1}$, which of the following is equivalent to $2i(i^3 - 4i)$?

    F. -6
    G. $-6i^2$
    H. 6
    J. 7
    K. 10

IF YOU FINISH BEFORE TIME IS CALLED, CHECK YOUR WORK ON THIS SECTION ONLY. DO NOT WORK ON ANY OTHER SECTION IN THE TEST.

STOP

Section 3: Reading Test

18 Minutes—20 Questions

Directions: The Reading Test consists of four passages, each followed by five questions. After reading a passage, select the best answer and fill in the corresponding circle on the answer sheet. You may look back in the passages as you answer the questions.

Passage I

Prose Fiction

The following is an excerpt from *Anne of Green Gables*, a novel written in 1908 by Lucy Maud Montgomery. The story is set in Green Gables, a farm on Prince Edward Island in Canada owned by siblings Matthew and Marilla Cuthbert. Mrs. Rachel, a neighbor of the Cuthberts, is a well-known gossip.

Mrs. Rachel, before she had fairly closed the door, had taken a mental note of everything that was on that table. There were three plates laid, so that Marilla must be expecting
(5) some one home with Matthew to tea; but the dishes were everyday dishes and there was only crab-apple preserves and one kind of cake, so that the expected company could not be any particular company. Yet what of
(10) Matthew's white collar and the sorrel mare? Mrs. Rachel was getting fairly dizzy with this unusual mystery about quiet, unmysterious Green Gables.

"Good evening, Rachel," Marilla said
(15) briskly. "This is a real fine evening, isn't it? Won't you sit down? How are all your folks?"

Something that for lack of any other name might be called friendship existed and always had existed between Marilla Cuthbert and
(20) Mrs. Rachel, in spite of—or perhaps because of—their dissimilarity.

Marilla was a tall, thin woman, with angles and without curves; her dark hair showed some gray streaks and was always twisted up
(25) in a hard little knot behind with two wire hairpins stuck aggressively through it. She looked like a woman of narrow experience and rigid conscience, which she was; but there was a saving something about her mouth which, if it
(30) had been ever so slightly developed, might have been considered indicative of a sense of humor.

"We're all pretty well," said Mrs. Rachel. "I was kind of afraid YOU weren't, though,
(35) when I saw Matthew starting off today. I thought maybe he was going to the doctor's."

Marilla's lips twitched understandingly. She had expected Mrs. Rachel up; she had known that the sight of Matthew jaunting off so
(40) unaccountably would be too much for her neighbor's curiosity.

"Oh, no, I'm quite well although I had a bad headache yesterday," she said. "Matthew went to Bright River. We're getting a little boy
(45) from an orphan asylum in Nova Scotia and he's coming on the train tonight."

If Marilla had said that Matthew had gone to Bright River to meet a kangaroo from Australia Mrs. Rachel could not have been
(50) more astonished. She was actually stricken dumb for five seconds. It was unsupposable that Marilla was making fun of her, but Mrs. Rachel was almost forced to suppose it.

"Are you in earnest, Marilla?" she
(55) demanded when voice returned to her.

"Yes, of course," said Marilla, as if getting boys from orphan asylums in Nova Scotia were part of the usual spring work on any well-regulated Avonlea farm instead of being
(60) an unheard of innovation.

Mrs. Rachel felt that she had received a severe mental jolt. She thought in exclamation points. A boy! Marilla and Matthew Cuthbert

(65) of all people adopting a boy! From an orphan asylum! Well, the world was certainly turning upside down! She would be surprised at nothing after this! Nothing!

(70) "What on earth put such a notion into your head?" she demanded disapprovingly. This had been done without her advice being asked, and must perforce be disapproved.

1. It can be inferred that Mrs. Rachel's dizziness is due to:

   A. the speed with which she hurried to the Cuthbert's farm.
   B. the inexplicable series of events leading up to this conversation.
   C. her fear that Marilla and Matthew were about to embark on a dangerous undertaking.
   D. her concern about Matthew's illness.

2. The physical description of Marilla suggests which of the following?

   F. Despite her circumscribed life, she is capable of seeing humor in life's situations.
   G. She is a warm, motherly woman with a soft, endearing manner.
   H. With very little persuasion, she would be willing to bend her moral code.
   J. Although she lives on a farm, she is sophisticated and urbane.

3. The reference to the kangaroo (line 48) suggests all of the following EXCEPT:

   A. the preposterous nature of the idea that Marilla and Matthew would adopt a child.
   B. Mrs. Rachel's astonishment that this turn of events could have transpired without her awareness.
   C. Avonlea farm is located in the Australian outback.
   D. taking in a child from an orphan asylum is not an everyday occurrence.

4. It can be reasonably inferred from the passage that:

   F. the close relationship between Mrs. Rachel and Marilla is based on the similarity of their lives and circumstances.
   G. Mrs. Rachel's surprise is a direct reflection of her inattention to detail and lack of perceptiveness.
   H. Mrs. Rachel prides herself on her ability to be well informed about events in her neighborhood.
   J. many farmers had previously adopted young orphans to help with the work on the farm.

5. The narrator's tone in the last sentence of the passage (lines 69–71) is:

   A. humorously ironic.
   B. contemptuously hostile.
   C. intensely disapproving.
   D. unabashedly sentimental.

Passage II

Social Science

The following passage is adapted from *The Life of Abraham Lincoln* written by Henry Ketcham in 1901. In this excerpt, the author describes the events leading up to Lincoln's taking office.

South Carolina was the first state to secede, and since Fort Sumter commanded Charleston Harbor, it instantly became the focus of national interest. The Secretary of War, Floyd,
(5) had so dispersed the little army of the United States that it was impossible to command the few hundred men necessary adequately to garrison the United States forts. As matters in and about Charleston grew threatening, Major
(10) Anderson, who was in command of the twin forts, Moultrie and Sumter, decided to abandon the former and do his utmost to defend the latter. The removal was successfully accomplished in the night, and when the fact was discovered it

(15) was greeted by the South Carolinians with a howl of baffled wrath. Buchanan had endeavored to send provisions. The steamer, *Star of the West,* had gone there for that purpose, but had been fired on by the South Carolinians and

(20) forced to abandon the attempt.

When Lincoln took the government at Washington, it may well be believed that he found matters in a condition decidedly chaotic. His task was many sided, a greater task than

(25) that of Washington as he had justly said. First, of the fifteen slave states seven had seceded. It was his purpose to hold the remaining eight, or as many of them as possible. Of this number, Delaware and Maryland could have been held

(30) by force. Kentucky and Missouri, though slave states, remained in the Union. The Union party in Tennessee, under the lead of Andrew Johnson, made a strong fight against secession, but failed to prevent the ordinance.

(35) The next task of Lincoln was to unite the North as far as possible. The difficulty of doing this has already been set forth. On the other hand there was in the North a sentiment that had been overlooked. It was devotion to the

(40) flag. Benjamin F. Butler, though an ardent democrat, had cautioned his southern brethren that while they might count on a large pro-slavery vote in the North, war was a different matter. The moment you fire on the flag, he said, you

(45) unite the North; and if war comes, slavery goes.

Not the least task of the President was in dealing with foreign nations. The sympathies of these, especially England and France, were ardently with the South. They would eagerly

(50) grasp at the slightest excuse for acknowledging the Southern Confederacy as an independent nation. It was a delicate and difficult matter so to guide affairs that the desired excuse for this could not be found.

(55) The tactics of the southerners were exceedingly exasperating. They kept "envoys" in Washington to deal with the government. Of course these were not officially received. Lincoln sent them a copy of his inaugural

(60) address as containing a sufficient answer to their questions. But they stayed on, trying to spy out the secrets of the government, trying

to get some sort of a pledge of conciliation from the administration, or, what would

(65) equally serve the purpose, to exasperate the administration into some unguarded word or act. Their attempts were a flat failure.

6. It can be reasonably inferred from the passage that the author believes that Lincoln was:

   F. overwhelmed by the formidable task he faced in Washington.

   G. able to handle the day-to-day practicalities, but unable to deal competently with the larger issues.

   H. a shrewd politician who manipulated his enemies into failure.

   J. a pragmatic leader who was an accomplished multi-tasker.

7. All of the following contributed to the "howl of baffled wrath" (line 16) EXCEPT:

   A. the tactics of Secretary of State Floyd regarding the positioning of troops.

   B. Major Anderson's decision to concentrate his forces at Fort Sumter.

   C. the secession of South Carolina.

   D. the attempted landing of the *Star of the West*.

8. It can be inferred from the passage that:

   F. although many in the North were sympathetic to the slaveholders, patriotism and belief in the Union were strong enough to unite the region.

   G. the Northern manufacturers depended on slave labor for raw materials and would not support the Union against the Confederacy.

   H. President Lincoln was so embroiled in domestic issues, international affairs were of little concern.

   J. had President Lincoln agreed to answer questions from leaders of the Confederacy, he could have averted the Civil War.

9. According to the passage, Lincoln faced all of the following difficulties EXCEPT:

    A. the presence of Southern spies in Washington.

    B. keeping Kentucky and Missouri in the Union.

    C. maintaining the support of European nations.

    D. holding on to the support of the pro-slave faction in the North.

10. The word "delicate" in line 52 suggests:

    F. the debated issues concerned matters that could easily erupt in scandal.

    G. without tactful diplomacy by Lincoln, European nations would side with the South.

    H. the relationship between England and France was fragile.

    J. escalating tensions between the North and the South had resulted in an uneasy truce.

Passage III

Humanities

The following passage is adapted from the *Memoir of Jane Austen* written by Austen's nephew, James Edward Austen-Leigh, in 1871.

Jane Austen lived in entire seclusion from the literary world: neither by correspondence, nor by personal intercourse was she known to any contemporary authors. It is probable that
(5) she never was in company with any person whose talents or whose celebrity equaled her own; so that her powers never could have been sharpened by collision with superior intellects, nor her imagination aided by their casual sug-
(10) gestions. Whatever she produced was a genuine home-made article. Even during the last two or three years of her life, when her works were rising in the estimation of the public, they did not enlarge the circle of her acquain-
(15) tance. Few of her readers knew even her name,

and none knew more of her than her name. I doubt whether it would be possible to mention any other author of note, whose personal obscurity was so complete. Even those great
(20) writers who hid themselves amongst lakes and mountains associated with each other; and though little seen by the world were so much in its thoughts that a new term, 'Lakers,' was coined to designate them. A few years ago, a
(25) gentleman visiting Winchester Cathedral desired to be shown Miss Austen's grave. The verger, as he pointed it out, asked, "Pray, sir, can you tell me whether there was anything particular about that lady; so many people
(30) want to know where she was buried?" During her life the ignorance of the verger was shared by most people; few knew that "there was anything particular about that lady."

It was not till towards the close of her life,
(35) when the last of the works that she saw published was in the press, that she received the only mark of distinction ever bestowed upon her; and that was remarkable for the high quarter whence it emanated rather than for
(40) any actual increase of fame that it conferred. It happened thus. In the autumn of 1815 she nursed her brother Henry through a dangerous fever and slow convalescence at his house in Hans Place. He was attended by one of the
(45) Prince Regent's physicians. All attempts to keep her name secret had at this time ceased, and though it had never appeared on a title-page, all who cared to know might easily learn it: and the friendly physician was aware that
(50) his patient's nurse was the author of "Pride and Prejudice." Accordingly he informed her one day that the Prince was a great admirer of her novels; that he read them often, and kept a set in every one of his residences; that he
(55) himself therefore had thought it right to inform his Royal Highness that Miss Austen was staying in London, and that the Prince had desired Mr. Clarke, the librarian of Carlton House, to wait upon her. The next day
(60) Mr. Clarke made his appearance, and invited her to Carlton House, saying that he had the Prince's instructions to show her the library

and other apartments, and to pay her every possible attention. The invitation was of (65) course accepted, and during the visit to Carlton House Mr. Clarke declared himself commissioned to say that if Miss Austen had any other novel forthcoming she was at liberty to dedicate it to the Prince. Accordingly such a (70) dedication was immediately prefixed to "Emma," which was at that time in the press.

11. The author uses the example of the "Lakers" (line 23) to:

    A. contrast one author's absolute isolation to the relative isolation of other authors.

    B. emphasize the prominence of a group of writers who frequented the Lake District in England.

    C. prove that living in proximity to natural beauty is inspirational to novelists.

    D. parallel the geographical segregation of a group of authors to the emotional alienation of Jane Austen.

12. The word "collision" in line 8 most nearly means:

    F. smash.

    G. explosion.

    H. accident.

    J. interaction.

13. The main idea of the second paragraph is:

    A. as Jane Austen interacted more with literary figures of her day, she increased the circle of her acquaintants to include the Prince Regent.

    B. through an accidental connection occasioned by the illness of her brother, Jane Austen learned of the Prince Regent's affection for her novels.

    C. Jane Austen dedicated her novel *Emma* to the Prince Regent because he was instrumental in saving the life of her brother Henry.

    D. few people, other than the Prince Regent, knew where Jane Austen was buried.

14. The use of the phrase "genuine home-made article" (lines 10–11) suggests that:

    F. Jane Austen was so rustic and modest that she even made her own clothes.

    G. the refinement and sophistication of Jane Austen's style came from the superior company with which she most often socialized.

    H. Jane Austen's life was so circumscribed that no association with other writers or literary critics influenced her style.

    J. it is impossible for an author to write authentically about experiences in life without first-hand knowledge.

15. Jane Austen dedicated *Emma* to the Prince Regent because:

    A. she had long cherished a secret love for the prince.

    B. the prince allowed her access to his library so that she could do research for her next novel.

    C. the prince's personal physician had saved the life of Jane Austen's beloved brother Henry.

    D. the prince suggested that Jane Austen was permitted to dedicate her next novel to him.

Passage IV

Natural Science

The following passage is an excerpt from *A History of Science,* Volume 2 written by Henry Smith William in 1904. The author discusses experiments by the noted American statesman, author, and scientist Benjamin Franklin (1706–1790) as Franklin investigates the nature of electricity.

According to Franklin's theory, electricity exists in all bodies as a "common stock," and tends to seek and remain in a state of equilibrium, just as fluids naturally tend to seek a (5) level. But it may, nevertheless, be raised or lowered, and this equilibrium be thus disturbed. If a body has more electricity than its

normal amount it is said to be POSITIVELY electrified; but if it has less, it is NEGATIVELY
(10) electrified. An over-electrified or "plus" body tends to give its surplus stock to a body containing the normal amount; while the "minus" or under-electrified body will draw electricity from one containing the normal amount.

(15) Working along lines suggested by this theory, Franklin attempted to show that electricity is not created by friction, but simply collected from its diversified state, the rubbed glass globe attracting a certain quantity of
(20) "electrical fire," but ever ready to give it up to any body that has less. He explained the charged Leyden jar by showing that the inner coating of tin-foil received more than the ordinary quantity of electricity, and in consequence
(25) is POSITIVELY electrified, while the outer coating, having the ordinary quantity of electricity diminished, is electrified NEGATIVELY.

These studies of the Leyden jar, and the studies of pieces of glass coated with sheet
(30) metal, led Franklin to invent his battery, constructed of eleven large glass plates coated with sheets of lead. With this machine, after overcoming some defects, he was able to produce electrical manifestations of great force—
(35) a force that "knew no bounds," as he declared ("except in the matter of expense and of labor"), and which could be made to exceed "the greatest know[n] effects of common lightning."

(40) This reference to lightning would seem to show Franklin's belief, even at that time, that lightning is electricity. Many eminent observers, such as Hauksbee, Wall, Gray, and Nollet, had noticed the resemblance between electric
(45) sparks and lightning, but none of these had more than surmised that the two might be identical. In 1746, the surgeon, John Freke, also asserted his belief in this identity. Winkler, shortly after this time, expressed the same
(50) belief, and, assuming that they were the same, declared that "there is no proof that they are of different natures"; and still he did not prove that they were the same nature.

16. The primary purpose of this passage is to:

   F. prove that Benjamin Franklin was the forerunner of modern physicists.

   G. argue that much of what scientists now know about electricity is derived from Benjamin Franklin's experiments.

   H. explain Benjamin Franklin's theory of electricity and his subsequent experiments to prove it.

   J. hypothesize that Benjamin Franklin was not an original thinker but one who copied the efforts of other scientists.

17. Franklin used the Leyden jar to:

   A. show how the inner coating is negatively charged and will thus attract electricity from the positively charged outer coating.

   B. prove conclusively that friction creates electricity.

   C. substantiate his theory that electricity seeks to remain in a state of balance.

   D. re-create conditions under which he could harness electricity to a light bulb.

18. The experiments with the Leyden jar led Franklin to:

   F. reject his theory in favor of that of John Freke.

   G. construct a device with which he could produce forceful electrical manifestations.

   H. theorize that electricity from lightning is of a different nature than that produced by a battery.

   J. overcome the skepticism of those who doubted his findings.

19. The author mentions Hauksbee, Wall, Gray, and Nollet as examples of men who:

    A. published findings similar to Franklin's but received no public credit.

    B. noted many of the same observations as Franklin but failed to make key connections.

    C. decried the experiments of men like Franklin as outlandish and absurd.

    D. jealously guarded their own experiments and prevented Franklin from building on their findings.

20. The purpose of rubbing a glass globe (lines 18–19) is to:

    F. make it clean enough to see the sparks within it.

    G. modify the electrical equilibrium of the glass.

    H. prepare it to receive liquid that will allow the electrical current to pass through.

    J. ground it so that any shock will pass through the jar into the cloth.

IF YOU FINISH BEFORE TIME IS CALLED, CHECK YOUR WORK ON THIS SECTION ONLY. DO NOT WORK ON ANY OTHER SECTION IN THE TEST.

Section 4: Science Test

18 Minutes—20 Questions

Directions: The Science Test consists of five passages; each passage is followed by several questions. After reading each passage, select the best answer to each question and fill in the corresponding circle on the answer sheet. Refer to the information in the passages as often as necessary to respond to the questions. Use of a calculator is NOT permitted on this test.

Passage I

Newton's Law of Cooling states that the rate of loss of heat from a body is proportional to the difference between the temperature of the body and the temperature of the surroundings. This law applies only to small ranges in temperature as are typical in the natural world.

Students were asked to experimentally verify Newton's Law of Cooling by analyzing the cooling of water over time. First, a sample of water was heated to just over 50°C. Then the beaker was transferred to an insulated surface on the lab bench and the initial temperature was immediately recorded at 50°C. As the water in the beaker was allowed to cool, the temperature to 0.1°C was recorded at 2-minute intervals and the change in water temperature (ΔT) over that interval was determined. Later, the average temperature of the water (T_w) over each interval was calculated, as was D_T, the difference between T_w and the temperature of the room (T_R). Finally, the ratio between ΔT and D_T was computed. The collective data were recorded in Table 1. (**Note:** Although the temperature is used here instead of the actual heat of the water sample, the constant mass present in the sample allows the use of temperature as an approximation for heat; $T_R = 20°C$.)

Table 1					
Time (min)	Temperature (°C)	ΔT (°C)	T_w (°C)	$D_T = T_w - T_R$ (°C)	$\dfrac{\Delta T}{D_T}$
0	50.0				
2	46.4	3.6	48.2	28.2	0.128
4	43.2	3.2	44.8	24.8	0.129
6	40.4	2.8	41.8	21.8	0.128
8	37.9	2.5	39.2	19.2	0.130
10	35.7	2.2	36.8	16.8	0.131

1. According to the data in Table 1, the largest change in temperature in any interval was observed after which minute?

   A. 2
   B. 4
   C. 6
   D. 8

2. As the water cools:

   F. the temperature of the water decreases at a constant rate over the entire 10-minute period.
   G. the change in the temperature of the water is inversely proportional to the difference between the temperature of the water and the temperature of the room.
   H. the temperature of the water decreases, reaches room temperature, and then increases slightly.
   J. the change in the temperature of the water is directly proportional to the difference between the temperature of the water and the temperature of its surroundings.

3. Students generated the following graph of D_T versus ΔT:

   Which of the following statements is supported from the graph and the data in Table 1?

   A. The increasing slope in the graph is evidence against Newton's Law of Cooling.
   B. Any slight variation in the data from the slope of 0.13 is evidence against Newton's Law of Cooling.
   C. The relatively constant slope in the graph supports Newton's Law of Cooling.
   D. Although a constant rate of cooling is demonstrated by the graph, further calculations need to be made to verify Newton's Law of Cooling.

4. The experiment was continued for several minutes past the 10-minute interval and then stopped. The difference between the temperature of the water and the temperature of the room was calculated to be 10°C at this stopping point. What was the approximate ΔT recorded for the water sample?

   F. 13.0°C
   G. 7.5°C
   H. 1.3°C
   J. 10.3°C

Passage II

The enzyme lactase catalyzes the breakdown of the disaccharide lactose, a sugar common in milk and other dairy foods, into the monosaccharides glucose and galactose according to the following reaction:

$$\text{Lactose + water} \xrightarrow{\text{Lactase}} \text{glucose + galactose}$$

A research group is performing quality-control experiments on commercially available lactase supplements that are designed to combat lactose-intolerance when taken prior to the consumption of lactose-rich foods. The condition of lactose-intolerance can cause painful gastrointestinal symptoms in affected individuals and is often associated with avoidance of the consumption of dairy products.

Experiment 1

Researchers test the effects of temperature on lactase activity when pH remains constant. Samples of lactase are either heated or cooled to various temperatures and then added to the same volume of lactose solution and allowed to react for 60 seconds. The reaction is then stopped by adding a concentrated salt solution. The rate of glucose formation in micromoles (μmol) per milliliter (mL) of solution is then measured and used to assess the reaction rate, and thus the effectiveness of the lactase supplement in digesting lactose. The data collected are shown in Table 1.

Table 1	
Temperature (°C)	Glucose formation (μmol/mL)
10	0.4
25	8.2
40	15.1
55	0.6
70	0.1

Experiment 2

Researchers test the effects of pH on lactase activity when temperature remains constant at 22°C (room temperature). The same general procedure is followed except that the pH of the lactose solution is altered just before the lactase enzyme is added. This is achieved by adding a relative amount of acid or base. The data collected are shown in Table 2.

Table 2	
pH	Glucose formation (μmol/mL)
1.5	0.7
4.0	1.3
6.5	18.8
8.0	10.6
10.5	0.2

The lactase supplement is designed to be swallowed by a lactose-intolerant individual before the consumption of dairy products. The average pH values of some segments of the human digestive tract (at normal body temperature) are presented in Table 3.

Table 3	
Digestive tract structure	**Average pH**
Mouth	7.0
Upper stomach	5.0
Lower stomach	2.0
Small intestine (upper)	7.5
Large intestine	6.0

Note: Structures are listed in the order in which food flows through the tract.

5. Normal human body temperature is around 37°C. According to the data in Table 1, the product tested:

   A. is likely to be effective at body temperature.
   B. is not likely to be effective at body temperature.
   C. is likely to work at normal body temperatures but not just above or below body temperature.
   D. may or may not be effective at body temperature; it is impossible to tell with the information provided.

6. Which of the following graphs accurately depicts the relationship between pH and the rate of glucose formation presented in Table 2?

7. Which of the following statements is consistent with the data presented in Tables 1 and 2?

   A.   As the temperature or the pH increases, the rate of glucose formation steadily increases.

   B.   As the temperature or the pH increases, the rate of glucose formation steadily decreases.

   C.   An increase in temperature causes an increase in pH, which in turn causes an increase in glucose formation.

   D.   The highest rates of reaction are at a pH of 6.5 and a temperature of 40°C.

8. If a separate trial were run repeating Experiment 2 and the rate of glucose formation was measured at 15.9 μmol/mL, the associated pH is likely to be:

   F.   12

   G.   3

   H.   9

   J.   7

9. The lactase enzyme is a protein, and proteins are known to denature (structurally break down and lose function) at relatively extreme temperatures and pH conditions. Lactase naturally works in the cells of the small intestine. Given the information presented in Table 3, which of the following statements presents a potential problem with the effectiveness of the lactase supplement as it travels through the human digestive tract?

   A.   The lactase supplement could denature at any point along the digestive tract due to the variable pH conditions present.

   B.   If denaturation is not reversible, then the activity of the lactase supplement might be diminished by the low pH in the stomach before reaching the small intestine.

   C.   The lactase supplement could denature at any point along the digestive tract due to the variable temperature conditions present.

   D.   Denaturation of the lactase supplement due to temperature or pH should not take place at any point along the digestive tract.

Passage III

In light of current concerns over global climate change and the perception of an increase in the number of annual hurricanes worldwide, many researchers have further investigated variables that affect hurricane intensity and frequency. A recent study examined the relationship between sea surface temperature (SST) and seasonal hurricane activity in a local region. It was commonly understood by scientists before the study that the SST positively affects the number of hurricanes observed, but debate remained regarding the way in which the SST is measured.

Hypothesis 1

The local SST in the region in isolation is responsible for affecting variations in local hurricane activity.

Hypothesis 2

The SST in the region relative to the SST in the tropics affects variations in local hurricane activity.

The actual number of hurricanes was recorded in a local region over a 10-year period and compared to the predications made by Hypotheses 1 and 2. The data are presented in Table 1. The correlation of each set of predictions to the observed values over the 10-year period is also shown; the closer the calculated correlation is to 1, the more reliable the prediction made by that hypothesis. (**Note:** Percent error is a measure of the closeness of the prediction to the observed value: A negative percent error indicates that the prediction was lower than the actual value, and a positive percent error indicates that the prediction was higher than the actual value. Percent errors of ±5 percent are considered reliable.)

Table 1					
Year	Number of Hurricanes Recorded	Hypothesis 1		Hypothesis 2	
		Prediction	% Error	Prediction	% Error
1	79	76	−3.80	82	3.80
2	92	92	0.00	91	−1.09
3	89	80	−10.10	88	−1.12
4	86	90	4.65	93	8.14
5	103	96	−6.80	102	−0.97
6	115	100	−13.00	116	0.87
7	121	117	−3.31	122	0.82
8	109	105	−3.67	113	3.67
9	99	94	−5.05	100	1.01
10	111	103	−7.21	110	−0.90
Total	1004	953	−5.08	1019	1.49
Correlation	(1)	0.93		0.98	

10. According to the information presented in the passage:

    F. the scientific community is debating the cause of the SST change.

    G. the hypotheses are in agreement about the way in which the SST is measured in order to assess its effects on annual hurricane frequency.

    H. global warming is causing an increase in hurricane frequency.

    J. the scientific community was in agreement before the study that the local SST was related to the frequency of hurricanes in a year.

11. In year two of the study:

    A. Hypothesis 2 was a better predictor of hurricane number than Hypothesis 1.

    B. more hurricanes were recorded than in any other year of the study.

    C. both Hypotheses 1 and 2 were good predictors of hurricane number, but Hypothesis 1 was better.

    D. neither hypothesis proved to be a good model for hurricane prediction.

12. According to the data presented in Table 1:

    F. Hypothesis 1 is more strongly supported than Hypothesis 2.

    G. Hypothesis 2 is more strongly supported than Hypothesis 1.

    H. Hypotheses 1 and 2 are supported with equal strength statistically.

    J. Hypothesis 1 is supported more strongly in the second half of the study than Hypothesis 2.

Passage IV

Solubility describes the ability for one substance (the solute) to dissolve in another substance (the solvent) and is affected by temperature, pressure, and other factors. Solubility curves are often generated to easily predict the solubility of a given substance under a certain set of conditions. Above any line, the solution is called supersaturated and some of the solute will not completely dissolve. Below any line, the solution is instead unsaturated, meaning that the solvent could dissolve more solute if added. On the line, the solution is exactly saturated.

Experiment 1

Industrial chemists were interested in the relationship between the temperature of a substance and its solubility. They tested a variety of substances for their solubility in 100 grams (g) of water at varying temperatures and constant pressure. The data are displayed in Figure 1.

Figure 1

Experiment 2

Of interest also to the chemists was the relationship between the number of carbon atoms present in a substance and the solubility of that substance in water. The solubility of various carbon-containing substances was tested in 110 g water at room temperature (20°C) and constant pressure. The solubilities of all substances tested that contained the same number of carbon atoms (but possessed different functional groups) were averaged. The data are shown in Figure 2. Some of the carbon-containing substances tested were primary alcohols, hydrocarbon molecules that contain the hydroxyl (−OH) functional group positioned at one end of the molecule. The solubility of each alcohol is listed separately from the other carbon-containing compounds in Table 1.

Figure 2

Table 1		
Alcohol name	Alcohol structure	Solubility (g alcohol/110 g H_2O)
Methanol	CH_3OH	Unlimited
Ethanol	CH_3CH_2OH	Unlimited
Propanol	$CH_3(CH_2)_2OH$	Unlimited
Butanol	$CH_3(CH_2)_3OH$	8.954
Pentanol	$CH_3(CH_2)_4OH$	2.904
Hexanol	$CH_3(CH_2)_5OH$	0.673

13. In Experiment 1, which of the following situations results in the highest solubility in 100 g of water?

    A. NaCl at 90°C
    B. KNO_3 at 45°C
    C. NH_3 at 15°C
    D. $KClO_3$ at 80°C

14. All of the following in Experiment 1 can be characterized as having solubilities in water that increase with temperature EXCEPT:

    F. NaCl
    G. NH_3
    H. KCl
    J. KNO_3

15. According to the information presented in Figure 2 and Table 1:

    A. all alcohols become insoluble in water at some concentration.
    B. any alcohol with more than two carbons has limited solubility in water.
    C. as the number of carbon atoms in an alcohol increases, its solubility in water increases.
    D. as the number of carbon atoms in an alcohol increases, its solubility in water decreases.

16. A chemist desires an aqueous solution of any substance that can keep its solubility fairly constant over a wide temperature range and has a minimum saturation of 20 g of solute per 100 g of water at 0°C. Which of the following substances would be best suited for this purpose?

    F. Hexanol
    G. NaCl
    H. KNO$_3$
    J. NH$_3$

Passage V

The life span of a cell from the time it is produced from its parent cell to the point that it completes a division is called the cell cycle. The cell cycle has two main phases: interphase and mitosis. During interphase, the cell metabolizes, grows, regulates its internal environment, and carries out most normal life processes. When a cell is triggered to divide, the mitosis phase begins. Mitosis is technically the division of the cell's nucleus, which may or may not be followed by the division of the rest of the cell (cytokinesis). Mitosis is broken down into four main phases (sequentially: prophase, metaphase, anaphase, and telophase) based upon the coordinated movement of the cell's chromosomes.

Students in a biology class were asked to use a compound light microscope to analyze the length of time needed to complete each phase of mitosis in onion root tip cells, which require 720 minutes to complete the entire cell cycle. They first counted the number of cells observed in each phase (interphase and mitosis) and calculated the relative percent of cells in each phase; they then used this information to determine the time required to complete each phase according to the following equation:

$$\text{Time for phase X (min)} = \frac{\text{\# of cells in phase X}}{\text{total \# of cells observed} \times 720 \text{ min}}$$

The percent of onion root tip cells observed in each phase and the calculated time needed to complete each phase are presented in Table 1.

Table 1		
Phase	% of cells in phase	Time required to complete phase (min)
Interphase	57	410.4
Prophase	27	194.4
Metaphase	8	57.6
Anaphase	5	36.0
Telophase	3	21.6

The students were then asked to compare this data with results from a research study concerning the cell cycle in normal and cancerous cells. The time needed by normal human skin cells and cancerous human skin cells to complete each phase is listed in Table 2.

Table 2		
	Time required to complete phase (min)	
Phase	**Normal human skin cell**	**Cancerous human skin cell**
Interphase	1380	1050
Prophase	41	33
Metaphase	8	8
Anaphase	3	3
Telophase	8	6

17. According to the passage and the data in Table 1, which phase of mitosis requires the longest amount of time to complete?

    A. Interphase
    B. Telophase
    C. Anaphase
    D. Prophase

18. Which of the following graphs correctly represents the data presented in Table 1?

19. Which of the following statements is consistent with the data presented in Tables 1 and 2?

    A.   Regardless of the cell type, one should expect to find the smallest proportion of any sample of cells in metaphase.

    B.   Regardless of the cell type, one should expect to find the largest proportion of any sample of cells in interphase.

    C.   In onion root cells, most cells tend to be in interphase; in human skin cells, most cells tend to be in prophase.

    D.   In human skin cells, most cells tend to be in interphase; in onion root cells, most cells tend to be in prophase.

20. Regarding the data shown in Table 2, cancerous human skin cells are different from normal human skin cells in that cancerous cells require:

    F.   less time to complete the cell cycle.

    G.   more time to complete the cell cycle.

    H.   less time to complete each phase of mitosis.

    J.   more time to complete each phase of mitosis.

IF YOU FINISH BEFORE TIME IS CALLED, CHECK YOUR WORK ON THIS SECTION ONLY. DO NOT WORK ON ANY OTHER SECTION IN THE TEST.

Section 5: Writing Test

30 Minutes

Directions: Think about the issue presented below. Then plan and write an essay in which you support your position with specific reasons and examples. You may choose to support one of the positions stated in the prompt or you may create an original perspective. Be sure to support your position with specific reasons and examples.

Many educators assert that the American education system is not working. They believe that one way to correct this failure is to ensure that high schools across the country teach all of the knowledge essential to send well-educated students on to universities, colleges, community colleges, or the workforce. To accomplish this goal, they have proposed a universal curriculum, one that will be implemented in all public high schools across the country. With this mandated curriculum, they believe, American high school students will rival students from any other country in the world. Others, however, believe that each school district should have the right to determine its own curriculum. They say that what is right for Los Angeles, California, may not be right for Ogunquit, Maine. In your opinion, should there be a mandated national curriculum?

IF YOU FINISH BEFORE TIME IS CALLED, CHECK YOUR WORK ON THIS SECTION ONLY. DO NOT WORK ON ANY OTHER SECTION IN THE TEST.

Scoring the Diagnostic Test

Answer Key

Section 1: English Test

1. D (UM)	15. C (RH)	29. C (RH)
2. H (UM)	16. F (UM)	30. J (RH)
3. B (UM)	17. B (UM)	31. A (UM)
4. G (UM)	18. G (RH)	32. G (UM)
5. C (UM)	19. A (UM)	33. A (RH)
6. H (UM)	20. F (UM)	34. J (UM)
7. D (UM)	21. C (UM)	35. A (UM)
8. J (RH)	22. J (UM)	36. G (UM)
9. B (RH)	23. A (RH)	37. C (UM)
10. J (UM)	24. J (UM)	38. H (UM)
11. A (RH)	25. C (RH)	UM = Usage/Mechanics
12. J (RH)	26. G (RH)	RH = Rhetorical Skills
13. A (UM)	27. C (UM)	
14. H (RH)	28. H (UM)	

Section 2: Mathematics Test

1. D (EA)	13. B (GT)	25. E (EA)
2. J (EA)	14. F (AG)	26. G (EA)
3. E (EA)	15. D (EA)	27. C (GT)
4. H (GT)	16. G (AG)	28. K (AG)
5. D (EA)	17. D (EA)	29. E (GT)
6. G (AG)	18. G (GT)	30. K (AG)
7. C (GT)	19. C (GT)	EA = Pre-Algebra/Elementary Algebra
8. F (GT)	20. J (AG)	
9. B (AG)	21. A (EA)	AG = Intermediate Algebra/ Coordinate Geometry
10. J (GT)	22. K (AG)	
11. E (AG)	23. E (EA)	GT = Plane Geometry/ Trigonometry
12. H (EA)	24. K (AG)	

Section 3: Reading Test

1. B (AL)
2. F (AL)
3. C (AL)
4. H (AL)
5. A (AL)
6. J (SS)
7. C (SS)
8. F (SS)
9. B (SS)
10. G (SS)
11. A (AL)
12. J (AL)
13. B (AL)
14. H (AL)
15. D (AL)
16. H (SS)
17. C (SS)
18. G (SS)
19. B (SS)
20. G (SS)

AL = Arts/Literature

SS = Social Studies/Sciences

Section 4: Science Test

1. A (DR)
2. J (DR)
3. C (DR)
4. H (DR)
5. A (RS)
6. G (RS)
7. D (RS)
8. J (RS)
9. B (RS)
10. J (CV)
11. C (CV)
12. G (CV)
13. B (RS)
14. G (RS)
15. D (RS)
16. G (RS)
17. D (DR)
18. H (DR)
19. B (DR)
20. F (DR)

DR = Data Representation

RS = Research Summaries

CV = Conflicting Viewpoints

Answer Explanations

Section 1: English Test

Passage I

1. **D.** The subject of the sentence is **cats,** so the verb must be the plural **are known.** Choice A is redundant because the word **famous** is already in the sentence. Choices B and C are incorrect because both use the singular form of the verb. (*Chapter V: Section D.9.*)

2. **H.** Commas are necessary between the parenthetical phrase **as the breed is known** and the rest of the sentence and between parallel adjectives **solid, stocky.** (*Chapter V: Section C.4.*)

3. **B.** In any sentence, to achieve parallelism with correlative conjunctions (**either...or**) whatever follows the word **either** must be in the same structure as what follows the word **or.** Choices A, C, and D are not parallel. (*Chapter V: Section D.5.*)

4. **G.** The present perfect tense is formed by the present tense of **have** and the past participle of the verb. The past participle of **arise** is **arisen.** Choice H incorrectly uses the simple past tense, and Choices F and J incorrectly use the past tense form of the verb **arose** instead of the past participle **arisen.** (*Chapter V: Section D.10.*)

5. **C.** This question tests your ability to recognize correct verb form in context. The context of the sentence should lead you to the correct form **was about to close.** Be sure to read the whole sentence as you make your choice. Choice A is not idiomatic English; Choice B is the incorrect tense; Choice D gives the wrong meaning to the sentence. (*Chapter V: Section D.10.*)

6. **H.** This punctuation question tests your understanding of the semicolon and the comma. The semicolon is incorrectly used in the passage, so Choice F is incorrect. (*Chapter V: Section C.3.*) Choice G uses the incorrect plural pronoun **their** to refer to the singular antecedent **cat.** (*Chapter V: Section D.1.*) Choice J incorrectly omits the comma after **mouser.** (*Chapter V: Section C.4.*)

7. **D.** This is a rhetoric question designed to test your understanding of writing style. It also tests your knowledge of vocabulary. Choices A, B, and C all indicate the cat's persistence. Choice D, **resigned to,** does not. **Resigned to** in this sentence would mean the cat is sadly accepting defeat. (*Chapter V: Section E.1.*)

8. **J.** Another rhetoric question, this question tests your understanding of organization. If you read the sentence in the passage that would follow the additional sentence in the question, you will see that both sentences say essentially the same thing, and the original sentence is a more fitting conclusion in any case. Therefore, the addition would be unnecessary. (*Chapter V: Section E.3.*)

9. **B.** Rhetoric again. Stylistically, Choice B is very wordy. All of the other choices are appropriate. (*Chapter V: Section D.2.*)

10. **J.** This question involves both pronoun and apostrophe issues. The correct pronoun is **their** because the antecedent is the plural noun **cats.** Thus, Choices F and G are incorrect. (*Chapter V: Section D.1.*) Also, the possessive pronoun **its** never takes an apostrophe (Choice F), and Choice G uses the singular possessive **kitten's** rather than the plural possessive **kittens'.** Choice H correctly uses **their** but omits the necessary apostrophe for **kittens.** (*Chapter V: Section C.1.*)

11. **A.** This rhetoric question tests your understanding of the correct transitional words for this situation. Choices B and C use contrast words; no contrast is indicated in the sentence. Choice D is not appropriate to begin paragraph 4 because it does not logically follow the previous transitional word that begins paragraph 3. *(Chapter V: Section E.3.)*

12. **J.** The sentence begins with the word **Today,** so it would be redundant to use any of the other choices. The underlined portion should be omitted. *(Chapter V: Section D.2.)*

13. **A.** No change is needed because the pronoun **it** refers to the gene and **became** is the proper verb form. *(Chapter V: Sections D.1 and D.10.)*

14. **H.** This is a rhetoric question about organization. The best place to put this sentence would be after the last sentence of paragraph 4 because it logically continues the information about the "cabbit." *(Chapter V: Section E.3.)*

15. **C.** This is not a formal, scholarly essay. It contains no statistical information, and it does not conclusively disprove any theories. *(Chapter V: Section E.)*

Passage II

16. **F.** No change is needed. The past participle **built** is the proper verb form to begin the participial phrase. *(Chapter V: Section D.10.)*

17. **B.** The singular antecedent **wall** takes the singular pronoun **it.** *(Chapter V: Section D.1.)* Logically, the present tense verb **winds** is preferable to the present progressive tense **is winding** in this sentence. *(Chapter V: Section D.10.)*

18. **G.** This is a wordiness error. Choices F, H, and J are all redundant in that they add unneeded words that restate what a defensive fortification is. *(Chapter V: Section D.2.)*

19. **A.** No change is needed. The singular subject **Each** takes the singular form of the verb **was.** *(Chapter V: Section D.1.)*

20. **F.** No change is needed. Choices G and H incorrectly add commas, and Choice J incorrectly uses a semicolon. *(Chapter V: Sections C.3 and C.4.)*

21. **C.** This sentence has a comma splice error. *(Chapter V: Section D.11.)* Choice B also is a comma splice, and Choice D incorrectly uses the semicolon (if **with** were deleted, Choice D would be correct). Choice C correctly divides the sentence into two sentences.

22. **J.** This is a question about parallelism and correlative conjunctions. The conjunctions "not only" and "but also" are correlative conjunctions (conjunctions that occur in pairs). The words or phrases that follow one correlative conjunction must be parallel to those that follow the other conjunction. In this sentence, **not only** is followed by a verb (**was**) while **but also** is followed by an adjective modifying a noun (**horse-pulled wagons**). The correct phrasing would be: "The wall was wide enough not only for troops but also for horse-pulled wagons …" The only parallel answer is Choice J. *(Chapter V: Section D.5.)*

23. **A.** The information is an interesting detail about the soldiers. It is not a transition (Choice B), it is not an anecdote (a short, personal story, Choice C), and it does not contrast with the preceding sentence (Choice D). *(Chapter V: Section E.)*

24. **J.** This is an idiom question. Only Choice J is idiomatically correct. *(Chapter V: Section D.3.)*

25. **C.** The correct transitional word to begin this sentence is Choice C, **However.** The information in the sentence contrasts the idea in the preceding sentence, and only Choice C provides the logical transition to a different idea. (*Chapter V: Section E.3.*)

26. **G.** The original phrase **connected together with each other** is redundant, as are Choices H and J. (*Chapter V: Section D.2.*)

27. **C.** The plural subject **sections** needs the plural form of the verb **are.** (*Chapter V: Section D.9.*)

28. **H.** This is a noun agreement problem. The plural noun **people** must match the plural noun **cameras.** (*Chapter V: Section D.9.*)

29. **C.** Choices A and B are irrelevant to the passage and inconsistent with its tone. Choice D is not an effective conclusion. (*Chapter V: Section E.1.*)

Passage III

30. **J.** The correct word is **fewer,** which should be used with the plural phrase "five films." Use **less** or **lesser** for singular or whole quantities. (*Chapter V: Section D.7.*)

31. **A.** No change is needed. This is a correct use of the colon. (*Chapter V: Section C.2.*)

32. **G.** The underlined portion should be omitted to achieve parallelism of items in the series. (*Chapter V: Section D.5.*)

33. **A.** The best transitional word for emphasis is **Indeed.** (*Chapter V: Section E.3.*)

34. **J.** The possessive form **bird's** is incorrect here. Choice G uses the incorrect singular pronoun **its** to refer to the plural antecedent **birds.** Choice J correctly uses the plural (not the possessive) form of **birds** and the correct plural pronoun **their.** (*Chapter V: Section C.1.*)

35. **A.** No change is needed because the plural subject **birds** needs the plural form of the verb **have** and the past participle **become.** (*Chapter V: Sections D.9 and D.10.*)

36. **G.** You must omit the underlined portion because the modifying phrase that begins the sentence (**Clumsy on land, yet graceful in the water**) modifies **penguins,** not **scientists.** (*Chapter V: Section D.4.*)

37. **C.** Choice C is idiomatically incorrect. All the other choices are acceptable. (*Chapter V: Section D.3.*)

38. **H.** The correct idiom is **protected from** not **protected away from.** (*Chapter V: Section D.3.*)

Section 2: Mathematics Test

1. **D.** The sum of m and n could be even or odd. However, 2 times this sum, $2(m + n)$, is always even, thus Choice D is correct. Another way to approach the question is to substitute different integers for m and n and to check each choice. (*Chapter VIII: Section B.*)

2. **J.** The expression $2(2^2) = 2^1(2^2) = 2^3$ and, therefore, $2^3 = 2^k$, and $k = 3$. (*Chapter VIII: Section F.*)

3. **E.** Since Mary was x years old 6 years ago, she is now $(x + 6)$. Bill was $2x$ years old 6 years ago, and thus, he is now $(2x + 6)$. The sum of their current ages is $(x + 6) + (2x + 6)$, which is $(3x + 12)$. (*Chapter IX: Section G.*)

4. **H.** Triangles ADE and ABC are similar. The ratio of AD to AB is $\frac{1}{3}$, and thus, the ratio of DE to BC is $\frac{1}{3}$. Therefore, $\frac{DE}{BC} = \frac{1}{3}$ and $\frac{3}{BC} = \frac{1}{3}$. So, $BC = 9$. *(Chapter XII: Section D.)*

5. **D.** There are 3 types of tables and 2 types of chairs. For each type of table, there are two choices for chairs. Therefore, there are 6 different dining room sets. *(Chapter VIII: Section J.)*

6. **G.** Since $y + x = 1$, you have $y = 1 - x$. Thus, $xy = -2$ becomes $x(1 - x) = -2$ and $x - x^2 = -2$ and $x^2 - x - 2 = 0$. Factor and you have $(x - 2)(x + 1) = 0$ and $x = 2$ or $x = -1$. Since x is negative, $x = -1$ is the only solution. *(Chapter X: Section F.)*

7. **C.** Since the $m\angle ACD = 140$, the $m\angle ACB = 40$. The $m\angle ACB$ and the $m\angle ABC$ are the same because they are base angles of an isosceles triangle. Therefore, $2x + 40 + 40 = 180$ and $x = 50$. *(Chapter XII: Section A.)*

8. **F.** The two intersecting lines create two pairs of vertical angles. Thus, $4y = 80$ and $y = 20$, and $2x = 100$, which leads to $x = 50$. Therefore, only statement I is true. *(Chapter XII: Section A.)*

9. **B.** You have $f(1) = 1^2 + 4 = 5$. Thus, $3f(1) = 15$ and $3f(1) + 2 = 17$. *(Chapter X: Section G.)*

10. **J.** The figure can be obtained by translating the graph of $y = -|x|$ (which is in the shape of an upside-down "v") 3 units to the left and 1 unit up. You could also enter the given equations into your calculator and examine their graphs. *(Chapter XII: Section I.)*

11. **E.** The slope of a line is defined as $m = \dfrac{y_2 - y_1}{x_2 - x_1}$. Therefore, the slope of the line $\overrightarrow{AB}$ is
$$m = \frac{4 - (-8)}{-2 - (-6)} = \frac{4 + 8}{-2 + 6} = \frac{12}{4} = 3.$$ *(Chapter XI: Section E.)*

12. **H.** You have $k - 0.25k = 24$, and, thus, $0.75k = 24$. Dividing both sides by 0.75 gives you $k = 32$. *(Chapter VIII: Section G.)*

13. **B.** Since $\overline{AC}$ is a diameter, angle B is inscribed in a semicircle, and thus, it is a right angle, and $\triangle ABC$ is a right triangle. You are given that $AB = BC$. Using the Pythagorean theorem, you obtain 8 for both AB and BC:

$$x^2 + x^2 = \left(8\sqrt{2}\right)^2$$
$$2x^2 = 128$$
$$x^2 = 64$$
$$x = \pm 8$$

Thus $AB = 8$ and $BC = 8$.

Since the diameter of the circle is $8\sqrt{2}$, the radius of the circle is $4\sqrt{2}$, and thus the area of the semicircle is 16π: $A = \dfrac{\pi r^2}{2} = \dfrac{\pi\left(4\sqrt{2}\right)^2}{2} = \dfrac{\pi(4)(4)(2)}{2} = \dfrac{32\pi}{2} = 16\pi$.

The area of the triangle is $\left(\dfrac{1}{2}\right)(8)(8)$, which is 32. The area of the two shaded regions is the difference of the semicircle and the triangle. Thus, the area of the two shaded regions is $16\pi - 32$. (*Chapter XII: Section G.*)

14. **F.** The standard equation of a circle is $(x - h)^2 + (y - k)^2 = r^2$, where (h,k) is the center and r is the radius. In this case, the radius is 1. Thus, the area of the circle is $\pi(1)^2$ or simply π. (*Chapter XI: Section B.*)

15. **D.** Begin with the equation $2n^2 = 4n$ and rewrite it as $2n^2 - 4n = 0$. Factor and obtain $2n(n - 2) = 0$, and thus $n = 0$ or $n = 2$. Since n is positive, n is 2. (*Chapter IX: Section F.*)

16. **G.** The midpoint formula is $\left(\dfrac{x_1 + x_2}{2}, \dfrac{y_1 + y_2}{2}\right)$. Therefore, $\dfrac{(4 + k)}{2} = 2$ or $4 + k = 4$ or $k = 0$. (*Chapter XI: Section G.*)

17. **D.** Mary paid $0.80 for the first doughnut and had $3.20 left. Divide $3.20 by $0.40, and you have 8. Thus, Mary bought a total of 9 doughnuts. (*Chapter IX: Section G.*)

18. **G.** The cosine function is defined as $\dfrac{\text{adjacent leg}}{\text{hypotenuse}}$. The adjacent leg to $\angle A$ is $\overline{AC}$. Using the Pythagorean theorem, you have $(AC)^2 + 12^2 = 13^2$ or $AC = 5$. Thus, $\cos A = \dfrac{5}{13}$. (*Chapter XIII: Section A.*)

19. **C.** The diameter of the circle is 20, and the diameter is also a diagonal of the square. The area of a square can be obtained by either $(s)^2$ or $\dfrac{(d)^2}{2}$, where s is a side and d is a diagonal. Thus, the area of the square is $\dfrac{(20)^2}{2}$ or 200. You could also have found the side of the square by using the Pythagorean theorem or the special 45°-45° right triangle relationship. (*Chapter XII: Section E.*)

20. **J.** This is an arithmetic sequence. The formula for the nth term of an arithmetic sequence is $a_0 + (n - 1)d$. Thus, the 5th term $= 0 + (5 - 1)(5) = 20$, and the 15th term $= 0 + (15 - 1)(5) = 70$. The sum of the two terms is 90. (*Chapter X: Section K.*)

21. **A.** The coordinate of B is -1.5 and $2C$ is -1. The sum of $B + 2C$ is -2.5. Thus, the point is A. (*Chapter VIII: Section C.*)

22. **K.** If a function f is an odd function, then $f(x) = -f(-x)$. In Choice K, $f(x) = x^5 - 2x^3$ and $-f(-x) = -[(-x)^5 - 2(-x)^3] = -(-x^5 + 2x^3) = x^5 - 2x^3$. Thus, $f(x)$ is an odd function. An alternate solution is to enter the given functions into your calculator and see which graph has point symmetry at the origin. (*Chapter X: Section G.*)

23. **E.** Using your calculator, you have $\left(8^{\frac{2}{3}}\right) = 4$. Then, $4\left(n^{\frac{1}{4}}\right) = 16$ and $\left(n^{\frac{1}{4}}\right) = 4$. Raise both sides of the equation to the 4th power; you have $n = 256$. (*Chapter IX: Section B.*)

24. **K.** Set $2n^2 + 3 = 35$ and solve for n. You have $2n^2 = 32$, which leads to $n = 4$ or -4. For the other choices, n would not be an integer. You could also have done this problem by trial and error and substituted small integers for n. (*Chapter X: Section A.*)

25. **E.** The probability of "getting at least one head" = 1 − the probability of getting 2 tails. The probability of getting 2 tails is $\left(\frac{1}{2}\right)\left(\frac{1}{2}\right) = \frac{1}{4}$. Thus, the probability of getting at least one head is $\frac{3}{4}$. (*Chapter VIII: Section K.*)

26. **G.** Set $B = \{2, 1, 0, -2, -3, -4\}$. The median is the middle number, and in this case, $\frac{(0 + -2)}{2}$ or −1. (*Chapter VIII: Section L.*)

27. **C.** Triangle *EHG* is a right triangle. Using the Pythagorean theorem, you can find *EG*. You have $6^2 + 4^2 = EG^2$ or $EG = \sqrt{52}$. Similarly, triangle *AEG* is a right triangle. Using the Pythagorean theorem again, you have $2^2 + \sqrt{52}^2 = AG^2$ or $AG = \sqrt{56}$. (*Chapter XII: Section F.*)

28. **K.** Since $\log_2 8 = 3$ and $\log_5 25 = 2$, you have $3 + 2 = \log_3 x$, or $5 = \log_3 x$. Thus, $x = 3^5$ or 243. (*Chapter X: Section H.*)

29. **E.** Since $\sin^2 \theta + \cos^2 \theta = 1$, you have $\cos^2 \theta = 1 - \sin^2 \theta$ or $\cos \theta = \pm\sqrt{1 - \sin^2 \theta}$. Since $0 < \theta < \frac{\pi}{2}$, $\cos \theta = \sqrt{1 - \sin^2 \theta}$. Thus, the expression $\frac{\cos \theta}{\sqrt{1 - \sin^2 \theta}}$ is equivalent to $\frac{\cos \theta}{\cos \theta}$ or 1. (*Chapter XIII: Section E.*)

30. **K.** Applying the distributive property, you have $2i(i^3 - 4i) = 2i^4 - 8i^2$. Since $i^4 = 1$ and $i^2 = -1$, the expression $2i^4 - 8i^2$ becomes $2(1) - 8(-1) = 2 + 8$ or 10. (*Chapter X: Section J.*)

Section 3: Reading Test

Passage I

1. **B.** According to the passage, Mrs. Rachel is getting dizzy because of "this unusual mystery about quiet, unmysterious Green Gables." It is clear from the passage that she is a woman who likes to know everything that is going on. The idea that a major event could occur in her neighborhood without her knowledge is extremely disturbing to her. (*Chapter VI: Section C.5.*)

2. **F.** The passage implies that Marilla has led a circumscribed (restricted) life. She is described as "a woman of narrow experience" (line 27). The details about her mouth (lines 28–32) suggest she has a sense of humor. (*Chapter VI: Section C.5.*)

3. **C.** In an EXCEPT question, three of the answers are correct and one is incorrect. Since the information in the introductory notes states that the Green Gables farm is in Canada, Choice C is clearly wrong. (*Chapter VI: Section C.5.*)

4. **H.** This is a generalization question. The whole passage suggests that Mrs. Rachel has a need to be informed on every event that occurs in Avonlea. In fact, she becomes upset at the notion that a major event is taking place without her knowledge. (*Chapter VI: Section C.7.*)

5. **A.** In the last sentence, the narrator sums up Mrs. Rachel's attitude, that anything done without her advice MUST be disapproved of, with an ironic tone. The humor is gentle, but the tone of the entire passage does not indicate any hostility, so Choice B is incorrect. Eliminate Choice C because the narrator does not share Mrs. Rachel's disapproval. The sentence is not sentimental at all, so Choice D is incorrect. (*Chapter VI: Section C.8.*)

Passage II

6. **J.** This question asks you to generalize about Lincoln, to take everything that you learned about him in the passage and boil it down to one statement that summarizes his character. Since the passage makes clear that Lincoln handled the crises well, Choices F and G are incorrect. Since the evidence in the passage suggests that Lincoln was a practical man rather than a manipulator (Choice H) and that he was able to handle multiple problems simultaneously, Choice J is the best answer. (*Chapter VI: Section C.7.*)

7. **C.** The "howl of baffled wrath" was the reaction of the South Carolinians to the news that Fort Moultrie was no longer being defended. This retreat occurred because Floyd did not have enough men (Choice A), so Major Anderson decided to remove his troops from Fort Moultrie and concentrate on defending Fort Sumter (Choice B). The South Carolinians had been expecting provisions from the *Star of the West,* but these could not be unloaded (Choice D). Thus, all of the choices except Choice C contributed to the feelings of anger. (*Chapter VI: Section C.5.*)

8. **F.** The answer to this implied detail question can be inferred from paragraph 3 (lines 35–43). It suggests that while some Northerners were sympathetic to the pro-slave position, the preservation of the Union was their priority. (*Chapter VI: Section C.5.*)

9. **B.** Choices A, C, and D are all mentioned in the passage as difficulties Lincoln faced. Kentucky and Missouri had remained in the Union (lines 30–31). Nowhere in the passage does it state that keeping these states in the union posed a problem for Lincoln. (*Chapter VI: Section C.5.*)

10. **G.** This vocabulary question requires that you consider the context carefully. Any "delicate" political situation will need careful diplomacy. The passage does not indicate that the relationship between England and France was fragile (Choice H) or that a truce was likely (Choice J) or that a scandal might erupt (Choice F). (*Chapter VI: Section C.9.*)

Passage III

11. **A.** The author mentions the "Lakers" as an example of writers who were isolated from the world, but who remained in contact with each other, in contrast to Jane Austen who had no contact with other writers. (*Chapter VI: Section C.6.*)

12. **J.** This vocabulary question tests your ability to understand the meaning of a simple word with multiple meanings. In the context of the passage, the word does not indicate any smash, explosion, or accident. It is used to emphasize Jane Austen's isolation in that she had no "interaction" with other intellectuals. (*Chapter VI: Section C.9.*)

13. **B.** All of the choices have some connection to events in the second paragraph, but only Choice B is accurate. Choice A is inaccurate because there is no evidence Jane Austen actually met the Prince Regent. Choice C is inaccurate because there is no evidence that the prince had anything to do with saving Jane Austen's brother. Choice D is off topic. There is no indication the prince knew where Jane Austen was buried. (*Chapter VI: Section C.5.*)

14. **H.** The passage repeatedly emphasized Jane Austen's isolation from the literary world. There is no evidence to support Choice F, Choice G contradicts the information in the passage, and Choice J is proved wrong by the popularity of Jane Austen's novels. (*Chapter VI: Section C.1.*)

15. **D.** This detail from the last paragraph is supported by the events described in the last two sentences of the passage. There is no evidence to support Choice A, B, or C. (*Chapter VI: Section C.5.*)

Passage IV

16. **H.** The primary purpose is to explain Franklin's theory. Choices F and G are not supported by textual evidence and Choice J is not accurate according to the passage. (*Chapter VI: Section C.1.*)

17. **C.** According to the passage, Franklin used the Leyden jar to prove that electricity seeks to "remain in a state of equilibrium" (lines 3–4). Franklin disagreed with Choice B. Choice A reverses the charges of the coating on the jar. Choice D is not covered in the passage. (*Chapter VI: Section C.5.*)

18. **G.** This cause and effect and sequence of events question asks you to follow the logic of the passage. Franklin took what he learned from the Leyden jar and applied it to the construction of a battery which, in turn, enabled him to "produce electrical manifestations of great force" (lines 33–34). He did not reject his theory (Choice F) or theorize that electricity is different from lightning (Choice H). There is no evidence in the passage to support his having to overcome skepticism (Choice J). (*Chapter VI: Section C.6.*)

19. **B.** To answer this detail question correctly, you must go back to the text, identify the four men, and note why they are mentioned. The passage indicates they all saw the "resemblance between electric sparks and lightning, but none of these had more than surmised that the two might be identical" (lines 44–47). Thus, they failed to make key connections. (*Chapter VI: Section C.5.*)

20. **G.** You must infer the answer to this detail question from lines 18–21 which state, "the rubbed glass globe attracting a certain quantity of 'electrical fire,' but ever ready to give it up to any body that has less." Choice H is incorrect because no liquid is placed in the jar. There is no indication that the jar will cause a shock (Choice J), and the cleanliness of the jar does not seem to be an issue (Choice F). (*Chapter VI: Section C.5.*)

Section 4: Science Test

Passage I

1. **A.** The largest change in temperature ($\Delta T = 3.6°C$) is observed after the first 2-minute interval. All other observed ΔT values in Table 1 are lower than $3.6°C$.

2. **J.** Although the temperature of the water does decrease, it is not at a constant rate (ΔT changes in each interval). Since $\dfrac{\Delta T}{D_T}$ is approximately equal to 0.13 in each interval, Choice J is strongly supported by the data.

3. **C.** The graph clearly demonstrates a strong correlation between ΔT and D_T such that $\dfrac{\Delta T}{D_T}$ is constant (lies approximately on a straight line). Although there are very slight variations from $\dfrac{\Delta T}{D_T} = 0.13$ in the data, this is insignificant and negligible. This could very easily be attributed to equipment error (low accuracy or poor calibration), human error in taking the measurement, and/or rounding in the calculations.

4. **H.** If $D_T = 10°C$, then $\Delta T = 10°C \times 0.13 = 1.3$. This is true because $\dfrac{\Delta T}{D_T} = 0.13$ (constant).

Passage II

5. **A.** The value lies between 25°C and 40°C, and in that range there is moderate to high glucose production (8.2–15.1 µmol/mL). The enzyme would therefore be effective at that temperature. There is also sufficient evidence to suggest that just above and below normal body temperature (36°–38°C), the enzyme would be either as effective or slightly less effective than at 37°C. It appears to only significantly lose effectiveness at more extreme temperatures.

6. **G.** Table 2 demonstrates that as pH increases, the rate of glucose formation increases, peaks, and then decreases. This graph is consistent with that relationship, for as the curve is read in the direction of increasing x-values, the corresponding y-values first increase, peak (around 19 µmol/mL), and then decrease.

7. **D.** Table 1 indicates that the highest rate of glucose formation observed is 15.1 µmol/mL, which corresponds to 40°C. Table 2 demonstrates that the highest rate of glucose formation is 18.8 µmol/mL, which corresponds to a pH of 6.5. Table 1 indicates that as temperature increases, the rate of glucose formation increases, peaks, and then decreases. A similar pattern is observed in Table 2 for pH.

8. **J.** The new value of 15.9 µmol/mL lies between two possible sets of observed values for glucose formation: 1.3–18.8 or 18.8–10.6 (i.e., just before or after the maximum rate of glucose production). The possible pH value then is somewhere between 4.0 and 8.0, but likely very close to 6.5. The closest answer is 7.

9. **B.** Table 3 indicates that just before the lactase supplement reaches the cells of the small intestine (where it will be working at a pH of 7.5), it passes through the stomach where the pH of 2 is much lower. Using Table 2, it is logical to predict that the lactase supplement would not be very effective in the stomach at that pH, which is consistent with the notion that the supplement would denature at low pH. If the denaturation is not reversible, when the supplement reaches the small intestine, it may no longer function properly.

Passage III

10. **J.** The passage states that even before the study, the scientific community was in agreement about a relationship between SST and hurricane frequency. The debate concerned the way in which the local SST was determined (i.e., whether the local SST should be measured relative to the tropical SST or on its own).

11. **C.** According to Table 1, Hypothesis 1 predicted the exact number of hurricanes observed in that year (0% error). Hypothesis 2 was also very close, but underpredicted the value by 1 (−1.09% error). Therefore, both hypotheses could be considered reliable since they fall within the ±5% range. Regarding hurricane numbers, there were more hurricanes recorded in years 5–10 than in year 2, when they numbered only 92.

12. **G.** According to Table 1, the correlation of Hypothesis 1 is 0.93 and the correlation of Hypothesis 2 is 0.98. Because the closer the correlation value is to 1, the stronger the hypothesis is considered, Hypothesis 2 is more strongly supported by the data overall.

Passage IV

13. **B.** According to Figure 1, the curve with the highest solubility at 45°C is KNO_3. The corresponding y-value on that curve where $x = 45$ is approximately 70 g of KNO_3 per 100 g of water. Each of the other suggested solubilities (40 g for NaCl at 90°C, 60 g for NH_3 at 15°C, and 40 g for $KClO_3$ at 80°C) is below that of KNO_3.

14. **G.** Examining the solubility curve for NH_3, it is obvious that as the temperature increases (moving along the x-axis from left to right), the solubility decreases (values along the y-axis become smaller). Each of the other solubility curves (NaCl, KCl, $KClO_3$, and KNO_3) demonstrates an increase in solubility with an increase in temperature (i.e., the y-values increase as the x-values increase).

15. **D.** According to Figure 2, as the number of carbon atoms present in any carbon-containing molecule increases (i.e., the x-values increase), the solubility of that molecule in 110 g of water decreases (i.e., the y-values decrease). According to Table 1, the solubilities of alcohols with 1–3 carbon atoms are unlimited, but as the number of carbon atoms present in an alcohol increases beyond 4, the solubility decreases sharply.

16. **G.** NaCl has a minimal change in solubility over a wide range of temperatures (e.g., 37 g at 0°C and 40 g at 100°C) and a minimum saturation of 37 g of solute in 100 g of water. It meets both criteria desired by the chemist. Hexanol demonstrates a lower solubility than desired (<1 g/110 g water), while KNO_3 and NH_3 vary widely as temperature increases. The solubility for KNO_3 increases from 12 g at 0°C to 150 g at 77°C, while the solubility for NH_3 decreases from 91 g at 0°C to 7 g at 100°C.

Passage V

17. **D.** According to the passage, mitosis includes prophase, metaphase, anaphase, and telophase (it does not include interphase). Table 1 demonstrates that the longest phase of mitosis then is prophase at 194.4 minutes. Both telophase and anaphase were calculated to require times lower than that of prophase (21.6 minutes and 36.0 minutes, respectively).

18. **H.** Of all the phases studied, interphase was found to be the most commonly observed (57% of all cells examined were in this phase) and thus required the longest time to complete (57% of 720 minutes, or 410.4 minutes). From there, the length of time required to complete the phase decreased for each successive phase as the cell progressed through mitosis.

19. **B.** According to Table 1, most onion root cells examined were in interphase. According to Table 2, interphase took the longest time to complete of any phase for both normal and cancerous human skin cells. It can be deduced then that most of the human skin cells observed under the microscope were in interphase. The smallest percentage of onion root cells observed in any phase was in telophase (see Table 1) and the smallest percentage of human skin cells observed was in anaphase (regardless of whether normal or cancerous, see Table 2).

20. **F.** According to Table 2, cancerous human skin cells require less time than normal human skin cells to complete each phase except metaphase and anaphase. For those two phases, the same amount of time is required for normal and cancerous cells. The entire cell cycle (interphase + mitosis) must then be shorter for cancerous cells (1100 minutes) than for normal cells (1440 minutes).

Section 5: Writing Test

Sample Scored Essays

Essay receiving a score of 2:

The United States was founded on principles of choice. Without being allowed to choose students can't follow there intrests. They can't determine there own curriculum to spelcialize in what they want.

I personally benefit from specialization as I can choose the courses I am interested in. I like the sciences and can take more science courses which is good for me. This way I can have a career in science. If I had to take the courses that the National says I have to take, I could not take all the science I want.

Specialization makes way for advancement. Because of flexibles schedules science courses may be taken. Students can get ahead and be on the way to there futures.

An inflexible cirruculum disables specialization. Students could become bored an have to take courses they don't want. This would ruin education in America.

Explanation of score of 2:

Essays that earn a score of 2 demonstrate poor understanding of the task. This essay implies a position: Students should be allowed to follow their interests. This position suggests the writer would not support a national curriculum. However, the student equates a local curriculum with specialization, a connection he/she does not clarify. In addition, little specific evidence is given to support the position. The writer does not acknowledge a counterargument, does not provide development of ideas, and does not use transitional phrases to establish coherence. Language use throughout the essay is weak, sentence structure is simple, and vocabulary is basic. The essay is also marred by spelling and grammatical errors (*intrests, there own, spelcialize, cirruculum*).

Essay receiving a score of 4:

As a current high school student about to embark on a journey through college, it would be appropriate to reflect on the curriculum I have learned and its use for me in the future. I was educated based on a set curriculum established by my school district which had to meet state and national requirements. Looking back, I believe it would be more effective if a national curriculum was established. However, I do not believe this should serve as the only curriculum being taught. The best, most practicle and effective educational curriculum would be a hybrid of national educational basics combined with district cirriculums.

When being taught in a public school environment students are being educated by a set cirriculum basis established most probably by their district. This approach allows each district to teach their students in a manner that is interesting for their specific environment and unique needs. This approach allows for teachers to adapt their teaching based on the unique characteristics of their students. Thus, this current method allows for the incorporation of district, regional, and state bias due to the flexibility in the dirriculum. This is most clearly exhibited in social studies classes. For example, the inclusion of the state's history would be relevant as would lessons in the specific geography of the area. Students who live in the desert could have different lessons than those who live in the city. Teachers could also adjust the pace to meet the needs of their students.

On the other hand, the national curriculum would further advance the student in a public school. The federal government would create and distribute a curriculum composed by teachers and specialists from throughout the country whose sole job is to create this unbiased, comprehensive learning package.

This would expel any bias in the learning process and would also make sure students learn all the basic skills they need to function in the global workforce. The problem with this idea is that it places yet another burden on the federal government and also allows more government interference in daily life.

The hybrid/district curriculum is the most comprehensive approach that would provide the most effective learning experience for students in the 21st century. Individual districts are still able to provide unique requirements for their students while also adhearing to a unified national curriculum which would allow for a set standard of learning quality and material throughout the United States schooling system.

Explanation of score of 4:

Essays that earn a score of 4 are adequate to the task. This essay takes a position: The best, most practical and effective educational curriculum would be a hybrid of national educational basics combined with district curriculums. Although this essay takes a more creative, original position than most 4 essays, the writer does only an adequate job of supporting his/her assertions. The supporting evidence, for the most part, remains rather general and vague: *The federal government would create and distribute a curriculum composed by teachers and specialists from throughout the country whose sole job is to create this unbiased, comprehensive learning package.* The writer never clarifies the "hybrid" quality of his/her proposal or explains why this hybrid would be better than either a local or national curriculum. This essay does demonstrate a basic organizational plan and does establish coherence using transitional words *(thus, for example, on the other hand)*. There are a few spelling errors *(practicle, cirriculums, adhearing)*, and the writer does have a tendency to lose control of his/her long sentences (*The federal government would create and distribute a curriculum composed by teachers and specialists from throughout the country whose sole job is to create this unbiased, comprehensive learning package.* and *Individual districts are still able to provide unique requirements for their students while also adhearing to a unified national curriculum which would allow for a set standard of learning quality and material throughout the United States schooling system.*).

Essay receiving a score of 6:

The American education system has always valued the idea of teaching a curriculum based upon the cultural interests and customs surrounding the student. Implementing a national curriculum eliminates the influence of cultural nuances specific to each school and limits the extent to which teachers can incorporate creative elements into both their methods of teaching and their lesson plans. Many blame the supposed "decline" in public education in the United States on the lack of a national curriculum and assert that the implementation of a national core curriculum could reverse this decline and restore the international reputation of the American educational system. What is needed, they assert, is a method of ensuring that all students receive a solid education in the core subjects. However, these supporters do not realize that it is, in fact, the lack of a standard curriculum that enables American students to flourish—something that ultimately cannot be measured by test scores. With more academic freedom, students can expand their interests, analyze their own capabilities beyond testing skills, and exercise their creativity.

In all levels of schooling, students are constantly reminded that they should learn solely for the sake of gaining knowledge, not for test scores and grades. Thus, implementing a standard curriculum is very hypocritical. Proponents of a national curriculum are focusing solely on American students' performance on international assessments as compared to students of other nations. Essentially, it is our students' "lagging" performance on these assessments that supporters of a national curriculum believe prompts the need for change in our education system. By creating a core curriculum, federal officials are ultimately teaching students that test scores and grades are much more crucial than learning for the pure enjoyment of obtaining new knowledge.

Furthermore, a national standard curriculum promotes cookie-cutter education in which students are limited in what they can learn and what they can do with this knowledge. This type of education system stifles creativity and intellectual curiosity and produces more students of similar interests, talents, and goals. Moreover, implementing a national curriculum is unfair to students whose academic needs are based largely on their surroundings and can most accurately be determined by their respective districts.

Not only is a standard national curriculum unfair to students, but it also undermines the ability of teachers and school officials to do their jobs. By intervening in the educational process, the government is essentially saying that teachers and administrators are doing a poor job of preparing students for college and for their futures. In essence, this movement implies that some "specialists" hired by the government know better than local professional educators what is most valuable for students, an attitude that undermines morale and questions the ability and dedication of teachers.

Ultimately, implementing a national curriculum is not the way to reform education in America. It limits the capabilities of both students and teachers, and its restricting effects will harm, not help, the academic success and reputation of our educational system.

Explanation of score of 6:

This essay is insightful, well-written, and effective. The writer clearly recognizes the complexity of the issue and addresses the counterargument. (*Many blame the supposed 'decline' in public education in the United States on the lack of a national curriculum and assert that … a national core curriculum could reverse this decline … What is needed … is a method of ensuring that all students receive a solid education in the core subjects.*) The writer then presents his or her position to refute the counterargument in a well-organized coherent essay. Transitional phrases are used effectively (*furthermore, not only, ultimately*), and the sentence structure is varied. The writer's vocabulary is appropriate, and the essay is free from grammatical and stylistic errors. Overall, this is an outstanding response.

Scoring Worksheets

Sections 1–4

English Test

Number Correct

Usage/Mechanics (UM) Subscore Area   _____ (25)

Rhetorical Skills (RH) Subscore Area   _____ (13)

Total Number Correct for English Test (UM + RH)   _____ (38)

Raw Score (Total Number Correct × 2)   _____

Mathematics Test

Number Correct

Pre-Algebra/Elementary Algebra (EA) Subscore Area _____ (11)

Intermediate Algebra/Coordinate Geometry (AG) Subscore Area _____ (10)

Plane Geometry/Trigonometry (GT) Subscore Area _____ (9)

Total Number Correct for Math Test (EA + AG + GT) _____ (30)

Raw Score (Total Number Correct × 2) _____

Reading Test

Number Correct

Social Studies/Sciences (SS) Subscore Area _____ (10)

Arts/Literature (AL) Subscore Area _____ (10)

Total Number Correct for Reading Test (SS + AL) _____ (20)

Raw Score (Total Number Correct × 2) _____

Science Test

Number Correct

Data Representation (DR) Subscore Area _____ (8)

Research Summaries (RS) Subscore Area _____ (9)

Conflicting Viewpoints (CV) Subscore Area _____ (3)

Total Number Correct for Science Test (DR + RS + CV) _____ (20)

Raw Score (Total Number Correct × 2) _____

Test	Raw Score	Scale Score
English		
Mathematics		
Reading		
Science		
Sum of Scale Scores (English + Mathematics + Reading + Science)		
Composite Score (sum ÷ 4)		

Note: To obtain your scale score, refer to the conversion table on page 337.

Section 5: Writing Test

To obtain your Writing Test score refer, to the following rubric. Then compare your essay to the scored essays on pages 63–65. It may be helpful to have another person, ideally your English teacher, give feedback on your essay.

The Rubric

Score of 6

- Takes a clear position on the question
- Acknowledges the complexity of the issue by considering more than one side
- Develops ideas with specific and logical details
- Maintains focus on the issue
- Shows evidence of an effective organizational plan
- Uses transitional words and phrases to achieve coherence
- Varies sentence structure
- Employs interesting and appropriate vocabulary
- Is free of most grammatical errors

Score of 5

- Takes a position on the question
- Recognizes that there may be other sides to the issue
- Develops ideas with references that are logical and specific
- Maintains focus on the issue
- Has an organizational plan that may be formulaic
- Shows effort to connect ideas with transitional words
- Demonstrates some sentence variety
- Uses appropriate vocabulary
- Is relatively free of serious grammatical errors

Score of 4

- Understands the question and takes a position on the issue
- May provide some acknowledgement of other positions on the issue
- Adequately develops argument with reasons and examples
- Maintains focus, though may digress slightly
- Presents a simple but apparent organizational plan
- Shows some effort to use transitions
- Attempts to vary sentences and use appropriate vocabulary
- Has grammatical errors, but they do not prevent the reader from understanding

Score of 3

- Shows limited understanding of the question
- Attempts to develop a position
- Develops reasons and examples without specific details
- May shift focus and rely on repetition
- Has a simple structure with few transitional words
- Employs basic sentence structure and vocabulary
- Has grammatical errors that may distract the reader and prevent understanding

Score of 2

- Shows poor understanding of the question and may not take a position
- Does not support a position with appropriate reasons or examples
- Demonstrates weak development; may rely on repetition of the prompt
- May have a hazy focus or irrelevant information
- Uses few, if any, transitions
- Contains very basic sentences and simple vocabulary
- Has frequent grammatical errors that may prevent understanding

Score of 1

- Shows little or no understanding of the question
- Does not support a position with reasons or examples
- May simply repeat ideas from the prompt rather than develop anything original
- May lack focus and be incoherent
- Uses basic sentence structure and possibly inappropriate word choice
- Is rife with grammatical errors that prevent understanding

Score of 0

- Blank, illegible, not on topic

V. English Test

Format

The English Test consists of five passages. There are about 15 questions per passage for a total of 75 questions to be completed in 45 minutes. On the ACT English Test, the passages are on the left side of the page and the questions are on the right side.

Content

The purpose of the ACT English Test is to test your knowledge of standard written English. This is the formal "language" used by educated Americans. For the most part, you do not have to know how to identify nouns, verbs, participles, or gerunds; you just have to know how to use them correctly. Since the ACT English Test is an editing and revising test, you will have to know the grammatical rules only as they apply to the context of the passages.

There are two categories of questions on the English Test:

- 40 **Usage/Mechanics** questions test your knowledge of punctuation, grammar and usage, and sentence structure.
- 35 **Rhetorical Skills** questions test your understanding of the decisions writers make about diction, style, organization, and writing strategy.

Parts of each of the passages are underlined. Some questions ask you to consider the underlined portion and determine whether or not a usage or mechanics error is present. You are offered four answer choices. If you think the underlined part is correct, you may select the NO CHANGE option (if it is offered as a choice). Or, you may consider the other options. Some questions ask you to consider the sentence, paragraph, or passage as a whole.

What is *NOT* on the ACT English Test: You will not be tested on spelling or vocabulary (other than an occasional diction question that asks you to choose the best word for the context). You will not have to identify the parts of speech or the parts of a sentence. No reading comprehension questions are given on the English Test. The reading comprehension questions are found in Section 3 of the ACT (the Reading Test).

A. Usage and Mechanics

The Usage and Mechanics questions will test your ability to recognize and use standard written English. You will be tested on your knowledge of punctuation, such as the proper use of apostrophes, colons, semicolons, commas, question marks, dashes, and exclamation points. In addition, you will be tested on your skills in revising sentence structure and correcting grammatical errors.

- Begin each passage by reading through the entire passage quickly, noting the organization, style, and tone.
- Consider the correctness of the underlined portion of the text within the context of the sentence and the whole essay.

- Note the differences among the answer choices. Be aware that some choices will correct the original error but create a new error.

- After you select an answer, reread the entire sentence to make sure it makes sense within the original context.

- Watch out for redundancies. Examine the phrasing **before or after** the underlined part for words or phrases that make the answer you have chosen redundant.

- Be careful about two-part questions and interrelated questions. In some cases, your answer to one question will impact your answer to the next question.

- Watch out for questions that ask you which answer would **NOT** be correct in the context of the passage. Some question will state, "All of the following are acceptable EXCEPT …" In these questions, three of the choices are **correct;** your task is to find the one that is **incorrect.**

B. Important Terms to Know

- A **clause** is group of words that contains a subject and a verb.
- A **main clause** or **independent clause** is a clause that expresses a complete thought.

  Example: The music on my iPod is a mixture of rock and country songs.

- A **subordinate clause** or **dependent clause** does not express a complete thought.

  Example: Since the music on my iPod is a mixture of rock and country songs

- A **sentence** contains a subject and a verb and expresses a complete thought.

  Example: Max is so excited about his new computer.

- A **sentence fragment** is missing one of the elements of a complete sentence.

  Example: Max being excited about his new computer (no verb)

  Example: Being excited about his new computer (no subject, no verb)

  Example: Since Max is excited about his new computer (incomplete thought)

- A **run-on sentence** combines two or more sentences with incorrect punctuation.

  Example: Max is excited about his new computer he just got it last night.

C. Understanding Mechanics

Mechanics refers to the little details of standard written English. On the ACT, mechanics questions test your knowledge of the rules of punctuation.

1. The Apostrophe

The apostrophe is used to indicate possession in nouns and to indicate missing letters in contractions.

a. To Indicate Possession

Singular nouns: The possessive form of singular nouns is made by adding **'s** to the word.

Example: cat + 's = cat's

The **cat's** bowl is filled with milk.

Example: Noah + 's = Noah's

The blanket is tucked into **Noah's** crib.

Singular nouns that end in s: In most cases, singular nouns that end in **s** follow the same rule. However, in some cases, it becomes difficult to pronounce the word in its possessive form. In these cases, just the apostrophe alone may be added after the last **s** in the word.

Example: Lois + 's = Lois's

Lois's car is parked behind the school.

Exception: The possessive form of **witness** is **witness' (or witness's)**

The witness' (or witness's) testimony was the deciding factor in the case.

Plural nouns: If the plural form of the noun does not end in **s,** form the plural by adding 's.

Example: children + 's = children's

The children's murals decorated the auditorium.

Plural nouns that end in s: If the plural form of the noun ends in **s,** add only the apostrophe to make it possessive.

Example: teachers + ' = teachers'

The teachers' cafeteria is located in the rear of the building.

Joint ownership: When two people own something together, the apostrophe is used only with the name of the last person mentioned.

Example: Jane and David's house

Indefinite pronouns: The possessive form of indefinite pronouns is formed by adding 's.

Example: one + 's = one's

It is important to protect one's identity from theft.

> IMPORTANT: The possessive forms of personal pronouns never require an apostrophe.
>
> Never use the apostrophe with these pronouns: my, his, hers, its, ours, yours, theirs, who.
>
> These apostrophe errors will appear frequently on the test, and you can quickly eliminate choices that contain *its', yours', theirs', ours', hers',* or *his'.*
>
> Note: *Who's* is the contraction of *who is*; the possessive form of *who* is *whose.*
>
> Example: We should determine who's going on the field trip so we know whose car to take.

b. In Contractions

The apostrophe indicates that one or more letters has been omitted in a contraction.

Example: it is = it's (**Note:** This is not the possessive form of **its,** which has no apostrophe.)

Example: who is = who's (**Note:** This is not the possessive of **who,** which is **whose.**)

Example: would have = would've (**Note:** It is never correct to write **would of, could of,** or **should of.**)

Examples

For the following sentences, choose the correct word:

> 1. The (rivers, rivers', river's) current was so strong we hardly had to paddle the canoe.

river's. The possessive of a singular noun is formed by adding **'s.**

> 2. I have found (its, it's) not hard to understand the lyrics to the song.

it's. The contraction of *it is* is **it's.**

> 3. The four (reader's, readers, readers') responses were recorded in their logs.

readers'. The possessive of a plural noun is formed by adding the apostrophe after the **s.**

> 4. After the summer, the song lost (its, it's, its') meaning to me.

its. The possessive pronoun *its* is already in the possessive form. It does not take an apostrophe.

> 5. The juniors wished that (their's, theirs', theirs) had been the winning float.

theirs. The possessive pronoun *theirs* is already in the possessive form. It does not take an apostrophe.

> 6. I would (of, have) left earlier if I had known it was going to snow.

have. *Would of* is never correct.

2. Colons

The colon indicates a pause in the sentence. It is used before a list; before a long, formal statement; and before an explanatory statement.

a. Before a List

Use a colon before a list of items, including a list that is introduced by the words *the following* or *as follows.*

> Example: Our tour included all of the following cities: London, Paris, Rome, and Florence.

Note: Do not use a colon right after a verb or a preposition.

Example: The distinguishing characteristics of collies <u>are</u> long pointy snouts, distinctive color coats, bushy tails, and affectionate dispositions. (no colon after a verb)

Example: You can learn about cities in France <u>by</u> looking in an encyclopedia, reading a book about Europe, or looking on the Internet. (no colon after a preposition)

b. Before a Long, Formal Statement

Use a colon to introduce a formal quotation. In this case, begin the quotation with a capital letter.

> Example: President Lincoln began the Gettysburg Address with these words: "Four score and seven years ago our fathers brought forth on this continent, a new nation, conceived in Liberty, and dedicated to the proposition that all men are created equal."

c. Before an Explanatory Statement

Use a colon after a main clause when it is followed by a second clause or phrase that offers an explanation or a restatement of the first clause. In this case, if the statement after the colon is a complete clause and is important, you may begin it with a capital letter. (This is not a hard and fast rule. You will see it both ways: both with and without the capital letter.)

> Example: Our all-day fishing expedition did not live up to our expectations: The weather was nasty and the fish did not bite. (complete clause after the colon)
> Example: Iago was driven by one deep desire: to destroy Othello. (phrase after the colon)

Examples

Rewrite the following sentences, correcting the punctuation:

> 1. I love the words of Queen Elizabeth's speech to her troops "Let tyrants fear, I have always so behaved myself that, under God, I have placed my chiefest strength and safeguard in the loyal hearts and good-will of my subjects."

I love the words of Queen Elizabeth's speech to her troops: "Let tyrants fear, I have always so behaved myself that, under God, I have placed my chiefest strength and safeguard in the loyal hearts and good-will of my subjects."

> 2. My chemistry teacher covered all of the following topics atomic structure, thermodynamics, and bonding.

My chemistry teacher covered all of the following topics: atomic structure, thermodynamics, and bonding.

> 3. Only four students were chosen to go to the finals Ellen, Stan, Charlie, and Devika.

Only four students were chosen to go to the finals: Ellen, Stan, Charlie, and Devika.

> 4. My favorite writers are Dostoyevsky, Fitzgerald, Faulkner, and Wharton.

My favorite writers are Dostoyevsky, Fitzgerald, Faulkner, and Wharton. (no colon needed after a verb)

> 5. My grandfather had one ambition in life to live to be one hundred years old.

My grandfather had one ambition in life: to live to be one hundred years old.

> 6. Galileo spent the last years of his life under house arrest he was condemned by the church for his heliocentric views.

Galileo spent the last years of his life under house arrest: He was condemned by the church for his heliocentric views.

3. Semicolons

The semicolon is used to join main clauses, between main clauses connected by a conjunctive adverb or a connecting phrase, between main clauses if there is a comma within one or both clauses, and between items in a series if there are commas within the series.

a. Join Main Clauses

Use the semicolon between closely related main clauses in a compound sentence when the main clauses are not connected by a conjunction.

> Example: You may find the movie appropriate for young children; Sydney does not.

b. Connection between Main Clauses

The semicolon is used between main clauses connected by a conjunctive adverb or a connecting phrase.

> Example: We enjoyed watching *Iron Man 2;* however, we thought the special effects were better in the first movie. (**Note:** Use a semicolon before the conjunctive adverb and a comma after it.)

> Example: My computer has been causing many problems; in fact, it totally crashed last week. (**Note:** Use a semicolon before the connecting phrase and a comma after it.)

Common conjunctive adverbs: indeed, furthermore, however, moreover, besides, consequently, nevertheless, therefore, yet, instead

Common connecting phrases: in fact, for example, for instance, that is, at the same time, on the other hand (**Note:** Use the semicolon only when these phrases connect two **main** clauses.)

c. Separate Main Clauses

The semicolon is used between main clauses if there is a comma within one or both clauses, or between items in a series if there are commas within the series.

Use the semicolon for clarity between clauses when there are commas within a clause.

> Example: If you leave early, we will not finish the project; but if you stay, we will complete the assignment.

Use the semicolon for clarity between items in a series that contains a comma.

Example: On our cruise, we stopped at Miami, Florida; San Juan, Puerto Rico; and Nassau, Bahamas.

Examples

Punctuate the following sentences correctly:

> 1. I enjoyed seeing Madonna perform live my mother did not.

I enjoyed seeing Madonna perform live; my mother did not.

> 2. My social studies teacher, a graduate of UCLA, is an expert on the history of California in fact, he is writing his thesis on the Gold Rush.

My social studies teacher, a graduate of UCLA, is an expert on the history of California; in fact, he is writing his thesis on the Gold Rush.

> 3. I thought I could handle two AP courses at the same time however, I find I am too stressed to do well in either class.

I thought I could handle two AP courses at the same time; however, I find I am too stressed to do well in either class.

> 4. Justin Timberlake's North American tour includes stops in Memphis, Tennessee Atlanta, Georgia Boston, Massachusetts and Toronto, Canada.

Justin Timberlake's North American tour includes stops in Memphis, Tennessee; Atlanta, Georgia; Boston, Massachusetts; and Toronto, Canada.

> 5. When I finish the report, I will be glad to help you together we will complete the diagrams.

When I finish the report, I will be glad to help you; together we will complete the diagrams.

Or: When I finish the report, I will be glad to help you, and together we will complete the diagrams.

4. Commas

Commas are used for many purposes:

- To separate items in a series
- Before a conjunction that joins main clauses
- To set off any expressions that interrupt the sentence
- With a direct quotation
- To set off an appositive

- With a non-restrictive clause or phrase
- To set off geographical names, addresses, and dates
- To separate two adjectives when the word **and** can be inserted between them
- To separate contrasting parts of a sentence
- After an introductory phrase or clause

a. Separate Items in a Series

Commas are used to separate items in a series.

> Example: Michael likes to listen to Ne-Yo, Kanye West, and Coldplay. (words in a series)
>
> Example: We put up new wallpaper in our bedroom, in the dining room, and in the kitchen. (phrases in a series)
>
> Example: I told you that the taxi arrived late, that the concert was disappointing, and that the entire evening was a disaster. (clauses in a series)

b. Join Main Clauses

Use a comma before a coordinating conjunction that joins main clauses. FANBOYS is an acronym that will help you remember the coordinating conjunctions: For, And, Nor, But, Or, Yet, So.

> Example: *C.S.I.* is my favorite TV program, but my friend finds it too gory to watch.

c. Set off Expressions

Commas are used to set off expressions that interrupt the sentence. Parenthetical expressions are set off with commas.

> Example: The winner of *American Idol,* I am sure, will have a great-selling album.
>
> Example: Phillip Phillips, for example, was number 1 on the charts.

Words used in direct address are set off with commas.

> Example: Sunil, your brother is looking for you.

Introductory words are set off with commas.

> Example: Well, there certainly are a lot of comma rules.

d. Direct Quotation

Commas are used with a direct quotation.

> Example: My English teacher announced, "All students should be reading for thirty minutes every night."
>
> Example: "Run four laps," the coach yelled, "and then meet me on the field."

e. Set Off an Appositive

Commas are used to set off an appositive. An **appositive** is a word or phrase that follows a noun or pronoun to explain or identify it.

Example: The movie, a horror film starring Courteney Cox, grossed 120 million dollars. (*a horror film starring Courteney Cox* is the appositive phrase.)

Note: You do not have to use commas with a one-word appositive that is closely related to the word it modifies.

Example: My aunt Judy wears the most glamorous outfits.

Example: My friend Myrna is a fabulous tennis player.

f. Non-restrictive Clause or Phrase

Commas are used with non-restrictive clauses or phrases. A non-restrictive clause or phrase is not essential to the meaning of the sentence.

Example: My cousin, the one who lives in Chicago, worked for Habitat for Humanity last summer. (*the one who lives in Chicago* is the non-restrictive clause: it is not essential to the meaning of the sentence.)

Example: The book that is on reserve is the one I need for my research. (*that is on reserve* is a restrictive clause: it is essential to the meaning of the sentence.)

Example: The book, which I got as a gift last year, has been very valuable for my research. (*which I got as a gift last year* is a non-restrictive clause: it is not essential to the meaning of the sentence.)

If you are not sure if the clause or phrase is essential or non-essential, here are some clues to help you:

Try leaving out the clause or phrase. Does the sentence still make sense?

Try moving the clause or phrase to a different position in the sentence. Does the sentence still make sense?

If your answer is *yes* to one or both of these questions, then the clause or phrase is non-restrictive (not essential to the sentence) and should be set off with commas.

g. Geographical Names, Addresses, and Dates

Use commas to set off geographical names, addresses, and dates.

Example: We visited the pumpkin farm in Weston, Connecticut, last week.

Example: The presidential election will determine who lives at 1600 Pennsylvania Avenue, Washington, D.C.

Example: Rona met her husband on August 6, 1999, in Omaha, Nebraska.

h. Separate Two Adjectives

Use a comma to separate two adjectives when the word *and* can be inserted between them.

Example: The basketball coach wants to recruit Josh for the team because of his tall, muscular physique.

Note: Do not use a comma if you would not use the word *and* between the adjectives.

Example: Sun Valley is an expensive winter resort. (You would not say "expensive and winter resort.")

i. Separate Contrasting Parts of a Sentence

Use a comma to separate contrasting parts of a sentence.

Example: The red car parked in my space is Jan's, not Jeff's.

j. Introductory Phrase or Clause

Use a comma after an **introductory adverb clause** that begins with a subordinating conjunction such as after, although, as, because, before, if, since, though, until, unless, when, whenever, where, while.

Example: Until I save all the work I have done, do not turn off the computer.

Use a comma after a **participial phrase** (a participle is a form of a verb that functions like an adjective to modify a noun or pronoun).

Example: Stamping her foot angrily, Ella refused to leave the toy store. (The phrase *Stamping her foot angrily* is a participial phrase modifying Ella.)

Use a comma after an **infinitive phrase** (to + verb).

Example: To make a call on the iPhone, simply say the name of the person to whom you wish to speak.

Use a comma after a long prepositional phrase or a series of prepositional phrases.

Example: In the middle of a long conversation, my cell phone battery died.

k. Avoid the Comma Splice Error

A frequent error on the ACT is the **comma splice error:** two main clauses joined by a comma. Do not use a comma to join two main clauses *unless* they are very brief.

Acceptable: I came, I saw, I conquered.

Not acceptable: I entered the classroom quietly, all the students were silently reading their response journals.

Correct a comma splice by using a semicolon, adding a conjunction, or making one of the main clauses into a subordinate clause.

Examples

Punctuate the following sentences correctly:

> 1. The European Conference on Artificial Intelligence will be held in Lisbon Portugal on April 10 2014.

The European Conference on Artificial Intelligence will be held in Lisbon, Portugal, on April 10, 2014.

> 2. Well I thought the class trip to Mount Rushmore National Memorial Keystone South Dakota would be fabulous but the reality surpassed my expectations.

Well, I thought the class trip to Mount Rushmore National Memorial, Keystone, South Dakota, would be fabulous, but the reality surpassed my expectations.

> 3. My uncle a math teacher in Memphis went to China on a teacher exchange.

My uncle, a math teacher in Memphis, went to China on a teacher exchange.

> 4. I have always found that my best subject is science not math.

I have always found that my best subject is science, not math.

> 5. The new science lab was amazing and we couldn't wait to try the new microscopes.

The new science lab was amazing, and we couldn't wait to try the new microscopes.

> 6. Although I am a good golfer I am unable to defeat my younger brother at Wii golf.

Although I am a good golfer, I am unable to defeat my younger brother at Wii golf.

> 7. "The winner of the debate contest" the principal announced "will go on to compete in the state finals."

"The winner of the debate contest," the principal announced, "will go on to compete in the state finals."

> 8. On the day of the ACT Test be sure to bring no. 2 pencils an eraser your ID and your admission ticket.

On the day of the ACT Test, be sure to bring no. 2 pencils, an eraser, your ID, and your admission ticket.

> 9. My old class picture which was packed in a carton in the garage clearly shows the braces I wore on my teeth for two years.

My old class picture, which was packed in a carton in the garage, clearly shows the braces I wore on my teeth for two years.

> 10. Barking loudly enough to wake the neighbors my new dog was a noisy unhappy pet.

Barking loudly enough to wake the neighbors, my new dog was a noisy, unhappy pet.

5. The Dash

Use the dash to indicate an important or abrupt break in thought or before a summary.

a. Abrupt Break in Thought

The dash gives the information that is set off special emphasis or indicates a sudden change in thought.

> Example: When I left my laptop on the plane, it was lost—or so I thought until the flight attendant came running after me.

> Example: Those rights that Americans hold dear—life, liberty, the pursuit of happiness—are not universally respected.

Note: When the dash sets off a part of the sentence, unless the sentence ends with that part, be sure to use a second dash (not a comma as you'll see in some incorrect answer choices).

Not acceptable: Four of the horses entering the starting gate—Afleet Alex, Trampoline, Winner Takes All, and Fascinating Filly, struggled impatiently against the handlers trying to calm them.

Acceptable: Four of the horses entering the starting gate—Afleet Alex, Trampoline, Winner Takes All, and Fascinating Filly—struggled impatiently against the handlers trying to calm them.

b. Before a Summary

Use the dash before a summary. In these cases, the dash and the colon are interchangeable. The dash is used after items in a series to indicate a summarizing statement.

> Example: Cupcakes, ice cream, cookies—the dessert buffet was filled with all my favorite confections.

6. The Parentheses

Use the parentheses to enclose additional material or explanatory information that might be interesting to know but is not of major importance to the text. Information that is enclosed in parentheses can usually be removed from the text without changing the meaning or losing any essential information.

> Example: When she moved to Indiana, Ms. North had to go through the complete process (certification, competency tests, interviews) to get her teaching license.

You could use a colon here for more emphasis since it is a list, or use a dash for strong emphasis. In this sentence, the material is rather unimportant to the main meaning of the sentence, so the parentheses are the proper punctuation.

Punctuation of parentheses can be tricky. Periods and other end punctuation are placed outside the close of a parenthesis. No punctuation mark may be placed before a parenthesis, but a comma can follow one. When the information enclosed in the parentheses is a complete sentence, treat it as such: Start with a capital letter and end with a period. A question mark or exclamation point, if it is part of the parenthetical material, can go inside a parenthesis, but another punctuation mark is needed to close the sentence:

> Example: I brought a ghoulish selection of costumes to the Halloween party (skeletons, goblins, and zombies!).

> Example: The Stone family has built a new home overlooking the river. (Their apartment in the city was too small.)

Examples

Punctuate the following sentences correctly:

---

1. Cilantro, chipotle, wasabi these spices have become popular with adventurous cooks.

Cilantro, chipotle, wasabi—these spices have become popular with adventurous cooks.

---

2. Florence called Firenze in Italy is a small city of breathtaking beauty.

Florence (called Firenze in Italy) is a small city of breathtaking beauty.

---

3. My sister Ann can you believe it got the lead role in the school play.

My sister Ann—can you believe it—got the lead role in the school play.

---

4. Most of the boys on the basketball team in fact all but two made all-state.

Most of the boys on the basketball team—in fact, all but two—made all-state.

---

5. It is a tradition in my family that holidays even Thanksgiving are potluck.

It is a tradition in my family that holidays (even Thanksgiving) are potluck.

7. Question Marks and Exclamation Marks

Question marks and exclamation marks are end marks that indicate the writer's intention: to ask a question or to make a strong or startling statement.

a. Question Marks

Use a question mark at the end of an interrogative sentence. An interrogative sentence is one that asks a question.

> Example: Do you have plans for vacation?

Do not use a question mark with an indirect question.

Example: Mr. Ramirez wants to know who won the game.

b. Exclamation Marks

Use an exclamation mark after a startling statement or at the end of an exclamatory sentence.

Example: Wow! I passed my road test!

Examples

Punctuate the following sentences:

1. Did you see that funny pets video on *YouTube*

Did you see that funny pets video on *YouTube*?

2. It was great

It was great!

3. I wonder if Louis saw the game last week

I wonder if Louis saw the game last week. (indirect question)

4. We won Can you believe it

We won! Can you believe it?

5. Have we changed quarterbacks

Have we changed quarterbacks?

D. Grammar and Usage

"PRIMPED CATS" is a mnemonic (a formula used to improve the memory). Each letter stands for a grammatical error you will encounter on the ACT English Test. Remember this mnemonic, and you are well on your way to ACT English success.

P—Pronoun errors   C—Comparisons

R—Redundancy   A—Agreement

I—Idioms   T—Tense

M—Modification   S—Sentence structure

P—Parallelism

E—Errors with adjectives/adverbs

D—Diction

1. Pronoun Errors

Pronouns are words that are used to replace nouns. The noun that the pronoun replaces is called the **antecedent.** Usually, but not always, the antecedent comes before the pronoun.

a. Pronoun Antecedent Agreement Errors

A pronoun must agree with its antecedent in gender and number. On the ACT English Test, always go back and reread the entire sentence to find the antecedent for the pronoun.

If the antecedent of a pronoun is singular, the pronoun must be singular. If the antecedent is plural, the pronoun must be plural.

If the antecedent is feminine, the pronoun must be feminine. If the antecedent is masculine, the pronoun must be masculine.

> Example: Debbie brought her laptop to the Math Challenge. (**Debbie** is the feminine singular antecedent for the feminine singular pronoun **her.**)
>
> Example: The **students** brought **their** laptops to the Math Challenge. (**Students** is the plural antecedent for the plural pronoun **their.**)

If the antecedent refers to both genders, the phrase "his or her" is acceptable to avoid sexist language. When this phrasing is repeated several times in a sentence or paragraph, it may become awkward; avoid the problem by using the plural form.

> Awkward: Every one of the students put his or her laptop on his or her desk.
>
> Better: The students put their laptops on their desks.

b. Indefinite Pronouns

When indefinite pronouns are antecedents, determine whether they are singular or plural.

Singular indefinite pronouns:

anybody	everybody	nobody
anyone	everyone	one
each	neither	somebody
either	no one	someone

Example: **Each** of the boys on the team took **his** trophy home.

Example: **Everyone** chose **his or her** favorite novel.

Exceptions: Sometimes, with **everyone** and **everybody,** the sense of the sentence is compromised when the singular pronoun is used. In these cases, the plural form is acceptable.

Awkward: **Everyone** in the crowd stood and applauded when **he or she** saw the float.

Better: **Everyone** in the crowd stood and applauded when **they** saw the float.

Plural Indefinite Pronouns:

both	many
few	several

Singular or Plural Indefinite Pronouns (depending on how they are used):

all	most	some
any	none	

Example: Some of the play has lost **its** meaning. (singular in meaning)

Example: Some of the houses have lost **their** roofs. (plural in meaning)

c. Singular Antecedents and Singular Pronouns

Two or more singular antecedents joined by *or* or *nor* take the singular pronoun.

Example: Either Marlee or Olivia will bring **her** car to the football game.

Example: Neither Eli nor Jaxon has taken **his** road test.

d. Clear Antecedents

To avoid vague pronoun references on the ACT English Test, be sure you can pinpoint the antecedent of the pronoun. Every pronoun must clearly refer to a specific antecedent.

Vague: In the newspaper **it** says that more young people voted this year than last year. (The pronoun **it** has no antecedent.)

Better: The article in the *Tribune* states that more young people voted this year than last year.

Vague: Jessica wants to be a doctor because **it** is so rewarding. (The pronoun **it** has no antecedent.)

Better: Jessica wants to be a doctor because the work is so rewarding.

Vague: Barbara came late to every meeting, **which** annoyed her supervisor. (**Which** is a vague pronoun because it has no antecedent.)

Better: Barbara came late to every meeting, a habit that annoyed her supervisor.

Or even better: Barbara's chronic lateness annoyed her supervisor.

Vague: Students are coming to school on time, bringing their books to class, and taking notes regularly. **This** helps the school receive federal funds. (**This** is a vague pronoun because it has no antecedent.)

Better: Students are coming to school on time, bringing their books to class, and taking notes regularly. The improved attendance helps the school receive federal funds.

e. Pronoun Case Errors

If you have ever wondered whether to write *I* or *me*, you have encountered a **pronoun case** problem. Pronouns change their form depending on how they are used. The different forms of the pronouns are called **cases.** Pronouns have three cases: **nominative, objective,** and **possessive.**

Nominative	Objective	Possessive
I	me	my, mine
we	us	our, ours
you	you	your, yours
he	him	his
she	her	her, hers
it	it	its
they	them	their, theirs
who	whom	whose

The **nominative case** of pronouns is used when the pronoun is the subject or the predicate nominative.

The **objective case** is used when the pronoun is the object of a verb or the object of a preposition.

The **possessive case** is used to indicate possession.

On the ACT English Test, you will have to decide which form of the pronoun to select. First, look at the whole sentence and determine what role the pronoun plays in the sentence. Is it the subject or the predicate nominative? Then use the nominative case. Is it the object of a verb or the object of a preposition? Then choose the objective case. Is the pronoun showing ownership? Then use the possessive case.

Nominative case: The pronoun is the subject.

Example: **He** and **I** want to be lab partners in chemistry.

Example: Judy and **she** went shopping for decorations for the prom.

Example: **Who** is going to be class president next year?

The pronoun is the **predicate nominative** (word in the predicate part of the sentence that is linked to the subject).

Example: The winners must have been **they.**

Example: The team captains are Sophie and **she.**

Objective case: The pronoun is the **object of a verb** (direct object or indirect object).

> Example: Alexis gave **her** the gift. (**Her** is the indirect object of the verb **gave.**)

> Example: Hayley invited Juan and **him** to the dance. (**Juan** and **him** are the direct objects of the verb **invited.**)

The pronoun is the **object of a preposition.**

> Example: The head of the committee wanted to share the responsibility with **them.** (**Them** is the object of the preposition **with.**)

> Example: To **whom** should I address the letter of recommendation? (**Whom** is the object of the preposition **to.**)

Possessive case: Use the possessive case to show ownership and before a gerund (-ing form of a verb used as a noun).

> Example: The director appreciates **your** being prompt for all rehearsals. (**Your** is the possessive pronoun used before the gerund **being.**)

> Example: **His** quick thinking saved the day. (**His** is the possessive pronoun used before the gerund **thinking.**)

Examples

Select the correct pronoun:

---

1. This birthday present is from Julia and (I, me).

This birthday present is from Julia and **me.**

---

2. The Intel Corporation awarded Ronni and (she, her) the prize.

The Intel Corporation awarded Ronni and **her** the prize.

---

3. No one objected to (he, him, his) bringing a date to the prom.

No one objected to **his** bringing a date to the prom.

---

4. Neither the seniors nor (us, we) have won the play contest.

Neither the seniors nor **we** have won the play contest.

---

5. Neither of these journals has all (its, their) entries.

Neither of these journals has all **its** entries.

6. Each of the participants presented (his or her, their) experiment(s) to the panel.

Each of the participants presented **his or her** experiment to the panel.

7. Russ and Jenn brought (his, their) calculators to the exam.

Russ and Jenn brought **their** calculators to the exam.

8. It is silly to let this disagreement come between you and (she, her).

It is silly to let this disagreement come between you and **her.**

9. I can't wait to find out if the champion is (her, she).

I can't wait to find out if the champion is **she.**

10. (Who, Whom) do you think should lead the group?

Who do you think should lead the group?

2. Redundancy

In standard written English, conciseness is a goal. It is best to express your ideas in as few well-chosen words as possible. On the ACT English Test, always be alert for such repetitive and wordy expressions as:

true fact	round in shape
important essentials	close proximity
two equal halves	new innovations
consensus of opinion	the future to come
unexpected surprise	due to the fact that
various different	ten years in age
extreme in degree	problem that needs a solution
large in size	

On the English Test, you will often have to go back to the beginning of a sentence (before the underlined part) and read all the way to the end of the sentence (past the underlined part) to check for redundancies.

Example. At the present time, the problem the community is currently facing must be addressed.

At first reading, you may think the underlined part of the sentence is grammatically correct. You'd be right. *However,* if you reread the sentence from the beginning, you will see the phrase *At the present time.* This phrase makes the word *currently* redundant. You will have to find a choice that eliminates this redundancy. You will also be expected to recognize words whose meanings are so similar that to use both words is redundant.

Example: In the **predictable** and **foreseeable** future new sources of energy will be necessary for survival.

The use of both **predictable** and **foreseeable** is redundant; you would choose an answer that eliminates one of these words.

Examples

Rewrite the following sentences to avoid redundancies and wordiness. Your answers might be slightly different. Do not worry if this is the case; your goal is to eliminate the redundant expressions.

1. By associating and connecting together, the two teams were able to come up with a new innovation.

By connecting, the two teams were able to come up with an innovation.

2. We chose a sign that was large in size due to the fact that we hoped every person and all people would be able to see it.

We chose a large sign so everyone could see it.

3. Every year the teachers do an annual review of their classroom supplies.

The teachers do an annual review of their classroom supplies.

4. I told you the reason why you should take the ACT is because it is a good test.

I told you to take the ACT because it is a good test.

5. Larry will tell you the honest truth about his past experience.

Larry will tell you the truth about his experiences.

6. It is the consensus of opinion that we should advance forward and join together to solve the problems that need solutions.

The consensus is that together we can advance and solve the problems.

7. The population of cougars began to decline and wane following the influx of humans into the area.

The population of cougars began to decline following the influx of humans into the area.

3. Idioms

Idioms are expressions or verb phrases that are used in English. The problem on the ACT English Test arises when a cliché appears (avoid them) or when the incorrect preposition is used with a verb. Unfortunately, there are no rules … you just need to know what is accepted as correct. Usually, you can trust your "ears"—go with what sounds right.

Some common idioms are as follows:

abide by	conform to	opinion of
agree to (something)	consists of	participate in
agree with (someone)	depend on	prefer to
apply for	differ from	preoccupied with
approve of	discriminate against	prohibited from
argue about (something)	escape from	protect from
argue with (someone)	in contrast to	relevant to
arrived at	insensitive to	subscribe to
believe in	insight into	succeeded in
capable of	insist upon	tendency to
comment on	method of	
complain about	object to	

Some common clichés to avoid are as follows:

the whole nine yards	selling like hotcakes
white (pale) as a ghost (sheet)	as easy as stealing candy from a baby
faster than the speed of light	quiet as a mouse
as light as a feather	slow as a turtle
fought an uphill battle	slept like a baby
sadder but wiser	free as a bird
blind as a bat	hit the nail on the head
since the dawn of time	bite the bullet

Examples

Correct the idiom errors in the following sentences:

---

1. Ignacio proved that he was capable to rebuild the engine on the '62 Chevy.

Ignacio proved that he was **capable of rebuilding** the engine on the '62 Chevy.

---

2. While I was reading *Macbeth,* I was amazed that Shakespeare had such insight on ambitious leaders who ruthlessly seize power.

While I was reading *Macbeth,* I was amazed that Shakespeare had such **insight into** ambitious leaders who ruthlessly seize power.

> 3. Alex tried to get his mother's attention, but she was preoccupied on the complicated recipe she was preparing.

Alex tried to get his mother's attention, but she was **preoccupied with** the complicated recipe she was preparing.

> 4. Contrasting with the ornate style of Gothic architecture, modern geometric buildings have clean lines and sharp edges.

In contrast to ornate Gothic architecture, modern geometric buildings have clean lines and sharp edges.

> 5. Because my dad is such a great cook, my family prefers eating at home rather than eating in restaurants.

Because my dad is such a great cook, my family prefers eating at home **to** eating in restaurants.

> 6. Arthur went into the new sales program as blind as a bat, but faster than the speed of light his product was selling like hotcakes.

Arthur was inexperienced at selling but quickly became successful. (eliminate all clichés)

4. Modification

On the ACT English Test, always go back and reread the entire sentence to check for proper modification. Modifiers are words, phrases, or clauses that describe, change, or specify other parts of a sentence.

a. Misplaced Modifiers

Modifiers are often participial phrases:

> Example: **Riding on the bus,** we read the article in the paper. (**Riding on the bus** describes **we.**)

> Example: As I turned the corner, I heard my dog **barking loudly. (Barking loudly** describes the **dog.**)

Sometimes modifiers are infinitive phrases:

> Example: **To understand English grammar,** students must practice writing and speaking correctly. (**To understand English grammar** modifies **students.**)

In English, changes in word order (syntax) lead to changes in meaning. A modifier that is misplaced can cause confusion.

> Examples:
>
> Maria spotted an orange cat sitting on a bench eating a sandwich. (The cat is sitting and eating.)
>
> Sitting on a bench eating a sandwich, Maria spotted an orange cat. (Maria is sitting and eating.)
>
> Sitting on a bench, Maria spotted an orange cat eating a sandwich. (Maria is sitting and the cat is eating.)

To avoid confusion, always place modifying phrases and clauses as close as possible to the words they modify.

b. Dangling Modifiers

Dangling modifiers have no word or phrase to modify.

> Confusing: Standing on the bridge overlooking the city, the buildings look like children's toys. (Who is standing? Certainly not the buildings.)

To correct dangling modifiers, add the missing words or revise the sentence.

> Revised: Standing on the bridge overlooking the city, George thought the buildings looked like children's toys.
>
> Or: As George stood on bridge overlooking the city, the buildings looked like children's toys.

Examples

Revise the following sentences to correct the modification errors. Your answers may vary, but be sure to eliminate all modification confusion.

---

1. Athena found her cell phone walking home from practice.

Walking home from practice, Athena found her cell phone.

---

2. To order safely from the Internet, your credit card should be protected.

To order safely from the Internet, you should be sure your credit card is protected.

---

3. Looking up at the sky, the eclipse was both magnificent and frightening.

Looking up at the sky, we discovered the eclipse was both magnificent and frightening.

---

4. While working out in the gym, my leg muscle cramped.

While I was working out in the gym, my leg muscle cramped.

---

5. Ashley wore her new bag over her shoulder which she had just purchased at the mall.

Ashley wore her new bag, which she had just purchased at the mall, over her shoulder.

---

6. Perhaps best known for convincing her husband to murder the king, Lady Macbeth's rampant ambition became uncontrollable.

Perhaps best known for convincing her husband to murder the king, Lady Macbeth allowed her rampant ambition to become uncontrollable.

5. Parallelism

Parallel ideas should be in the same grammatical form. On the ACT English Test, always go back and reread the entire sentence to check the parallelism.

When you join ideas using conjunctions, they should be in the same form. Nouns should be joined with nouns, prepositional phrases joined with prepositional phrases, and clauses joined with clauses.

> Unparallel nouns: Martin Luther King, Jr., was honored for his courage, faith, and he was willing to stick to his beliefs.
>
> Parallel nouns: Martin Luther King, Jr., was honored for his courage, faith, and perseverance.
>
> Unparallel verb phrases: I like to ski, to hike, and swimming.
>
> Parallel verb phrases: I like to ski, to hike, and to swim. (Also: I like to ski, hike, and swim.)
>
> Unparallel prepositional phrases: We left the party early because of the inclement weather, and it was late.
>
> Parallel prepositional phrases: We left the party early because of the inclement weather and because of the lateness of the hour.
>
> Unparallel clauses: Hamlet found it difficult to believe that his father had died of natural causes and in the innocence of his uncle.
>
> Parallel clauses: Hamlet found it difficult to believe that his father had died of natural causes and that his uncle was innocent.

Correlative conjunctions, which always occur in pairs, can be tricky; be sure what comes after the first conjunction is parallel to what comes after the second conjunction.

Correlatives are as follows: both … and, either … or, neither … nor, not only … but also.

> Unparallel: The car wash **not only** did a great job on my car, **but also** on my brother's.
>
> Parallel: The car wash did a great job **not only** on my car, **but also** on my brother's.
>
> Unparallel: The general had **neither** the support of his troops **nor** did he have the loyalty of his officers.
>
> Parallel: The general had **neither** the support of his troops **nor** the loyalty of his officers.

Examples

Revise the following sentences to correct the errors in parallelism. Your answers may vary slightly.

> 1. Julius Caesar could not be sure that he had the support of the common people or if the other senators would stand by him.

Julius Caesar could not be sure that he had the support of the common people or the other senators.

> 2. Brutus was ambitious, gullible, and he thought a lot about his own motives.

Brutus was ambitious, gullible, and introspective.

> 3. I either want to do my English research paper on Ernest Hemingway or F. Scott Fitzgerald.

I want to do my English research paper on either Ernest Hemingway or F. Scott Fitzgerald.

> 4. Galileo not only believed that the earth was round but also that it rotated around the sun.

Galileo believed not only that the earth was round but also that it rotated around the sun.

> 5. Those who try sky diving both know the thrill of freefall and the excitement of flying.

Those who try sky diving know both the thrill of freefall and the excitement of flying.

6. Errors with Adjectives/Adverbs

To answer these questions on the ACT English Test, you will need to know the difference between adjectives and adverbs. Adjectives are used to modify nouns. They usually answer such questions as "Which?" "What kind?" and "How many?" Adverbs are used to modify verbs, adjectives, or other adverbs. They usually answer such questions as "How?" "When?" and "To what extent?"

a. Comparisons

Use the **comparative** form of the adjective to compare *two* nouns or pronouns. The comparative is formed in two ways. For one-syllable adjectives, add *–er* (also used for some two-syllable adjectives).

> Example: Of the two boys, Troy is the younger.
> Example: Samantha is the funnier of the two sisters.

For most two-syllable-or-more adjectives, put "more" in front of the word.

> Example: Sydney's flowers are more fragrant than mine.
> Example: My computer is more efficient than Herb's.

Use the **superlative** form of the adjective to compare *three or more* nouns or pronouns. The superlative form is formed in two ways: For one-syllable adjectives, add *–est* (also used for some two-syllable adjectives).

> Example: Amy is the youngest girl in the class.
> Example: The happiest (or most happy) teacher in the district is Sarah.

For most two-syllable adjectives, put "most" in front of the word.

> Example: Jana won the award for the most cautious driver.

Some irregular comparison forms are as follows:

	Comparative	Superlative
good	better	best
bad	worse	worst
little	less or lesser	least
much	more	most
far	farther or further	farthest or furthest

Some adjectives are absolute values and cannot be intensified with **more** or **most**:

complete	round	totally
correct	square	unique
perfect	superior	
preferable	supreme	

b. Adjective/Adverb Confusion

Use an adjective to modify a noun or a pronoun and use an adverb to modify a verb, an adjective, or another adverb.

> Incorrect: The children's choir sang so beautiful that the audience was moved to tears. (incorrectly uses the adjective **beautiful** instead of the adverb **beautifully** to modify the verb "sang")

> Correct: The children's choir sang so beautifully that the audience was moved to tears. (correctly uses the adverb **beautifully** to modify the verb "sang")

Examples

Correct the errors in the following sentences:

---

1. Of the jaguar and the hyena, the jaguar is the fastest.

Of the jaguar and the hyena, the jaguar is the **faster.**

---

2. When she won the lottery, my neighbor was the most happiest woman in town.

When she won the lottery, my neighbor was the **happiest** (or **most happy**) woman in town.

---

3. The fire chief was impressed by how speedy we all exited the building during the fire drill.

The fire chief was impressed by how **speedily** we all exited the building during the fire drill.

4. I thought the stuffed animal I bought for my little sister was more cuter than the one she has on her bed.

I thought the stuffed animal I bought for my little sister was **cuter** than the one she has on her bed.

5. When we measured all ten basketball players, Jamal was the taller.

When we measured all ten basketball players, Jamal was the **tallest.**

6. Among all the pottery on display, Russell's was the most unique.

Among all the pottery on display, Russell's was **unique.**

7. Diction

Diction means word choice. A diction error occurs when a word is used incorrectly or inappropriately.

Commonly misused words:

among/between:	use **between** for two people or things (between my brother and me)
	use **among** for three or more (among all my friends)
fewer/less:	use **fewer** for anything you can count (fewer times at bat)
	use **less** for whole quantities (less pain)
their/there/they're:	use **their** for the plural possessive pronoun (their notebooks)
	use **there** for place (I put it there)
	use **they're** as a contraction of *they are* (they're coming home)
amount/number:	use **amount** for whole quantities (amount of homework)
	use **number** for things you can count (number of math problems)
who's/whose:	use **who's** as a contraction of *who is* (who's your buddy)
	use **whose** for possessive form of who (whose book is that)
bad/badly:	use **bad** (adjective) after a linking verb (Sue feels bad)
	use **badly** (adverb) to describe how something is being done (he sings badly)

Examples

Correct the diction errors in the following sentences:

1. The chemistry teacher divided the unknowns between the four groups.

The chemistry teacher divided the unknowns **among** the four groups.

> 2. I hope I have less pages to read than you do.

I hope I have **fewer** pages to read than you do.

> 3. The coach took a survey to see whose going to the clinic on Saturday.

The coach took a survey to see **who's** going to the clinic on Saturday.

> 4. Tracy and Lauren left there books outside, and their going to be so sorry when they're is a thunderstorm.

Tracy and Lauren left **their** books outside, and **they're** going to be so sorry when **there** is a thunderstorm.

> 5. The amount of physics problems we have to do is not terrible, especially if we divide them among the two of us.

The **number** of physics problems we have to do is not terrible, especially if we divide them **between** the two of us.

> 6. I tried to find Linda so I could apologize because I felt so badly about the argument.

I tried to find Linda so I could apologize because I felt so **bad** about the argument.

8. Comparisons

To check comparisons on the ACT English Test, always go back and reread the entire sentence.

a. Illogical Comparisons

Use the word *other* or the word *else* to compare one thing or person to the rest of the group.

> Illogical comparison: Our debate team won more prizes than any team. (illogical because your team is one of the competing teams)
> Logical comparison: Our debate team won more prizes than any **other** team.

b. Unbalanced Comparisons

Comparisons must be balanced and parallel. Use the word *than* or *as* to balance the sentence.

> Unbalanced: The mathletes won as many points, if not more than, their opponents.
> Balanced: The mathletes won **as** many points **as,** if not more **than,** their opponents.

c. Faulty Comparisons

You must compare like things ... apples to apples, not apples to oranges.

> Faulty: After tasting all the exotic dishes at the ethnic food fair, I found I like the foods from India better than China. (comparing **foods** to **China**)
>
> Correct: After tasting all the exotic dishes at the ethnic food fair, I found I like the foods from India better than the foods (or those) from China. (comparing foods to foods)

> Faulty: Our track star was more dominant than the previous years. (comparing the track star to years)
>
> Correct: Our track star was more dominant than those in previous years. (comparing **star** to **those** or **track stars**)

Examples

Correct the comparison errors in the following sentences:

> 1. The music of Rascal Flatts is as good as Sugarland.

The music of Rascal Flatts is as good as **that of** Sugarland.

> 2. Rachel felt her poetry was better than any other student in the writing class.

Rachel felt her poetry was better than **that of** any other student in the writing class.

> 3. My car is cleaner than any car in the parking lot.

My car is cleaner than any **other** car in the parking lot.

> 4. It was clear that the flowers from the local garden shop were fresher than the florist.

It was clear that the flowers from the local garden shop were fresher than **those from** the florist.

> 5. The movie *Diehard 3* was as suspenseful, if not more suspenseful than, the prequel.

The movie *Diehard 3* was as suspenseful **as,** if not more suspenseful than, the prequel.

> 6. The Spanish restaurant on South Street is better than any restaurant in town.

The Spanish restaurant on South Street is better than any **other** restaurant in town.

9. Agreement

Agreement questions usually refer to errors in subject-verb agreement or noun agreement. Your task will be to make sure all verbs agree with their subjects in gender and number and all noun references agree in number.

a. Agreement of Subject and Verb

A verb must agree with its subject in number. A singular subject takes the singular form of a verb; a plural subject takes the plural form of the verb.

> Singular: My **answer agrees** with yours. (one answer)
>
> Plural: My **answers agree** with yours. (more than one answer)

Note: While most nouns form the plural by adding the letter s, most verbs in their plural form do not end in the letter s.

Phrases may intervene between the subject and the verb. In most cases, to ensure agreement, ignore the intervening phrase.

> Example: My answers **on the test** agree with yours. (**on the test** is a prepositional phrase)

Intervening **prepositional phrases** do not affect agreement of subject and verb, so the best approach is to cross out or bracket intervening phrases. This will avoid confusion.

Note: The subject of a sentence is NEVER part of a prepositional phrase.

> Example: The sleeping **cabin** with a bathroom and two beds **is** available.

To check agreement on the ACT, go back and reread the entire sentence. Bracket the intervening phrase:

> The sleeping **cabin** [with a bathroom and two beds] **is** available.

Be sure to find the subject and match it with the verb.

> Example: Studying for final exams helps me do well on the test.

Bracket the intervening phrases:

> **Studying** [for final exams] **helps** me do well on the test.
> **Studying** is the singular subject; **helps** is the singular form of the verb.

Sometimes on the ACT English Test passages, multiple phrases intervene.

> Example: The photographs of the family taken in the field beyond the house show a group of smiling people of all ages.

Follow the same procedure and reread the entire sentence bracketing the phrases.

> The **photographs** [of the family taken in the field beyond the house] **show** a group of smiling people of all ages.

Photographs is the plural subject; **show** is the plural form of the verb.

Intervening **parenthetical or explanatory phrases** also do not affect agreement of subject and verb, so the best approach is to cross out or bracket intervening phrases. This will avoid confusion.

> Example: My cousin, along with ten of her closest friends, volunteers in a hospital.

Bracket the intervening phrase or phrases and match the subject with the verb:

My **cousin,** [along with ten of her closest friends,] **volunteers** in a hospital.

Example: Our chapter of DECA, like all the other chapters in the surrounding districts, attends the state competition.

Our **chapter** [of DECA,] [like all the other chapters in the surrounding districts,] **attends** the state competition.

Example: Julius Caesar, accompanied by many of the deceitful senators, was approached by a soothsayer who warned him of danger.

Julius Caesar, [accompanied by many of the deceitful senators,] **was** approached by a soothsayer who warned him of danger.

Singular **indefinite pronouns** take the singular form of the verb; plural indefinite pronouns take the plural form of the verb.

Example: **Each** of the games on the computer **requires** skillful manipulation. (singular)

Example: **Both** of the games on the computer **require** skillful manipulation. (plural)

Agreement problems also occur with *either ... or* and *neither ... nor*. Singular subjects joined by these correlative conjunctions are singular.

Example: Either the **novel** or the **play is** acceptable.

Plural subjects joined by these correlative conjunctions are plural.

Example: Neither the **trees** nor the **bushes were** damaged by the fire.

When one subject is singular and one subject is plural, the verb agrees with the closer subject.

Example: Neither the **parents** nor the little **girl is** afraid of spiders.

Example: Either the **coach** or my **parents are driving** to the game.

Inverted sentences will be tricky on the ACT because you will encounter the verb before the subject. Again, the key to success is to find the subject, wherever it is in the sentence.

Note: The words *here* and *there* are never subjects.

Example: Two months before the hurricane there **were** warning **signs.** (Plural subject **signs** agrees with the plural form of the verb **were.**)

Example: There **are** many **problems** with the economy today. (Plural subject **problems** agrees with the plural form of the verb **are.**)

Be sure to read the whole sentence through to find the subject.

Example: Onto the field **march** the **band** and **the color guard.** (Plural subjects **band** and **color guard** agree with the plural form of the verb **march.**)

Example: Over the trees **flies** a small **bird.** (Singular subject **bird** agrees with singular form of the verb **flies.**)

b. Noun Agreement

Use a singular noun to refer to a singular noun and a plural noun to refer to a plural noun ... sounds logical, right? Yet, problems do arise.

Example: People who wish to be a teacher should apply here.

This sentence is incorrect because the plural noun **people** requires the plural noun **teachers** to be logical.

Correct: **People** who wish to be **teachers** should apply here.
Incorrect: Tourists with a visa must sign in at Passport Control.
Correct: **Tourists** with **visas** must sign in at Passport Control.

Examples

Select the best word in the following sentences:

> 1. Into every life (come, comes) some issues that perplex us.

Into every life **come** some issues that perplex us.

> 2. A carton of books (is, are) ready to be opened and stacked on the shelves.

A carton of books **is** ready to be opened and stacked on the shelves.

> 3. Neither the cats nor the dog (is, are) in the house.

Neither the cats nor the dog **is** in the house.

> 4. Each of the sentences on the bulletin boards (was, were) written by a student.

Each of the sentences on the bulletin boards **was** written by a student.

> 5. (Does, Do) either of the maps show the Himalayan Mountains?

Does either of the maps show the Himalayan Mountains?

> 6. One of the puzzling aspects of the physics equations (is, are) the vector analysis.

One of the puzzling aspects of the physics equations **is** the vector analysis.

10. Tense

Verbs tell the action or state of being in a sentence. They are also the **time** words, the principal indicators of **tense.** Tense errors come up fairly frequently on the ACT. As you read, be aware of the tense of the passage and note any inconsistencies.

The six tenses in English are as follows:

Present	Past	Future
(action taking place in the present)	(action that has already taken place in the past)	(action that will take place in the future)
I walk	I walked	I will walk
He, she, it walks	He, she, it walked	He, she, it will walk
They walk	They walked	They will walk

Present Perfect	Past Perfect	Future Perfect
(action that began in the past and continues into the present)	(action that began in the past and was completed before some other action)	(action completed in the future before some other action in the future)
I have walked	I had walked	I will have walked
He, she, it has walked	He, she, it had walked	He, she, it will have walked
They have walked	They had walked	They will have walked

Perfect tenses are always formed by using **have, has,** or **had** + the **past participle** form of the verb.

You also have the option of using the **progressive** form (-ing) in each tense to show ongoing action:

Present Progressive: I am walking	*Present Perfect Progressive:* I have been walking
Past Progressive: I was walking	*Past Perfect Progressive:* I had been walking
Future Progressive: I will be walking	*Future Perfect Progressive:* I will have been walking

The **present participle** is the –ing form of the verb: walking. (These –ing forms cannot be verbs alone; they need a helping verb.)

The **past participle** is the –ed, –d, –t, –en, –n form of the verb: walked. Many verbs have irregular forms:

Present	Past	Past Participle
arise	arose	(have) arisen
become	became	(have) become
bring	brought	(have) brought
catch	caught	(have) caught
do	did	(have) done
drink	drank	(have) drunk
drive	drove	(have) driven
eat	ate	(have) eaten
fall	fell	(have) fallen
fly	flew	(have) flown
lend	lent	(have) lent
ring	rang	(have) rung
sing	sang	(have) sung
swim	swam	(have) swum
write	wrote	(have) written

Often verbs occur in verb phrases with a helping verb and a main verb. Some verbs like **do, have,** and **be** can be either main verbs or helping verbs.

Example: Roberto will **do** his homework. (main verb)

Example: Roberto and Anna **do need** to practice their duet. (helping verb)

As you read the passages on the ACT English Test, watch for sentences that have illogical shifts in tense or that use incorrect verb forms.

Illogical shift: He **searched** for signs of deer when he **notices** the tracks.

Correct: He **is searching** for signs of deer when he **notices** the tracks. (present)

Or: He **was searching** for signs of deer when he **noticed** the tracks. (past)

Check the tense of the passage to determine whether the sentence should be in the present or past.

Incorrect verb form: We were shocked that he **had drank** all the water in the canteen.

Correct: We were shocked that he **had drunk** all the water in the canteen.

Examples

Write the correct form of the italicized verb in the blank:

1. I was pleased to discover that I had _____ a mile. *swim*

swum

2. By the next meet, I will have _____ my own record. *beat*

beaten

3. When I woke up, I found that two inches of snow had _____. *fall*

fallen

4. At last week's meeting, I _____ a presentation. *give*

gave

5. Joan _____ her dog to school yesterday. *bring*

brought

6. Once the bell has _____, we can leave for the beach. *ring*

rung

11. Sentence Structure

Questions on sentence structure test your ability to recognize run-on sentences, sentence fragments, and complete sentences. They also test your ability to recognize the relationship between main clauses and subordinate clauses.

a. Run-on Sentences

Two or more complete thoughts joined in one sentence without proper punctuation constitute a run-on sentence.

> Example: The lecture was on the life cycle of the frog it seemed to go on for hours.

The run-on can be corrected in several ways:

1. Break the sentence up into separate sentences.
   The lecture was on the life cycle of the frog. It seemed to go on for hours.
2. Join the main clauses with a semicolon.
   The lecture was on the life cycle of the frog; it seemed to go on for hours.
3. Change one or more of the main clauses to a subordinate clause.
   Because the lecture was on the life cycle of the frog, it seemed to go on for hours.
4. Use a comma and a conjunction.
   The lecture was on the life cycle of the frog, and it seemed to go on for hours.
5. Use the semicolon and a conjunctive adverb.
   The lecture was on the life cycle of the frog; consequently, it seemed to go on for hours.

The comma splice: The most common run-on occurs when a comma joins two sentences.

> Example: Serena really likes Aaron, she thinks he can help her achieve her goals.

Correct the comma splice by any one of the run-on correction methods.

> Example: Serena really likes Aaron; she thinks he can help her achieve her goals.

b. Sentence Fragments

Most sentence fragments are phrases or subordinate clauses. Very often on the ACT English Test a participial phrase or an infinitive phrase will be a choice, but a complete sentence is needed.

> Example: Being interested in setting up a charity auction. (participial phrase)
> Example: To be interested in setting up a charity auction. (infinitive phrase)
> Example: Since we are all interested in setting up a charity auction. (subordinate clause)

To avoid fragments, remember:

- A sentence must have a subject and a verb and express a complete thought.
- No word ending in –ing can stand alone as a verb without a helping verb (except one-syllable verbs like sing and ring).

Examples

Correct the following sentences. Answers may vary.

> 1. Raghav being the highest scoring quarterback on the football team.

Raghav has been the highest scoring quarterback on the football team.

> 2. Many people think dogs make the best pets, cats are affectionate, too.

Many people think dogs make the best pets, but cats are affectionate, too.

> 3. Hoping to fill all the seats in the auditorium for the school musical.

We are hoping to fill all the seats in the auditorium for the school musical.

> 4. Pearl loves to go to Florida, she has so many friends and relatives to visit there.

Pearl loves to go to Florida because she has so many friends and relatives to visit there.

> 5. Not only did the class picnic get rained out on Saturday, but cancelled forever.

Not only did the class picnic get rained out on Saturday, but it was also cancelled forever.

> 6. The TV show *Lost* was filmed in Hawaii, the lucky cast got to live there.

The TV show *Lost* was filmed in Hawaii; the lucky cast got to live there.

E. Rhetoric

Rhetoric questions focus on style, writing strategy, and organization. You are asked to make decisions similar to those that writers make when they revise their work.

1. Style

The five passages on the ACT English Test will vary in style. You are expected to note the style (sometimes referred to as the writer's voice) and take it into consideration as you answer questions about the writers' decisions. Some passages, especially those written in first person (I) by a teenager, will have an informal, even breezy, style, but rarely will slang expressions be correct. Many passages are objective and informational; these will have a straightforward and unemotional style. Most questions will involve choices in diction and wordiness.

---

1. My cousin Larry is one of the funniest people I know. I see him every day because we attend the same school. He is very clever and never fails to make me laugh with his <u>nutty, crazy stuff that makes me giggle</u>.

    A. NO CHANGE
    B. idiosyncratic and comedic jocularity.
    C. quirky humor and silly jokes.
    D. perspicacious awareness of absurdity.

In this question, you should note that the excerpt is written in an informal style. Therefore, Choice B and Choice D are far too formal for this passage. Choice A, although informal, borders on slang and is wordy and imprecise. Choice C is the best phrasing for the underlined words.

---

2. The Board of Education has issued a statement regarding the dress code for high schools in the district. The code includes a definition of what constitutes "proper attire." The reason for the new code is <u>because some kids come to school dressed to the nines.</u>

    F. NO CHANGE
    G. that some students have been dressing too formally.
    H. because of kids' wearing formal clothes.
    J. because of kids who wear formal attire.

This excerpt is written in a more formal style than the previous example. The underlined portion is not acceptable; it contains a usage error and a cliché. *The reason … is because* is not standard English. It should be rewritten as *The reason … is that*. In addition, *dressed to the nines* is a cliché and should be changed to more original phrasing. Choice H repeats the usage error. Choice J also has the usage error. Choice G is correct.

In answering style questions, keep in mind that active verbs are preferable to passive ones.

    Example: **He designed the posters.** (active verb) is preferable to **The posters were designed by him.** (passive).

2. Writing Strategy

These questions ask you to consider the appropriateness of the writer's strategy in either a portion of the passage or the entire passage. As you read, consider the following questions: Which is the best choice for the writer to accomplish his or her purpose? Which choice shows his or her awareness of the audience? Which choice is more effectively written? Is every piece of information relevant to the focus of the passage?

(The following is an adaptation of an essay written in 1921 by T. S. Eliot)

The modern dramatist, and probably the modern audience, is terrified of the myth. The myth is imagination and it is also criticism, <u>and the two are one.</u> The Seventeenth Century had its own machinery of virtues
₁

and vices, as we have, but its drama is a <u>criticism about humanity</u> far more serious than its conscious moral
₂

judgments. "Volpone" does <u>not merely show</u> that wickedness is punished; it criticises humanity by intensifying
₃

wickedness. <u>When I read "Volpone," I found it difficult to follow the stage directions.</u>
₄

---

1. If the writer were to delete the underlined portion, the paragraph would primarily lose

   A. a contrast to the idea that preceded it.
   B. an emphatic assertion.
   C. a detail that adds specificity to the sentence.
   D. a foreshadowing of the conclusion.

B. If the writer deletes the underlined portion, he will lose an emphatic assertion (Choice B). An emphatic assertion is a strong statement. The writer has stated that myth is both imagination and criticism. Now he reiterates the point with emphasis. The statement is not a contrast (Choice A) or a detail (Choice C). In no way does it foreshadow a conclusion (Choice D).

---

2. Which of the following is the best alternative to the underlined part?

   F. criticism towards humanity
   G. criticism toward humanity
   H. criticism referring to humanity
   J. criticism of humanity

J. This is an idiom question. The correct preposition to use with **criticism** is **of** (Choice J).

---

3. Which of the following alternatives to the underlined part would NOT be acceptable?

   A. not only show
   B. not show
   C. not merely illustrate
   D. not only demonstrate

B. In this sentence, **merely** and **only** can be used interchangeably before the verb. The verbs **show, demonstrate,** and **illustrate** are equally appropriate in this sentence. Choice B, which omits the word **merely,** changes the meaning of the sentence and is not acceptable.

4. The writer is considering leaving out this sentence. Should he delete it?

    F.   No, because his opinion adds liveliness to the essay.

    G.   No, because the reader always wants to know what the writer is thinking.

    H.   Yes, because it is irrelevant to the focus of the essay.

    J.   Yes, because it is a detail that might enhance the reader's understanding of the paragraph.

H. The writer should delete the sentence (Choice H) because it is irrelevant to the paragraph. The writer never mentioned stage directions, and his opinion, at this point in the paragraph, is not relevant.

3. Organization

Questions on organization deal with the order and coherence of ideas in the passages. One of the keys to achieving coherence is the effective use of transitional words and phrases.

a. Order and Coherence

You will notice as you read the ACT English Test passages that sometimes the sentences in the passage are numbered, and sometimes the paragraphs are numbered. This numbering tells you that you will encounter questions about order. Use the context clues to help you determine the best order. For example, if a person or place is mentioned by name, ask yourself, "Has this name been introduced or identified?" If the introduction comes later in the passage, then you know you must logically rearrange the order of the sentences. The same holds true for paragraph order. Use logic and look for clues to what happens next within the passage.

    (1) Last summer I went on vacation with my family to England. (2) Since we had landed in London, we had to rent a car to drive to their house. (3) Several times we got lost and had to ask for directions. (4) While we were there, we decided to visit some cousins who live in Ludlow, a small city near the border of Wales. (5) To our embarrassment and to the amusement of those we stopped, we frequently mispronounced the names of the towns along the way. (6) The drive itself was an adventure. (7) How could we know the British often drop syllables from names?

1. The passage is best organized in which order?

    A.   1, 4, 2, 3, 5, 6, 7

    B.   2, 1, 6, 5, 4, 7, 3

    C.   2, 6, 1, 3, 7, 4, 5

    D.   1, 4, 2, 6, 3, 5, 7

D. The logical order is Choice D:

    (1) Last summer I went on vacation with my family to England. (4) While we were there, we decided to visit some cousins who live in Ludlow, a small city near the border of Wales. (2) Since we had landed in London, we had to rent a car to drive to their house. (6) The drive itself was an adventure. (3) Several times we got lost and had to ask for directions. (5) To our embarrassment and to the amusement of those we stopped, we frequently mispronounced the names of the towns along the way. (7) How could we know the British often drop syllables from names?

b. Transitional Words and Phrases

Transitional words and phrases link ideas and indicate the relationship of ideas within a sentence, a paragraph, or a passage. They are essential tools for a writer who wants to achieve a clear and logical flow of ideas.

Important Transitional Words and Phrases			
Words used to indicate an example		**Words used to show a result**	
for example		consequently	
for instance		hence	
specifically		accordingly	
		therefore	
Words used to indicate a reason		**Words used to indicate more information**	
as		besides	
because		in addition	
since		moreover	
due to		furthermore	
Words used to contrast		**Words used to show similarity**	
although		another	
but		similarly	
however		likewise	
in contrast		also	
nevertheless		again	
whereas		in the same way	
while		too	
yet		equally	
on the other hand			
still			
despite			
Words used to establish time relationships		**Words used for emphasis**	
before	later	then	indeed
during	soon	then again	clearly
after	next	once	to be sure
at last	until	at the same time	without doubt
at this point	recently	assuredly	

Examples

Select the best transitional word or phrase to fit in the sentences:

---

1. Our lacrosse team has lost every game so far; _____, they are expected to win today.

   A. similarly
   B. nevertheless
   C. in addition
   D. recently

B. nevertheless (contrast)

---

2. I heard it is raining heavily in Denver, _____ it is sunny in Topeka.

   F. then
   G. but
   H. likewise
   J. consequently

G. but (contrast)

---

3. The report on upgrading the reading program showed serious weaknesses in some programs; _____, it recommended several steps to redress the problems.

   A. although
   B. furthermore
   C. likewise
   D. whereas

B. furthermore (more information)

---

4. I have traveled to many states; _____, I have been to New York, California, Florida, and Nevada.

   F. in addition
   G. however
   H. therefore
   J. for example

J. for example (an example)

VI. Reading Test

A. Overview of the ACT Reading Test

The Reading Test consists of four passages: Prose Fiction, Humanities, Social Science, and Natural Science. After each section, there are 10 questions based on the information stated or implied in the passage. You have 35 minutes to read the passages and answer the 40 questions.

Prose Fiction: This passage is usually an excerpt from a short story or a novel. You are reading to understand the mood of the selection, the narration of events (plot), and the characters as they are revealed by their words, their actions, and the responses of the other characters to them.

Humanities: This passage describes or analyzes works of art, presents information about an artist, or is a memoir. The Humanities passage tests your ability to comprehend, analyze, and ascertain point of view.

Social Science: This passage is an informative presentation of material that has been gathered by research. It is similar to a chapter in your social studies textbook. To answer the questions, you will often have to follow the chronology of the events in the passage, understand the ramifications of political actions, or make conclusions about psychological experiments.

Natural Science: This passage tests your ability to read about science-related topics. The questions require you to understand the sequence of events, recall facts, and draw conclusions.

B. General Strategies for the Reading Test

- Read the passage actively. Think about what you are reading as you read.
- Answer all questions based on information directly stated in the passage or implied by the passage. Do not rely on your own knowledge of the topic.
- Take note of names, dates, places, and events that may show up in the questions. Circle or underline them as you read.
- As you read, think about the main idea of the passage and the author's purpose in writing it.
- Don't get bogged down with a difficult sentence or two. Keep reading; the point may become clear as you go on.
- Read the questions carefully; be sure you know exactly what you are being asked.
- The questions do not go in the order of the passage. The first question, for example, may deal with information in the last paragraph of the passage.
- Some questions are EXCEPT or NOT questions. In these cases, you are looking for the answer choice that is NOT true.
- Do not feel you must rely on your memory; go back and refer to the text as often as necessary.
- For detail questions, go back and skim until you find the reference. Some of the questions will ask you to recall very specific information.

- If you are unsure of an answer, make your best guess and move on. Remember, there is no guessing penalty on the ACT, so do not leave any answers blank.
- Be aware of time; you can't leisurely read the passages. You have about 8½ minutes to read and answer the 10 questions on each passage.

C. Types of Reading Questions

The reading questions will test your ability to read and comprehend passages similar to those you will encounter in college. To answer the questions, you will need to understand both what is directly stated in the passage and what is implied by the author. You don't need any previous knowledge of the topics; all the information you need to answer the questions is contained in the passages, so don't hesitate to look back as you answer.

1. Main Idea

Main idea questions test your ability to figure out the author's primary point in writing the passage. Often, rereading the first two sentences in each paragraph will help you. Most authors refer to their main idea in the topic sentence(s) of each paragraph. Look for the common thread, the idea that each paragraph supports.

2. Main Conflict Questions

Main conflict questions refer to the opposing sides in the primary struggle within the prose fiction passage. The struggle may be between two characters, between a character and a facet of nature, or between two facets of nature.

3. Passage-as-a-Whole Questions

Questions about the passage as a whole refer to the main point of the entire passage, not just a portion.

4. Main Point of a Paragraph

These questions ask you to identify the main point of one particular paragraph. First, be sure you are looking at the correct paragraph; perhaps mark in brackets as a reminder. Check the line numbers in the questions carefully. Then identify the topic sentence of the paragraph (usually, but not always, the first sentence). Follow the author's logic in the paragraph. Ask yourself, "What point is he/she trying to prove?" The answer to this question should correspond to one of the answer choices.

Practice 1: Main Conflict Question

The following excerpt is from *The Autobiography of Benjamin Franklin* written in 1771.

It was about this time I conceiv'd the bold and arduous project of arriving at moral perfection. I wish'd to live without committing any fault at any time; I would conquer all that either natural inclination, custom, or company might lead me into. As I knew, or thought I knew, what was right and wrong,

(5) I did not see why I might not always do the one and avoid the other. But I soon found I had undertaken a task of more difficulty than I had imagined. While my care was employ'd in guarding against one fault, I was often surprised by another; habit took the advantage of inattention; inclination was sometimes too strong for reason. I concluded, at length, that the mere speculative conviction that it was our interest to be completely virtuous was not sufficient to prevent our slipping; and that the contrary habits must be broken, and good ones acquired and established, before we can have any dependence on a (10) steady, uniform rectitude of conduct.

---

1. The main conflict in this passage is between:

   A. Franklin's need for independence and his employer's need for assistance.
   B. Franklin's desire to be virtuous and his tendency toward wrongdoing.
   C. Franklin's belief in good habits and his code of conduct.
   D. Franklin's inclination to be alone and his natural need for company.

B is correct. Franklin states he conceived the idea of living a life of "moral perfection." Then he writes, "But I soon found I had undertaken a task of more difficulty than I had imagined." It was more difficult because he found his desire to be good "was not sufficient to prevent our slipping." So, even though he wanted to be good, he could not help slipping back into bad habits. All the wrong answer choices (Choices A, C, and D) count on your reading quickly and pouncing on words in the choices that look familiar because they are also in the passage.

Practice 2: Main Idea Question

The following excerpt is from *Democracy in America* written by Alexis de Tocqueville in 1840.

In the United States the majority undertakes to supply a multitude of ready-made opinions for the use of individuals, who are thus relieved from the necessity of forming opinions of their own. Everybody there adopts great numbers of theories, on philosophy, morals, and politics, without inquiry, upon public trust; and if we look to it very narrowly, it will be perceived that religion herself holds her sway there, much less (5) as a doctrine of revelation than as a commonly received opinion. The fact that the political laws of the Americans are such that the majority rules the community with sovereign sway, materially increases the power which that majority naturally exercises over the mind. For nothing is more customary in man than to recognize superior wisdom in the person of his oppressor. This political omnipotence of the majority in the United States doubtless augments the influence which public opinion would obtain without it over the (10) mind of each member of the community; but the foundations of that influence do not rest upon it.

---

2. Which of the following best states the main idea of this paragraph?

   F. America is a nation founded on the premise that the convictions of the individual are more powerful than the will of the majority.
   G. The foundation of political power in this country rests in the hands of those with superior wisdom.
   H. The beliefs of the majority in America are sovereign and inform the opinions of the individual.
   J. Because it is a country ruled by the majority, the United States is politically omnipotent.

H is correct. The main idea is stated in the first sentence of the passage. Choice F is the opposite of his thesis, Choice G is a misreading of his point that the individual believes the majority has superior wisdom, and Choice J is unsupported by any evidence in the passage.

5. Detail Questions

Questions about details in a passage will ask you to identify and analyze details that the author uses to support his or her thesis. Details will usually be in the form of facts, names, examples, illustrations, places, or evidence from research.

a. Directly Stated Details

Directly stated details should be locatable within the passage. Identify the paragraph that most likely contains the information; then skim until you find the specific piece of information you need.

b. Implied Details

Some details are implied by the information in the text. In these cases, you must "read between the lines" to find the implied detail.

Practice 3: Detail Questions

This passage is an excerpt from *The Birds of America* written by John James Audubon in 1839.

> Previous to my visit to the Florida Keys, I had seen but few Frigate-birds, and those only at some distance, while I was on the Gulf of Mexico, so that I could merely recognize them by their mode of flight. On approaching Indian Key, however, I observed several of them, and as I proceeded farther south, their numbers rapidly increased; but on the Tortugas very few were observed. This bird rarely travels farther
> (5) eastward than the Bay of Charleston in South Carolina, although it is abundant in all seasons from Cape Florida to Cape Sable, the two extremes of the peninsula. How far south it may be found I cannot tell.

---

3. Before the author traveled to the Florida Keys, he had:

   A. widely studied the Frigate-birds in their natural habitat.
   B. been part of a scientific expedition that had explored all of the Florida peninsula to find the rare Frigate-bird.
   C. doubted the existence of the nearly extinct bird.
   D. not seen Frigate-birds close up, but had observed them in flight.

D is correct. The author directly states: "Previous to my visit to the Florida Keys, I had seen but few Frigate-birds, and those only at some distance." None of the other choices are supported by the text.

---

4. Where would one be most likely to see a flock of Frigate-birds?

   F. On the islands in the Bay of Charleston off the east coast of South Carolina
   G. Off the coast of Miami Beach
   H. On Cape Sable Island in Canada
   J. On an American Indian reservation in Arizona

G is correct. The author states the Frigate-bird "is abundant in all seasons from Cape Florida to Cape Sable, the two extremes of the peninsula." From this statement, you may infer that the birds are abundant anywhere along the coast of Florida. Choice F is incorrect because the author states, "This bird rarely travels farther eastward than the Bay of Charleston in South Carolina." Choice H is meant to distract you with an island that has the same name as Cape Sable in Florida; however, this passage solely concerns Florida. Choice J is obviously wrong; however, it is a distracter because Indian Key was mentioned in the passage.

6. Relationships

Some questions will test your ability to note relationships among ideas, facts, examples, or illustrations.

a. Comparison/Contrast

Comparison/contrast questions test your ability to note similarities and differences between the elements in a passage. For these questions, you must make connections between ideas, engage in critical thinking, and reflect on similarities and differences. Look for words like **compare, contrast, similarities,** and **differences** to help you locate the answer in the text.

b. Cause and Effect

Cause and effect questions test your ability to see how one event or situation is responsible for another. The cause is what made something happen; the effect is the result of the cause.

c. Sequence of Events

Sequence of events questions test your ability to follow a series of events in the order in which they occurred. Some order may be chronological (time) or spatial (large to small, east to west, top to bottom) or specific to general (or general to specific).

7. Generalizations

A **generalization** question asks you to consider the information in the passage and reduce it to a single statement. You may have to characterize a person about whom you have been reading, condense a process, or draw a conclusion about a subject.

Practice 4: Relationship and Generalization Questions

The following is adapted from "The Custom-House," the introductory chapter of *The Scarlet Letter,* written by Nathaniel Hawthorne in 1850.

But, one idle and rainy day, it was my fortune to make a discovery of some little interest. Poking and burrowing into the heaped-up rubbish in the corner, unfolding one and another document, and reading the names of vessels that had long ago foundered at sea or rotted at the wharves . . . I chanced to lay my hand on a small package, carefully done up in a piece of ancient yellow parchment. This envelope had
(5)   the air of an official record . . . There was something about it that quickened an instinctive curiosity, and made me undo the faded red tape that tied up the package, with the sense that a treasure would here be brought to light. Unbending the rigid folds of the parchment cover, I found it to be a commission . . . in favour of one Jonathan Pue, as Surveyor of His Majesty's Customs for the Port of Salem . . . Nothing, if I rightly call to mind, was left of my respected predecessor, save an imperfect skeleton, and some frag-
(10)   ments of apparel, and a wig of majestic frizzle, which, unlike the head that it once adorned, was in very

satisfactory preservation. But, on examining the papers which the parchment commission served to envelop, I found more traces of Mr. Pue's mental part, and the internal operations of his head . . .

They were documents, in short, not official, but of a private nature, or, at least, written in his private capacity, and apparently with his own hand. I could account for their being included in the heap of
(15) Custom-House lumber only by the fact that Mr. Pue's death had happened suddenly, and that these papers, which he probably kept in his official desk, had never come to the knowledge of his heirs, or were supposed to relate to the business of the revenue. On the transfer of the archives to Halifax, this package, proving to be of no public concern, was left behind, and had remained ever since unopened.

The ancient Surveyor—being little molested, I suppose, at that early day with business pertaining to
(20) his office—seems to have devoted some of his many leisure hours to researches as a local antiquarian . . .

But the object that most drew my attention to the mysterious package was a certain affair of fine red cloth, much worn and faded. There were traces about it of gold embroidery, which, however, was greatly frayed and defaced, so that none, or very little, of the glitter was left. It had been wrought, as was easy to perceive, with wonderful skill of needlework; and the stitch (as I am assured by ladies conversant with
(25) such mysteries) gives evidence of a now forgotten art, not to be discovered even by the process of picking out the threads. This rag of scarlet cloth—for time, and wear, and a sacrilegious moth had reduced it to little other than a rag—on careful examination, assumed the shape of a letter. It was the capital letter A. . . .

---

5. What is the correct sequence of events?

   A. The narrator found the cloth, discovered the commission of Mr. Pue, and poked around the accumulated garbage in the corner of the room.

   B. The narrator opened the parchment package, did research, and found the scarlet cloth before Mr. Pue died.

   C. The narrator poked around the rubbish, found and opened the parchment package, discovered Mr. Pue's documents, and found the scarlet cloth.

   D. After Mr. Pue died, the narrator found the scarlet cloth, undid the faded red tape, and read the documents.

C is correct. Refer to the passage and locate each event. Choice A is incorrect because the narrator found the package when he poked around the rubbish. In Choice B, Mr. Pue dies last; since he left the package when he died, the order is incorrect. Choice D reverses the order: The cloth is in the package tied with the red tape.

---

6. The author is intrigued by the scarlet cloth for all of the following reasons EXCEPT:

   F. It is evidence of the forgotten art of needlework.

   G. It is a curious find among the papers of a surveyor.

   H. Although it is quite old, it has been mysteriously preserved in good condition.

   J. He is an instinctively curious man.

H is correct. The narrator states the cloth has been reduced to little more than a rag by time and wear and moths.

7. In the passage, the author creates a contrast between:

    A. idle curiosity and fascinating discovery.
    B. sensationalistic expectation and official bookkeeping.
    C. eager anticipation and disappointing reality.
    D. youthful enthusiasm and mature practicality.

A is correct. The narrator is just passing time on an idle, rainy day when he unexpectedly discovers the mysterious embroidered cloth. He appears fascinated by his discovery, not disappointed (Choice C) or practical (Choice D). He certainly had no sensationalistic expectation, and bookkeeping does not figure into his reaction (Choice B).

8. Based on the evidence in the passage, the narrator is best described as:

    F. a humorless and pompous bureaucrat.
    G. an unromantic and meticulous organizer.
    H. an imaginative and somewhat ironic observer.
    J. a piously devoted antiquarian.

H is correct. The narrator's imagination is captured by the scrap of scarlet cloth; his irony is apparent in his comments about his deceased predecessor, Mr. Pue: "a wig of majestic frizzle, which, unlike the head that it once adorned, was in very satisfactory preservation" (lines 10–11). There is no evidence of pomposity, and he does display ironic humor, so Choice F is incorrect. Choice G does not consider his imagination (unromantic), and he is just poking around rubbish, not organizing it. The narrator refers to Mr. Pue, not himself, as an antiquarian (Choice J).

8. Author's Voice and Method

These questions refer to the author's tone and attitude toward his or her subject and the way in which he or she presents ideas. Questions may be about the author's craft as well as his or her point of view. Look for clues in the diction (word choice) in the passage. Is it positive and generally a tribute to the person or event? Does it point out the weaknesses or failures of a plan or a design? Also, if a question asks you to consider the purpose of a paragraph, think about what that paragraph contributes to the passage as a whole. Ask yourself what the passage would lose if that paragraph were to be omitted.

9. Vocabulary in Context

Vocabulary-in-context questions ask about the meaning of a word or a short phrase as it is used in the passage. Often words that have multiple meanings are selected. You must find the appropriate choice for the context. The best technique is to go back to the text, circle the word or phrase, and reread the whole sentence. Then replace the circled word or phrase with the words in the answer choices. Select the answer choice that is consistent with the original meaning of the sentence.

Practice 5: Author's Voice and Method and Vocabulary Questions

The following passage is an excerpt from *The Age of Innocence* written by Edith Wharton in 1920. Newland Archer, a wealthy young gentleman, is at the opera observing an innocent young woman whom he plans to marry.

He did not in the least wish the future Mrs. Newland Archer to be a simpleton. He meant her (thanks to his enlightening companionship) to develop a social tact and readiness of wit enabling her to hold her own with the most popular married women of the "younger set," in which it was the recognised custom to attract masculine homage while playfully discouraging it. If he had probed to the bottom of his
(5) vanity (as he sometimes nearly did) he would have found there the wish that his wife should be as worldly-wise and as eager to please as the married lady whose charms had held his fancy through two mildly agitated years; without, of course, any hint of the frailty which had so nearly marred that unhappy being's life, and had disarranged his own plans for a whole winter.

How this miracle of fire and ice was to be created, and to sustain itself in a harsh world, he had never
(10) taken the time to think out; but he was content to hold his view without analyzing it, since he knew it was that of all the carefully-brushed, white-waistcoated, button-hole-flowered gentlemen who succeeded each other in the club box, exchanged friendly greetings with him, and turned their opera-glasses critically on the circle of ladies who were the product of the system. In matters intellectual and artistic Newland Archer felt himself distinctly the superior of these chosen specimens of old New York gentility; he had probably
(15) read more, thought more, and even seen a good deal more of the world, than any other man of the number. Singly they betrayed their inferiority; but grouped together they represented "New York," and the habit of masculine solidarity made him accept their doctrine on all the issues called moral. He instinctively felt that in this respect it would be troublesome—and also rather bad form—to strike out for himself.

9. It can be inferred from the passage that the author views Newland Archer as:

   A. a confident man who does not rely on the judgments of others to give him authority.
   B. a rather egotistical gentleman with pretensions to superiority.
   C. a naïve fellow who lacks the sophistication of "New York gentility."
   D. a newcomer to society who believes he must conform to the standards of those who set the rules.

B is correct. Archer is presented as a man with an inflated sense of his own self-worth. He believes he is "superior" to the other men. Choice A is incorrect: Although Archer is confident, he does rely on the judgments of others. Choice C is incorrect because Archer is quite sophisticated. Choice D is also incorrect; nothing in the passage indicates that Archer is a newcomer to society.

10. Which of the following best describes the function of the author's parenthetical comments in lines 1–2 and line 5?

   F. They underscore her faith in Archer's good judgment.
   G. They ironically comment on Archer's egotism.
   H. They present the first indication that the author is hostile to Archer.
   J. They present a contrast between the public Archer and the private Archer.

G is correct. The author's parenthetical comments are ironic and reveal her acknowledgment of Archer's vanity. Choice F is incorrect because the comments don't emphasize Archer's good judgment. Choice H is incorrect because the author isn't hostile to Archer. Choice J is incorrect because no contrast is evident in the passage.

11. The reference to "this miracle of fire and ice" (line 9) indicates that the narrator believes:

    A. Archer has set unreasonable standards for his future wife.

    B. Archer's future will be juxtaposed between the joy of passion and the bleakness of despair.

    C. the harshness of the world will intrude on Archer's neat plan for marriage to his intended bride.

    D. the tragedy of the opera will be a direct contrast to the happiness of Archer's marriage.

A is correct. By using the term "miracle," the author implies Archer has set unreasonable standards for his wife. Choices B, C, and D are incorrect because the phrase refers only to Archer's future wife, not to his future, the world, or the opera.

12. The word "fancy" in line 6 most nearly means:

    F. embellishment.

    G. interest.

    H. daydream.

    J. enthusiasm.

G is correct. A "lady whose charms had held his fancy" held his *interest.* None of the other choices fit the context.

13. The sentence "Singly they betrayed their inferiority; but grouped together they represented 'New York,' and the habit of masculine solidarity made him accept their doctrine on all the issues called moral" (lines 16–17) functions in the passage to present the narrator's view that:

    A. Archer's arrogance does not extend to challenging the collective values of his clique in society.

    B. because Archer believes himself a cut above the other men, he is unwilling to conform to their collective values.

    C. Archer feels betrayed by the members of society who disapprove of his choice of his future bride.

    D. because of the superiority of his education and the breadth of his reading, Archer believes he should be the moral compass of his social set.

A is correct. The fact that Archer would "accept their doctrine on all the issues called moral" suggests that he didn't challenge the moral values of the group, an implication that makes Choice B incorrect. There is no indication that Archer feels betrayed, so Choice C is incorrect. Archer doesn't believe he should be the moral compass (Choice D) because he isn't a leader; he's a follower of the values of the group.

14. The description of the men as "carefully-brushed, white-waistcoated, button-hole-flowered gentlemen" (line 11) reveals all of the following EXCEPT:

    F. the importance of conformity in appearance.

    G. the habit of masculine solidarity.

    H. the emphasis on individualism and assertiveness.

    J. the superficiality of a society that values conventionality.

H is correct. The lines indicate that the men are concerned about their appearance (Choice F), believe in masculine superiority (Choice G), and accept the importance of conventionality (Choice J).

D. Practice Questions

The following passage is adapted from *Manners, Customs, and Dress During the Middle Ages and During the Renaissance Period* written by Paul Lacroix circa 1874.

Charlemagne took as much pains with the administration of his palace as he did with that of his States. For instance, he not only interested himself in his warlike and hunting equipages, but also in his kitchen and pleasure gardens. He insisted upon knowing every year the number of his oxen, horses, and goats; he calculated the produce of the sale of fruits gathered in his orchards, which were not required (5) for the use of his house; he had a return of the number of fish caught in his ponds; he pointed out the shrubs best calculated for ornamenting his garden, and the vegetables which were required for his table.

The Emperor generally assumed the greatest simplicity in his dress. His daily attire consisted of a linen shirt and drawers, and a woolen tunic fastened with a silk belt. Over this tunic he threw a cloak of blue stuff, very long behind and before, but very short on each side, thus giving freedom to his arms to (10) use his sword, which he always wore. On his feet he wore bands of stuffs of various colors, crossed over one another, and covering his legs also. In winter, when he traveled or hunted on horseback, he threw over his shoulders a covering of otter or sheepskin.

He was most simple as regards his food and drink, and made a habit of having pious or historical works read to him during his repasts. He devoted the morning, which with him began in summer at (15) sunrise, and in winter earlier, to the political administration of his empire. He dined at twelve with his family; the dukes and chiefs of various nations first waited on him, and then took their places at the table, and were waited on in their turn by the counts, prefects, and superior officers of the court who dined after them. When these had finished the different chiefs of the household sat down, and they were succeeded lastly by servants of the lower order, who often did not dine till midnight, and had to content (20) themselves with what was left. When occasion required, however, this powerful Emperor knew how to maintain the pomp and dignity of his station; but as soon as he had done what was necessary, either for some great religious festival or otherwise, he returned, as if by instinct, to his dear and native simplicity.

It must be understood that the simple tastes of Charlemagne were not always shared by the princes (25) and princesses of his family, nor by the magnates of his court. Poets and historians have handed down to us descriptions of hunts, feasts, and ceremonies, at which a truly Asiatic splendor was displayed. Eginhard, however, assures us that the sons and daughters of the King were brought up under their father's eye in liberal studios; that, to save them from the vice of idleness, Charlemagne required his sons to devote themselves to all bodily exercises, such as horsemanship, handling of arms, etc., and his (30) daughters to do needlework and to spin. From what is recorded, however, of the frivolous habits and irregular morals of these princesses, it is evident that they but imperfectly realized the end of their education.

Science and letters, which for a time were brought into prominence by Charlemagne and also by his son Louis, who was very learned and was considered skilful in translating and expounding Scripture, were, (35) however, after the death of these two kings, for a long time banished to the seclusion of the cloisters, owing to the hostile rivalry of their successors, which favored the attacks of the Norman pirates. All the monuments and relics of the Gallo-Roman civilization, which the great Emperor had collected, disappeared in the civil wars, or were gradually destroyed by the devastations of the northerners.

During the first period of feudalism, that is to say from the middle of the ninth to the middle of the (40) twelfth centuries, the inhabitants of castles had little time to devote to the pleasures of private life. They had not only to be continually under arms for the endless quarrels of the King and the great chiefs; but they had also to oppose the Normans on one side, and the Saracens on the other, who, being masters of

the Spanish peninsula, spread like the rising tide. It is true that the Carlovingian warriors obtained a handsome and rich reward for these long and sanguinary efforts, for at last they seized upon the
(45) provinces and districts which had been originally entrusted to their charge, and the origin of their feudal possession was soon so far forgotten, that their descendants pretended that they held the lands, which they had really usurped regardless of their oath, from heaven and their swords. It is needless to say, that at that time the domestic life in these castles must have been dull and monotonous; although, according to M. Guizot, the loneliness which was the result of this rough and laborious life, became by degrees the
(50) pioneer of civilization.

"When the owner of the fief left his castle, his wife remained there, though in a totally different position from that which women generally held. She remained as mistress, representing her husband, and was charged with the defense and honor of the fief. This high and exalted position, in the center of domestic life, often gave to women an opportunity of displaying dignity, courage, virtue, and intelli-
(55) gence, which would otherwise have remained hidden, and, no doubt, contributed greatly to their moral development, and to the general improvement of their condition.

"The importance of children, and particularly of the eldest son, was greater in feudal houses than elsewhere. The eldest son of the noble was, in the eyes of his father and of all his followers, a prince and heir-presumptive, and the hope and glory of the dynasty. These feelings, and the domestic pride and
(60) affection of the various members one to another, united to give families much energy and power. Add to this the influence of Christian ideas, and it will be understood how this lonely, dull, and hard castle life was, nevertheless, favorable to the development of domestic society, and to that improvement in the condition of women which plays such a great part in the history of our civilization."

Whatever opinion may be formed of chivalry, it is impossible to deny the influence which this
(65) institution exercised on private life in the Middle Ages. It considerably modified custom, by bringing the stronger sex to respect and defend the weaker. These warriors, who were both simple and externally rough and coarse, required association with women to soften them. In taking women and helpless widows under their protection, they were necessarily more and more thrown in contact with them. A deep feeling of veneration for woman, inspired by Christianity, and, above all, by the worship of the
(70) Virgin Mary, ran throughout the songs of the troubadours, and produced a sort of sentimental reverence for the gentle sex, which culminated in the authority which women had in the courts of love.

1. In this passage, Charlemagne is generally characterized as:

   A. a ruthless dictator driven by ambition.
   B. an elegant courtier with refined manners and rarefied tastes.
   C. an uncouth barbarian who disdained the trappings of civilization.
   D. a strong but unassuming ruler who was involved in all aspects of his domain.

2. The author's purpose in writing this passage is most likely to:

   F. point out the differences between life in France before and after the rule of Charlemagne.
   G. present a portrait of the internal workings of the household of the Emperor.
   H. argue that the Age of Chivalry was actually marred by serious religious conflicts.
   J. hypothesize that Charlemagne was responsible for the improvement in the lives of the peasants.

3. The purpose of the second and third paragraphs (lines 7–23) is to:

    A. show how Charlemagne brought an emphasis on science and learning to the court.

    B. explain why Charlemagne was regarded as the ruler who most democratized the court in the Middle Ages.

    C. argue that Charlemagne was responsible for reorganizing the hierarchy of the social order in Medieval France.

    D. substantiate the assertion that Charlemagne did not leave the administration of his household to others.

4. According to the passage, all of the following were habits of Charlemagne EXCEPT:

    F. He enjoyed listening to religious tracts while he dined.

    G. He usually appeared dressed in simple apparel.

    H. He insisted upon knowing exactly how many goats were born each year.

    J. He rose at sunrise, summer and winter.

5. It can be inferred from the passage that the position of women in the Middle Ages:

    A. changed radically in that they no longer had the right to govern their households.

    B. improved during those periods when their husbands were not in residence.

    C. was unprecedented in that for the first time women were no longer considered property of their husbands.

    D. degenerated as the status of first-born sons was elevated to new heights.

6. According to M. Guizot, the loneliness and monotony of castle life had what effect?

    F. It led warriors to fight among themselves to combat boredom.

    G. Clinical depression reached epidemic proportions.

    H. Lords declared war on neighboring fiefs to gain land and power.

    J. It led to the rise of civilization as it fostered the development of domestic society.

7. According to the passage, both Christianity and chivalry:

    A. engendered feelings of respect and protectiveness in men toward women.

    B. increased the likelihood that the eldest son would become a scholar.

    C. stimulated scientific thought and inspired a renewed interest in the Gallo-Roman relics.

    D. elevated the status of servants in the household of Charlemagne.

8. It can be inferred from the passage that the daughters of Charlemagne:

    F. inspired the troubadours to write love songs dedicated to them.

    G. disappointed their father by their frivolous and immoral behavior.

    H. were highly skilled in martial arts including horsemanship and weaponry.

    J. displayed the dignity, courage, and elegance expected of royal princesses.

9. According to the passage, what was a direct result of the deaths of Charlemagne and his son Louis?

   A. Women achieved prominence in the fields of art and music.
   B. Studies in science and religion were relegated to religious orders.
   C. New rulers arose who restored pomp and dignity to the court.
   D. Feelings of domestic pride diminished, and household rivalries marred family gatherings.

10. The phrase "but imperfectly realized the end of their education" (lines 31–32) suggests:

    F. the princesses did not know when they had completed their education.
    G. Charlemagne thought it unwise to educate the daughters in the royal household.
    H. education was so primitive during the Middle Ages that most knowledge was inaccurate or incomplete.
    J. the outcome of the princesses' education was not what had been intended.

Answer Explanations

1. **D.** Charlemagne is presented as a man of simple dress who involved himself in the internal workings of his empire. The passage doesn't indicate that he is ruthless (Choice A), elegant (Choice B), or uncouth (Choice C).

2. **G.** The focus of the passage is a description of how Charlemagne ran his household. Nothing is mentioned of the differences in life in France before and after his rule, so Choice F is incorrect. The passage doesn't argue or hypothesize, so Choices H and J are incorrect.

3. **D.** The second and third paragraphs continue the description of Charlemagne's involvement in the day-to-day running of his household. A discussion of science and learning doesn't occur until paragraph 5 (Choice A). The passage doesn't indicate that Charlemagne democratized the court (Choice B) or reorganized the hierarchy of the social order (Choice C).

4. **J.** According to lines 14–15 of the passage, Charlemagne rose "in summer at sunrise, and in winter earlier."

5. **B.** See paragraph 7 (lines 51–56). A wife's position was elevated when her husband was away from home, but the passage doesn't state that wives were no longer property of their husbands (Choice C). Their position didn't degenerate (Choice D) or change radically (Choice A).

6. **J.** According to M. Guizot, "this lonely, dull, and hard castle life was, nevertheless, favorable to the development of domestic society" (lines 61–62). This contradicts Choice G. No mention is made in the passage of the boredom causing fights (Choice F) or wars (Choice H).

7. **A.** The last two paragraphs of the passage discuss the effects of chivalry and Christianity, especially their emphasis on the defense of women. Choices B, C, and D are not mentioned in the passage as relevant to the principles of chivalry and Christianity.

8. **G.** The passage makes it clear that Charlemagne wanted his children to occupy themselves with useful skills. The reader can infer that the "frivolous habits and irregular morals" (lines 30–31) of the princesses would have disappointed their pragmatic father. Choice F is not mentioned in the passage with regard to the princesses. Choice H refers to Charlemagne's sons, not his daughters. Choice J is contradicted by the description of the princesses in the passage.

9. **B.** According to the passage, the study of science and letters declined after the deaths of Charlemagne and his son Louis (paragraph 5, lines 33–38). Choices A, C, and D aren't mentioned as results of the deaths of these two men.

10. **J.** The phrase suggests that the princesses' education didn't fulfill Charlemagne's intentions for them. Because they are described as frivolous and immoral, it can be inferred that they lacked maturity and engaged in idle foolishness. The passage indicates that Charlemagne did value education, so Choice G is incorrect. Choice F is a misreading of the phrase, and Choice H is an inaccurate representation of the information in the passage.

VII. Strategies for Solving ACT Math Problems

You have 60 minutes to answer 60 questions in the Math Section. The 60 questions are roughly divided as follows:

- 14 Pre-Algebra Problems
- 10 Elementary Algebra Problems
- 9 Intermediate Algebra Problems
- 9 Coordinate Geometry Problems
- 14 Plane Geometry Problems
- 4 Trigonometry Problems

On the average, you have about 1 minute per question. Do not linger on any question. Move on.

Do the easy questions first. All questions are worth the same amount of credit. There is no partial credit for any of the questions. You do not need to show work for your answers.

There is no penalty for an incorrect answer. For questions that you do not know how to solve, make an educated guess.

Read, Read, Read. Read each question carefully, particularly with a word problem. Know what information is given to you and determine what the question is asking you to find. Be sure to answer the question.

If a problem contains a graph or a chart, read the labeling of the chart and the scale for the axes carefully. For example, one unit on the x-axis may represent 1 hour, but one unit on the y-axis may represent 10 miles.

Be careful if a problem changes its unit of measurement. For example, a problem may state that a train traveled 180 miles in 3 hours and ask you to find the number of minutes the train will take to cover a distance of 20 miles. You will need to convert hours to minutes.

If a problem involves an equation, sometimes the solution to the equation may not be the final answer to the question. Be sure to know what the question is asking you to find and answer the question.

Sometimes it is easier to work backward by trying each of the given choices as the final answer. Often, you will be able to eliminate a couple of the choices immediately.

If you have trouble solving a problem involving a literal equation with several variables, try substituting numbers for some of the variables and then solve. For example, to solve the equation $at + b = c$ for t, you might substitute numbers for a, b, and c, such as 2, 4, and 8, respectively, and obtain $2t + 4 = 8$. Solve $2t + 4 = 8$ and obtain $t = 2$. Check the given choices for t using $a = 2$, $b = 4$, and $c = 8$ and see which choice is equivalent to $t = 2$. It is possible that substituting random numbers may produce a solution that satisfies more than one of the given choices, especially with problems involving inequalities. In that case, try substituting another set of numbers, find a solution, and look among the given choices for the one that satisfies both solutions.

If a problem contains decimal numbers, do not round off these numbers until the final answer. Carry all decimal numbers at least two more decimal places than the question requires for the final answer, and round the final answer at the last step.

 Before the ACT Mathematics Test, clear all entries (for variables) in your graphing calculator by resetting your RAM. For example, you might have stored a numerical value to the variable x; clear all such entries before the test.

Be sure to remember whether your calculator is set to degree mode or radian mode.

Lastly, trust your instincts. Your first approach to solve a problem is usually the correct one.

Good luck! You can do it.

VIII. Applying Pre-Algebra Skills

On the ACT Mathematics Test, approximately 14 out of the 60 questions are pre-algebra questions. You'll be tested on your pre-algebra skills, which include the concepts of real numbers, linear equations, simple probability, data interpretation, and simple statistics. The practice problems in this chapter are designed to help you review many of the pre-algebra skills. Work the problems, and check your answers with the given explanations.

A. Real Numbers

1. If $x^2y = 16$ and $xyz = 0$, which of the following must be true?

   A. $x > 0$
   B. $y < 0$
   C. $y = 0$
   D. $z < 0$
   E. $z = 0$

E is correct because $xyz = 0$; at least one of the variables x, y, or z must be 0. If either $x = 0$ or $y = 0$, the product x^2y would have to equal 0. Since $x^2y = 16$, which implies that neither x nor y is 0, the factor that equals zero must be z.

2. Which of the following expressions has a negative value if $p < 0$ and $q < 0$?

   F. $2pq$
   G. $-p^2q$
   H. $\dfrac{p}{q}$
   J. $|-p + q|$
   K. $2p + 3q$

K is correct. One approach is to assign numerical values to p and q and substitute them in the algebraic expression of each of the five choices. For example, let $p = -2$ and $q = -3$. Thus, in Choice F, $2pq = 2(-2)(-3) = 12$; in Choice G, $-p^2q = -(-2)^2(-3) = 12$; in Choice H, $\dfrac{p}{q} = \dfrac{-2}{-3} = \dfrac{2}{3}$; in Choice J, $|-p + q| = |-(-2) + (-3)| = 1$; and in Choice K, $2p + 3q = 2(-2) + 3(-3) = -13$, which is a negative value. When evaluating the numerical expressions, you must follow PEMDAS, the order of operations: **P**arenthesis, **E**xponents, **M**ultiplication, **D**ivision, **A**ddition, and **S**ubtraction. Multiplication and division are performed from left to right. For example, $40 \div 4 \times 2 = 10 \times 2 = 20$. Addition and subtraction are also performed from left to right. If you are using a calculator, you could just enter the entire numerical expression as shown above. The calculator will follow PEMDAS.

B. Integers

---

1. Which of the following is NOT a factor of 72?

   A. 8
   B. 16
   C. 24
   D. 36
   E. 72

B is correct. A number is a factor of 72 if the remainder is zero when 72 is divided by the number. If you divide 72 by 8, 24, 36, or 72, the remainder is zero. If you divide 72 by 16, the remainder is 8. Thus, 16 is not a factor of 72. Alternatively, the prime factorization of 72 is (2)(2)(2)(3)(3), and the prime factorization of 16 is (2)(2)(2)(2). Since 16 has four factors of 2 and 72 has only three factors of 2, 16 cannot be a factor of 72.

---

2. If n is a positive integer, which of the following expressions always represents an odd integer?

   F. $n + 5$
   G. $2n - 4$
   H. $3n + 3$
   J. $6n + 3$
   K. $n^2 + 1$

J is correct. Test each choice by substituting values for n. Because even/odd results are influenced by whether the number substituted is even or odd, you must use an even number and an odd number when you test. When you substitute 4 for n, $n + 5 = 9$, $2n - 4 = 4$, $3n + 3 = 15$, $6n + 3 = 27$, and $n^2 + 1 = 17$. Choice G is eliminated. Then substitute 3 for n in the remaining choices: $n + 5 = 8$, $3n + 3 = 12$, $6n + 3 = 21$, and $n^2 + 1 = 10$. The expression that represents an odd integer is $6n + 3$.

---

3. If n and k are both prime numbers, which of the following is NOT a possible value of nk?

   A. 10
   B. 13
   C. 33
   D. 35
   E. 49

B is correct. Each choice, except for Choice B, may be expressed as a product of two prime numbers: $10 = (5)(2)$, $33 = (3)(11)$, $35 = (7)(5)$, $49 = (7)(7)$. Choice B, 13, can never be expressed as a product of primes because 13 is a prime number and has only 1 and itself as factors, and 1 is not a prime number.

4. If a positive integer, n, is divisible by 2, 5, and 6, which of the following must also be divisible by 2, 5, and 6?

   F. $n + 10$
   G. $n + 12$
   H. $n + 13$
   J. $n^2 - 13$
   K. $2n + 30$

K is correct. Since n is a positive integer divisible by 2, 5, and 6, a possible value for n is 30. Now substitute 30 for n in the given choices, and you have $n + 10 = 40$, $n + 12 = 42$, $n + 13 = 43$, $n^2 - 13 = 887$, and $2n + 30 = 90$. Only Choice K produces an answer that is divisible by 2, 5, and 6. Thus, $2n + 30$, Choice K, is the correct answer. You could also use a different approach that is based on the fact that if two numbers are divisible by 2, 5, and 6, then their sum, difference, and product are also divisible by 2, 5, and 6. Inspecting the given choices, you have n, n^2, and $2n$ all divisible by 2, 5, and 6. Looking at the constants in the given choices, you have 10, 12, and 13 not divisible by 2, 5, and 6, and thus, Choices F, G, H, and J are eliminated. For Choice K, you know that 30 is divisible by 2, 5, and 6. Therefore, the sum $2n + 30$, Choice K, is divisible by 2, 5, and 6.

C. Fractions and Decimals

1. If $b < -1 < a < 0$, which of the following has the smallest value?

   A. $-b^3$
   B. $-b$
   C. ab
   D. $-a^2$
   E. a^3

D is correct. You can either consider each choice or select values and substitute. If you consider each choice:

- Choice A: Since b is less than -1, b^3 is also less than -1, and $-b^3$ is greater than 1.
- Choice B: Since b is less than -1, $-b$ is more than 1.
- Choice C: Since a and b are both negative, their product is positive, and ab is positive.
- Choice D: Since a^2 is always positive, $-a^2$ is negative.
- Choice E: Since a is negative, a^3 is negative.

Since negative numbers are smaller than positive numbers, Choices A, B, and C are eliminated. For example, a^3 and $-a^2$ are both between -1 and 0; if you let $a = -0.5$, then $a^3 = -0.125$ and $-a^2 = -0.25$. Thus, $-a^2 < a^3$. The smallest value is $-a^2$.

If you substitute values, let $b = -10$ and $a = -0.5$, then $-b^3 = 1000$, $-b = 10$, $ab = 5$, $-a^2 = -0.25$, and $a^3 = -0.125$. The smallest value is -0.25, which is $-a^2$.

2. On the number line, a, b, c, d, and e are equally spaced between -2 and 1. Which of the following fractions has the greatest value?

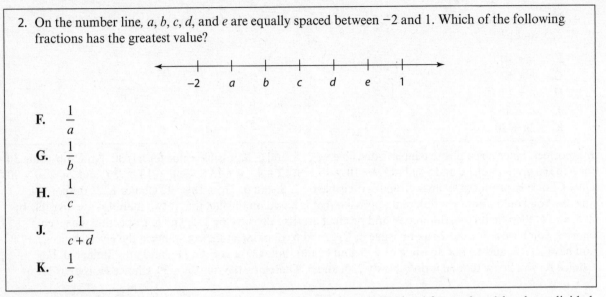

  F. $\dfrac{1}{a}$

  G. $\dfrac{1}{b}$

  H. $\dfrac{1}{c}$

  J. $\dfrac{1}{c+d}$

  K. $\dfrac{1}{e}$

K is correct. The length of the segment from -2 to 1 is 3. Because the interval from -2 to 1 has been divided into 6 equal segments, each segment is 0.5 in length, and $a = -1.5$, $b = -1$, $c = -0.5$, $d = 0$, and $e = 0.5$. Since a, b, and c are negative and $d = 0$, when evaluated, Choices F, G, H, and J will be negative. Since e is positive, only the value of Choice K is positive.

The greatest value must be $\dfrac{1}{e}$.

3. As part of the high school physical fitness program, each of the 180 students in a school was required to sign up for exactly one activity: soccer, baseball, table tennis, or volleyball. If $\dfrac{1}{2}$ of the students signed up for soccer, $\dfrac{1}{3}$ signed up for baseball, and of the remaining students, twice as many signed up for volleyball as table tennis, how many students signed up for table tennis?

  A. 5
  B. 10
  C. 15
  D. 20
  E. 30

B is correct. Since $\dfrac{1}{2}$ of the students signed up for soccer, $\dfrac{1}{2}(180)$ or 90 students signed up for soccer. Since $\dfrac{1}{3}$ of the students signed up for baseball, $\dfrac{1}{3}(180)$ or 60 students signed up for baseball. The $180 - (90 + 60)$ or 30 remaining students played table tennis or volleyball, and of these students, twice as many signed up for volleyball than signed up for table tennis. The number of students who signed up for table tennis, x, can be obtained from the equation $2x + x = 30$. Thus $x = 10$.

4. What is the least common denominator when adding the fractions $\frac{x}{6}$, $\frac{1}{12}$, and $\frac{y}{18}$?

    F.   6

    G.   18

    H.   36

    J.   216

    K.   1296

H is correct. One approach to the problem is to test each number in the choices beginning with the smallest. Remember that the least common denominator (LCD) must be divisible by all three denominators: 6, 12, and 18. Thus, 36 is the LCD. Another approach is to express each denominator as a product of its prime factors. Thus, $6 = 2 \times 3$, $12 = 2 \times 2 \times 3$, and $18 = 2 \times 3 \times 3$. The LCD must contain the prime factors of all three denominators. Therefore, the LCD $= 2 \times 2 \times 3 \times 3$ or 36.

D. Absolute Value

1. What is the value of $|-6 + 4(-5)|$?

    A.   −26

    B.   −10

    C.   10

    D.   26

    E.   50

D is correct. Remember the absolute value of a number is always greater than or equal to zero. First, evaluate the expression by following *PEMDAS*, the order of operations (see page 127). Thus,

$$|-6 + 4(-5)| = |-6 - 20| = |-26| \text{ or } 26$$

2. If a and b are nonzero numbers and $|a + b| = |a| + |b|$, then which of the following must be true?

    F. $a = b$

    G. $ab > 0$

    H. $ab < 0$

    J. $a > b$

    K. $b > a$

G is correct. The equation $|a + b| = |a| + |b|$ is true only when both a and b are positive or both are negative. For example, $|3 + 4| = |3| + |4|$ and $|(-3) + (-4)| = |-3| + |-4|$. If a and b have different signs, the equation is false, $|-3 + 4| \neq |-3| + |4|$. Therefore, the choice that must be true is $ab > 0$.

3. In the xy-plane, which of the following points lies on the graph of the equation $-2|x| + y = 2$?

 A. $(-3,8)$
 B. $(-1,0)$
 C. $(0,-2)$
 D. $(4,-1)$
 E. $(6,-2)$

A is correct. If a point lies on the graph of an equation, then the coordinates of the point satisfy the equation. Substitute the coordinates of each point in the five choices into the equation and check. In Choice A, using $x = -3$ and $y = 8$, you have $-2|-3| + 8 = 2$, or $-6 + 8 = 2$, or $2 = 2$. Thus, the coordinates satisfy the equation. The point that is on the graph is $(-3,8)$. Since Choice A worked, there is no need to try the other answer choices.

E. Scientific Notation

1. What is the value of $(3.5 \times 10^8)(4.8 \times 10^{-2})$?

 A. 16.8×10^{-14}
 B. 1.68×10^5
 C. 1.68×10^4
 D. 1.68×10^7
 E. 16.8×10^7

D is correct. Apply the commutative property of multiplication and rewrite $(3.5 \times 10^8)(4.8 \times 10^{-2})$ as $(3.5 \times 4.8) \times (10^8 \times 10^{-2})$, which is equivalent to $16.8 \times 10^{8 + (-2)}$ or 16.8×10^6. Then express 16.8×10^6 in scientific notation, and you have $1.68 \times 10 \times 10^6$ or 1.68×10^7.

2. What is the value of $\dfrac{2.4 \times 10^{-2}}{6 \times 10^{-6}}$?

 F. 4×10^{-7}
 G. 4×10^{-4}
 H. 4×10^3
 J. 4×10^4
 K. 4×10^7

H is correct. Dividing 2.4 by 6, you have 0.4, and dividing 10^{-2} by 10^{-6}, you have $10^{-2 - (-6)}$ or 10^4. Thus, $\dfrac{2.4 \times 10^{-2}}{6 \times 10^{-6}} = 0.4 \times 10^4$, which is equivalent to $(4 \times 10^{-1}) \times 10^4$ or 4×10^3.

F. Exponents and Radicals

1. If $5^4(5^a) = 5^{20}$, what is the value of a?

   A. 5
   B. 6
   C. 10
   D. 16
   E. 80

D is correct. Since you are trying to find an exponent, express each side as a power with the same base and set the exponents equal. Since $5^4(5^a) = 5^{(4+a)}$, you can set $5^{(4+a)} = 5^{20}$ and $4 + a = 20$ or $a = 16$.

2. If $\sqrt[3]{x} = 2$ and $y^2 = 16$, which of the following could be a value of $x - y$?

   F. −8
   G. −2
   H. 6
   J. 8
   K. 12

K is correct. Since $\sqrt[3]{x} = 2$, raise both sides to the third power, and you have $\left(\sqrt[3]{x}\right)^3 = (2)^3$ or $x = 8$, and since $y^2 = 16$, $y = \pm 4$. Therefore, $x - y$ could be $8 - 4 = 4$ or $8 - (-4) = 12$, which is the only correct answer shown in the choices.

3. What is the value of $\sqrt[3]{8} + \left(\dfrac{1}{2}\right)^{-2} - 4^0$?

   A. 0
   B. $\dfrac{5}{4}$
   C. 3
   D. 5
   E. 7

D is correct. Evaluating each term, you have $\sqrt[3]{8} = 2$, $\left(\dfrac{1}{2}\right)^{-2} = \left(\dfrac{2}{1}\right)^2 = 4$, and $-4^0 = -1$. Therefore, $\sqrt[3]{8} + \left(\dfrac{1}{2}\right)^{-2} - 4^0 = 2 + 4 - 1$ or 5.

G. Percents

1. If n is a positive number, which of the following represents $2n$ percent of 150?

   A. $3n$
   B. $30n$
   C. $60n$
   D. $75n$
   E. $300n$

A is correct. Since $2n\%$ is $\dfrac{2n}{100}$, then $2n\%$ of 150 is equivalent to $\dfrac{2n}{100}(150) = 3n$.

2. The accompanying circle graph shows how John's salary in 2013 was determined. If John earned a total of $18,000 in overtime pay in 2013, how much did he receive as bonuses?

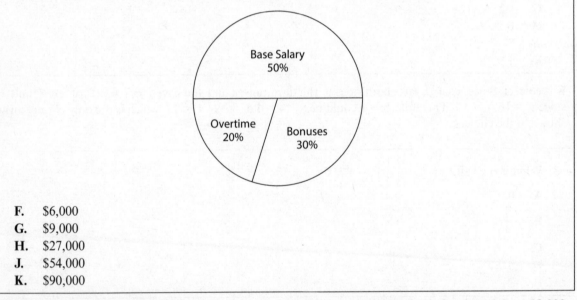

   F. $6,000
   G. $9,000
   H. $27,000
   J. $54,000
   K. $90,000

H is correct. Let x be John's annual salary. Since the overtime pay was 20% of John's salary, $0.2x = 18,000$ or $x = 90,000$. Since the bonuses were 30% of John's salary, $0.3x = 0.3(90,000) = 27,000$. Thus, John's bonuses for 2013 were $27,000. You can also do this problem by setting up a proportion to find the bonuses. Let y be the bonuses. Then $\dfrac{0.2}{18,000} = \dfrac{0.3}{y}$ or $0.2y = (0.3)(18,000)$. Thus, $y = 27,000$.

3. Two rounds of auditions were being held to select 40 students for a new chorus that was being formed. In the first round of auditions, 30 students were selected, 80% of whom were girls. If 25% of the members of the chorus had to be boys, how many boys had to be selected in the second round of auditions?

A. 4
B. 6
C. 8
D. 10
E. 12

A is correct. If 25% of the 40 chorus members must be boys, there must be a total of 0.25(40) = 10 boys selected. In the first round, since 80% of the 30 students were girls, 20% of the 30 students were boys and 20% of 30 is 0.20(30) = 6. Since 10 boys are needed and 6 were already selected, in the second round, the number of boys selected must be 10 − 6 or 4.

H. Ratios and Proportions

1. If $\frac{2}{5}$ of a number is 30, what is $\frac{1}{3}$ of the number?

A. 4
B. 10
C. 12
D. 25
E. 75

D is correct. Let x be the number. Since $\frac{2}{5}$ of the number is 30, you have $\frac{2}{5}x = 30$ or $x = 75$. Thus, $\frac{1}{3}$ of the number is $\frac{1}{3}(75)$ or 25. You can also do this problem by using a proportion: $\frac{\frac{2}{5}}{30} = \frac{\frac{1}{3}}{x}$. Thus, $\frac{2}{5}x = \frac{1}{3}(30)$, or $x = 25$.

2. On a blueprint for an office building, 6 in represents 45 ft. Using this scale, how many inches on the blueprint represent 30 ft?

F. 1.5
G. 2
H. 2.5
J. 3
K. 4

K is correct. To find the number of inches on the blueprint, x, use the proportion $\frac{6}{45} = \frac{x}{30}$.

Thus, $45x = 6(30)$ or $x = 4$. Notice that you do not have to convert inches to feet. When you set up a proportion, corresponding quantities must have the same unit of measurement. In this problem, you are comparing inches on the blueprint to height measured in feet. Both blueprint numbers are in the same units, inches, and both heights are in the same units, feet, and so the proportion may be set up. If the height of one building were given in feet and the height of the other building were given in inches, you would have to convert both to feet or both to inches before the proportion could be set up.

---

3. Erica and Niki were the only candidates running for president of the senior class. When the votes were tallied, the ratio of the number of votes that Erica received to the number of votes that Niki received was 3 to 2. If 60 students voted for Erica, how many students voted in the election?

    A.   20
    B.   40
    C.   60
    D.   80
    E.   100

E is correct. To find the number of votes that Niki received, x, solve the proportion $\dfrac{3}{2} = \dfrac{60}{x}$ or $x = 40$. Since 60 students voted for Erica and 40 voted for Niki, the number of students who voted is $60 + 40$ or 100.

I. Linear Equations

---

1. If $2x + 3y = 10$, what is the value of $4x + 6y$?

    A.   15
    B.   20
    C.   30
    D.   40
    E.   60

B is correct. The question did not ask for the individual values of x and y, but instead the value of $4x + 6y$. Notice that $4x + 6y = 2(2x + 3y)$. Multiply both sides of the equation $2x + 3y = 10$ by 2 and you have $2(2x + 3y) = 20$. Thus, $4x + 6y = 20$.

---

2. If $8 - 2(x + 1) = 4x$, what is the value of x?

    F. -3
    G. -1
    H.   1
    J. $\dfrac{7}{6}$
    K.   3

H is correct. Begin by applying the distributive property, and you have $8 - 2x - 2 = 4x$, which is equivalent to $6 - 2x = 4x$. Adding $2x$ to both sides of the equation, you have $6 = 6x$ or $x = 1$.

3. What is the value of n if $\frac{1}{2}n - \frac{1}{3}n = 6$?

A. -36

B. -6

C. 1

D. 6

E. 36

E is correct. One approach to the problem is to multiply every term of the equation by 6, the least common denominator (LCD) of 2 and 3: $6\left(\frac{1}{2}n\right) - 6\left(\frac{1}{3}n\right) = 6(6)$, which is equivalent to $3n - 2n = 36$ or $n = 36$.

J. Counting Problems

1. At a restaurant, the menu consists of 2 varieties of salad, 5 different entrées, and 3 desserts of which one is apple pie. If the Tuesday night dinner special consists of 1 salad, 1 entrée, and apple pie for dessert, how many different Tuesday night dinner specials are there?

A. 5

B. 7

C. 10

D. 15

E. 30

C is correct. Use the Fundamental Counting Principle to determine the number of different dinner specials. Since there are 2 choices for salad, 5 choices for the entrée, and 1 choice for dessert because dessert must be apple pie, there are (5)(2)(1), or 10 different dinner specials.

2. The junior class is holding an election for president, vice president, and secretary, and 6 students are candidates. If any of the candidates could be elected president, vice president, or secretary, but no one can hold more than 1 position, how many different outcomes are possible?

F. 6

G. 20

H. 36

J. 72

K. 120

K is correct. This is a permutation problem because order matters (you could have the same three students elected to different positions). For example: Mary could be elected president, Bill vice president, and Janet secretary; or Bill could be elected president, Janet vice president, and Mary secretary. Thus, the number of different outcomes is $_6P_3$, which is 6(5)(4) or 120.

3. What is the total number of distinct diagonals that can be drawn in an octagon? (An octagon has 8 sides.)

    A. 7
    B. 20
    C. 28
    D. 40
    E. 56

B is correct.

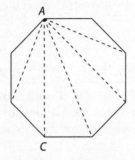

There are 8 vertices in an octagon. From each vertex, 5 diagonals can be drawn. You have (8)(5) or 40 diagonals. However, each diagonal was counted twice. For example, a diagonal drawn from vertex A to C is the same as the diagonal drawn from vertex C to A. Therefore, the total number of distinct diagonals in an octagon is $\frac{40}{2}$ or 20.

4. If the local post office has only three denominations of stamps available—$0.01 stamps, $0.10 stamps, and $0.20 stamps—how many different sets of the three kinds of stamps can be used to form $0.41?

    F. 4
    G. 5
    H. 8
    J. 9
    K. 10

J is correct. This problem involves not only selecting from three subgroups of stamps, but also factoring in the values of these stamps. This is not a permutation or combination problem. To solve this problem, list all the possible outcomes. Summarizing the outcomes, you have the following table:

$0.01	$0.10	$0.20
1	0	2
1	2	1
11	1	1
21	0	1
1	4	0
11	3	0
21	2	0
31	1	0
41	0	0

There are 9 possible combinations of stamps to make $0.41.

K. Probability

1. If a number is randomly selected from the set {1, 2, 3, 4, 5, 6, 7, 8, 9}, what is the probability that it will be a prime number?

   A. $\dfrac{2}{9}$

   B. $\dfrac{3}{9}$

   C. $\dfrac{4}{9}$

   D. $\dfrac{5}{9}$

   E. 3

C is correct. $P(\text{a prime number}) = \dfrac{\text{number of prime numbers in the set}}{\text{total number of elements in the set}}$.

There are 4 prime numbers in the set: 2, 3, 5, 7. There are 9 numbers in total. Therefore, the probability of getting a prime number is $\dfrac{4}{9}$.

2. Janet labeled all her books in her classroom as either fiction or nonfiction. She has 30 nonfiction books. If a book is picked at random, the probability that it is fiction is $\dfrac{3}{5}$. What is the total number of books in her classroom?

   F. 50
   G. 60
   H. 75
   J. 90
   K. 150

H is correct. Since $P(\text{fiction}) = \frac{3}{5}$, $P(\text{nonfiction}) = 1 - \frac{3}{5} = \frac{2}{5}$. Use x to represent the total number of books. There are 30 nonfiction books. Therefore, $\frac{\text{the number of nonfiction books}}{\text{total number of books}} = \frac{2}{5}$ or $\frac{30}{x} = \frac{2}{5}$, which is equivalent to $2x = 30(5)$ or $x = 75$. There are 75 books in total in Janet's classroom.

---

3. Victoria has 3 quarters and 2 dimes in her piggybank. If 2 coins are taken out of the piggybank at random, what is the probability that both coins are dimes?

   A. $\frac{1}{20}$

   B. $\frac{1}{10}$

   C. $\frac{2}{5}$

   D. $\frac{2}{3}$

   E. $\frac{4}{5}$

B is correct. $P(2 \text{ dimes}) = \frac{\text{number of ways of picking 2 dimes}}{\text{total number of ways of picking 2 coins from 5 coins}}$. The number of ways of picking 2 dimes is $_2C_2$ or 1. The number of ways of picking 2 coins from 5 coins is $_5C_2$ or 10. Therefore, $P(2 \text{ dimes}) = \frac{1}{10}$. Another approach is as follows:

$P(2 \text{ dimes}) = P(\text{first coin is a dime}) \times P(\text{second coin is a dime}) = \frac{2}{5}\left(\frac{1}{4}\right) = \frac{1}{10}$.

---

4. In a box, there are 10 red balls and 8 blue balls. What is the minimum number of balls that have to be removed in order for the probability of picking a red ball at random from the box to be $\frac{2}{3}$?

   F. 0
   G. 2
   H. 3
   J. 4
   K. 6

H is correct. The probability of picking a red ball equaling $\frac{2}{3}$ implies that the total number of balls in the box has to be divisible by 3. Initially, there are 10 red and 8 blue balls in the box totaling 18, which is divisible by 3. However, the probability of picking a red ball is $\frac{10}{18}$, which is $\frac{5}{9}$ not $\frac{2}{3}$. The next number divisible by 3 is 15. If there are 15 balls in the box and the probability of picking a red ball is $\frac{2}{3}$, then you have $\frac{x}{15} = \frac{2}{3}$, x being the number of red balls. Solve the proportion and note that $x = 10$. So you need 10 red balls and 5 blue balls. Since there are 10 red and 8 blue balls initially, you must remove 3 blue balls from the box.

L. Mean, Median, and Mode

1. If the average (arithmetic mean) of 6, m, and n is 10, what is the average of m and n?

   A. 4
   B. 12
   C. 18
   D. 24
   E. 36

B is correct. Knowing the average implies knowing the sum. Since $\frac{6+m+n}{3} = 10$, you know that $6 + m + n = 30$ by multiplying both sides of the equation by 3. Then $m + n = 24$, and the average of m and n is $\frac{m+n}{2}$, which is $\frac{24}{2}$ or 12.

2. If the average (arithmetic mean) of x and $3x - 4$ is p and the average of $6 - 2x$ and $14 - 2x$ is q, what is the average of p and q?

   F. 4
   G. 16
   H. $4 - 2x$
   J. $2x + 4$
   K. $8x + 16$

F is correct. Since the average of x and $3x - 4$ is p, you have $p = \frac{(x)+(3x-4)}{2} = \frac{4x-4}{2} = 2x - 2$. Similarly, $q = \frac{(6-2x)+(14-2x)}{2} = \frac{20-4x}{2} = 10 - 2x$. The average of p and q can be obtained by $\frac{(2x-2)+(10-2x)}{2} = \frac{8}{2} = 4.$

3. Rebecca's test grades in her math class for the first quarter are 90, 84, 80, 92, 84, and 98. Of the 6 grades in the first quarter, if p is the mean, q is the median, and r is the mode, which of the following inequalities is true?

   A. $r < q < p$
   B. $r < p < q$
   C. $p < r < q$
   D. $q < p < r$
   E. $p < q < r$

A is correct. The mean is the average: $p = \dfrac{90 + 84 + 80 + 92 + 84 + 98}{6} = 88$. The median is q, which is the middle value of 80, 84, 84, 90, 92, 98 or $\dfrac{84 + 90}{2} = 87$. The mode is r, which is the value that appears the most often: 84. Thus, $r < q < p$.

4. Given $3x - 2$, $-\dfrac{1}{x}$, and x^2, if x^2 is the median, which of the following could be the value of x?

   F. -3

   G. -2

   H. $-\dfrac{1}{2}$

   J. $\dfrac{1}{2}$

   K. 3

H is correct. Substitute the given numbers into the three expressions:

x	$3x - 2$	x^2	$-\dfrac{1}{x}$
-3	-11	9	$\dfrac{1}{3}$
-2	-8	4	$\dfrac{1}{2}$
$-\dfrac{1}{2}$	$-3\dfrac{1}{2}$	$\dfrac{1}{4}$	2
$\dfrac{1}{2}$	$-1\dfrac{1}{2}$	$\dfrac{1}{4}$	-2
3	7	9	$-\dfrac{1}{3}$

Notice that when $x = -\dfrac{1}{2}$, you have $-3\dfrac{1}{2}$, $\dfrac{1}{4}$, and 2, making x^2 the median.

M. Data Interpretation

1. In the accompanying diagram, the line graph shows the number of books sold by Whitman Bookstore in each month from January to May. What percent of the number of books sold in February is equal to the number of books sold in May?

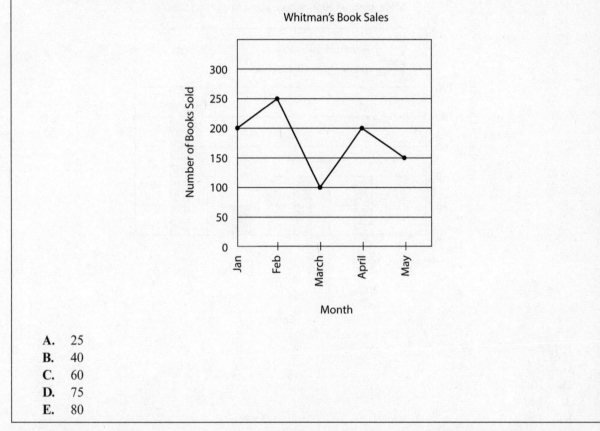

Whitman's Book Sales

   A.   25
   B.   40
   C.   60
   D.   75
   E.   80

C is correct. According to the graph, you know that the number of books sold in February is 250 and the number of books sold in May is 150. Use the proportion $\dfrac{150}{250} = \dfrac{x}{100\%}$, which is equivalent to $x = \dfrac{100(150)}{250}\%$ or 60%.

2. In 2013, students who attended Washington High School or Adams High School were allowed to participate in only one sport for the year: tennis, soccer, swimming, or basketball. Based on the information provided in the accompanying bar graph, how many more students at Washington High School than at Adams High School participated in a sport in 2013?

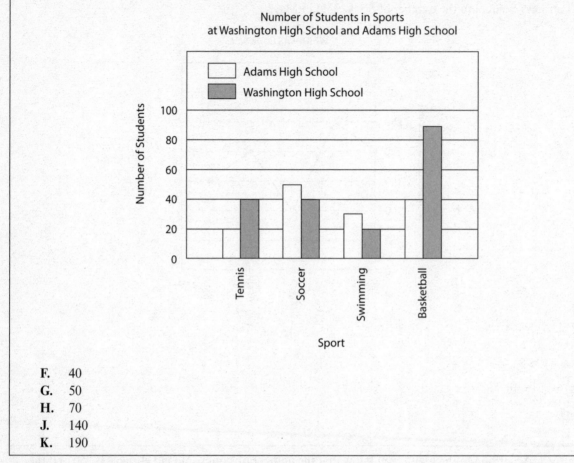

Number of Students in Sports
at Washington High School and Adams High School

F. 40
G. 50
H. 70
J. 140
K. 190

G is correct. At Washington High School, 40 students played tennis, 40 played soccer, 20 swam, and 90 played basketball, totaling 40 + 40 + 20 + 90 = 190 students who participated in a sport. At Adams High School, 20 students played tennis, 50 played soccer, 30 swam, and 40 played basketball, totaling 20 + 50 + 30 + 40 = 140 students who participated in a sport. The difference between the number of students who participated in a sport at Washington High School and at Adams High School is 190 − 140 = 50.

3. In the accompanying diagram, the double line graph shows the revenues and expenses of Concord Electronics for the past five years. Which year had the greatest profit?

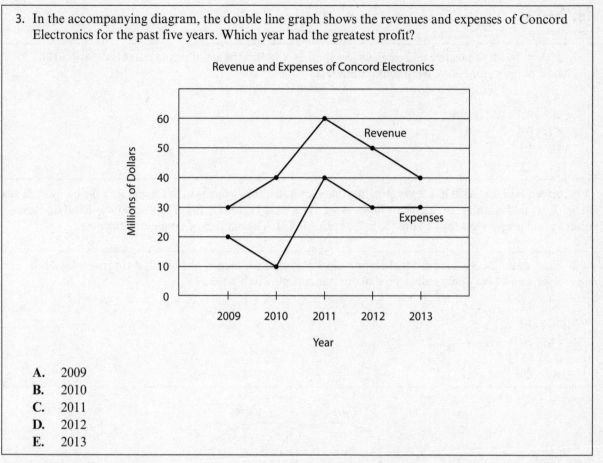

Revenue and Expenses of Concord Electronics

A. 2009
B. 2010
C. 2011
D. 2012
E. 2013

B is correct. Profit = Revenue − Expenses. According to the line graph, in 2010, revenue was $40 million and expenses were $10 million. Profit for that year was $30 million, the largest for the five years.

	2009	2010	2011	2012	2013
Revenue	30	40	60	50	40
Expenses	20	10	40	30	30
Profit	10	30	20	20	10

N. Sets

1. If A is the set of positive odd integers less than 24 and B is the set of prime numbers less than 20, how many numbers are common to both sets?

    A. 7
    B. 8
    C. 9
    D. 10
    E. 12

A is correct. Because Set B has fewer elements than Set A, list the elements in Set B and see how many elements in Set B are odd integers. The elements in Set B are {2, 3, 5, 7, 11, 13, 17, 19}. The elements in Set B that are positive odd integers less than 24 are {3, 5, 7, 11, 13, 17, 19}. The number of common elements is 7.

2. Each of the 24 students in Mr. Martin's class plays tennis, soccer, or both. If 4 students play both sports and 8 play only tennis, how many students play only soccer?

    F. 12
    G. 14
    H. 16
    J. 18
    K. 20

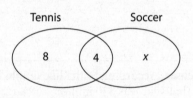

F is correct.

Set up a Venn diagram with x representing the number of students who only play soccer. Because 4 students play in both sports and 8 students play only tennis, the number of students who only play soccer is $24 - (8 + 4) = 24 - 12 = 12$.

3. When x is a member of Set A, the value of $\sqrt{x^2} + x$ is also a member of Set A. Which of the following could be Set A?

  A. $\{-2, 1\}$
  B. $\{-1, 0\}$
  C. $\{-1, 0, 1\}$
  D. $\{0, 1\}$
  E. $\{0, 1, 2\}$

B is correct. Substituting gives the results listed in the following table.

x	-2	-1	0	1	2
$\sqrt{x^2} + x$	0	0	0	2	4

Of the choices, the only set that satisfies the condition is $\{-1, 0\}$.

IX. Solving Elementary Algebra Problems

On the ACT Mathematics Test, approximately 10 out of the 60 questions are elementary algebra questions. You'll be tested on your elementary algebra skills, which include working with algebraic expressions, polynomials, exponents, and quadratic equations. The practice problems in this chapter are designed to help you review many of the elementary algebra skills. Work the problems, and check your answers with the given explanations.

A. Rational Expressions

1. For all values of x not equal to 4, which of the following expressions is equivalent to $\dfrac{x^2-16}{2x-8}$?

   A. $\dfrac{x-4}{2}$

   B. $\dfrac{x}{2}+4$

   C. $x+2$

   D. $\dfrac{x+2}{2}$

   E. $\dfrac{x+4}{2}$

E is correct. Factoring both the numerator and denominator of $\dfrac{x^2-16}{2x-8}$, you have $\dfrac{(x+4)(x-4)}{2(x-4)}$, which is equivalent to $\dfrac{x+4}{2}$.

2. For all values of x not equal to ± 2, which of the following is equivalent to the sum of $\dfrac{1}{x+2}+\dfrac{1}{2-x}$?

   F. $\dfrac{1}{x+1}$

   G. $\dfrac{2}{x+2}$

   H. $\dfrac{1}{x^2-1}$

   J. $\dfrac{1}{x^2}$

   K. $\dfrac{-4}{x^2-4}$

K is correct. Multiply both the numerator and denominator of $\dfrac{1}{2-x}$ by -1 and you have $\dfrac{-1}{x-2}$. Now $\dfrac{1}{x+2}+\dfrac{1}{2-x}$ becomes $\dfrac{1}{x+2}-\dfrac{1}{x-2}$. The least common denominator (LCD) of $(x+2)$ and $(x-2)$ is $(x+2)(x-2)$. Therefore, $\dfrac{1}{x+2}-\dfrac{1}{x-2}=\dfrac{1(x-2)-1(x+2)}{(x+2)(x-2)}=\dfrac{x-2-x-2}{(x+2)(x-2)}$ or $\dfrac{-4}{x^2-4}$.

B. Properties of Exponents

1. If $3^n + 3^n + 3^n = 9^6$, what is the value of n?

    A. 2
    B. 3
    C. 4
    D. 11
    E. 12

 D is correct. Since you are trying to find an exponent, express each side as a power with the same base and then set the exponents equal.

Since $3^n + 3^n + 3^n = 3(3^n) = (3^1)(3^n) = 3^{n+1}$ and since $9^6 = (3^2)^6 = 3^{12}$, you know that $3^{n+1} = 3^{12}$ and $n + 1 = 12$ or $n = 11$.

2. If $(2x^2)^3 = 8x^n$ for all values of x, what is the value of n?

    F. 3
    G. 4
    H. 5
    J. 6
    K. 7

J is correct. Since you are trying to find an exponent, express each side as a power with the same base and set the exponents equal. Since $(2x^2)^3 = 8x^6$ and $(2x^2)^3 = 8x^n$, you know that $8x^6 = 8x^n$ or $n = 6$.

3. If $n^a = 5$ and $n^b = 25$, what is the value of n^{2a+b}?

    A. 25
    B. 35
    C. 125
    D. 625
    E. 3125

D is correct. Since $n^{2a+b} = (n^a)(n^a)(n^b)$ and $n^a = 5$ and $n^b = 25$, you know that $n^{2a+b} = (5)(5)(25)$. The value of n^{2a+b} is 625.

C. Factoring Polynomials

---

1. Which of the following is equivalent to $3x^2 - 11x + 10$ for all values of x?

    A. $(x + 5)(3x + 2)$
    B. $(x - 5)(3x - 2)$
    C. $(x + 2)(3x + 5)$
    D. $(x - 2)(3x + 5)$
    E. $(3x - 5)(x - 2)$

E is correct. One approach to the problem is to multiply the two binomials in each of the five choices and check the results. In Choice E, $(3x - 5)(x - 2) = 3x^2 - 6x - 5x + 10$, which is equivalent to $3x^2 - 11x + 10$, the result that we want. Another approach is to factor the trinomial $3x^2 - 11x + 10$. The possible pairs of factors of $+10$ are $\{1, 10\}$, $\{-1, -10\}$, $\{2, 5\}$, and $\{-2, -5\}$. Since the coefficient of x is -11, only the pairs $\{-1, -10\}$ and $\{-2, -5\}$ are possible. Thus, checking the possible pairs of factors, you have $(3x - 2)(x - 5)$, $(3x - 5)(x - 2)$, $(3x - 1)(x - 10)$, and $(3x - 10)(x - 1)$. Only the product $(3x - 5)(x - 2)$ is $3x^2 - 11x + 10$.

---

2. What is the value of c if $(x - 5)$ is a factor of $3x^2 - 14x + c$ for all values of x?

    F. -15
    G. -5
    H. 5
    J. 6
    K. 15

G is correct. If $(x - 5)$ is a factor of $3x^2 - 14x + c$, then $x = 5$ is a root of the equation $y = 3x^2 - 14x + c$. In other words, if you substitute $x = 5$ in the equation, you'll have $y = 0$. Thus, $3(5)^2 - 14(5) + c = 0$, which is equivalent to $75 - 70 + c = 0$ or $c = -5$.

---

3. For all values of x and y, which of the following is a factor of $x^2 - 4y^2$?

    A. -4
    B. $x - y$
    C. $x + 4y$
    D. $x - 2y$
    E. $2(x + y)$

D is correct. Rewrite $x^2 - 4y^2$ as $(x)^2 - (2y)^2$, which is now expressed as the difference of two squares. Thus, $(x)^2 - (2y)^2 = (x - 2y)(x + 2y)$, with $x - 2y$ as a factor.

4. What is the greatest common factor of $12x^2y$, $15xy^2$, and $18xy$ for all values of x and y?

    F. $2xy$
    G. $3xy$
    H. $3x^2y^2$
    J. $180xy$
    K. $180x^2y^2$

G is correct. Begin with the coefficients 12, 15, and 18. The prime factors are $12 = 2 \times 2 \times 3$, $15 = 3 \times 5$, and $18 = 2 \times 3 \times 3$. Therefore, the greatest common factor (GCF) is 3. The GCF of x^2y, xy^2, and xy is xy. Thus, the GCF of $12x^2y$, $15xy^2$, and $18xy$ is $3xy$.

D. Adding and Subtracting Polynomials

1. What polynomial must be subtracted from $x^2 - 4$ so that the difference is $2x^2 - 3x + 1$?

    A. $-x^2 + 3x - 5$
    B. $x^2 - 3x + 5$
    C. $-x^2 - 3x + 1$
    D. $x^2 + 3x + 5$
    E. $3x^2 - 3x - 3$

A is correct. Subtract each polynomial in the five choices from $x^2 - 4$ and check the result. Begin with Choice A and you have $(x^2 - 4) - (-x^2 + 3x - 5) = x^2 - 4 + x^2 - 3x + 5$ or $2x^2 - 3x + 1$, the desired result. There is no need to check the other answer choices.

2. If the length of a rectangle is represented by $2x$ and the width by $3x + 1$, what is the perimeter of the rectangle in terms of x?

    F. $x + 1$
    G. $5x + 1$
    H. $10x + 2$
    J. $10x + 4$
    K. $6x^2 + 2x$

H is correct. The perimeter of a rectangle equals twice the length plus twice the width. Thus, the perimeter is $2(2x) + 2(3x + 1)$, which is equivalent to $4x + 6x + 2$ or $10x + 2$.

E. Multiplying and Dividing Polynomials

1. For all values of x, which of the following is equivalent to $(2x - 1)^2$?

    A. $4x - 2$
    B. $4x^2 + 1$
    C. $4x^2 - 2x + 1$
    D. $4x^2 - 4x + 1$
    E. $4x^2 + 4x + 1$

D is correct. Rewrite $(2x - 1)^2$ as $(2x - 1)(2x - 1)$ and multiply. Thus, $(2x - 1)(2x - 1) = 4x^2 - 2x - 2x + 1$ or $4x^2 - 4x + 1$.

2. For all values of $x \neq 0$, which of the following is equivalent to $\dfrac{3x^6 - 2x^4 + x^2}{x^2}$?

    F. $3x^3 - 2x^2 + x$
    G. $3x^3 - 2x^2 + 1$
    H. $3x^4 - 2x^2$
    J. $3x^4 - 2x^2 + 1$
    K. $3x^4 - 2x^4$

J is correct. The expression $\dfrac{3x^6 - 2x^4 + x^2}{x^2}$ is equivalent to dividing each term in the numerator by the denominator x^2. Thus $\dfrac{3x^6}{x^2} - \dfrac{2x^4}{x^2} + \dfrac{x^2}{x^2} = 3x^4 - 2x^2 + 1$. Remember that when you divide monomials with the same base, you subtract exponents.

F. Quadratic Equations

1. If x is a real number, how many values of x satisfy the equation $(x + 10)^2 = 25$?

    A. 0
    B. 1
    C. 2
    D. 3
    E. 4

C is correct. Instead of multiplying $(x + 10)(x + 10)$ and then factoring to solve the quadratic equation $x^2 + 20x + 75 = 0$, keep the equation in its original form and find the square root of both sides. Thus, $(x + 10) = \pm 5$. Solving the equations $x + 10 = 5$ and $x + 10 = -5$, you have $x = -5$ or $x = -15$. Therefore, there are two values of x satisfying the given equation.

2. Which of the following is a solution to the equation $y^2 = 4y$?

    F.   −4
    G. −2
    H. 0
    J.   8
    K. 16

H is correct. Rewrite $y^2 = 4y$ by subtracting $4y$ from both sides of the equation. Thus, you have $y^2 − 4y = 0$. Factor $y^2 − 4y = 0$, and you have $y(y − 4) = 0$. Therefore, either $y = 0$ or $y − 4 = 0$, which is equivalent to $y = 4$. The solutions are 0 and 4, but only 0 is shown among the given choices.

3. Which of the following equations has both $x = h$ and $x = −k$ as roots?

    A. $x^2 + x(h − k) − hk = 0$
    B. $x^2 − x(h − k) + hk = 0$
    C. $x^2 + x(k − h) + hk = 0$
    D. $x^2 + x(h − k) + hk = 0$
    E. $x^2 + x(k − h) − hk = 0$

E is correct. Since the roots of the equation are $x = h$ and $x = −k$, then the equation could be written as $(x − h)(x − (−k)) = 0$, which is equivalent to $(x − h)(x + k) = 0$. Multiplying $(x − h)(x + k)$, you have $x^2 + kx − hx − hk = 0$ or $x^2 + x(k − h) − hk = 0$.

G. Word Problems

1. Three times a number is the same as the number added to 60. What is the number?

    A. 15
    B. 20
    C. 30
    D. 45
    E. 180

C is correct. Let x be the number. Then you have $3x = x + 60$, which is equivalent is to $2x = 60$, or $x = 30$. The number is 30. You could also solve the problem by substituting each answer choice to see which one works.

2. Rebecca has twice as much money as Rachel. If Rebecca gives Rachel $60, then the two of them will have the same amount of money. How much money did Rebecca have originally?

   F. $60
   G. $90
   H. $120
   J. $180
   K. $240

K is correct. Let x be the amount of money that Rachel has. Then $2x$ represents the amount of money that Rebecca has. Since Rebecca gave Rachel $60 and they have the same amount of money, you can write the equation $2x - 60 = x + 60$. Subtracting x from both sides of the equation, you have $x - 60 = 60$ or $x = 120$. Thus, Rachel has $120, and Rebecca has $240. You could also solve this problem by substituting each answer choice to see which one works.

3. There are 200 marbles in a box. All the marbles are either red or blue. If there are 40 more red marbles than blue marbles, how many red marbles are there in the box?

   A.   40
   B.   80
   C.   120
   D.   160
   E.   180

C is correct. Let x be the number of blue marbles and $x + 40$ be the number of red marbles. Since there are 200 marbles in the box, you have $x + x + 40 = 200$, which is equivalent to $2x + 40 = 200$ or $x = 80$. Thus, the number of red marbles is $x + 40$ or 120. You could also solve this problem by substituting each answer choice to see which one works.

4. Erica used a car service that charges $5 per mile plus an initial fee of $20. If the total cost for the car service was $110, what was the distance traveled in miles?

   F.   16
   G.   18
   H.   20
   J.   22
   K.   26

G is correct. Let x be the number of miles of Erica's trip. Then $5x + 20 = 110$, which is equivalent to $5x = 90$ or $x = 18$. Thus, the distance of Erica's trip is 18 miles. You could also solve this problem by substituting each answer choice to see which one works.

X. Studying Intermediate Algebra

On the ACT Mathematics Test, approximately 9 out of the 60 questions are intermediate algebra questions. You'll be tested on your intermediate algebra skills, which include working with rational and algebraic expressions, equations and inequalities, logarithmic and exponential functions, complex numbers, sequences, and matrices. The practice problems in this chapter are designed to help you review many of the intermediate algebra skills. Work the problems, and check your answers with the given explanations.

A. Algebraic Expressions

---

1. If you hire Mary's Car Service to drive you across town, you will be charged $10 plus $2 for each $\frac{1}{4}$ mile. Which of the following represents the total number of dollars that you would be charged if the trip is n miles?

   A. $2n$
   B. $10 + 2n$
   C. $10 + 4n$
   D. $10 + 8n$
   E. $12n$

D is correct. Because you are charged $2 for each $\frac{1}{4}$ mile, the charge for each mile is 4($2) = $8 and the charge for n miles would be $8n$. The total charge, in dollars, is $10 + 8n$.

---

2. If Janet is n years old, Karen is 2 years younger than Janet, and Mary is 4 years more than twice Janet's age, which of the following represents how many years older Mary is than Karen?

   F. 2
   G. $n - 2$
   H. n
   J. $n + 2$
   K. $n + 6$

K is correct. Because Janet's age is n, Karen's age is $(n - 2)$ and Mary's age is $2n + 4$. Since Mary is older than Karen, the difference in their ages is $(2n + 4) - (n - 2)$, which is equivalent to $2n + 4 - n + 2$ or $n + 6$.

3. Points A, B, C, and D lie on the same line. If B is the midpoint of $\overline{AC}$, C is the midpoint of $\overline{BD}$, and $AD = 12k$, what is the length of $\overline{BD}$ in terms of k?

   A. $2k$
   B. $4k$
   C. $6k$
   D. $8k$
   E. $10k$

D is correct.

Since B is the midpoint of $\overline{AC}$, $AB = BC$. Since C is the midpoint of $\overline{BD}$, $BC = CD$. Since $AB = BC$ and $BC = CD$, you know that $AB = BC = CD$. Because $AB + BC + CD = AD$ and $AD = 12k$, each segment is $4k$ in length. $BC + CD = 4k + 4k = 8k$ and thus $BD = 8k$.

4. Let n^* be defined as $n^* = n^2 - 3n$ for all integers n. What is the value of n^* if $n = -4$?

   F. -28
   G. -4
   H. 4
   J. 16
   K. 28

K is correct. Substitute -4 for n and do the arithmetic: $(-4)^2 - 3(-4) = 16 + 12$ or 28.

B. Algebraic Expressions Involving Absolute Value

1. $10 - |n + 2| = 4$

   If n is a negative number, what is the value of n?

   A. -2
   B. -6
   C. -8
   D. -10
   E. -16

C is correct. The equation is equivalent to $6 = |n + 2|$. In this form you can see that $n + 2 = 6$ or $n + 2 = -6$, and you have $n = 4$ or $n = -8$. Since n is a negative number, $n = -8$.

2. If x is a negative integer, $\left|\dfrac{x}{2}-1\right| < 2$, what is the value of x?

    F. -4

    G. -3

    H. -2

    J. -1

    K. 0

J is correct. The inequality $\left|\dfrac{x}{2}-1\right| < 2$ is equivalent to $-2 < \left(\dfrac{x}{2}-1\right) < 2$. Adding 1 to all three parts, you have $-1 < \dfrac{x}{2} < 3$. Multiplying by 2, you have $-2 < x < 6$. Since x is a negative integer, $x = -1$.

3. If $\left|\dfrac{k}{3}-4\right| = \dfrac{k}{3}-4$, what is the smallest possible value for k?

    A. -12

    B. 0

    C. 8

    D. 12

    E. 15

D is correct. The absolute value of a quantity must be greater than or equal to 0. Since $\left|\dfrac{k}{3}-4\right| = \dfrac{k}{3}-4$, you have $\dfrac{k}{3}-4 \geq 0$. Solve the inequality, and you have $\dfrac{k}{3} \geq 4$ or $k \geq 12$. Thus, the smallest value for k is 12.

C. Algebraic Expressions Involving Exponents and Radicals

1. If x is a positive integer, $x^a = \dfrac{x^4}{x^b}$, and $x^a = x^2(x^b)$, what is the value of b?

    A. 4

    B. 2

    C. 1

    D. 0

    E. -2

C is correct. Since you are trying to find an exponent, express each side as a power with the same base and set the exponents equal. Since $x^a = \dfrac{x^4}{x^b}$ and $\dfrac{x^4}{x^b} = x^{4-b}$, you know that $x^a = x^{4-b}$ and $a = 4 - b$. Since $x^a = x^2(x^b)$ and $x^2(x^b) = x^{2+b}$, you know that $x^a = x^{2+b}$ and $a = 2 + b$. Solving the system $a = 4 - b$ and $a = 2 + b$, you have $4 - b = 2 + b$, or $b = 1$.

2. What is the value of $x^2 + x^{\frac{1}{4}}$ if $\sqrt{x} = 4$?

   F. 4.5
   G. 5
   H. 20
   J. 254
   K. 258

K is correct. Squaring both sides of the equation $\sqrt{x} = 4$, you have $x = 16$. Therefore, $x^2 + x^{\frac{1}{4}} = (16)^2 + (16)^{\frac{1}{4}} = 256 + 2$ or 258.

3. Which of the following has the greatest value if $0 < x < 1$?

   A. $\sqrt[3]{x}$
   B. $\sqrt{x}$
   C. x
   D. x^2
   E. x^3

A is correct. One approach to the problem is to assign a numerical value to x. For example, let $x = 0.5$, then $\sqrt[3]{x} = \sqrt[3]{0.5} \approx 0.79$, $\sqrt{x} = \sqrt{0.5} \approx 0.71$, $x = 0.5$, $x^2 = (0.5)^2 = 0.25$, and $x^3 = (0.5)^3 = 0.125$. Therefore, $\sqrt[3]{x}$ has the greatest value.

4. If $\sqrt{x+1} - 2 = 7$, what is the value of x?

   F. 24
   G. 26
   H. 80
   J. 81
   K. 82

H is correct. Isolate the radical by adding 2 to both sides of the equation, and you have $\sqrt{x+1} = 9$. Squaring both sides gives you $x + 1 = 81$ or $x = 80$. Checking $x = 80$ with the original equation, you have $\sqrt{80+1} - 2 = 7$ or $7 = 7$.

D. Equations

---

1. For which positive number is 16 times the cube root of the number the same as the number?

    A. 4

    B. 8

    C. 10

    D. 32

    E. 64

E is correct. If x is the number, then $16\left(\sqrt[3]{x}\right) = x$. Cubing both sides, you have $4096x = x^3$ or $x^3 - 4096x = 0$. Factoring the equation $x^3 - 4096x = 0$, you have $x(x^2 - 4096) = 0$. Thus $x = 0$ or $x = \pm\sqrt{4096} = \pm64$. Since x is a positive number, $x = 64$.

---

2. If $a > b$ and $ay - by = 4$, what is the value of y when $(a - b)^2 = 4$?

    F. 0

    G. 1

    H. 2

    J. 4

    K. 8

H is correct. Since $(a - b)^2 = 4$, you know that $(a - b) = \pm2$. Because $a > b$, you know $a - b > 0$ and $a - b = 2$. To find y when $a - b = 2$, express $ay - by = 4$ in the factored form: $y(a - b) = 4$. Now substitute 2 for $(a - b)$. Then $(y)(2) = 4$ and $y = 2$.

---

3. If $(a - 1)(b + 2)(c - 3) = 0$, what is the smallest value for $a^2 + b^2 + c^2$?

    A. 0

    B. 1

    C. 4

    D. 9

    E. 14

B is correct. In order for $(a - 1)(b + 2)(c - 3)$ to have a value of zero, only one of the following three conditions must be met: $a = 1$ or $b = -2$ or $c = 3$. If you let $a = 1$ and then choose to let $b = 0$ and $c = 0$, the product of $(a - 1)(b + 2)(c - 3)$ will be zero and the value of $a^2 + b^2 + c^2$ will be the smallest value possible or $(1)^2 + (0)^2 + (0)^2 = 1$.

E. Inequalities

---

1. If $\frac{1}{6} < \frac{3}{n} < \frac{1}{4}$, how many integral values of n are possible?

    A.   1
    B.   3
    C.   5
    D.   6
    E.   7

C is correct. The inequality $\frac{1}{6} < \frac{3}{n} < \frac{1}{4}$ is equivalent to $\frac{1}{6} < \frac{3}{n}$ and $\frac{3}{n} < \frac{1}{4}$. Solving $\frac{1}{6} < \frac{3}{n}$, you have $n < 18$. Similarly, solving $\frac{3}{n} < \frac{1}{4}$, you have $12 < n$ or $n > 12$. Since $n > 12$ and $n < 18$, n must be 13, 14, 15, 16, or 17. There are 5 integral values for n.

---

2. Five years ago, Mary was at least 3 more than twice Karen's age. If k represents Karen's age now and m represents Mary's age now, which of the following describes the relationship of their ages 5 years ago?

    F. $m > 2k + 3$
    G. $m > 2k - 3$
    H. $m + 5 > 2(k + 5) - 3$
    J. $m - 5 \leq 2(k + 5) + 3$
    K. $m - 5 \geq 2(k - 5) + 3$

K is correct.

	Current age	Age 5 years ago
Mary	m	$m - 5$
Karen	k	$k - 5$

Five years ago, Mary's age was $m - 5$ and Karen's age was $k - 5$. If 5 years ago Mary had been 3 years more than twice Karen's age, the relationship of their ages would have been described as $m - 5 = 2(k - 5) + 3$. Since 5 years ago, Mary was *at least* 3 years more than twice Karen's age, the equation becomes an inequality: $m - 5 \geq 2(k - 5) + 3$.

3. If a and b are positive integers and $(a - b)^2 = 36$, which of the following must be true?

    A. $a^2 + b^2 < 36$

    B. $a^2 + b^2 > 36$

    C. $a^2 + b^2 = 36$

    D. $a^2 - b^2 = 36$

    E. $a - b = 6$

B is correct. Since $(a - b)^2 = a^2 - 2ab + b^2$, you know that $a^2 - 2ab + b^2 = 36$ or $a^2 + b^2 = 36 + 2ab$. Because a and b are positive integers, $2ab$ is positive. Thus, $a^2 + b^2 = 36 + 2ab$ is equivalent to $a^2 + b^2 = 36 + $ (a positive number). Therefore, $a^2 + b^2 > 36$.

F. Systems of Equations

1. If $4a - 5b = 20$ and $b = 4$, what is the value of $2b + 5a$?

    A. -42

    B.   0

    C.   8

    D.   30

    E.   58

E is correct. Since $b = 4$ and $4a - 5b = 20$, you know that $4a - 5(4) = 20$ or $4a = 40$ or $a = 10$. Because $a = 10$ and $b = 4$, $2b + 5a = 2(4) + 5(10)$ or 58.

2. If $a > 0$, $c > 0$, $a^2b = 9$, and $bc^2 = 25$, what is the value of abc?

    F.   15

    G.   25

    H.   45

    J.   75

    K.   225

F is correct. When you multiply the equations $a^2b = 9$ and $bc^2 = 25$, you have $(a^2b)(bc^2) = (9)(25)$ or $a^2b^2c^2 = 225$ and $abc = \pm15$. Because $a > 0$ and $c > 0$ and $a^2b = 9 > 0$, you know that $b > 0$. Thus, $abc = 15$.

3. At the beginning of the school year, Caitlin paid $22 for 4 pens and 3 notebooks. Two months later, she decided to buy 6 more of the same pens and 5 more of the same notebooks before the price changed. If she spent $35 on these additional pens and notebooks, what was the cost, in dollars, of 1 notebook?

   A. 2

   B. $2\frac{1}{2}$

   C. 4

   D. 5

   E. 8

C is correct. Let p be the price of a pen and n be the price of a notebook, then $4p + 3n = 22$ and $6p + 5n = 35$. To solve for n, multiply the first equation by -3 and the second by 2 and then add them together:

$$
\begin{array}{r}
-12p - 9n = -66 \\
12p + 10n = 70 \\
\hline
n = 4
\end{array}
$$

The number of dollars that 1 notebook cost was 4.

G. Functions

1. If $f(x) = x^2 - 4$ and $g(x) = x + 2$, then what is the value of $f(g(-4))$?

   A. -8
   B. -4
   C. 0
   D. 4
   E. 8

C is correct. Begin by evaluating $g(-4)$, which is $g(-4) = (-4) + 2$ or -2. Therefore, $f(g(-4)) = f(-2)$, and evaluating $f(-2)$, you have $f(-2) = (-2)^2 - 4 = 4 - 4$ or 0.

2. If the function f is defined by $f(x) = 2x - 6$, which of the following is equivalent to $5f(x) + 10$?

   F. $10x - 40$
   G. $10x - 20$
   H. $10x + 4$
   J. $10x + 20$
   K. $7x + 4$

G is correct. Since $f(x) = 2x - 6$, you have $5f(x) + 10 = 5(2x - 6) + 10$, which is equivalent to $10x - 20$.

3. The life expectancy of a certain virus is given by the function $L(t) = \dfrac{12t + 36}{t + 1}$, $t \leq 120$, where t is the temperature in Celsius of the environment in which the virus is placed, and L is the number of minutes that the virus will survive in that environment. What is the change in life expectancy, in minutes, if the temperature is raised from 7°C to 23°C?

   A. −16
   B. −2
   C. 15
   D. 16
   E. 30

B is correct. At 7°C, the life expectancy of the virus is $L(7) = \dfrac{12(7) + 36}{7 + 1} = \dfrac{120}{8} = 15$ minutes, and at 23°C it is $L(23) = \dfrac{12(23) + 36}{23 + 1} = \dfrac{312}{24} = 13$ minutes. Therefore, the change in life expectancy is $13 - 15$ or −2 minutes.

4. Some of the values of the function f are shown in the accompanying table. If a function h is defined by $h(x) = 2f(x - 1)$, what is the value of $h(2)$?

x	f(x)
−3	−1
−2	0
−1	4
0	2
1	−3
2	4
3	5

   F. −6
   G. −3
   H. 4
   J. 5
   K. 7

F is correct. Since $h(x) = 2f(x - 1)$, $h(2) = 2f(2 - 1)$ or $h(2) = 2f(1)$. The table shows that $f(1) = -3$. Thus, $2f(1) = 2(-3)$ or −6.

H. Logarithmic and Exponential Functions

1. If $\log_x 16 = 2$, what is the value of x?

   A. -4

   B. $\dfrac{1}{4}$

   C. $\dfrac{1}{2}$

   D. 4

   E. 8

D is correct. One of the properties of a logarithm is that if $a > 0$, $a \neq 1$, and $\log_a b = c$, then $a^c = b$. Since $\log_x 16 = 2$, you have $x^2 = 16$ and $x = \pm 4$. Since $x > 0$, you have $x = 4$.

2. If $3(5^x) = 375$, what is the value of x?

   F. 3

   G. 25

   H. 120

   J. 125

   K. 625

F is correct. Begin by dividing both sides of the equation by 3, and you have $5^x = 125$. Notice that $125 = 5^3$ and rewrite $5^x = 125$ as $5^x = 5^3$. Thus, $x = 3$.

3. If $\log_4 32 + \log_4 2 = \log_{2} x$, what is the value of x?

   A. 3

   B. 8

   C. 32

   D. 68

   E. 128

B is correct. One of the properties of a logarithm is that if a, b, and $c > 0$, and $a \neq 1$, then $\log_a(bc) = \log_a b + \log_a c$. Therefore, rewrite $\log_4 32 + \log_4 2$ as $\log_4(32)(2)$, which is equivalent to $\log_4(64)$ and $\log_4(64) = 3$ since $4^3 = 64$. Now that the left side of the equation is 3, you have $3 = \log_{2} x$, which is equivalent to $2^3 = x$ or $x = 8$.

I. Modeling

> 1. In a printing company, if one machine can print 600 copies in 12 hours, how many hours would it take to print 1200 copies with three identical machines working together?
>
>   **A.** 4
>   **B.** 6
>   **C.** 8
>   **D.** 10
>   **E.** 12

C is correct. Since it takes 12 hours for one machine to print 600 copies, it would take 24 hours for one machine to print 1200 copies. If three machines worked together to print 1200 copies, it would take $\frac{24}{3}$ or 8 hours. You could also use an inverse proportion. The more machines you use, the less time it would require to print 1200 copies.

Number of machines	Hours	# of copies
1	24	1200
3	x	1200

Since the number of copies is the same, you have $(1)(24) = (3)(x)$ or $x = 8$ hours.

> 2. If Marissa drove for h hours at an average rate of m miles per hour and then she drove for k hours at an average rate of n miles per hour, what is the total distance, in miles, that she drove?
>
>   **F.** $m + n$
>   **G.** $\dfrac{m + n}{h + k}$
>   **H.** $\dfrac{m}{h} + \dfrac{n}{k}$
>   **J.** $(h + k)(m + n)$
>   **K.** $mh + nk$

K is correct. Since Distance = Rate × Time, when Marissa drove for h hours at an average of m miles per hour, the distance was mh miles. Similarly, when she drove for k hours at an average rate of n miles per hour, the distance was nk miles. The total distance, in miles, is $mh + nk$.

3. In a music class with 22 students, each student plays only the violin, plays only the cello, or plays both. If 4 students play both the violin and the cello, and of the remaining students, twice as many play the violin as play the cello, how many students play only the cello?

 A. 4
 B. 6
 C. 8
 D. 10
 E. 12

B is correct.

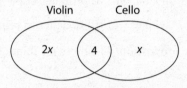

Set up a Venn diagram with x representing the number of students who play only the cello and $2x$ representing the number of students who play only the violin. Since there are 22 students in the class, $2x + x + 4 = 22$. Solve the equation, and you find $x = 6$. The number of students who play only the cello is 6.

4. Mrs. Cohen bought a box of individually wrapped chocolates and decided to give the chocolates to her students. If she gave each student 2 pieces of chocolate, 25 pieces would be left in the box. If she gave each student 3 pieces, 5 pieces would be left in the box. How many students are in her class?

 F. 15
 G. 20
 H. 30
 J. 40
 K. 65

G is correct. If x is the number of students in Mrs. Cohen's class and y is the number of pieces of chocolate in the box, then $2x + 25 = y$ and $3x + 5 = y$ or $2x + 25 = 3x + 5$ and $x = 20$. The number of students in Mrs. Cohen's class is 20.

J. Complex Numbers

1. Given $i^2 = -1$, what is the value of $(3 - i)(3 + i)$?

   A. 5
   B. 8
   C. 10
   D. 12
   E. 13

C is correct. Multiply $(3 - i)$ and $(3 + i)$ by applying the distributive property, and you have $9 + 3i - 3i - i^2$ or $9 - i^2$. Since $i^2 = -1$, $9 - i^2 = 9 - (-1)$ or 10.

2. For $i^2 = -1$, what is the value of $2i^4 + i^3 - 3i^2 + i$?

   F. -1
   G. 1
   H. 5
   J. $-1 + 2i$
   K. $5 + 2i$

H is correct. Since $i^2 = -1$, you have $2i^4 = 2(1)$, $i^3 = -i$, and $-3i^2 = -3(-1) = 3$. Therefore, $2i^4 + i^3 - 3i^2 + i = 2 - i + 3 + i$ or 5.

3. For $i^2 = -1$, which of the following is equivalent to $\dfrac{1}{1+i} + \dfrac{1}{1-i}$?

   A. -2
   B. $-i$
   C. 0
   D. i
   E. 1

E is correct. Express both $\dfrac{1}{1+i}$ and $\dfrac{1}{1-i}$ in $a + bi$ form. Rewrite $\dfrac{1}{1+i}$ as $\dfrac{1}{1+i} \cdot \dfrac{1-i}{1-i} = \dfrac{1-i}{1-i^2} = \dfrac{1-i}{1-(-1)} = \dfrac{1-i}{2}$ or $\dfrac{1}{2} - \dfrac{i}{2}$. Also, rewrite $\dfrac{1}{1-i}$ as $\dfrac{1}{1-i} \cdot \dfrac{1+i}{1+i} = \dfrac{1+i}{1-i^2} = \dfrac{1+i}{1-(-1)} = \dfrac{1+i}{2}$ or $\dfrac{1}{2} + \dfrac{i}{2}$. Therefore, $\dfrac{1}{1+i} + \dfrac{1}{1-i} = \dfrac{1}{2} - \dfrac{i}{2} + \dfrac{1}{2} + \dfrac{i}{2}$ or 1.

An alternate solution is to add the two fractions as follows: $\dfrac{1}{1+i} + \dfrac{1}{1-i} = \dfrac{1-i+1+i}{(1+i)(1-i)} = \dfrac{2}{1-i^2} = \dfrac{2}{2} = 1$.

K. Patterns and Sequences

1. If the kth term of a sequence is defined as $5k - 1$, what is the value of the smallest term greater than 100?

   A. 20
   B. 21
   C. 104
   D. 109
   E. 504

C is correct. Since the value of the kth term is $5k - 1$, solve $5k - 1 > 100$, and you have $5k > 101$ or $k > 20.2$. Since k has to be an integer, and the smallest integer greater than 20.2 is 21, $k = 21$ and $5k - 1 = 104$, which is the smallest term greater than 100. Note that you can eliminate Choices A and B right away since they are both less than 100.

2. If the first term of a sequence is 2 and each successive term is found by multiplying the preceding term by -3, what is the sum of the fourth and fifth terms?

   F. -216
   G. -108
   H. 108
   J. 162
   K. 216

H is correct. Since this is a geometric sequence, using the formula $a_n = a_1(r^{n-1})$, you have the fourth term $a_4 = (2)(-3)^{(4-1)} = 2(-3)^3 = -54$ and the fifth term $a_5 = 2(-3)^{(5-1)} = 162$. The sum of the fourth and fifth terms is $162 + (-54)$ or 108.

3. $1^2, 2^2, 3^2, 4^2, \ldots$

   The first 4 terms of a sequence are shown here. If the sum of the first nth terms is greater than 100, what is the smallest value of n?

   A. 6
   B. 7
   C. 8
   D. 10
   E. 17

B is correct. To find when the sum will be more than 100, start adding the terms: $1^2 + 2^2 = 5$; $1^2 + 2^2 + 3^2 = 14$. When you reach $1^2 + 2^2 + 3^2 + 4^2 + 5^2 + 6^2 = 91$, and $1^2 + 2^2 + 3^2 + 4^2 + 5^2 + 6^2 + 7^2 = 140$, you know that the first time the sum is greater than 100 occurs when $n = 7$. The smallest value of n is 7.

L. Matrices

1. The matrices A and B are given here:

$$A = \begin{bmatrix} -4 & 0 \\ 2 & 1 \end{bmatrix} \text{ and } B = \begin{bmatrix} 3 & 2 \\ -1 & 5 \end{bmatrix}$$

If $X = 3A - 2B$, which of the following is X?

A. $\begin{bmatrix} -4 & 0 \\ 2 & 1 \end{bmatrix}$

B. $\begin{bmatrix} -1 & -2 \\ 3 & -4 \end{bmatrix}$

C. $\begin{bmatrix} -15 & -2 \\ 7 & 2 \end{bmatrix}$

D. $\begin{bmatrix} -6 & 4 \\ 4 & -13 \end{bmatrix}$

E. $\begin{bmatrix} -18 & -4 \\ 8 & -7 \end{bmatrix}$

E is correct. Since $X = 3A - 2B$, you have $X = 3\begin{bmatrix} -4 & 0 \\ 2 & 1 \end{bmatrix} - 2\begin{bmatrix} 3 & 2 \\ -1 & 5 \end{bmatrix} = \begin{bmatrix} -12 & 0 \\ 6 & 3 \end{bmatrix} - \begin{bmatrix} 6 & 4 \\ -2 & 10 \end{bmatrix}$

$$= \begin{bmatrix} -12-6 & 0-4 \\ 6-(-2) & 3-10 \end{bmatrix} = \begin{bmatrix} -18 & -4 \\ 8 & -7 \end{bmatrix}.$$

2. If $\begin{bmatrix} x & -6 \\ 3 & 10 \end{bmatrix} = \begin{bmatrix} 4 & 2y \\ 3 & 10 \end{bmatrix}$, what is the value of $x + y$?

F. -8
G. -4
H. -2
J. 1
K. 2

J is correct. Since the two matrices are equal, you have $x = 4$ and $-6 = 2y$ or $-3 = y$. Therefore, $x + y = 4 + (-3)$ or 1.

3. What is the matrix product of $\begin{bmatrix} 2 & -1 & 0 \end{bmatrix} \begin{bmatrix} 4 \\ 6 \\ -3 \end{bmatrix}$?

   A. $[-48]$

   B. $[-1]$

   C. $[2]$

   D. $\begin{bmatrix} 8 & -6 & 0 \end{bmatrix}$

   E. $\begin{bmatrix} 8 \\ -6 \\ 0 \end{bmatrix}$

C is correct. Since $\begin{bmatrix} 2 & -1 & 0 \end{bmatrix}$ is a 1×3 matrix and $\begin{bmatrix} 4 \\ 6 \\ -3 \end{bmatrix}$ is a 3×1 matrix, their product is a 1×1 matrix.

The product is $[2(4) + (-1)(6) + 0(-3)]$ or $[8 - 6 + 0]$, which is $[2]$.

XI. Answering Coordinate Geometry Questions

On the ACT Mathematics Test, approximately 9 out of the 60 questions are coordinate geometry questions. You'll be tested on many concepts of coordinate geometry, including your understanding of graphing points, lines, inequalities, conics, and other curves. You are also expected to know and apply the distance, midpoint, and slope formulas (see below). The practice problems in this chapter are designed to help you review many of the coordinate geometry concepts. Work the problems, and check your answers with the given explanations. Here are the distance, midpoint, and slope formulas for reference:

Given $A(x_1, y_1)$ and $B(x_2, y_2)$:

- The **distance** between A and B (the length of $\overline{AB}$): $d_{\overline{AB}} = \sqrt{(x_2 - x_1)^2 + (y_2 - y_1)^2}$

- The **midpoint** of $\overline{AB}$: $\left(\dfrac{x_1 + x_2}{2}, \dfrac{y_1 + y_2}{2} \right)$. Think of a midpoint as the "average."

- The **slope** of $\overline{AB}$: $m_{\overline{AB}} = \dfrac{y_2 - y_1}{x_2 - x_1}$.

A. Points, Lines, and Planes

1. Which of the following is a relation that contains the three ordered pairs (x,y) listed in the table?

x	0	1	2
y	0	3	8

   A. $y = 3x$
   B. $y = 3x^2$
   C. $y = x^3$
   D. $y = x^2 + 2x$
   E. $y = x^3 + 2x$

D is correct. A relation contains the given ordered pair if substituting the given value of x produces the given value of y. To determine which of the equations contains all three pairs, choose an equation and substitute $x = 0$. If the answer is $y = 0$, test the next value of x by substituting $x = 1$. If that answer is $y = 3$, test the third value of x by substituting $x = 2$. If the answer is $y = 8$, then the relation contains all three ordered pairs. Only $y = x^2 + 2x$ contains all three pairs.

Note: If you use a graphing calculator, you can solve this problem without substitution. Just use the [y₁=] function to enter each equation, and check for the three ordered pairs using [Table].

2. Which of the following points on the accompanying graph has coordinates that satisfy the equation, $-|x| + y = 2$?

F. A
G. B
H. C
J. D
K. E

F is correct. A point satisfies an equation if substituting produces an equation that is true. Substitute the coordinates of each point into the equation $-|x| + y = 2$. Only when the coordinates of A $(-1,3)$ are substituted is the resulting equation true: $-|-1| + 3 = -1 + 3 = 2$.

3. In the xy-plane, the point $(-4,-2)$ is on the line $-3x + y = k$. What is the value of k?

A. -14
B. -10
C. 10
D. 12
E. 18

C is correct. The coordinates of a point on a line satisfy the equation of the line. Therefore, substitute -4 for x and -2 for y in the equation $-3x + y = k$, and you have $-3(-4) + (-2) = k$ or $k = 10$.

4. In the xy-plane, two lines intersect at point $(1,k)$. If the equations of the two lines are $y = -x$ and $y = 2x + h$, what is the value of h?

    F. -3
    G. -1
    H. 0
    J. 1
    K. 3

F is correct. If two lines intersect, the coordinates of the intersection point satisfy the equations of both lines. Substitute $(1,k)$ into both equations, and you have $k = -1$ and $k = 2(1) + h$. Therefore, $-1 = 2 + h$ or $h = -3$.

B. Conic Sections and Other Curves

1. In an xy-coordinate plane, point C with coordinates $(2,1)$ is the center of a circle and point A with coordinates $(7,1)$ is on the circle. Which of the following could be the coordinates of point B, if B is also a point on the circle?

    A. $(-7,1)$
    B. $(1,7)$
    C. $(4,6)$
    D. $(6,4)$
    E. $(7,6)$

D is correct.

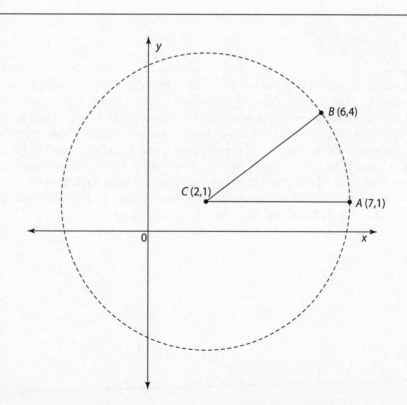

Since $\overline{CA}$ is a radius of the circle, the length of the radius of the circle is $\sqrt{(7-2)^2 + (1-1)^2} = 5$. Because B is a point on the circle, $\overline{CB}$ must also be a radius with length 5. Using the distance formula with each choice, only when the coordinates of B are $(6,4)$ does the length equal 5: $\sqrt{(6-2)^2 + (4-1)^2} = 5$.

> **Note:** You can save time if you graph the points. Since $\overline{CA}$ is horizontal, you can find the length of the radius using $7 - 2 = 5$, and you can see that Choices A, B, and E appear to be too far from C to be on the circle. Now only two points require checking with the distance formula.

---

2. Which of the following could be the equation of the graph in the accompanying figure?

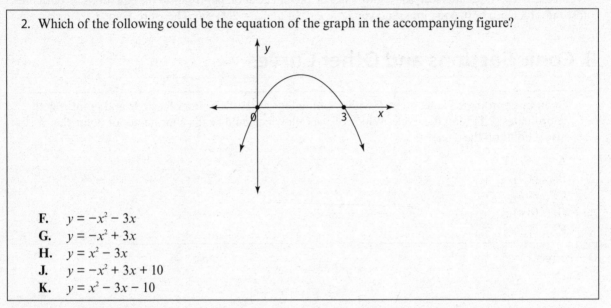

    F. $y = -x^2 - 3x$
    G. $y = -x^2 + 3x$
    H. $y = x^2 - 3x$
    J. $y = -x^2 + 3x + 10$
    K. $y = x^2 - 3x - 10$

G is correct. For a parabola written in the form of $y = ax^2 + bx + c$, c is the y-intercept, and if $a > 0$, then the parabola is concave up, and if $a < 0$, then the parabola is concave down. The parabola in the accompanying figure is concave down; therefore $a < 0$, thus eliminating Choices H and K. Also, the y-intercept in the accompanying parabola is 0, which implies that $c = 0$, thus eliminating Choice J. In addition, the x-intercepts of the accompanying parabola are 0 and 3, and therefore the roots of the equation must be 0 and 3. In Choice F, let $-x^2 - 3x = 0$, and you have $-x(x + 3) = 0$, which is equivalent to $x = 0$ or $x = -3$, which are not the roots of the accompanying parabola. In Choice G, letting $-x^2 + 3x = 0$, you have $x(-x + 3) = 0$ leading to $x = 0$ or $x = 3$ and, therefore, the roots of the equation are 0 and 3, which means Choice G, $y = -x^2 + 3x$, could be the equation of the accompanying parabola.

3. In an xy-coordinate plane, a circle in the second quadrant is tangent to the x-axis, the y-axis, and the line $x = -8$. If point $C(h,k)$ is the center of the circle, what is the value of $h + k$?

   A. −8
   B. −4
   C. 0
   D. 4
   E. 8

C is correct.

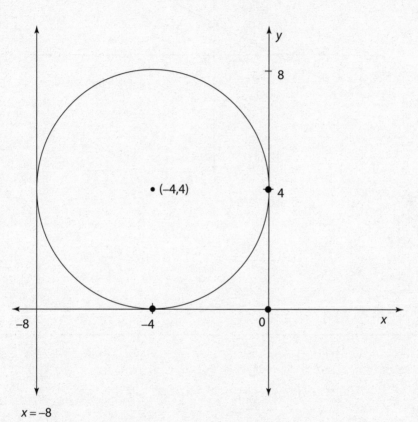

Draw a sketch of the coordinate plane and the line $x = -8$. Since the circle is tangent to both axes and the line $x = -8$, its diameter must be 8, which implies the radius is 4. Therefore, the center must be 4 units from all three lines, making its coordinates $(-4,4)$. Thus, the value of $h + k$ is $(-4) + (4)$ or 0.

177

4. In the standard (x,y) coordinate plane below, line ℓ is shown in the accompanying diagram. The graph of which of the following equations is the reflection of line ℓ on the y-axis?

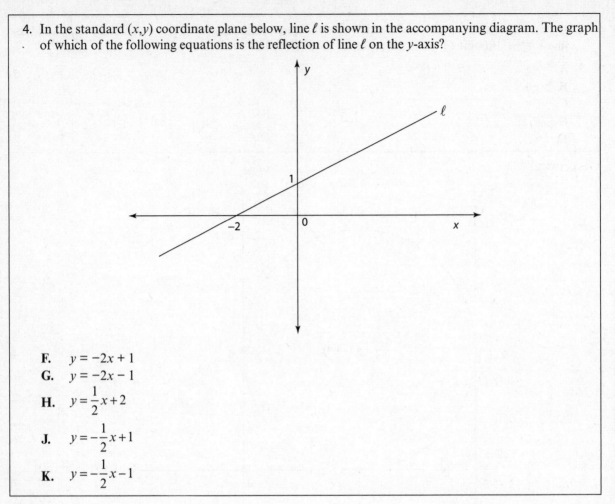

F. $y = -2x + 1$

G. $y = -2x - 1$

H. $y = \dfrac{1}{2}x + 2$

J. $y = -\dfrac{1}{2}x + 1$

K. $y = -\dfrac{1}{2}x - 1$

J is correct.

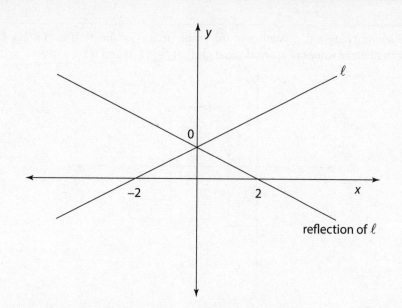

reflection of ℓ

The reflection of line ℓ on the y-axis is the mirror image of line ℓ with the y-axis as the mirror. The mirror image of the point $(-2,0)$ is $(2,0)$. This point $(0,1)$ is on the y-axis, and therefore, the mirror image of $(0,1)$ is itself. Now you have two points on the mirror image of line ℓ: $(2,0)$ and $(0,1)$. The slope of this mirror image is $\dfrac{1-0}{0-2} = -\dfrac{1}{2}$, and the equation is $y-1 = -\dfrac{1}{2}(x-0)$ or $y = -\dfrac{1}{2}x+1$.

Note: You could also enter the equations into your graphing calculator and see which one is the reflection of line ℓ.

5. In the accompanying diagram, a portion of the graph of $h(x)$ is shown. If $h(x) = h(x + 4)$ for all values of x, how many distinct values of x are there such that $h(x) = 0$ and $0 \le x \le 40$?

   A.   8
   B.   10
   C.   20
   D.   40
   E.   80

C is correct. The fact that $h(x) = h(x + 4)$ implies that $h(x)$ is periodic. That is to say that the graph repeats itself every 4 units. In this case, the portion of the graph will appear 10 times on the interval [0,40]. Also, the x-values satisfying $h(x) = 0$ are the x-intercepts. Since the graph crosses the x-axis twice for $0 \le x \le 4$, it will cross the x-axis 2(10) or 20 times for $0 \le x \le 40$.

C. Odd and Even Functions

1. A function f is an even function if $f(x) = f(-x)$ for all x in the domain of f. Which of the following is an even function?

   A. $f(x) = 4x$
   B. $f(x) = 2x^2 - 4x$
   C. $f(x) = (x - 2)^2$
   D. $f(x) = x^3 + 2$
   E. $f(x) = x^4 - 3$

E is correct. Apply the property $f(x) = f(-x)$ to the five choices by finding $f(-x)$ and comparing it with $f(x)$: Choice A, $f(-x) = 4(-x) = -4x \ne 4x$; Choice B, $f(-x) = 2(-x)^2 - 4(-x) = 2x^2 + 4x \ne 2x^2 - 4x$; Choice C, $f(-x) = (-x - 2)^2 = (-(x + 2))^2 = (x + 2)^2 \ne (x - 2)^2$; Choice D, $f(-x) = (-x)^3 + 2 = -x^3 + 2 \ne x^3 + 2$; and Choice E, $f(-x) = (-x)^4 - 3 = x^4 - 3$, which is the same as $f(x)$.

2. Which of the following functions is neither an odd function nor an even function?

F.

G.

H.

J.

K.

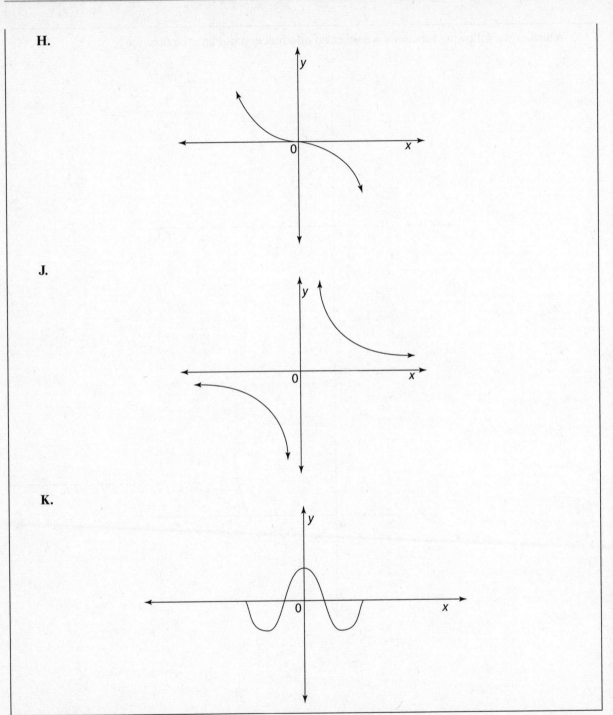

G is correct. The graph of an even function is symmetric with respect to the y-axis, and the graph of an odd function is symmetric with respect to the origin. The graph in Choice F is symmetric with respect to the y-axis; in Choice H, the origin; in Choice J, the origin; and in Choice K, the y-axis. The graph in Choice G is not symmetric with respect to the y-axis or the origin; thus, it is neither an even nor an odd function.

3. A function f is an odd function if $f(x) = -f(-x)$. Which of the following is an odd function?

   A. $f(x) = 3x + 5$
   B. $f(x) = x^2 - 1$
   C. $f(x) = (x + 1)^3$
   D. $f(x) = |x|$
   E. $f(x) = \dfrac{1}{x}$

E is correct. Apply the property $f(x) = -f(-x)$ to the five choices by finding $-f(-x)$ and checking it with $f(x)$. In Choice A, $-f(-x) = -(3(-x) + 5) = -(-3x + 5) = 3x - 5 \neq f(x)$. In Choice B, $-f(-x) = -((-x)^2 - 1) = -(x^2 - 1) = -x^2 + 1 \neq f(x)$. In Choice C, $-f(-x) = -(-x + 1)^3 = -((-(x - 1))^3) = -(-(x - 1)^3) = (x - 1)^3 \neq f(x)$. In Choice D, $-f(-x) = -|-x| = -|x| \neq f(x)$. In Choice E, $-f(-x) = -\dfrac{1}{-x} = \dfrac{1}{x} = f(x)$; therefore, the function in

Choice E is an odd function.

D. Graphing Inequalities

1. Which of the following inequalities has the graph shown in the accompanying figure?

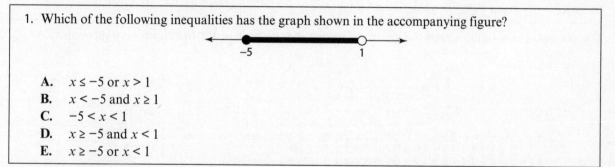

   A. $x \leq -5$ or $x > 1$
   B. $x < -5$ and $x \geq 1$
   C. $-5 < x < 1$
   D. $x \geq -5$ and $x < 1$
   E. $x \geq -5$ or $x < 1$

D is correct. The graph in the accompanying figure indicates a set of real numbers between -5 and 1 including -5 but not including 1. Using interval notation, this set is written as $[-5, 1)$. Using set builder notation, this set may be written as either $\{x | -5 \leq x < 1\}$ or $\{x | x \geq -5 \text{ and } x < 1\}$. Thus, the inequality in Choice D is the correct choice.

2. Which of the following systems of inequalities is represented by the shaded region in the accompanying figure?

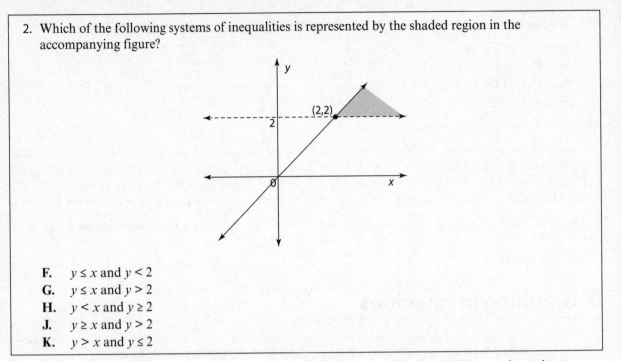

F. $y \le x$ and $y < 2$
G. $y \le x$ and $y > 2$
H. $y < x$ and $y \ge 2$
J. $y \ge x$ and $y > 2$
K. $y > x$ and $y \le 2$

G is correct. The solution sets of the system of inequalities for each of the five choices are shown here:

H.

J.

K.

Thus, the system of inequalities in Choice G is the correct choice.

E. Slopes

1. In the accompanying diagram, what is the slope of line ℓ?

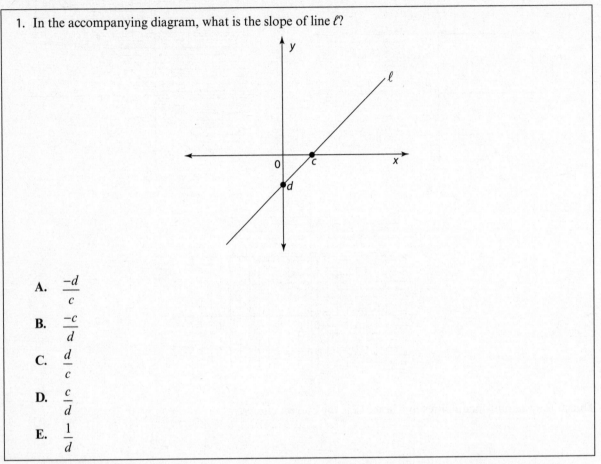

  A. $\dfrac{-d}{c}$

  B. $\dfrac{-c}{d}$

  C. $\dfrac{d}{c}$

  D. $\dfrac{c}{d}$

  E. $\dfrac{1}{d}$

A is correct. The coordinates of the two points are $(c,0)$ and $(0,d)$. The slope of a line passing through two given points is defined as $m = \dfrac{\Delta y}{\Delta x}$ or $\dfrac{y_2 - y_1}{x_2 - x_1}$. In this case, the slope of line ℓ is $m = \dfrac{0 - d}{c - 0}$ or $\dfrac{-d}{c}$. Remember that you must use the same order when subtracting the x and y coordinates.

2. In the accompanying diagram, if a line is drawn through any two of the given points, which of the following is the smallest possible value for the slope of the line?

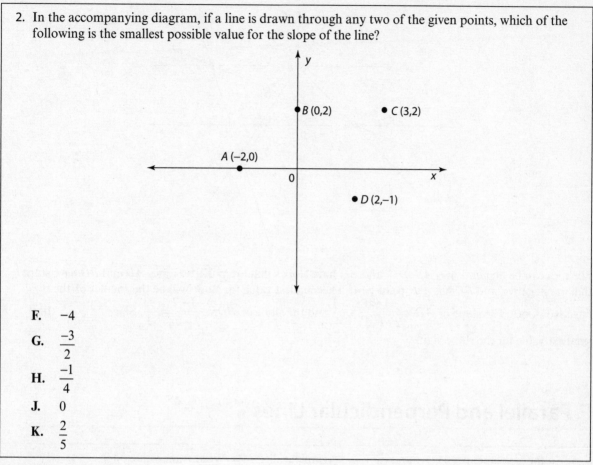

F. −4

G. $\dfrac{-3}{2}$

H. $\dfrac{-1}{4}$

J. 0

K. $\dfrac{2}{5}$

G is correct.

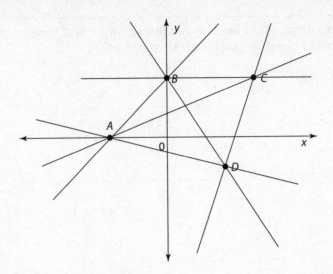

Six lines can be drawn. Lines $\overleftrightarrow{AB}$, $\overleftrightarrow{DC}$, and $\overleftrightarrow{AC}$ have slopes that are positive. Lines $\overleftrightarrow{AD}$ and $\overleftrightarrow{BD}$ have slopes that are negative, and $\overleftrightarrow{BC}$ has a slope of zero. The smallest value for slope will be the smaller of the two negative slopes. The slope of $\overleftrightarrow{AD} = \dfrac{-1-0}{2-(-2)} = \dfrac{-1}{4}$ and the slope of $\overleftrightarrow{BD} = \dfrac{-1-2}{2-0} = \dfrac{-3}{2}$. Since $\dfrac{-3}{2} < \dfrac{-1}{4}$, the smallest value for the slope is $\dfrac{-3}{2}$.

F. Parallel and Perpendicular Lines

1. In the xy-plane, $y = 4x + 1$ and $cx + 2y = d$ are parallel lines. What is the value of c?

   A. -8
   B. -4
   C. $-\dfrac{1}{4}$
   D. 4
   E. 8

A is correct. If two lines are parallel, their slopes are equal. The line $y = 4x + 1$ is written in slope-intercept form $y = mx + b$. The slope of this line is $m = 4$. To find the slope of $cx + 2y = d$, rewrite the equation in $y = mx + b$ form. Subtracting cx from both sides of the equation, you have $2y = -cx + d$, and dividing both sides by 2, you have $y = \dfrac{-cx}{2} + \dfrac{d}{2}$. Therefore, the slope of this line is $m = -\dfrac{c}{2}$. Since the two lines are parallel, the slopes are equal. Set $-\dfrac{c}{2} = 4$, and you have $c = -8$.

2. In the xy-plane, the coordinates of three given points are $A(2,4)$, $B(1,1)$, and $C(4,2)$. If line ℓ is drawn passing through point A and perpendicular to $\overline{BC}$, what is the slope of line ℓ?

    F. -3

    G. -1

    H. $-\dfrac{1}{3}$

    J. $\dfrac{1}{3}$

    K. 1

F is correct. Draw a sketch of the xy-plane including the points A, B, and C.

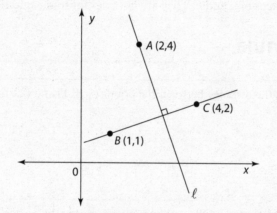

If two lines are perpendicular, their slopes are negative reciprocals. The slope of $\overline{BC}$ is $m_{\overline{BC}} = \dfrac{2-1}{4-1} = \dfrac{1}{3}$.

Therefore, the slope of a line perpendicular to $\overline{BC}$ is -3.

Note: The fact that the line passes through point A is not relevant. There are infinitely many lines perpendicular to $\overline{BC}$, and the slopes of all of these lines are -3.

G. Midpoints

1. On a number line, what is the midpoint of the line segment whose endpoints are -12 and -2?

    A. -14

    B. -7

    C. -5

    D. 5

    E. 7

B is correct. The midpoint of a line segment whose endpoints are two given numbers on a number line is equivalent to the average of the two numbers. In this case, the coordinate of the midpoint of -12 and -2 is $\dfrac{(-12)+(-2)}{2}$ or -7.

2. In the coordinate plane, if $M(2,-1)$ is the midpoint of the line segment joining points $A(4,a)$ and $B(0,b)$, what is the value of $a + b$?

    F. -2
    G. -1
    H. 0
    J. 3
    K. 6

F is correct. Applying the midpoint formula (see page 173), you have the coordinates of M as $\left(\dfrac{4+0}{2}, \dfrac{a+b}{2} \right)$. Since the coordinates of M are given as $(2,-1)$, you have $\dfrac{a+b}{2} = -1$ or $a + b = -2$. Notice that you do not need to find the individual values of a and b. They are not relevant to the question.

H. Distance Formula

1. In the xy-plane, what is the distance between the points $(-10,1)$ and $(2,6)$?

    A. 12
    B. 13
    C. 17
    D. $\sqrt{89}$
    E. $\sqrt{189}$

B is correct. The distance between two points can be found using the distance formula, $d = \sqrt{(x_2 - x_1)^2 + (y_2 - y_1)^2}$. In this case, $d = \sqrt{(2-(-10))^2 + (6-1)^2} = \sqrt{12^2 + 5^2} = \sqrt{144 + 25} = \sqrt{169}$ or 13.

2. In a coordinate plane, the distance between point $A(10,5)$ and point $B(-2,b)$ is 13. If $b > 0$, what is the value of b?

    F. -5
    G. 0
    H. 5
    J. 10
    K. 15

J is correct. Using the distance formula, you have $d_{\overline{AB}} = \sqrt{(10-(-2))^2 + (5-b)^2} = 13$, or $\sqrt{144 + (5-b)^2} = 13$. Square both sides of the equation, and you have $144 + (5-b)^2 = 169$ or $(5-b)^2 = 25$. Take the square root of both sides, and you get $5 - b = 5$ or $5 - b = -5$, which implies $b = 0$ or $b = 10$. Since $b > 0$, $b = 10$.

XII. Working with Plane Geometry

On the ACT Mathematics Test, approximately 14 of the 60 questions are plane geometry questions. You'll be tested on many concepts of plane geometry, including properties of angles, line segments, triangles, quadrilaterals, polygons, and circles. You are also expected to demonstrate an understanding of transformations, surface areas, volumes, and the techniques of proof. The practice problems in this chapter are designed to help you review many of the plane geometry concepts. Work the problems, and check your answers with the given explanations.

A. Measurement of Angles and Line Segments

1. The measure of the vertex angle of an isosceles triangle is 40 degrees. What is the measure, in degrees, of a base angle of the triangle?

   A. 40
   B. 60
   C. 70
   D. 80
   E. 90

C is correct.

In the accompanying diagram, x represents the degree measure of one of the base angles. Since the given triangle is isosceles, the measures of the base angles are equal. The sum of the measures of a triangle is 180 degrees. Therefore, you have $x + x + 40 = 180$ or $2x = 140$. Thus $x = 70$.

2. Line ℓ intersects $\overline{AB}$ and $\overline{BC}$ at D and E, respectively. What is the value of x?

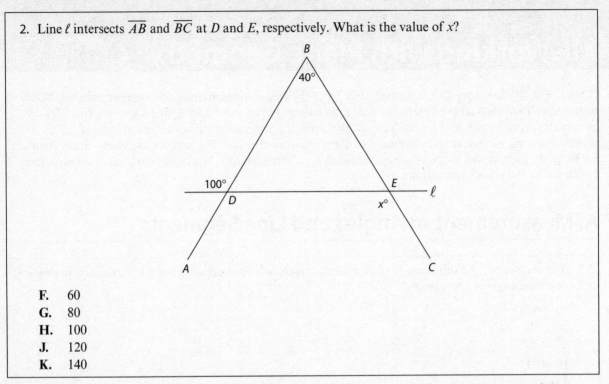

F. 60
G. 80
H. 100
J. 120
K. 140

J is correct. Since $m\angle BDE + 100 = 180$, $m\angle BDE = 80$. You know that the sum of the measures of the three angles of a triangle is 180 degrees. Therefore, $80 + 40 + m\angle BED = 180$ or $m\angle BED = 60$. Since $m\angle BED + x = 180$, you have $60 + x = 180$, or $x = 120$.

3. In the accompanying diagram, $ABCD$ is a parallelogram. What is the value of x?

Not drawn to scale

A. 60
B. 80
C. 100
D. 120
E. 150

E is correct. Opposite sides of a parallelogram are congruent; therefore, $BC = 6$. In the right triangle $\triangle BEC$, $BE = 3$ and $BC = 6$. Note that $\overline{BC}$ is the hypotenuse and $\overline{BE}$ is a leg. Since the length of the hypotenuse is twice the length of a leg, $\triangle BEC$ is a 30°-60° right triangle. Thus, the $m\angle C = 30$. Also, in parallelogram $ABCD$, $\angle D$ and $\angle C$ are supplementary. Therefore, $m\angle D = 150$.

---

4. Points A, B, C, and D lie on a line in that order. If C is the midpoint of $\overline{BD}$, $CD = 2AB$ and $AD = 60$, what is the length of $\overline{AC}$?

   F.   12
   G.   24
   H.   36
   J.   40
   K.   48

H is correct. Let $AB = x$. Since $CD = 2AB$, you have $CD = 2x$. Also, C is the midpoint of $\overline{BD}$; therefore, $BC = CD = 2x$. Since $AD = 60$, you have $x + 2x + 2x = 60$ or $5x = 60$, which leads to $x = 12$. The length of $\overline{AC}$ is $3x$ or $3(12)$, which is 36.

B. Properties of Triangles

---

1. Starting from home, Mary drove 5 miles due east to Bill's house. She then drove 6 miles due south to Karen's house. Mary then drove 3 miles due east to Janet's house. What is the distance, in miles, between Mary's house and Janet's house?

   A.   4
   B.   8
   C.   10
   D.   14
   E.   16

C is correct.

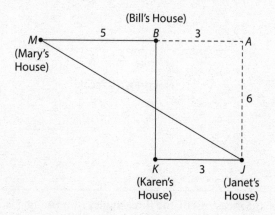

In the accompanying diagram of Mary's trip, if you extend $\overline{MB}$ to A and draw $\overline{AJ}$, ΔMAJ is a right triangle and quadrilateral $BAJK$ is a rectangle with $BA = KJ = 3$ and $BK = AJ = 6$. Since $AM = 8$, $(AM)^2 + (AJ)^2 = (MJ)^2$ or $8^2 + 6^2 = (MJ)^2$ and $MJ = 10$.

---

2. In ΔDEF, $DE = 6$ and $DF = 10$. What is the smallest possible integer length of side $\overline{EF}$?

    F. 4

    G. 5

    H. 6

    J. 15

    K. 16

G is correct.

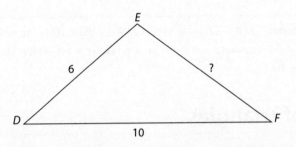

Since you are looking for the smallest possible length of $\overline{EF}$, assume that $\overline{EF}$ is not the longest side of ΔDEF. Applying the triangle inequality, you have $DE + EF > DF$ or $6 + EF > 10$, which is equivalent to $EF > 4$. Since EF is an integer, the smallest possible value for EF is 5.

---

3. In the accompanying diagram, a, b, and c are the lengths of the three sides of the triangle. Which of the following must be true?

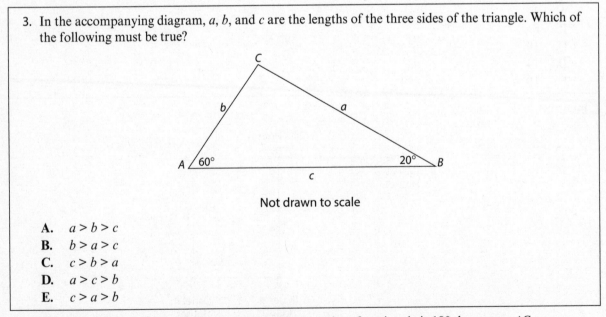

Not drawn to scale

    A. $a > b > c$

    B. $b > a > c$

    C. $c > b > a$

    D. $a > c > b$

    E. $c > a > b$

E is correct. Since the sum of the measures of the three angles of a triangle is 180 degrees, $m\angle C = 180 - 60 - 20 = 100$. In a triangle, the longest side is always opposite the biggest angle. Thus, $c > a > b$.

4. Given three points A, B, and C, if the distance between A and B is 5 and the distance between B and C is 12, what is the shortest possible distance between A and C?

F. 5
G. 7
H. 12
J. 13
K. 17

G is correct. Points A, B, and C either form a triangle, or they lie on the same line. If A, B, and C form a triangle, then $7 < AC < 17$ because the sum of the lengths of any two sides of the triangle must be greater than the third. If the points are collinear, then the shortest distance occurs when A is between B and C. Thus, $AC = 12 - 5 = 7$.

C. Properties of Quadrilaterals

1. In the accompanying diagram, $DEFG$ is a parallelogram. What is the length of $\overline{GH}$?

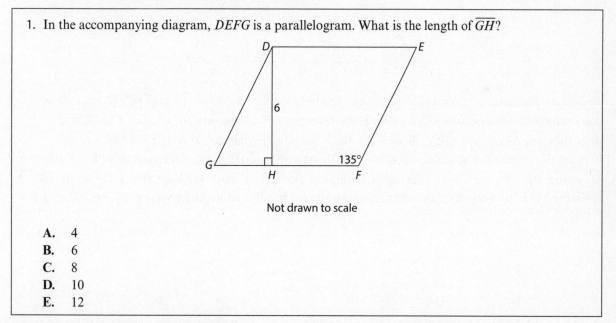

Not drawn to scale

A. 4
B. 6
C. 8
D. 10
E. 12

B is correct. Since $DEFG$ is a parallelogram, $m\angle G + m\angle F = 180$ degrees, which means $m\angle G + 135 = 180$ or $m\angle G = 45$. In the right triangle DGH, $m\angle G = 45$ implies that $m\angle GDH$ is also 45, and thus $\triangle DGH$ is isosceles. Therefore, $GH = DH$ or $GH = 6$.

2. In the accompanying diagram, $ABCD$ is an isosceles trapezoid with $\overline{AB} \parallel \overline{DC}$. If $AB = 8$, $DC = 16$, and the height of the trapezoid is 3, what is the perimeter of trapezoid $ABCD$?

   F.   29
   G. 34
   H. 40
   J.   42
   K. 44

G is correct.

To find the perimeter of trapezoid $ABCD$, you need to know the lengths of $\overline{AD}$ and $\overline{BC}$. To start, draw a line from point A intersecting $\overline{DC}$ at point E and from point B intersecting $\overline{DC}$ at point F to form two right triangles: $\triangle ADE$ and $\triangle BCF$. Since $\overline{AD}$ is the hypotenuse in right $\triangle ADE$, $(AD)^2 = (AE)^2 + (DE)^2$. Because the trapezoid is isosceles, $\overline{AD} \cong \overline{BC}$, $\triangle ADE \cong \triangle BCF$, and $DE = FC$. And since $AB = 8$, $EF = 8$. Therefore, $DE + EF + FC = 16$, making the lengths of $\overline{DE}$ and $\overline{FC}$ both 4. Also, $(AD)^2 = 3^2 + 4^2$, so $AD = 5$. Since the legs of an isosceles trapezoid are congruent, $BC = 5$. Therefore, the perimeter of $ABCD = 5 + 8 + 5 + 16 = 34$.

3. In the accompanying diagram, $ABCD$ is a rectangle with side $\overline{AB}$ containing points E and F and $AE = EF = FB$. If the area of $\triangle ADF$ is 12, what is the area of quadrilateral $FBCD$?

Not drawn to scale

   A.   12
   B.   24
   C.   30
   D.   36
   E.   48

B is correct.

Draw a perpendicular line from F to $\overline{DC}$, meeting $\overline{DC}$ at point G. Note that the area of $\triangle AFD$ equals the area of $\triangle FDG = 12$. Since $AE = EF = FB$, you have $FB = \frac{1}{2}AF$. The area of rectangle $FBCG = \frac{1}{2}AFGD$. The area of rectangle $AFGD = 24$, making the area of rectangle $FBCG = 12$. Therefore, the area of quadrilateral $FBCD$ is $12 + 12$ or 24.

D. Similarity

1. Kaela is 5 ft 6 in tall and casts a shadow that is 11 ft long. If Dan is standing behind Kaela, and he is 6 ft tall, how long is his shadow?

   A.   10 ft
   B.   11 ft
   C.   11 ft 6 in
   D.   12 ft
   E.   12 ft 6 in

D is correct.

Not drawn to scale

Dan

Kaela

6 ft

5.5 ft

11 ft

x

Since each triangle has a right angle and the triangles share an angle, they are similar. As long as all numbers are expressed in the same units with Kaela's height 5.5 ft instead of 5 ft 6 in, Dan's height can be found using the equation $\dfrac{\text{Kaela's height}}{\text{length of Kaela's shadow}} = \dfrac{\text{Dan's height}}{\text{length of Dan's shadow}}$ or $\dfrac{5.5}{11} = \dfrac{6}{x}$ or $5.5x = 66$ or $x = 12$. Dan's shadow is 12 ft long.

2. In the accompanying diagram, $\overline{DE} \parallel \overline{BC}$. If $AE = 2$, $EC = 4$, and $BC = 12$, find the length of $\overline{DE}$.

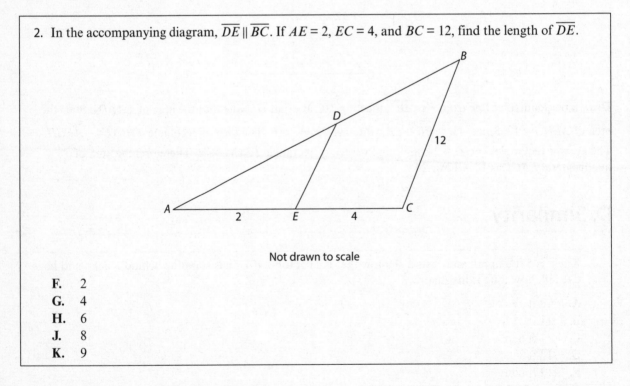

Not drawn to scale

   F. 2
   G. 4
   H. 6
   J. 8
   K. 9

G is correct. Because $\overline{DE} \parallel \overline{BC}$, congruent corresponding angles are formed with $\angle DEA \cong \angle BCA$ and $\angle ADE \cong \angle ABC$, and thus $\triangle ADE \sim \triangle ABC$. Since the triangles are similar, their corresponding sides are in proportion and $\dfrac{DE}{BC} = \dfrac{AE}{AC}$. Notice that $EC = 4$ may not be used in this proportion because $\overline{EC}$ is not a side of either triangle. To find DE, solve $\dfrac{DE}{BC} = \dfrac{AE}{AC}$ or $\dfrac{DE}{12} = \dfrac{2}{6}$ or $DE = 4$.

---

3. In the accompanying diagram, $\overline{AB} \parallel \overline{CD}$ and $\overline{AD}$ intersects $\overline{BC}$ at E. If $AB = 6$, $CD = 9$, and $BC = 30$, what is the length of $\overline{BE}$?

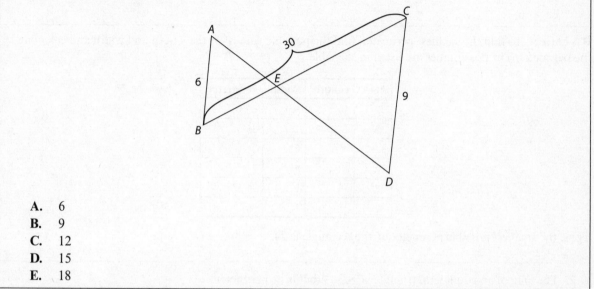

   A.   6
   B.   9
   C.   12
   D.   15
   E.   18

C is correct. Since $\overline{AB} \parallel \overline{CD}$, pairs of congruent alternate interior angles are formed, $\angle B \cong \angle C$ and $\angle A \cong \angle D$, and so $\triangle ABE \sim \triangle DCE$. Since the triangles are similar, corresponding sides are in proportion and $\dfrac{BE}{AB} = \dfrac{EC}{DC}$. To find BE, use x as the length of $\overline{BE}$ and $(30 - x)$ as the length of $\overline{EC}$: $\dfrac{x}{6} = \dfrac{30 - x}{9}$ or $9x = 6(30 - x)$ or $9x = 180 - 6x$ or $15x = 180$ or $x = 12$.

---

4. $\triangle LMN$ is similar to $\triangle PQT$. The area of $\triangle LMN$ is 16, and the length of its shortest side is 2. If the area of $\triangle PQT$ is 36, what is the length of its shortest side?

   F.   3
   G.   4.5
   H.   6
   J.   9
   K.   22

F is correct. Since $\triangle LMN \sim \triangle PQT$, the ratio of the areas is equal to the square of the ratio of any corresponding sides. Since the two shortest sides are a pair of corresponding sides, $\dfrac{16}{36} = \left(\dfrac{2}{x}\right)^2$ or $\dfrac{4}{9} = \dfrac{4}{x^2}$ or $4x^2 = 36$ or $x^2 = 9$ or $x = \pm 3$. Since x must be positive, $x = 3$. The length of the shortest side of $\triangle PQT$ is 3.

E. Areas and Perimeters

> 1. If the area of a rectangle is 32 and the measures of the length and width of the rectangle are integers, what is the smallest possible perimeter of the rectangle?
>
>   **A.** 12
>   **B.** 24
>   **C.** 36
>   **D.** 64
>   **E.** 66

B is correct. To find the smallest perimeter, find the possible values for the length and width and calculate the perimeter. The possibilities are listed in the table:

Area	Length	Width	Perimeter
32	1	32	66
32	2	16	36
32	4	8	24
32	8	4	24
32	16	2	36
32	32	1	66

Thus, the smallest possible perimeter of the rectangle is 24.

> 2. The area of an equilateral triangle is $9\sqrt{3}$. What is its perimeter?
>
>   **F.** 6
>   **G.** 12
>   **H.** 18
>   **J.** 24
>   **K.** 36

H is correct. Since the area of the equilateral triangle is $9\sqrt{3}$ and $A = \dfrac{s^2\sqrt{3}}{4}$, then $\dfrac{s^2\sqrt{3}}{4} = 9\sqrt{3}$ or $s^2 = 4(9)$ or $s = \pm 6$. Since s is the length of a side, $s = 6$, and the perimeter is 3(6) or 18.

> 3. If two sides of a triangle measure 6 and 8, what is the largest possible area for the triangle?
>
>   **A.** 7
>   **B.** 24
>   **C.** 32
>   **D.** 48
>   **E.** 64

B is correct.

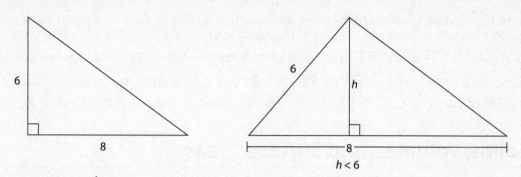

The area of a triangle is $\frac{1}{2}$(base)(height). The largest possible area for a triangle with two sides measuring 6 and 8 is the area of a right triangle with legs measuring 6 and 8. In this case, the area of the right triangle is $\frac{1}{2}$(6)(8) or 24. Notice that if the two sides 6 and 8 are not perpendicular, the altitude will be less than 6. Therefore, the area of the triangle would be less than 24.

4. In the accompanying diagram, *ABCD* and *CEFG* are squares. If *DE* = 2 and *DC* = 4, what is the area of the entire figure?

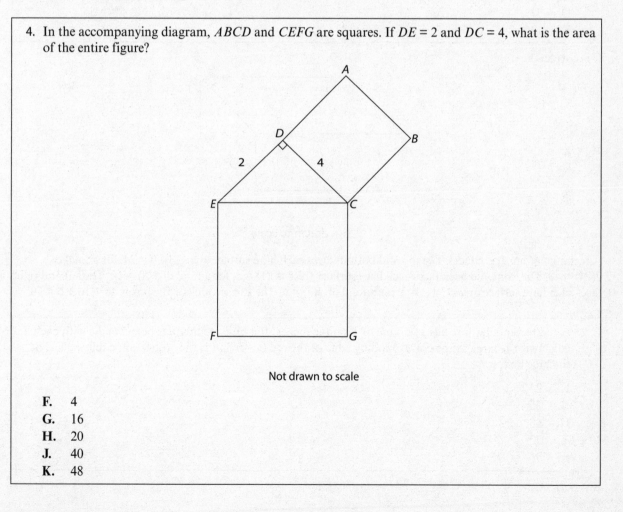

Not drawn to scale

   F.   4
   G. 16
   H. 20
   J.   40
   K. 48

J is correct. To find the total area of the figure, you must find the area of each square, the area of the triangle, and the sum of these areas. The area of square $ABCD = s^2 = 4^2 = 16$. The area of the right $\triangle DEC = \frac{1}{2}(DE)(DC) = \frac{1}{2}(2)(4) = 4$. Since $\overline{CE}$ is a side in square $CEFG$ and also the hypotenuse in $\triangle DEC$, the length of $\overline{CE}$ can be found using $(CE)^2 = (DE)^2 + (DC)^2$ or $(CE)^2 = (2)^2 + (4)^2$ or $CE = \pm\sqrt{20}$ or $CE = \sqrt{20}$, and the area of square $CEFG = s^2 = \left(\sqrt{20}\right)^2 = 20$. The area of the entire figure is $16 + 4 + 20 = 40$.

F. Solids, Volumes, and Surface Areas

1. If the length, width, and height of a rectangular box measure 8, 3, and 1, respectively, what is the total surface area of the box?

    A. 24
    B. 35
    C. 70
    D. 72
    E. 144

C is correct.

Not drawn to scale

A rectangular box has 6 faces. The top and bottom faces each have surface areas (8)(3) = 24, for a total of 2(24) = 48. The front and back faces each have surface areas (8)(1) = 8, for a total of 2(8) = 16. The left and right faces each have surface areas (3)(1) = 3, for a total of 2(3) = 6. The surface area of the box is 48 + 16 + 6 = 70.

2. A red rectangular box has a volume of 12 cubic inches. If a blue rectangular box is made with each edge twice as large as the corresponding edge of the red box, what is the volume, in cubic inches, of the blue box?

    F. 24
    G. 36
    H. 48
    J. 72
    K. 96

K is correct.

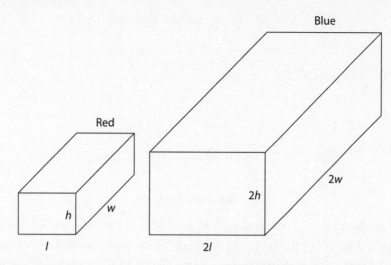

Since the volume of the red box is $(l)(w)(h)$ and the edges of the blue box are twice as large, the volume of the blue box is $(2l)(2w)(2h)$ or $8(lwh)$. The volume of the blue box is 8 times the volume of the red box, $8(12) = 96$.

---

3. If all faces of a pyramid (including the base) are equilateral triangles, and an edge of the pyramid measures 2 cm, what is the total surface area, in cm², of the pyramid?

    A. 4
    B. $3\sqrt{3}$
    C. $4\sqrt{3}$
    D. 8
    E. 16

C is correct. Since **all** faces of the pyramid are congruent equilateral triangles, the total surface area of the pyramid is 4 times the area of one of the triangles. Each edge of the pyramid is also a side of a triangle, and so the triangles are equilateral triangles with sides of length 2 cm, and the area of each triangle is $A = \dfrac{s^2\sqrt{3}}{4} = \dfrac{(2)^2\sqrt{3}}{4} = \sqrt{3}$. The total surface area of the pyramid is therefore $4\sqrt{3}$ cm².

---

4. A sphere with a diameter measuring 3 cm is inscribed in a cube. What is the length of a diagonal, in centimeters, of the cube?

    F. 3
    G. $3\sqrt{2}$
    H. $3\sqrt{3}$
    J. 6
    K. 27

H is correct.

Not drawn to scale

Since the diameter of the sphere is 3 cm, the length of each edge of the cube, including edges $\overline{AE}$, $\overline{EH}$, and $\overline{HG}$, is 3 cm. To find a diagonal of the cube, you must use the Pythagorean theorem twice, first to find EG and then to find AG. Since $\overline{EG}$ is the hypotenuse in right triangle ΔEHG, $(EG)^2 = 3^2 + 3^2 = \sqrt{18}$. Since $\overline{AG}$ is the hypotenuse in right triangle ΔAEG, $(AG)^2 = 3^2 + \left(\sqrt{18}\right)^2 = 9 + 18 = 27$ and $AG = \pm\sqrt{27} = \pm 3\sqrt{3}$. The length of a diagonal is $3\sqrt{3}$ cm.

G. Properties of Circles

1. In the accompanying diagram, O is the center of the circle. If the area of sector AOB is 25π, what is the length of $\overset{\frown}{AB}$?

   A.   5

   B.   10

   C. $\dfrac{5\pi}{2}$

   D. 5π

   E. 10π

D is correct. First, find the radius of the circle. Use the proportion $\dfrac{\text{area of sector } AOB}{\text{area of a circle}} = \dfrac{90}{360}$, which is equivalent to $\dfrac{25\pi}{\pi r^2} = \dfrac{1}{4}$ or $r^2 = 4(25)$. Thus, $r = 10$. Now use another proportion to find the length of $\overset{\frown}{AB}$, $\dfrac{\text{length of } \overset{\frown}{AB}}{\text{circumference of a circle}} = \dfrac{90}{360}$ or $\dfrac{\text{length of } \overset{\frown}{AB}}{2\pi(10)} = \dfrac{1}{4}$. Thus, the length of $\overset{\frown}{AB} = 5\pi$.

---

2. In the accompanying diagram, $\overline{AB}$ and $\overline{CD}$ are diameters of the circle. If length of $\overset{\frown}{AD}$ is 4π, what is the total area of the shaded regions?

F. 3π
G. 6π
H. 12π
J. 24π
K. 48π

H is correct. Begin by finding the area of the circle. To do that, you need to find the radius. Using the proportion $\dfrac{\text{length of } \overset{\frown}{AD}}{2\pi r} = \dfrac{120}{360}$, you have $\dfrac{4\pi}{2\pi r} = \dfrac{1}{3}$ or $r = 6$. The area of the circle is πr^2 or 36π. Since $\overline{AB}$ is a diameter, $m\angle DOB + 120 = 180$, and thus, $m\angle DOB = 60$. Also, $\angle AOC$ and $\angle DOB$ are vertical angles, and thus $m\angle AOC = 60$. Now use a proportion to find the area of sector DOB: $\dfrac{\text{area of sector } DOB}{\text{area of a circle}} = \dfrac{60}{360}$. The proportion is equivalent to $\dfrac{\text{area of sector } DOB}{36\pi} = \dfrac{1}{6}$ or area of sector $DOB = 6\pi$, and the total area of the shaded regions is $2(6\pi)$ or 12π.

3. In the accompanying diagram, a regular hexagon is inscribed in a circle. If $AB = 6$, what is the length of $\overset{\frown}{AB}$?

   A. 2
   B. π
   C. 2π
   D. 4π
   E. 6π

C is correct.

Draw radii $\overline{OA}$ and $\overline{OB}$. A regular hexagon is both equilateral and equiangular. Therefore, $m\angle AOB = \left(\dfrac{1}{6}\right)(360) = 60$. Also, $\overline{OA}$ and $\overline{OB}$ are radii and thus, $m\angle OAB = m\angle OBA = 60$, and $\triangle AOB$ is an equilateral triangle. To find the length of $\overset{\frown}{AB}$, use the proportion $\dfrac{\text{length of } \overset{\frown}{AB}}{\text{circumference of a circle}} = \dfrac{60}{360}$, which is equivalent to $\dfrac{\text{length of } \overset{\frown}{AB}}{2\pi(6)} = \dfrac{1}{6}$ or length of $\overset{\frown}{AB} = 2\pi$.

4. In the accompanying diagram, O is the center of the larger circle, and $\overline{OA}$ and $\overline{OB}$ are diameters of the smaller circles. If the length of $\overline{AB}$ is 12, what is the total area of the shaded regions?

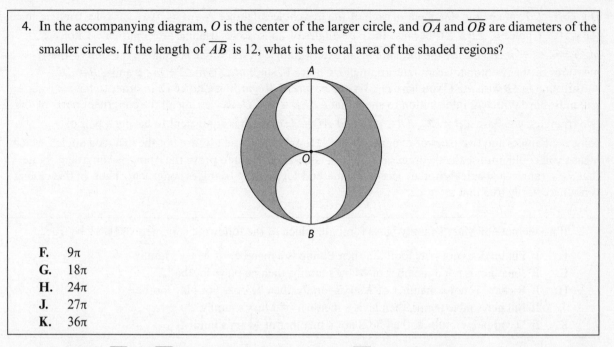

F. 9π
G. 18π
H. 24π
J. 27π
K. 36π

G is correct. Since $\overline{OA}$ and $\overline{OB}$ are radii of the larger circle and $\overline{AB}$ is 12, you have $OA = OB = 6$. The area of the larger circle is $\pi(6)^2$ or 36π. The two smaller circles are congruent, and the length of the radius for each of the small circles is 3. The area of each small circle is $\pi(3)^2$ or 9π, and the total area of both small circles is 18π. Therefore, the area of the shaded regions is $36\pi - 18\pi$ or 18π.

H. Concept of Proof

1. In the accompanying figure, $\overline{AB} \cong \overline{AC}$. Which of the following statements is NOT necessarily true?

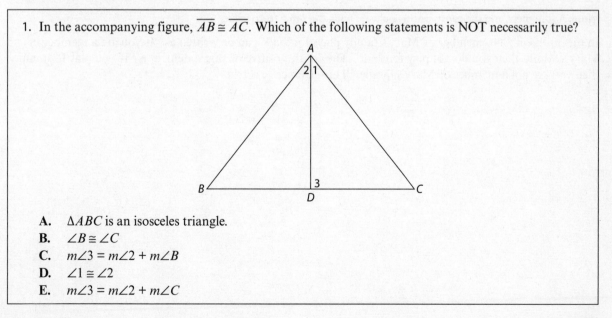

A. $\triangle ABC$ is an isosceles triangle.
B. $\angle B \cong \angle C$
C. $m\angle 3 = m\angle 2 + m\angle B$
D. $\angle 1 \cong \angle 2$
E. $m\angle 3 = m\angle 2 + m\angle C$

D is correct. Examine the statement in each of the five choices. Choice A, $\triangle ABC$ is an isosceles triangle since $\overline{AB} \cong \overline{AC}$. Choice B, $\angle B \cong \angle C$ because the base angles of an isosceles triangle are congruent. Choice C, $m\angle 3 = m\angle 2 + m\angle B$ because the measure of an exterior angle of a triangle is equal to the sum of the measures of the two nonadjacent interior angles. Choice E, since $m\angle 3 \cong m\angle 2 + m\angle B$ and $\angle B \cong \angle C$, substituting $m\angle B$ with $m\angle C$ you have $m\angle 3 \cong m\angle 2 + m\angle C$. Regarding Choice D, in order to have $\angle 1 \cong \angle 2$, you must have sufficient information to show that $\triangle ABD \cong \triangle ACD$. Reviewing all the congruent parts of the two triangles, you have $\angle B \cong \angle C$, $\overline{AB} \cong \overline{AC}$, and $\overline{AD} \cong \overline{AD}$, which is equivalent to having a pair of congruent angles and two pairs of congruent sides. However, $\angle B$ and $\angle C$ are not the included angles, which means you could not use the theorem *s.a.s.* $\cong$ *s.a.s.* (side-angle-side) to prove the triangles congruent. Note that *a.s.s.* (angle-side-side) is not an acceptable method for proving triangles congruent. Thus, in this case, it is not necessarily true that $\angle 1 \cong \angle 2$.

---

2. If no member of Mary's family plays football, which of the following statements MUST be true?

   F. If Phillip does not play football, then Phillip is a member of Mary's family.
   G. If Jonathan is not a member of Mary's family, then he plays football.
   H. If Richard is not a member of Mary's family, then he does not play football.
   J. If Bill plays table tennis, then he is a member of Mary's family.
   K. If David plays football, then he is not a member of Mary's family.

K is correct. Use reasoning skills. Since no one in Mary's family plays football, if you play football you are not in Mary's family. Another approach is to use formal logic. Here are some of the rules of logic:

- Statement: If A, then B.
- Converse: If B, then A.
- Inverse: If not A, then not B.
- Contrapositive: If not B, then not A.

Note: A statement and the contrapositive always have the same truth value.

In this problem, "No member of Mary's family plays football" can be written as "If you are a member of Mary's family, then you do not play football." The contrapositive of this statement is "If you play football, then you are not a member of Mary's family." Thus, Choice K is true.

I. Transformations

1. In the accompanying diagram, the graph of $y = f(x)$ is shown. Which of the following could be the graph of $f(x + 2)$?

A.

B.

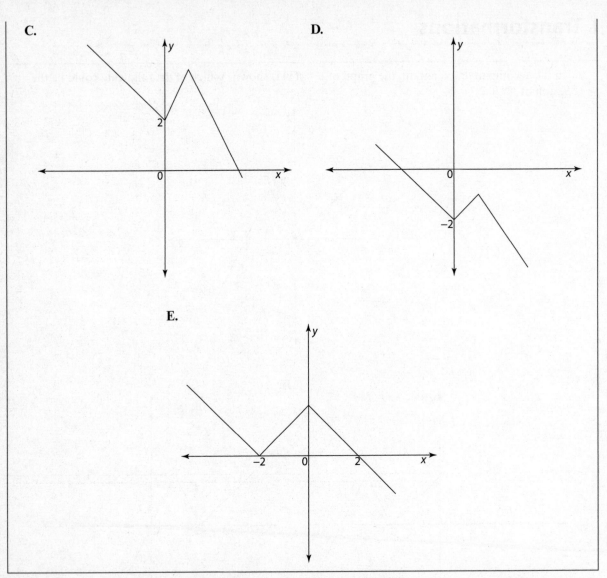

C.

D.

E.

B is correct. The graph of $f(x + 2)$ is the same as the graph of $f(x)$ shifted two units to the left. Therefore, $(0,0)$ is shifted to $(-2,0)$ and $(2,0)$ becomes $(0,0)$. Thus, Choice **B** is the graph of $f(x + 2)$.

2. In the accompanying diagram, a triangle and the line $y = x$ are shown. Which of the following would be the image of the triangle reflected in the line $y = x$?

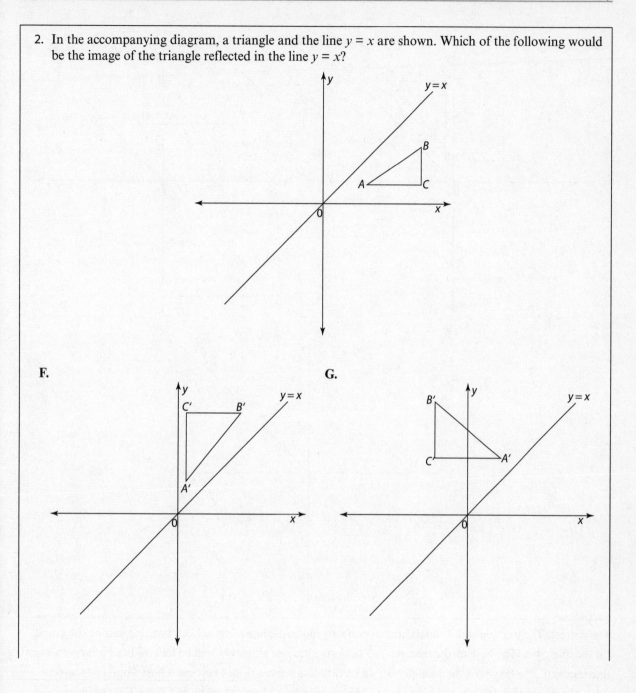

F.

G.

H.

J.

K.

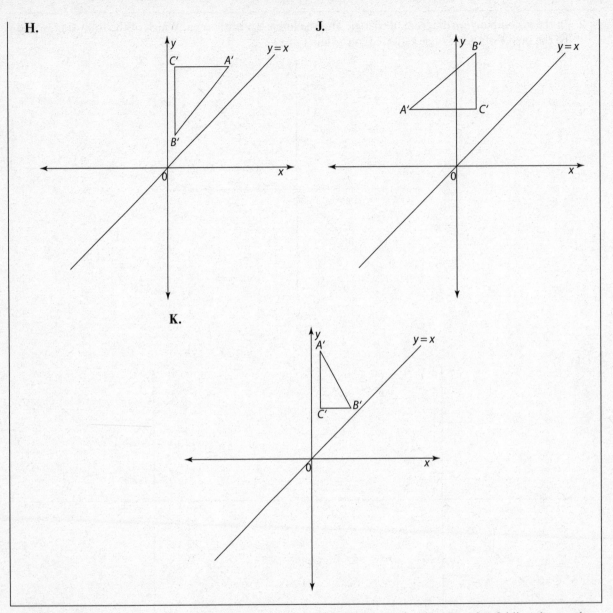

F is correct. The triangle and its image match perfectly along the line of reflection. Imagine folding the graph on the line $y = x$. The base of the triangle, $\overline{AC}$ (a horizontal line segment), will be reflected to become a vertical line segment. The height of the triangle, $\overline{BC}$ (a vertical line segment), will become a horizontal line segment. Also, the image of $\triangle ABC$ should have vertex A below side $\overline{BC}$. Thus, the graph in Choice F is the image.

3. In the accompanying diagram, the figure is a regular hexagon. How many lines of symmetry does the hexagon have?

   A. 1
   B. 2
   C. 3
   D. 4
   E. 6

E is correct.

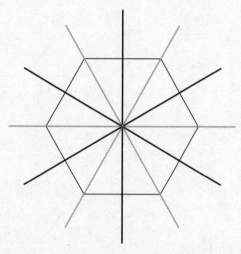

A line of symmetry divides a figure into two parts, each the mirror image of the other. As illustrated in the accompanying diagram, 6 such lines are possible.

XIII. Tackling Trigonometry

On the ACT Mathematics Test, approximately 4 of the 60 questions are trigonometry questions. You'll be tested on many concepts of trigonometry, including trigonometry of the right triangle, properties of trigonometric functions of non-acute angles, laws of sine and cosine, and graphs of trigonometric functions. You are also expected to know how to work with trigonometric identities and solve trigonometric equations. The practice problems in this chapter are designed to help you review many of the trigonometry concepts. Work the problems, and check your answers with the given explanations.

A. Trigonometry of the Right Triangle

1. In the accompanying figure, $\triangle DEF$ is a right triangle with $m\angle F = 90$, $DF = 5$, and $EF = \sqrt{11}$. What is $\cos D$?

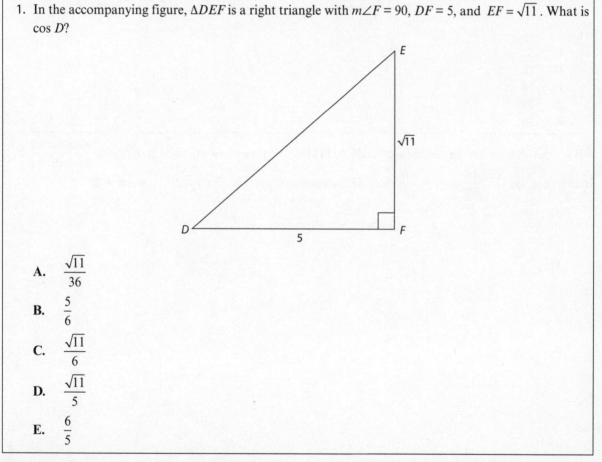

A. $\dfrac{\sqrt{11}}{36}$

B. $\dfrac{5}{6}$

C. $\dfrac{\sqrt{11}}{6}$

D. $\dfrac{\sqrt{11}}{5}$

E. $\dfrac{6}{5}$

B is correct. Remember the mnemonic SOHCAHTOA (see page 352). The cosine of an angle is the ratio $\dfrac{\text{adjacent leg}}{\text{hypotenuse}}$. In this case, $\cos D = \dfrac{DF}{DE}$. Using the Pythagorean theorem, you have $(DE)^2 = \left(\sqrt{11}\right)^2 + (5)^2$, which is equivalent to $(DE)^2 = 11 + 25$ or $(DE)^2 = 36$ or $DE = \pm 6$. Since $DE > 0$, you have $DE = 6$. Thus, $\cos D = \dfrac{5}{6}$.

2. In the accompanying figure, $\triangle ABC$ is a right triangle with $m\angle B = 90$ and $BC = 12$. If $\tan C = \dfrac{2}{3}$, what is the length of $\overline{AB}$?

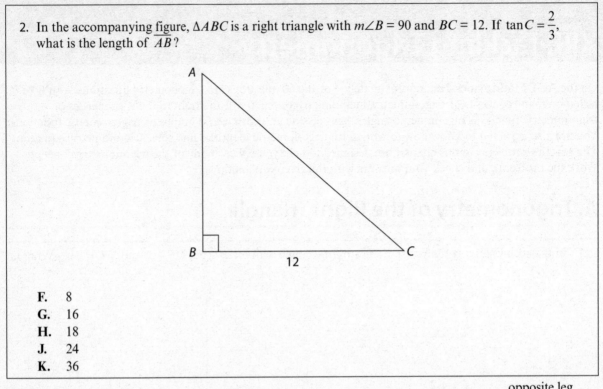

F. 8
G. 16
H. 18
J. 24
K. 36

F is correct. Remember the mnemonic SOHCAHTOA. The tangent of an angle is the ratio $\dfrac{\text{opposite leg}}{\text{adjacent leg}}$.

In this case, $\tan C = \dfrac{AB}{BC}$ or $\dfrac{2}{3} = \dfrac{AB}{12}$. Solving the equation, you have $3AB = 2(12)$ or $AB = 8$.

3. A 20-ft ladder is leaning against a wall of a building. The wall is perpendicular to the ground. If the ladder makes an angle of 52° with the ground, what is the distance, to the nearest tenth of a foot, from the foot of the ladder to the bottom of the wall?

   A. 12.3
   B. 12.4
   C. 15.7
   D. 15.8
   E. 25.6

A is correct.

Let x be the distance from the foot of the ladder to the bottom of the wall. Applying the cosine ratio, you have $\cos 52° = \dfrac{x}{20}$. Using a calculator, you have $\cos 52° = 0.6157$, and therefore, $0.6157 = \dfrac{x}{20}$ or $x = 12.314$ ft. Thus, the distance is 12.3 ft.

B. Trigonometric Functions of Non-Acute Angles

1. If $\cos\theta = \dfrac{-5}{13}$ and $\pi < \theta < \dfrac{3\pi}{2}$, what is the value of $\sin\theta$?

   A. $\dfrac{-12}{13}$

   B. $\dfrac{-5}{13}$

   C. $\dfrac{5}{13}$

   D. $\dfrac{5}{12}$

   E. $\dfrac{12}{13}$

A is correct.

One approach is to draw θ as illustrated in the accompanying figure. Using the Pythagorean theorem, you have $5^2 + (AB)^2 = 13^2$, which is equivalent to $25 + (AB)^2 = 169$ or $(AB)^2 = 144$ or $AB = \pm12$. Since AB is the length of a side of right $\triangle AOB$, $AB = 12$; however, note that the coordinates of point B are $(-5, -12)$. Remember the mnemonic CAST for determining the sign of a trigonometric function in each of the four quadrants.

The letter A in the first quadrant indicates that all functions are positive in that quadrant. The letter S in the second quadrant indicates that only sine and cosecant are positive in that quadrant. The letter T in the third quadrant indicates that only tangent and cotangent are positive in that quadrant. And lastly, the letter C in the fourth quadrant indicates that only cosine and secant are positive in that quadrant.

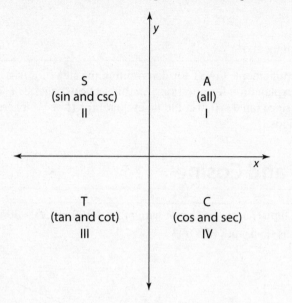

The sine ratio is negative in the third quadrant. Thus, $\sin\theta = \dfrac{-12}{13}$.

---

2. If $\sin\theta = -0.5$, which of the following could be true?

F. $\theta = \dfrac{\pi}{6}$

G. $\theta = \dfrac{\pi}{3}$

H. $\theta = \dfrac{5\pi}{6}$

J. $\theta = \dfrac{7\pi}{6}$

K. $\theta = \dfrac{5\pi}{3}$

J is correct. One approach is to substitute the value of θ in each of the five choices in the equation $\sin\theta = -0.5$ and see which is true. In Choice F, $\sin\left(\dfrac{\pi}{6}\right) = \dfrac{1}{2} \neq -0.5$; in Choice G, $\sin\left(\dfrac{\pi}{3}\right) = \dfrac{\sqrt{3}}{2} \neq -0.5$; in Choice H, $\sin\left(\dfrac{5\pi}{6}\right) = \dfrac{1}{2} \neq -0.5$; in Choice J, $\sin\left(\dfrac{7\pi}{6}\right) = -0.5$; and in Choice K, $\sin\left(\dfrac{5\pi}{3}\right) = \dfrac{-\sqrt{3}}{2} \neq -0.5$.

3. If $\sin \theta > 0$ and $\tan \theta < 0$, in which quadrant does θ lie?

    A. Quadrant I
    B. Quadrant II
    C. Quadrant III
    D. Quadrant IV
    E. Cannot be determined.

B is correct. Remember the mnemonic CAST for determining the sign of a trigonometric function in each of the four quadrants (see explanation for question 1 in this section, pages 218–219). Since $\sin \theta > 0$, θ could lie in quadrant I or II, and since $\tan \theta < 0$, θ could lie in quadrant II or IV. Therefore, θ lies in quadrant II, thus satisfying both conditions.

C. Laws of Sine and Cosine

1. In the accompanying figure, ΔDEF is shown with $m\angle F = 100$, $m\angle D = 30$, and $EF = 12$. Which of the following expressions is the length of $\overline{DF}$?

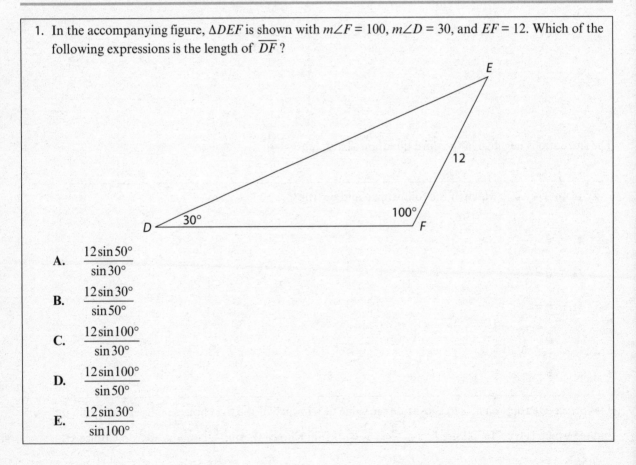

    A. $\dfrac{12 \sin 50°}{\sin 30°}$

    B. $\dfrac{12 \sin 30°}{\sin 50°}$

    C. $\dfrac{12 \sin 100°}{\sin 30°}$

    D. $\dfrac{12 \sin 100°}{\sin 50°}$

    E. $\dfrac{12 \sin 30°}{\sin 100°}$

A is correct. The Law of Sines states that the ratios of the sines of the angles of a triangle to the lengths of the sides opposite those angles are equal. Applying the Law of Sines, you have $\dfrac{\sin 30°}{12} = \dfrac{\sin E}{DF}$. Since $m\angle F = 100$ and $m\angle D = 30$, $m\angle E = 180 - 100 - 30 = 50$. Therefore, $\dfrac{\sin 30°}{12} = \dfrac{\sin 50°}{DF}$, which is equivalent to $(DF)\sin 30° = 12 \sin 50°$ or $DF = \dfrac{12\sin 50°}{\sin 30°}$.

---

2. In the accompanying figure, $\triangle ABC$ is shown with $AB = 8$, $AC = 5$, and $BC = 10$. Which of the following expressions is the measure of $\angle B$?

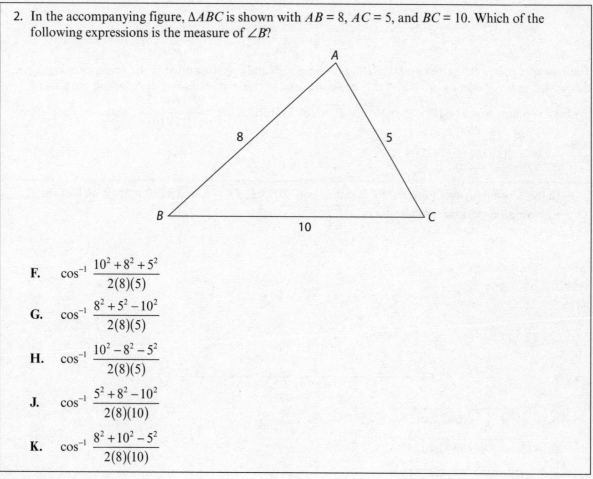

F. $\cos^{-1} \dfrac{10^2 + 8^2 + 5^2}{2(8)(5)}$

G. $\cos^{-1} \dfrac{8^2 + 5^2 - 10^2}{2(8)(5)}$

H. $\cos^{-1} \dfrac{10^2 - 8^2 - 5^2}{2(8)(5)}$

J. $\cos^{-1} \dfrac{5^2 + 8^2 - 10^2}{2(8)(10)}$

K. $\cos^{-1} \dfrac{8^2 + 10^2 - 5^2}{2(8)(10)}$

K is correct.

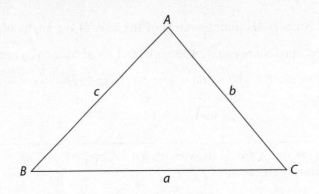

The Law of Cosines states that given $\triangle ABC$ with sides a, b, and c as illustrated in the accompanying figure, then $c^2 = a^2 + b^2 - 2ab \cos C$, $b^2 = a^2 + c^2 - 2ac \cos B$, and $a^2 = b^2 + c^2 - 2bc \cos A$. Applying the Law of Cosines, you have $5^2 = 8^2 + 10^2 - 2(8)(10) \cos B$, which leads to $\cos B = \dfrac{8^2 + 10^2 - 5^2}{2(8)(10)}$. Thus, the measure of $\angle B = \cos^{-1} \dfrac{8^2 + 10^2 - 5^2}{2(8)(10)}$.

---

3. In the accompanying figure, $\triangle DEF$ is shown with $DF = 6$, $EF = 7$, and $m\angle F = 25$. Which of the following expressions is the length of $\overline{DE}$?

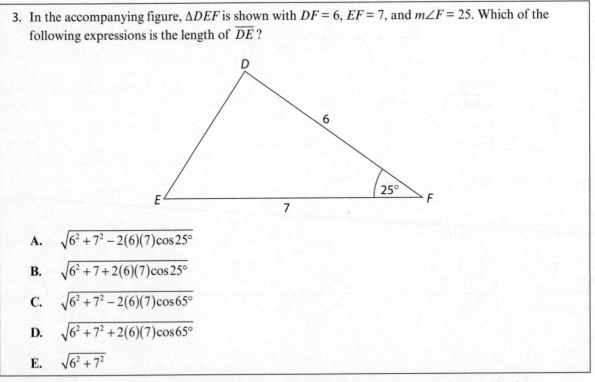

A. $\sqrt{6^2 + 7^2 - 2(6)(7)\cos 25°}$

B. $\sqrt{6^2 + 7 + 2(6)(7)\cos 25°}$

C. $\sqrt{6^2 + 7^2 - 2(6)(7)\cos 65°}$

D. $\sqrt{6^2 + 7^2 + 2(6)(7)\cos 65°}$

E. $\sqrt{6^2 + 7^2}$

A is correct. The Law of Cosines states that given $\triangle ABC$ with sides a, b, and c as illustrated in the accompanying figure, then $c^2 = a^2 + b^2 - 2ab \cos C$, $b^2 = a^2 + c^2 - 2ac \cos B$, and $a^2 = b^2 + c^2 - 2bc \cos A$. Applying the Law of Cosines, you have $(DE)^2 = 6^2 + 7^2 - 2(6)(7) \cos 25°$ or $DE = \pm\sqrt{6^2 + 7^2 - 2(6)(7)\cos 25°}$. Since $DE > 0$, you have $DE = \sqrt{6^2 + 7^2 - 2(6)(7)\cos 25°}$.

D. Graphs of Trigonometric Functions

1. The graph of a function $y = f(x)$ is shown in the accompanying figure. Which of the following could be the function f?

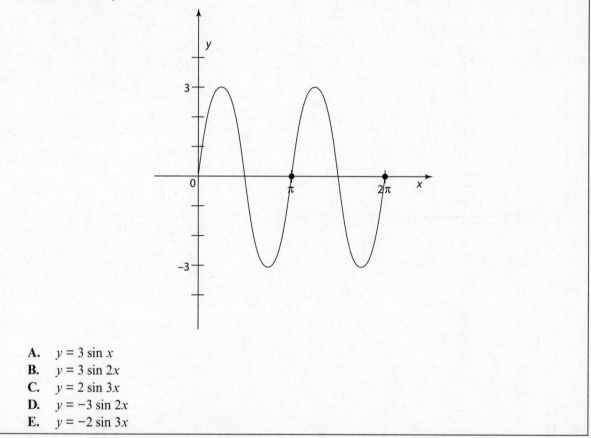

 A. $y = 3 \sin x$
 B. $y = 3 \sin 2x$
 C. $y = 2 \sin 3x$
 D. $y = -3 \sin 2x$
 E. $y = -2 \sin 3x$

B is correct. Since all five choices involve the sine function, you can assume that the given graph is that of a sine function. The given graph completes one cycle of the sine curve from $x = 0$ to $x = \pi$, which implies that the period of the function is π. Using the formula, $\text{period} = \dfrac{2\pi}{\text{frequency}}$, you have $\pi = \dfrac{2\pi}{\text{frequency}}$ or the frequency is 2. The graph also indicates that the range of the f is $-3 \le y \le 3$, which means the amplitude of f is 3. Thus, the sine function is $y = 3 \sin 2x$, where the amplitude is 3 and the frequency is 2.

2. In the accompanying figure, the graph of a function $y = a \cos x + d$ is shown. What is the value of a?

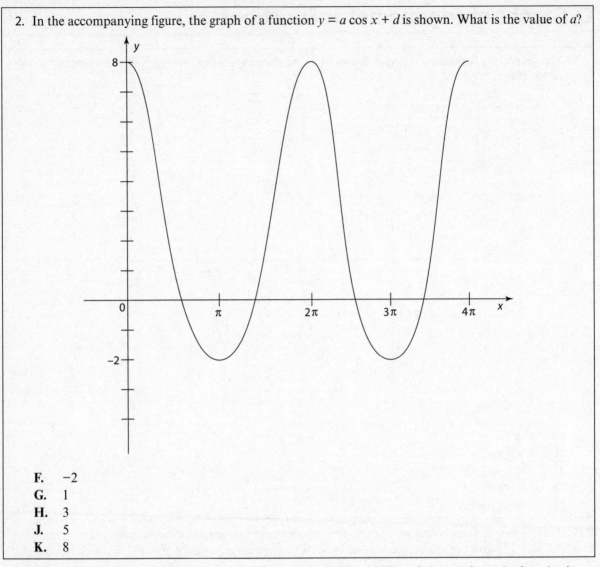

F. -2
G. 1
H. 3
J. 5
K. 8

J is correct. The graph shows that the range of f is $-2 \le y \le 8$. The midline of the graph can be found using the formula $y = \left(\dfrac{1}{2}\right)(\text{maximum value of } y + \text{minimum value of } y)$. Thus, you have $y = \dfrac{8 + (-2)}{2} = 3$. Thus, $y = 3$ is the midline, and the amplitude of the function is $8 - 3$ or 5. Therefore, the equation of the function is $y = 5\cos x + 3$, which means $a = 5$.

E. Trigonometric Identities

1. For all values of θ such that $0 < \theta < \dfrac{\pi}{2}$, which of the following is equivalent to $\csc \theta (1 - \cos^2 \theta)$?

   A. $\sin \theta$
   B. $\cos \theta$
   C. $\csc \theta$
   D. $\sec \theta$
   E. $\sin^2 \theta$

A is correct. Beginning with the Pythagorean identity $\sin^2 \theta + \cos^2 \theta = 1$, you can derive $\sin^2 \theta = 1 - \cos^2 \theta$. Also using the reciprocal identity $\csc \theta = \dfrac{1}{\sin \theta}$, you can rewrite $\csc \theta (1 - \cos^2 \theta)$ as $\dfrac{1}{\sin \theta}(\sin^2 \theta)$, which is equivalent to $\sin \theta$.

2.

θ	$\sin \theta$	$\cos \theta$
30°	$\dfrac{1}{2}$	$\dfrac{\sqrt{3}}{2}$
45°	$\dfrac{\sqrt{2}}{2}$	$\dfrac{\sqrt{2}}{2}$
60°	$\dfrac{\sqrt{3}}{2}$	$\dfrac{1}{2}$

Given the accompanying table of values and that $\sin(A + B) = \sin A \cos B + \cos A \sin B$, which of the following is the value of $\sin 75°$?

   F. $\sqrt{3}$

   G. 3

   H. $1 + \sqrt{6}$

   J. $\dfrac{1 + \sqrt{3}}{2}$

   K. $\dfrac{\sqrt{2} + \sqrt{6}}{4}$

K is correct. Applying the formula $\sin(A + B) = \sin A \cos B + \cos A \sin B$, you have $\sin 75° = \sin(30° + 45°) = \sin 30° \cos 45° + \cos 30° \sin 45°$. Using the given table of values,

$$\sin 75° = \left(\frac{1}{2}\right)\left(\frac{\sqrt{2}}{2}\right) + \left(\frac{\sqrt{3}}{2}\right)\left(\frac{\sqrt{2}}{2}\right) = \frac{\sqrt{2}}{4} + \frac{\sqrt{6}}{4} = \frac{\sqrt{2} + \sqrt{6}}{4}.$$

F. Solving Trigonometric Equations

---

1. If $2\cos\theta - 1 = 0$ and $0° < \theta < 90°$, what is the value of θ in degrees?

   A. $\dfrac{1}{2}$

   B. 30

   C. 45

   D. 60

   E. 120

D is correct. Adding 1 to both sides of the equation, $2\cos\theta - 1 = 0$, you have $2\cos\theta = 1$, which is equivalent to $\cos\theta = \dfrac{1}{2}$. Therefore, $\cos^{-1}(\cos\theta) = \cos^{-1}\left(\dfrac{1}{2}\right)$ or $\theta = \cos^{-1}\left(\dfrac{1}{2}\right)$. Using a calculator, you will find $\cos^{-1}\left(\dfrac{1}{2}\right) = 60°$ and thus, $\theta = 60°$.

---

2. If $2\sin^2 x = \sin x$ and $0 < x < \dfrac{\pi}{2}$, what is the value of x?

   F. 0

   G. $\dfrac{\pi}{6}$

   H. $\dfrac{\pi}{4}$

   J. $\dfrac{\pi}{3}$

   K. $\dfrac{\pi}{2}$

G is correct. Begin by solving for $\sin x$. Rewrite $2\sin^2 x = \sin x$ as $2\sin^2 x - \sin x = 0$. Factoring out $\sin x$, you have $\sin x(2\sin x - 1) = 0$, which implies $\sin x = 0$ or $2\sin x - 1 = 0$. If $\sin x = 0$, then $x = 0$, π, or 2π. If $2\sin x - 1 = 0$, then $\sin x = \dfrac{1}{2}$, and $x = \dfrac{\pi}{6}$ or $\dfrac{5\pi}{6}$. Since $0 < x < \dfrac{\pi}{2}$, the only solution is $x = \dfrac{\pi}{6}$.

XIV. Science Test

A. Overview

The ACT Science Test includes 40 multiple-choice questions distributed over 7 different passages. You will find between 5 and 7 questions that follow the text and data presented in any passage; the exact number of questions depends on the passage type under consideration.

No calculator is allowed, but it is completely unnecessary anyway. Any math calculations you will be asked to do involve simple arithmetic, and often it is not a specific calculation that matters as much as understanding the pattern or trend in the data displayed. In some instances, interpolation or extrapolation of graphs or data tables will be required.

The content of the ACT Science Test mirrors subject matter from the curricula typically found in the core science courses completed between grades 9 and 12 in American secondary schools. These include content from the following disciplines (examples of topics shown in parentheses):

- *Earth/Space Sciences* (geology, astronomy, meteorology, oceanography, and environmental sciences)
- *Biology* (biochemistry, cell biology, genetics, evolution, microbiology, botany, zoology, and ecology)
- *Chemistry* (properties and states of matter, chemical bonding, chemical reactions, solutions, acids and bases, kinetics and equilibria, gas laws, and organic chemistry)
- *Physics* (mechanics, energy, thermodynamics, electromagnetism, fluids, solids, and optics)

You should be prepared to take this test if you are in the process of completing a college-preparatory science course of study in secondary school (three years or more of science) and you have already completed two such courses. To ensure that you have a solid foundation in both the physical and life sciences and have been exposed to a wide range of topics within each discipline, it is helpful (but not required or necessary) to have completed a course in biology and a course in the physical sciences (or equivalents).

An important fact to remember is that this test is primarily concerned with your ability to think scientifically, not with your ability to recall specific information from any one discipline or course. Students taking this test are at different points in their science program, and the sequence of courses within the course of study can also vary greatly from school to school. This test must accommodate a diverse student pool with a wide range of specific scientific knowledge; most of the information necessary to understand a passage is presented either directly or implicitly within the passage itself.

B. General Strategies

Remember that pacing yourself throughout the test is essential for maximizing your success. Managing 40 questions distributed over 7 different passages in a 35-minute period can be stressful and doesn't allow much time for review of passages. (This amounts to an average of 5 minutes per section, but recall that sections will vary in the number of questions asked depending on the passage type.) It is highly recommended that you practice sample science questions in an authentic, test-like environment as much as possible, as you are more likely to be relaxed and confident on the actual test day. In other words, practice, practice, practice! The Cram Plans presented in this book will help you organize your practice schedule given your specific timeframe for review.

To think like a scientist, you should base your conclusions on a logical analysis of facts and objective observations. The **scientific method** is the organized approach to solving a problem and/or answering a question using logic and reasoning and integrating past scientific knowledge. It generally follows the sequence of steps below:

1. **Observation** involves using one or more of the five senses to perceive the world. Observations can be qualitative in nature (that is, involve the use of descriptive words) or quantitative in nature (that is, involve the use of descriptive numbers). An example of qualitative data is color (for example, blue or yellow); an example of quantitative data is length in meters (for example, 0.025 m or 1.37×10^{-6} cm).

2. **Forming a hypothesis** involves creating a statement that uses the independent and dependent variables present in an experimental design (see step 3) to predict the outcome of an experiment. A hypothesis is something of an "educated guess" based on direct observation and past scientific knowledge. A hypothesis should be testable and the tests replicable in order to be able to be tested scientifically.

3. **Experimentation** varies widely depending upon the scientific discipline involved and on the specific question posed, but is generally some form of controlled laboratory design. This includes a means of manipulating the independent variable and recording data describing the effect in the dependent variable. The independent variable is the factor that is selected by the experimenter to be altered during the course of the experiment and is the lone difference between the control group and the experimental group. The dependent variable is the observed result or outcome of the alteration of the independent variable.

4. **Data analysis** involves using the data collected during experimentation to create graphs, charts, and other visual representations that help clarify patterns in the data and verify the relationship between the independent and dependent variables tested in the experiment. Calculations are often performed to manipulate the data and to understand relationships between data values.

5. **Forming a conclusion** includes a summary of the findings of the experiment and omits a statement of support or rejection of the hypothesis. Any difference in the dependent variable between the control and experimental groups can be attributed to the independent variable, and the hypothesis can be supported. If no difference between the control and experimental groups is observed and the hypothesis is rejected, a new hypothesis might be proposed including observations made and conclusions drawn during this experiment. Only when a concept has stood the test of countless scientific experimentation over time (that is, is supported by overwhelming evidence) and helps establish an overarching idea or guiding principles to explain a natural phenomenon, might it be considered a theory (for example, the theory of relativity and the theory of evolution by natural selection).

Remember that scientific reasoning skills are emphasized over recall of any specific scientific content on the ACT Science Test. Do not use precious time reviewing such specific content before the ACT; your time is better spent practicing a variety of sample problems and exposing yourself to a variety of data presentation formats. The more exposure you have to concepts and experimental scenarios from a variety of scientific disciplines, and the more you practice reading and interpreting data presented in a variety of chart, table, and graphic forms, the more comfortable you will be addressing the passages and questions on the actual test. In addition to the sample problems and visual examples in this book, you can find countless other graphic and visual presentations of data in science textbooks and in (print or digital) journals and news articles. For more specific information, review the next section, "Visual Representations of Data."

C. Visual Representations of Data

The likelihood of formulating the correct answer for most of the questions in the ACT Science Test is directly related to your ability to read and interpret visual data. Understanding the way that data tables are organized and the way that graphs are structured will make it easier to understand the different displays of data that you are likely to encounter on the ACT Science Test, and will thus help to maximize your score. Descriptions of data tables and graphs are provided below along with examples from various science contexts. After reviewing those, it will be helpful to regularly review tables and graphs that you encounter in science and math textbooks, newspaper articles, and other sources of visual data displays.

1. Understanding Data Tables

A data table is a set of related data values organized into a series of vertical columns and horizontal rows creating a grid (or matrix). Data tables are useful in organizing, managing, and understanding large volumes of data and for discerning patterns and relationships between variables. There are often descriptive titles that summarize the nature of the data presented using the independent and dependent variables. The far left column generally contains data representing the independent variable; other columns usually contain information pertaining to the dependent variable.

An example of the range of recorded wavelengths and frequencies of light is shown in the following table:

Color of Light	Wavelength (nm)	Frequency (THz)
Red	780–622	384–482
Orange	622–597	482–503
Yellow	597–577	503–520
Green	577–492	520–610
Blue	492–455	610–659
Violet	455–390	659–769

Here, the color of observed light is the independent variable, and the wavelength of observed light (measured in nanometers) and the frequency of observed light (measured in terahertz) are the dependent variables. Note that the units used are given in parentheses in the heading of each column after the column title.

2. Understanding Graphs

Line graphs can show more detail than other types of graphs and are used when the independent variable (*x*-axis) represents a continuous quantity (for example, temperature in degrees Celsius). When the independent variable is instead a qualitative factor (e.g., whether the test subject received a pharmaceutical drug or a placebo), a bar graph is more appropriately used.

An example of a bar graph is shown here to represent the frequency that an interviewer received an affirmative response to a survey question:

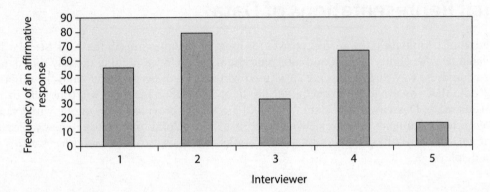

An example of a line graph is shown here to demonstrate the relationship between time (independent variable) and the growth of a plant seedling (dependent variable):

Line graphs you will encounter are likely to demonstrate data with one or more of the following trends:

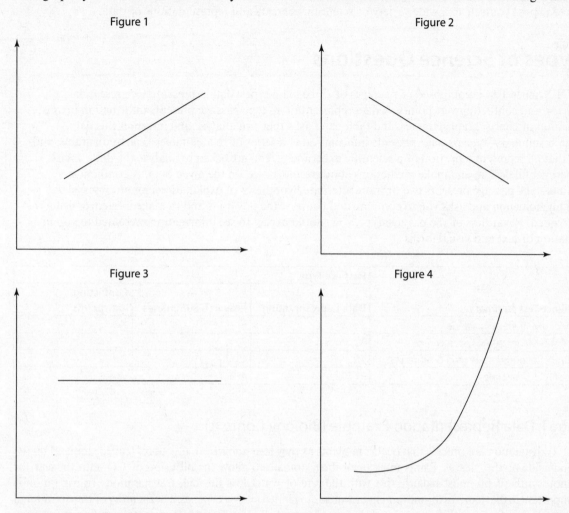

In Figure 1, the relationship between variables is direct and positive; as the value of x increases, so does the value of y. In Figure 2, the relationship between variables can be described as inverse and negative; as the value of x increases, the value of y decreases. In Figure 3, there is likely no meaningful relationship between variables; as x increases, y remains constant. Finally, in Figure 4, the relationship demonstrated is exponential; as x increases, y increases exponentially.

To summarize the approach to interpreting any visual representation of data, consider the following:

1. Read the labels and units carefully. Understand the type of measurement presented.
2. Consider the trend of data presented. Describe a relationship between the independent and dependent variables.
3. Extrapolate (extend the given data points in a logical predictive manner beyond what is directly presented) when appropriate to predict results. A line of best fit is typical for linear graphs.
4. Interpolate between points on a graph or in a data table to predict values to be expected at that point.

Don't forget to review figures in science and math textbooks and in newspaper, magazine, and journal articles to expose yourself to a wide variety of scientific contexts and representations of data.

D. Types of Science Questions

The ACT Science Test is composed of passages of three main types: data representation, research summaries, and conflicting viewpoints. A data representation–type passage presents information in any combination of charts, graphs, figures, and tables and asks that you analyze and interpret this data. A research summary–type passage presents information in a series of related tables, charts, diagrams, and graphs that all represent a portion of a scientific experiment. You are asked to analyze the data, assess the experimental design, and make predictions about results based on the given data. A conflicting viewpoints–type passage presents two or more alternate hypotheses or explanations for an observable natural phenomenon and asks you to compare and contrast the positions and to make inferences using the data provided. Regardless of the passage type, you should expect to see information presented to you in a combination of text and visual forms.

| | Passage Type | | |
ACT Science Test Summary	Data Representation	Research Summaries	Conflicting Viewpoints
Number of questions per passage	5	6	7
Number of passages on ACT Science Test	3	3	1
Total number of questions on ACT Science Test	15	18	7
Percent of ACT Science Test	37.5%	45%	17.5%

Passage I: Data Representation Example (Biology Context)

Transpiration is a process that occurs in plants as they lose water from tiny pores (called stomata) on the underside of their leaves. Plants must open their stomata to allow the diffusion of CO_2 into the leaf for photosynthesis but must balance this with the rate of water loss through transpiration. Transpiration is important in that it drives the movement of water into plant roots via osmosis. The quantity of transpirational water loss in leaves with the same surface areas but experiencing four environmental conditions (normal, windy, hot, and humid) was recorded in a botany laboratory; the data are shown in Table 1.

Table 1				
Time (min.)	Total Transpirational Water Loss (mL)			
	Normal	+ Wind	+ Heat	+ Humidity
5	0.2	0.3	0.2	0.05
10	0.5	0.6	0.4	0.15
15	0.7	1.1	0.7	0.35
20	1.0	1.5	1.1	0.45
25	1.2	1.8	1.5	0.5

1. According to Table 1, which type of condition is likely to encourage the least amount of transpiration from a plant leaf?

   A. normal
   B. windy
   C. hot
   D. humid

D is correct. High humidity (simulated in the lab through heavy misting of the plant leaf) was associated with only 0.5 mL of transpirational water loss, the lowest value of any of the four environmental conditions, including the normal control group. More water was present in the air and thus a smaller gradient was present to affect the movement of water from the leaf into the atmosphere.

2. The greatest quantity of water loss due to transpiration during any single 5-minute interval occurred under what set of conditions?

   F. normal
   G. windy
   H. hot
   J. humid

G is correct. The greatest amount of transpirational water loss during a 5-minute interval was recorded in the windy environment between the 10- and 15-minute intervals; the plant lost 0.5 mL of water. The wind contributed to a drier (less humid) environment, so there was an increased gradient present to affect the movement of water from the leaf into the atmosphere.

3. Which of the following graphs is consistent with the data presented in Table 1?

   A.

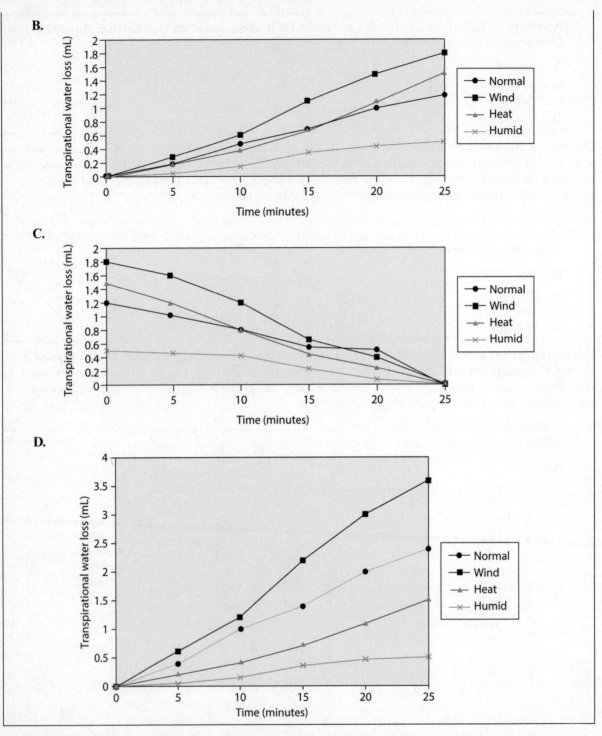

B.

C.

D.

B is correct. According to the data, the humid environment lost the least amount of water over time and the windy environment lost the most (for the reasons outlined earlier). Only the Choice B graph correctly displays all four lines.

4. What type of specific indoor environment could be inferred to necessitate the most frequent watering schedule for a common houseplant?

F. A dark hallway
G. Near an air conditioner
H. Under a table lamp
J. In a bathroom with a shower

G is correct. The fan involved in the operation of the air conditioner would simulate the windy environment in the experiment. A plant directly in the airflow would likely require a more frequent watering schedule due to increased transpiration.

5. Which of the following inferences is consistent with the data presented in this passage?

A. A plant in a hot, windy environment will transpire more than a plant in either a hot environment or a windy environment.
B. A plant in a very humid environment will transpire more than a plant in a moderately humid environment.
C. A plant in a very hot, sunny desert will transpire more in the winter than in the summer.
D. A plant in the dark will transpire equally if the environment is humid or dry.

A is correct. Since increased heat was associated with increased transpiration, and increased wind was also associated with increased transpiration, it is logical to infer that an environment that included both increased heat and wind would result in more transpiration than was recorded in either of the individual situations.

Passage II: Research Summaries Example (Chemistry Context)

The first step in the commercial production of fertilizer often involves the production of the main ingredient, ammonia (NH_3), according to the following equation:

$$N_{2(g)} + 3H_{2(g)} \leftrightarrow 2NH_{3(g)} + heat$$

This reaction is reversible as indicated by the double-headed arrow. According to Le Chatelier's Principle, a reversible reaction will work to reach equilibrium by favoring the direction of the reaction that will alleviate any stress on the system. For example, increasing the pressure on a system will encourage the reaction to proceed in the direction that favors the reduction of the pressure. In the reaction above to produce NH_3, an increase in pressure on the system would encourage the forward reaction that has fewer molecules (2 molecules of NH_3 product compared to the 4 total molecules of reactants), favoring the production of NH_3 for fertilizer. The pressure and temperature were adjusted while this reaction was being carried out; the data are shown in Tables 1 and 2.

Table 1		
Pressure (atm)	% NH_3 present	Temperature (°C)
50	40	200
100	70	200
200	80	200
300	90	200

Table 2		
Temperature (°C)	% NH$_3$ present	Pressure (atm)
200	90	400
300	80	400
400	50	400
500	30	400

Although applying Le Chatelier's Principle helps to understand the conditions under which the maximum amount of NH$_3$ can be generated, these conditions are not always practical in a real-world industrial setting. The same reaction was tested under a wider range of pressures and more detailed temperature data were recorded. The data were used to generate Figure 1. The pressure and temperature conditions that were determined to be economically and otherwise practically feasible are shaded in the figure.

Figure 1

Once ammonia is produced, it often is converted into other products for easier storage and handling. For instance, ammonia can first be converted into nitric acid (HNO$_3$) through oxidation, and that HNO$_3$ product can be combined with NH$_3$ to produce the final ammonium nitrate (NH$_4$NO$_3$) fertilizer product according to the following reactions:

$$NH_3 + 2O_2 \rightarrow HNO_3 + H_2O$$
$$NH_3 + HNO_3 \rightarrow NH_4NO_3$$

Although it is a desirable fertilizer because of its high nitrogen content, NH_4NO_3 must be stored and handled appropriately due to certain physical and chemical characteristics of the compound. Although stable at temperatures below 210°C, it will spontaneously decompose at or above that temperature and can become part of an explosive, self-sustaining reaction if certain catalysts are present. The solubility of NH_4NO_3 in water at various temperatures is shown in Table 3.

Table 3	
Temperature (°C)	Solubility of NH_4NO_3 (g/100 mL H_2O)
0	119
20	190
40	286
60	421
80	630
100	1024

6. According to Table 1, if another trial were conducted at 200°C and 55% of NH_3 were present at equilibrium, which of the following pressure values would be expected to be present?

   F. 40 atm
   G. 70 atm
   H. 250 atm
   J. 340 atm

G is correct. According to Table 1, a value of 55% NH_3 falls between the observed values of 40% NH_3 (at 50 atm) and 70% NH_3 (at 100 atm). A logical pressure then to associate with 55% NH_3 is 70 atm, a value that falls between the other two.

7. Which statement correctly describes the trend in the data presented in Table 2 when pressure is held constant?

   A. As the temperature of the system at equilibrium decreases, the percent of NH_3 present remains constant.
   B. As the temperature of the system at equilibrium increases, the percent of NH_3 present increases.
   C. As the temperature of the system at equilibrium decreases, the percent of NH_3 present decreases.
   D. As the temperature of the system at equilibrium increases, the percent of NH_3 present decreases.

D is correct. As the temperature values increase in the first column of Table 2, the corresponding percentages of NH_3 present at equilibrium decrease. For example, 200°C is associated with 90% NH_3, while 400°C is associated with 50% NH_3.

8. Using the data presented in Figure 1, which scenario for the production of NH_3 is both economically feasible and allows for a minimum of 30% NH_3 present at equilibrium?

   F. 150 atm; 300°C
   G. 250 atm; 400°C
   H. 300 atm; 300°C
   J. 550 atm; 200°C

G is correct. To be economically feasible, the point representing the set of conditions described must lie within the shaded area and at a point that is above 30% on the *y*-axis. The only option provided that meets the criteria is at 250 atm and 400°C. Any pressure value below 200 atm or above 500 atm would not qualify, nor would any temperature below 300°C.

9. If one industrial chemist wants to store the NH_4NO_3 by dissolving it in water at 50°C, what is a possible quantity of compound that could be dissolved in 100 mL of water according to the information presented in Table 3?

   A. 179 g
   B. 260 g
   C. 408 g
   D. 512 g

C is correct. Using the information in Table 3, the maximum quantity of NH_4NO_3 that can be completely dissolved in 100 mL of water at 40°C is 286 grams and at 60°C is 421 grams. The mass then that can be dissolved at 50°C must be between 286 and 421 grams; 408 grams meets this criterion.

10. The equilibrium constant (K_{eq}) is an important part of the proportion that predicts the concentrations of reactants and products present in a system at equilibrium such that for the generic reaction

$$aA + bB \rightarrow cC + dD, K_{eq} = \frac{[C]^c [D]^d}{[A]^a [B]^b}.$$

For the initial ammonia synthesis reaction $N_{2(g)} + 3H_{2(g)} \leftrightarrow 2NH_{3(g)} + \text{heat}$, the $K_{eq} = 4.50 \times 10^{-5}$ at 450°C. When the synthesis is repeated but the temperature is raised to 500°C, the $K_{eq} = 1.50 \times 10^{-5}$. Which statement best explains the significance of these results?

   F. As the temperature increases, the reverse reaction is favored to relieve the system of the added temperature stress; relatively less NH_3 will be present.
   G. As the temperature increases, the pressure also increases; this favors the reverse reaction and relatively more NH_3 will be present.
   H. As the temperature increases, the forward reaction is favored to relieve the system of the added temperature stress; relatively less NH_3 will be present.
   J. As the temperature increases, the pressure decreases; this favors the forward reaction and relatively less NH_3 will be present.

F is correct. According to Le Chatelier's Principle, a reversible reaction at equilibrium will favor the direction of the reaction that acts to relieve any stress placed on the system. If the temperature increases, then the reverse reaction will be favored to use heat energy; relatively less NH_3 will then be present.

Passage III: Conflicting Viewpoints Example (Earth/Space Sciences Context)

Much debate currently rages regarding the appropriate reaction to the global warming crisis. The world emissions of CO_2, a critical greenhouse gas that directly contributes to global warming, has increased dramatically the past 50 years. This increase can be directly attributed in part to the burning of fossil fuels (like oil, natural gas, and coal) for energy. Data regarding global CO_2 emissions from 1950–1995 and global use of fossil fuels throughout the 1970s are presented in Figures 1 and 2, respectively.

Figure 1

Figure 2

As efforts are made to convert U.S. energy sources to renewable, more environmentally-friendly options, different opinions arise regarding the type of renewable energy source that should be invested in to replace the current need for energy being met chiefly by the burning of fossil fuels. Relative global use of different energy sources, both conventional and renewable, from 1980 to 2005, is shown in Figure 3.

239

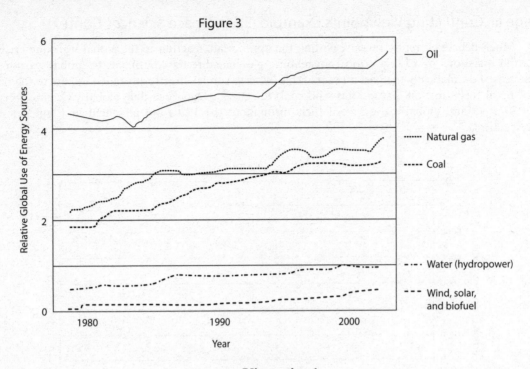

Figure 3

Viewpoint 1

Although much recent discussion of global warming and alternative energy sources has included the concepts of wind, solar, and water power, these energy sources are unreliable (e.g., cloudy days can interfere with solar power) and are not equally distributed across the country (e.g., low solar intensity in northern regions).

In order to encourage the United States to burn less fossil fuels for energy and thus to emit less of the greenhouse gas CO_2, the infrastructure must be converted to support the burning of biofuels like ethanol instead. When the corn or soybean is being grown, the plant is absorbing significant quantities of CO_2 from the atmosphere to use for photosynthesis. It thus naturally acts to detoxify the air of a greenhouse gas. When the ethanol is later burned for fuel, the CO_2 produced from the combustion is negated by the earlier absorption. Ethanol thus has a carbon-neutral footprint.

Viewpoint 2

While some biofuels might be useful and responsible renewable energy sources, soybean- and corn-based ethanol is actually contributing to global warming. The benefit gained from the absorption of CO_2 during the natural plant growth process is canceled out from the CO_2 released during the combustion process that allows the ethanol to be used as a fuel. Additionally, natural forests are being cleared and fields that are currently being used as farmlands are being converted to biofuel fields. This makes ethanol a producer of CO_2 when the global effect is considered.

A better alternative is utilizing a combination of renewable energy sources, like wind and solar. While it is true that not all countries and local regions have equal access to all forms of energy, if efforts are combined at all levels of government within the United States, and if those efforts are then coordinated between the United States and neighboring countries, and if multiple energy sources are utilized, the United States and its neighbors can free themselves of their dependence on burning fossil fuels, producing fewer CO_2 emissions and contributing less to global warming in the future.

11. Using Figures 1 and 2 and the information presented in the passage, which of the following statements is true?

    A. The United States is primarily responsible for the increase in CO_2 emissions observed over the past 50 years.

    B. Although CO_2 emissions increased dramatically from 1950 through 1995, recent evidence suggests that emissions are decreasing in more recent years.

    C. Replacing traditional methods of burning fossil fuels with renewable energy sources will reverse global warming.

    D. The burning of fossil fuels is directly related to the increase in CO_2 emissions and is thus directly related to the global warming crisis.

D is correct. The passage states that CO_2 emissions are directly related to the burning of fossil fuels, and the parallel curves presented in Figures 1 and 2 support that claim. Some of the other statements may seem true based on prior knowledge, but remember to base your conclusions on the evidence presented in the passage.

12. Which statement correctly summarizes the more recent data presented in Figure 3 regarding the global use of traditional and renewable energy sources?

    F. The use of all sources of energy was increasing at a steady rate between 1980 and 2005.

    G. While the use of many energy sources between 1980 and 2005 was increasing, the use of some renewable energy sources like solar and wind power remained relatively flat.

    H. The use of hydroelectric and nuclear power increased at the same rate from 1980 to 2005.

    J. While the use of all fossil fuels has continued to increase, the use of renewable energy like solar, wind, and biofuels actually decreased between 1980 and 2005.

G is correct. Figure 3 shows that the curves for all forms of energy except wind, solar, and biofuels are sloping upward over time and thus are increasing in usage. The curve for wind, solar, and biofuels is basically flat throughout the time period, a sharp contrast from the other curves.

13. According to Viewpoint 1, which statement is supported regarding ethanol?

    A. Burning ethanol is better than burning traditional oil because burning ethanol is not associated with releasing CO_2.

    B. Ethanol produces as much CO_2 as it absorbs, thus it is a carbon-neutral fuel.

    C. Ethanol is better for the environment because it is extracted from plants and is thus a natural alternative.

    D. Ethanol is not a suitable replacement for oil even though it is considered renewable.

B is correct. The main argument presented in Viewpoint 1 supports the use of ethanol as a biofuel and states that such biofuels are desirable because the plants grown for the process absorb as much CO_2 as they release when burned for energy.

14. Which of the following statements is consistent with Viewpoint 2 and presents a point of conflict with Viewpoint 1?

    F. Ethanol from soybeans is associated with less CO_2 than ethanol from corn and is thus preferable as a biofuel.

    G. Plants need CO_2 for photosynthesis and are therefore consumers of CO_2.

    H. If CO_2 emission data associated with using ethanol for fuel include the amount of land cleared for new biofuel fields, ethanol is a net producer of CO_2.

    J. Alternative energy like wind, water, and solar power is associated with fewer CO_2 emissions than the combustion of any fuel, traditional or renewable.

H is correct. The main argument presented in Viewpoint 2 contradicts that which is presented in Viewpoint 1. It claims that the biofuel fields are replacing farmlands and natural forests and thus are actually contributing to the global CO_2 emissions.

15. Which of the following statements might logically be made as a rebuttal from Viewpoint 1 to the perspective presented in Viewpoint 2?

    A. The efforts required to coordinate efforts at local and state levels within the United States and then between the United States and its neighbors are too complicated and expensive to be dependable or practical.

    B. Very few successful attempts have been made in recent years to increase the use of solar and wind power, so future attempts are also likely to be ineffective.

    C. Ethanol and other biofuels should be part of the combination of renewable energy sources to replace fossil fuels even though they are a net producer of CO_2.

    D. Nuclear energy should be utilized as much as possible because it is not associated with the same limitations as is ethanol.

A is correct. The only rebuttals that can be made logically with the evidence provided in the passage are that the solution presented in Viewpoint 2 would be ineffective for some reason or that the data can be challenged or contradicted by other data. The notion of coordinating efforts among different governments, countries, and energy sources speaks to the potential ineffectiveness of this solution.

In Passages I–III above, five sample questions were presented after each passage in order to provide a sufficient sampling of questions that you should expect to see for any passage type. Remember that on the actual ACT Science Test, you will be asked to primarily respond to questions associated with research summaries and data representation passage types, and only to respond to seven total questions within the one conflicting viewpoints passage.

XV. Writing Test

The ACT Writing Test is an essay in which you demonstrate your writing and thinking skills. This section of the ACT is optional and is administered after the four sections of the ACT are completed. If you choose to take the Writing Test, you will receive a separate Writing Test subscore that does not affect any of the other scores as well as a combined English/Writing score. The essay score is not calculated into the Composite score.

You will be required to write a 30-minute essay response to a prompt. The prompt will present two sides of a debatable issue that is familiar to high school students. You are asked to consider the problem, take a position, and support that position using reasons and examples. Past questions have concerned high school dress codes, mandated community service, and the value of extra-curricular activities.

The essay is holistically scored on a 6-point scale. Two graders will read each essay, and their scores will be added together. Thus, the highest score an essay can receive is a 12. The graders know you are writing this essay under pressure in 30 minutes so they are not looking for a polished piece of writing. Rather, they hope to see a thoughtful (and legible) first draft.

The rubric is included after the diagnostic test in Chapter IV (see pages 67–68).

A. Approach to the Essay: Thinking (2–3 minutes)

Thinking is the first (and often most important) step. As you read the prompt, think about the issue. What is your position on the issue? What are the reasons you feel this way? What examples could you use to support your position? Your answers to these questions will help you formulate your response.

Note: To support your position, do not ignore the counterargument (the other side of an issue). You strengthen your argument by defining the counterargument and then explaining why your position is stronger. Also, you can qualify an issue (limit or restrict the argument). Often an issue is complex, and under some conditions, you would support one side, while under other conditions, you would support the other. In this case, your thesis would clearly state the conditions affecting your position.

B. Approach to the Essay: Planning (2–3 minutes)

It is helpful to begin your planning by writing a thesis sentence, a one-sentence assertion that presents the position that your examples will prove. If you are still not sure exactly where you stand on the issue, do some brainstorming first: Think of all the examples, reasons, and ideas that will support each side and then determine on which side your argument will be stronger.

After you know your position, begin to plan your essay. List your thoughts on the question page in your test booklet. These notes can be very brief: just ideas for the examples you will use to support your position.

Always write from strength: It is important to choose logical, appropriate examples and specific references to support your thesis. You should avoid hypothetical examples or very broad generalizations; the strength of your essay is in the specific details. In addition, to ensure that you have something to write about, it is helpful to be aware of current debates in education. Read the newspapers and pay particular attention to issues that concern schools and high school students.

Note: Do not feel you must use multiple examples in your essay. Some very good essays present one fully developed example while others give two or three examples. The number of examples depends on how much you know about the issue and what you think is the most effective evidence to support your opinion. There is also no magic number of paragraphs that you must write. Essays should be organic; as you begin a new topic, start a new paragraph.

C. Approach to the Essay: Writing (18–22 minutes)

1. State Thesis Clearly in Introductory Paragraph

It is always to your advantage to pique your reader's interest in the opening paragraph. However, in a timed writing, you don't need a long introductory paragraph. Get to the point quickly so you have time to develop your argument. Make sure you establish your position and set up the development of your examples. Explaining the context of the issue is a good beginning point; in other words, set the scene. Clarify why this issue is a topic of debate. For example, if you are responding to a prompt asking you to present an argument for or against school uniforms, you might begin by discussing a situation in which some students arrive at school dressed inappropriately. You might give some specific examples of this ill-chosen attire. You would then state your position on the issue: Does the inappropriate dress warrant a change in a school's dress code to school uniforms? Or, is clothing just an expression of individual creativity that should be ignored? Is there a middle ground? Your answers to these questions form the basis of your thesis statement.

2. Develop Your Examples

In the topic sentence of your first body paragraph, state the example or the reason that you will develop. Then explain the reason/example so the reader understands why it supports your thesis. Try to give specific details. If you are writing about articles of clothing, describe them; about books, give the titles; about magazines, name them; about extracurricular activities, list the clubs.

3. Organize Coherently

Many students ask about a "formula" for the essay or about the required numbers of paragraphs. There is no specific plan or correct number of paragraphs to guarantee success on the Writing Test. The number of paragraphs will depend on the number of examples you choose to support your argument. Paragraphing should be logical: Each time you begin a new point, begin a new paragraph. As you develop your examples, be sure to use transitional phrases. These words and phrases are the key to coherence, and graders are trained to spot them. When you begin a new paragraph, use a phrase like "Another *advantage to school uniforms* . . . " or "*Uniformity in dress* also *fosters school unity.*" Use transitional phrases within the paragraph as well to help your ideas flow logically.

Transitional words and phrases link ideas and indicate the relationship of ideas within a sentence, a paragraph, or a passage. They are essential tools for a writer who wants to achieve a clear and logical flow of ideas.

Important Transitional Words and Phrases	
Words used to indicate an example	**Words used to show a result**
for example for instance specifically	consequently hence accordingly therefore
Words used to indicate a reason	**Words used to indicate more information**
as because since due to	besides in addition moreover furthermore
Words used to contrast	**Words used to show similarity**
although but however in contrast nevertheless whereas while yet on the other hand still despite	another similarly likewise also again in the same way too equally
Words used to establish time relationships	**Words used for emphasis**
before during after at last at this point later soon next until recently then then again once at the same time	indeed clearly to be sure without doubt assuredly

4. State the Counterargument

The prompt will state two points of view. You may choose one or the other, or you may present an original point of view. Whatever you choose, be sure to state the opposing position (the counterargument) and explain your reasons for rejecting it. This technique indicates your awareness of the complexity of the issue. Too often students make the mistake of reducing a complex issue to simple black-and-white terms. Introduce the counterargument with transitional words or phrases: "Granted . . . " or "It may be true that . . . " or "Some may say that . . . " and then respond to it with your argument.

For example: Some may say that teenagers use their clothing to express their artistic individuality, but painted and ripped jeans that reveal an inordinate amount of skin are a distraction in the classroom.

5. Use Active Verbs

To make your writing lively rather than flat, avoid state-of-being verbs (forms of the verb *to be*) and weak passive sentences. Also, avoid phrases like "I believe" and "I think" and clichés.

> *Weak:* I think people who dress to impress are silly.
> *Strong:* Clothing expresses both individuality and creativity.

6. Vary Sentence Structure

Most students have a tendency to write simple and compound sentences that follow the subject-verb pattern. Since you will have very little time to revise your essay, be aware of sentence structure as you write.

Start a sentence with a participial phrase:

> *Instead of:* I find it difficult to decide what to wear to school.
> *Write:* Standing in front of my closet, I search in vain for something comfortable to wear to school.

Start with a subordinate clause:

> When I get ready for school, I waste precious minutes deciding what to wear.

Start with an adverb:

> Frequently, students use their attire to express their individuality and creativity.

D. Proofread (2–3 minutes)

Try to allow time to read over your essay. Be sure your writing is legible. If you see a mistake, change it by crossing out neatly or erasing carefully. You may insert a word or phrase above the line with a carat (^). **Do not write outside the black lines in your test booklet.**

XVI. Full-Length Practice Test with Answer Explanations

Format of the ACT Practice Test

The Practice Test will cover four content areas: English, Mathematics, Reading, and Science. These tests are designed to measure your ability in these four areas and to predict your success in college. Each question on the test is numbered. Choose the best answer for each question and fill in the corresponding circle on the answer sheet provided.

For each question, be sure to fill in only one circle on your answer sheet. If you erase, do so completely, as the scoring device will pick up any stray marks. (Although this is a practice test and is not being mechanically scored, you should practice the way you would like to perform on the actual test.)

Your score will be based on the number of questions you have answered correctly during the time allowed for each section. No points will be deducted for incorrect answers. You should answer all questions, even if you are unsure and have to guess. It is advantageous to you to answer every question on the test.

If you finish a section before the allotted time runs out, you may not work on any other section. You may not go back to a previous section or move ahead to work on the next section.

You may use any open spaces on your test booklet for scrap.

The Practice Test also includes the optional Writing Test. The Writing Test is an essay in which you demonstrate your writing and thinking skills. It is administered after the four sections of the ACT are completed. For more on the Writing Test, see Chapter XV.

Timing: You will need 3 hours and 25 minutes to complete the Practice Test.

Test	# of Questions	# of Minutes
English	75	45
Mathematics	60	60
Reading	40	35
Science	40	35
Writing	1	30

After you complete the test, use the Answer Key (pages 314–315), the Scoring Worksheets (pages 335–336), and the Raw Score Conversions chart (page 337) to obtain your scaled scores.

To score the Writing Test (Essay), refer to the rubric on pages 67–68 and to the sample essays and their evaluations starting on page 332.

Answer Sheet

Section 1: English Test

1 Ⓐ Ⓑ Ⓒ Ⓓ	26 Ⓕ Ⓖ Ⓗ Ⓙ	51 Ⓐ Ⓑ Ⓒ Ⓓ
2 Ⓕ Ⓖ Ⓗ Ⓙ	27 Ⓐ Ⓑ Ⓒ Ⓓ	52 Ⓕ Ⓖ Ⓗ Ⓙ
3 Ⓐ Ⓑ Ⓒ Ⓓ	28 Ⓕ Ⓖ Ⓗ Ⓙ	53 Ⓐ Ⓑ Ⓒ Ⓓ
4 Ⓕ Ⓖ Ⓗ Ⓙ	29 Ⓐ Ⓑ Ⓒ Ⓓ	54 Ⓕ Ⓖ Ⓗ Ⓙ
5 Ⓐ Ⓑ Ⓒ Ⓓ	30 Ⓕ Ⓖ Ⓗ Ⓙ	55 Ⓐ Ⓑ Ⓒ Ⓓ
6 Ⓕ Ⓖ Ⓗ Ⓙ	31 Ⓐ Ⓑ Ⓒ Ⓓ	56 Ⓕ Ⓖ Ⓗ Ⓙ
7 Ⓐ Ⓑ Ⓒ Ⓓ	32 Ⓕ Ⓖ Ⓗ Ⓙ	57 Ⓐ Ⓑ Ⓒ Ⓓ
8 Ⓕ Ⓖ Ⓗ Ⓙ	33 Ⓐ Ⓑ Ⓒ Ⓓ	58 Ⓕ Ⓖ Ⓗ Ⓙ
9 Ⓐ Ⓑ Ⓒ Ⓓ	34 Ⓕ Ⓖ Ⓗ Ⓙ	59 Ⓐ Ⓑ Ⓒ Ⓓ
10 Ⓕ Ⓖ Ⓗ Ⓙ	35 Ⓐ Ⓑ Ⓒ Ⓓ	60 Ⓕ Ⓖ Ⓗ Ⓙ
11 Ⓐ Ⓑ Ⓒ Ⓓ	36 Ⓕ Ⓖ Ⓗ Ⓙ	61 Ⓐ Ⓑ Ⓒ Ⓓ
12 Ⓕ Ⓖ Ⓗ Ⓙ	37 Ⓐ Ⓑ Ⓒ Ⓓ	62 Ⓕ Ⓖ Ⓗ Ⓙ
13 Ⓐ Ⓑ Ⓒ Ⓓ	38 Ⓕ Ⓖ Ⓗ Ⓙ	63 Ⓐ Ⓑ Ⓒ Ⓓ
14 Ⓕ Ⓖ Ⓗ Ⓙ	39 Ⓐ Ⓑ Ⓒ Ⓓ	64 Ⓕ Ⓖ Ⓗ Ⓙ
15 Ⓐ Ⓑ Ⓒ Ⓓ	40 Ⓕ Ⓖ Ⓗ Ⓙ	65 Ⓐ Ⓑ Ⓒ Ⓓ
16 Ⓕ Ⓖ Ⓗ Ⓙ	41 Ⓐ Ⓑ Ⓒ Ⓓ	66 Ⓕ Ⓖ Ⓗ Ⓙ
17 Ⓐ Ⓑ Ⓒ Ⓓ	42 Ⓕ Ⓖ Ⓗ Ⓙ	67 Ⓐ Ⓑ Ⓒ Ⓓ
18 Ⓕ Ⓖ Ⓗ Ⓙ	43 Ⓐ Ⓑ Ⓒ Ⓓ	68 Ⓕ Ⓖ Ⓗ Ⓙ
19 Ⓐ Ⓑ Ⓒ Ⓓ	44 Ⓕ Ⓖ Ⓗ Ⓙ	69 Ⓐ Ⓑ Ⓒ Ⓓ
20 Ⓕ Ⓖ Ⓗ Ⓙ	45 Ⓐ Ⓑ Ⓒ Ⓓ	70 Ⓕ Ⓖ Ⓗ Ⓙ
21 Ⓐ Ⓑ Ⓒ Ⓓ	46 Ⓕ Ⓖ Ⓗ Ⓙ	71 Ⓐ Ⓑ Ⓒ Ⓓ
22 Ⓕ Ⓖ Ⓗ Ⓙ	47 Ⓐ Ⓑ Ⓒ Ⓓ	72 Ⓕ Ⓖ Ⓗ Ⓙ
23 Ⓐ Ⓑ Ⓒ Ⓓ	48 Ⓕ Ⓖ Ⓗ Ⓙ	73 Ⓐ Ⓑ Ⓒ Ⓓ
24 Ⓕ Ⓖ Ⓗ Ⓙ	49 Ⓐ Ⓑ Ⓒ Ⓓ	74 Ⓕ Ⓖ Ⓗ Ⓙ
25 Ⓐ Ⓑ Ⓒ Ⓓ	50 Ⓕ Ⓖ Ⓗ Ⓙ	75 Ⓐ Ⓑ Ⓒ Ⓓ

Section 2: Mathematics Test

1 Ⓐ Ⓑ Ⓒ Ⓓ Ⓔ	31 Ⓐ Ⓑ Ⓒ Ⓓ Ⓔ
2 Ⓕ Ⓖ Ⓗ Ⓙ Ⓚ	32 Ⓕ Ⓖ Ⓗ Ⓙ Ⓚ
3 Ⓐ Ⓑ Ⓒ Ⓓ Ⓔ	33 Ⓐ Ⓑ Ⓒ Ⓓ Ⓔ
4 Ⓕ Ⓖ Ⓗ Ⓙ Ⓚ	34 Ⓕ Ⓖ Ⓗ Ⓙ Ⓚ
5 Ⓐ Ⓑ Ⓒ Ⓓ Ⓔ	35 Ⓐ Ⓑ Ⓒ Ⓓ Ⓔ
6 Ⓕ Ⓖ Ⓗ Ⓙ Ⓚ	36 Ⓕ Ⓖ Ⓗ Ⓙ Ⓚ
7 Ⓐ Ⓑ Ⓒ Ⓓ Ⓔ	37 Ⓐ Ⓑ Ⓒ Ⓓ Ⓔ
8 Ⓕ Ⓖ Ⓗ Ⓙ Ⓚ	38 Ⓕ Ⓖ Ⓗ Ⓙ Ⓚ
9 Ⓐ Ⓑ Ⓒ Ⓓ Ⓔ	39 Ⓐ Ⓑ Ⓒ Ⓓ Ⓔ
10 Ⓕ Ⓖ Ⓗ Ⓙ Ⓚ	40 Ⓕ Ⓖ Ⓗ Ⓙ Ⓚ
11 Ⓐ Ⓑ Ⓒ Ⓓ Ⓔ	41 Ⓐ Ⓑ Ⓒ Ⓓ Ⓔ
12 Ⓕ Ⓖ Ⓗ Ⓙ Ⓚ	42 Ⓕ Ⓖ Ⓗ Ⓙ Ⓚ
13 Ⓐ Ⓑ Ⓒ Ⓓ Ⓔ	43 Ⓐ Ⓑ Ⓒ Ⓓ Ⓔ
14 Ⓕ Ⓖ Ⓗ Ⓙ Ⓚ	44 Ⓕ Ⓖ Ⓗ Ⓙ Ⓚ
15 Ⓐ Ⓑ Ⓒ Ⓓ Ⓔ	45 Ⓐ Ⓑ Ⓒ Ⓓ Ⓔ
16 Ⓕ Ⓖ Ⓗ Ⓙ Ⓚ	46 Ⓕ Ⓖ Ⓗ Ⓙ Ⓚ
17 Ⓐ Ⓑ Ⓒ Ⓓ Ⓔ	47 Ⓐ Ⓑ Ⓒ Ⓓ Ⓔ
18 Ⓕ Ⓖ Ⓗ Ⓙ Ⓚ	48 Ⓕ Ⓖ Ⓗ Ⓙ Ⓚ
19 Ⓐ Ⓑ Ⓒ Ⓓ Ⓔ	49 Ⓐ Ⓑ Ⓒ Ⓓ Ⓔ
20 Ⓕ Ⓖ Ⓗ Ⓙ Ⓚ	50 Ⓕ Ⓖ Ⓗ Ⓙ Ⓚ
21 Ⓐ Ⓑ Ⓒ Ⓓ Ⓔ	51 Ⓐ Ⓑ Ⓒ Ⓓ Ⓔ
22 Ⓕ Ⓖ Ⓗ Ⓙ Ⓚ	52 Ⓕ Ⓖ Ⓗ Ⓙ Ⓚ
23 Ⓐ Ⓑ Ⓒ Ⓓ Ⓔ	53 Ⓐ Ⓑ Ⓒ Ⓓ Ⓔ
24 Ⓕ Ⓖ Ⓗ Ⓙ Ⓚ	54 Ⓕ Ⓖ Ⓗ Ⓙ Ⓚ
25 Ⓐ Ⓑ Ⓒ Ⓓ Ⓔ	55 Ⓐ Ⓑ Ⓒ Ⓓ Ⓔ
26 Ⓕ Ⓖ Ⓗ Ⓙ Ⓚ	56 Ⓕ Ⓖ Ⓗ Ⓙ Ⓚ
27 Ⓐ Ⓑ Ⓒ Ⓓ Ⓔ	57 Ⓐ Ⓑ Ⓒ Ⓓ Ⓔ
28 Ⓕ Ⓖ Ⓗ Ⓙ Ⓚ	58 Ⓕ Ⓖ Ⓗ Ⓙ Ⓚ
29 Ⓐ Ⓑ Ⓒ Ⓓ Ⓔ	59 Ⓐ Ⓑ Ⓒ Ⓓ Ⓔ
30 Ⓕ Ⓖ Ⓗ Ⓙ Ⓚ	60 Ⓕ Ⓖ Ⓗ Ⓙ Ⓚ

CUT HERE

Section 3: Reading Test

1 Ⓐ Ⓑ Ⓒ Ⓓ	26 Ⓕ Ⓖ Ⓗ Ⓙ
2 Ⓕ Ⓖ Ⓗ Ⓙ	27 Ⓐ Ⓑ Ⓒ Ⓓ
3 Ⓐ Ⓑ Ⓒ Ⓓ	28 Ⓕ Ⓖ Ⓗ Ⓙ
4 Ⓕ Ⓖ Ⓗ Ⓙ	29 Ⓐ Ⓑ Ⓒ Ⓓ
5 Ⓐ Ⓑ Ⓒ Ⓓ	30 Ⓕ Ⓖ Ⓗ Ⓙ
6 Ⓕ Ⓖ Ⓗ Ⓙ	31 Ⓐ Ⓑ Ⓒ Ⓓ
7 Ⓐ Ⓑ Ⓒ Ⓓ	32 Ⓕ Ⓖ Ⓗ Ⓙ
8 Ⓕ Ⓖ Ⓗ Ⓙ	33 Ⓐ Ⓑ Ⓒ Ⓓ
9 Ⓐ Ⓑ Ⓒ Ⓓ	34 Ⓕ Ⓖ Ⓗ Ⓙ
10 Ⓕ Ⓖ Ⓗ Ⓙ	35 Ⓐ Ⓑ Ⓒ Ⓓ
11 Ⓐ Ⓑ Ⓒ Ⓓ	36 Ⓕ Ⓖ Ⓗ Ⓙ
12 Ⓕ Ⓖ Ⓗ Ⓙ	37 Ⓐ Ⓑ Ⓒ Ⓓ
13 Ⓐ Ⓑ Ⓒ Ⓓ	38 Ⓕ Ⓖ Ⓗ Ⓙ
14 Ⓕ Ⓖ Ⓗ Ⓙ	39 Ⓐ Ⓑ Ⓒ Ⓓ
15 Ⓐ Ⓑ Ⓒ Ⓓ	40 Ⓕ Ⓖ Ⓗ Ⓙ
16 Ⓕ Ⓖ Ⓗ Ⓙ	
17 Ⓐ Ⓑ Ⓒ Ⓓ	
18 Ⓕ Ⓖ Ⓗ Ⓙ	
19 Ⓐ Ⓑ Ⓒ Ⓓ	
20 Ⓕ Ⓖ Ⓗ Ⓙ	
21 Ⓐ Ⓑ Ⓒ Ⓓ	
22 Ⓕ Ⓖ Ⓗ Ⓙ	
23 Ⓐ Ⓑ Ⓒ Ⓓ	
24 Ⓕ Ⓖ Ⓗ Ⓙ	
25 Ⓐ Ⓑ Ⓒ Ⓓ	

Section 4: Science Test

1 Ⓐ Ⓑ Ⓒ Ⓓ	26 Ⓕ Ⓖ Ⓗ Ⓙ
2 Ⓕ Ⓖ Ⓗ Ⓙ	27 Ⓐ Ⓑ Ⓒ Ⓓ
3 Ⓐ Ⓑ Ⓒ Ⓓ	28 Ⓕ Ⓖ Ⓗ Ⓙ
4 Ⓕ Ⓖ Ⓗ Ⓙ	29 Ⓐ Ⓑ Ⓒ Ⓓ
5 Ⓐ Ⓑ Ⓒ Ⓓ	30 Ⓕ Ⓖ Ⓗ Ⓙ
6 Ⓕ Ⓖ Ⓗ Ⓙ	31 Ⓐ Ⓑ Ⓒ Ⓓ
7 Ⓐ Ⓑ Ⓒ Ⓓ	32 Ⓕ Ⓖ Ⓗ Ⓙ
8 Ⓕ Ⓖ Ⓗ Ⓙ	33 Ⓐ Ⓑ Ⓒ Ⓓ
9 Ⓐ Ⓑ Ⓒ Ⓓ	34 Ⓕ Ⓖ Ⓗ Ⓙ
10 Ⓕ Ⓖ Ⓗ Ⓙ	35 Ⓐ Ⓑ Ⓒ Ⓓ
11 Ⓐ Ⓑ Ⓒ Ⓓ	36 Ⓕ Ⓖ Ⓗ Ⓙ
12 Ⓕ Ⓖ Ⓗ Ⓙ	37 Ⓐ Ⓑ Ⓒ Ⓓ
13 Ⓐ Ⓑ Ⓒ Ⓓ	38 Ⓕ Ⓖ Ⓗ Ⓙ
14 Ⓕ Ⓖ Ⓗ Ⓙ	39 Ⓐ Ⓑ Ⓒ Ⓓ
15 Ⓐ Ⓑ Ⓒ Ⓓ	40 Ⓕ Ⓖ Ⓗ Ⓙ
16 Ⓕ Ⓖ Ⓗ Ⓙ	
17 Ⓐ Ⓑ Ⓒ Ⓓ	
18 Ⓕ Ⓖ Ⓗ Ⓙ	
19 Ⓐ Ⓑ Ⓒ Ⓓ	
20 Ⓕ Ⓖ Ⓗ Ⓙ	
21 Ⓐ Ⓑ Ⓒ Ⓓ	
22 Ⓕ Ⓖ Ⓗ Ⓙ	
23 Ⓐ Ⓑ Ⓒ Ⓓ	
24 Ⓕ Ⓖ Ⓗ Ⓙ	
25 Ⓐ Ⓑ Ⓒ Ⓓ	

CUT HERE

Section 5: Writing Test

CUT HERE

Section 1: English Test

45 Minutes—75 Questions

Directions: The English Test consists of five passages. In each passage, words and phrases are underlined and numbered. Following each passage are corresponding questions (on the actual exam, passages appear in the left-hand column, with corresponding questions in the right-hand column). Each question offers four alternatives for the underlined part. Consider the choices and then select the one that best fits the requirements of standard written English. Be sure to take into account the style and tone of the whole passage. If you think the word or phrase is correct as written, choose "NO CHANGE." For some of the questions, you will see a number in a box, which corresponds to a similar number within the passage. These questions ask about a section of the passage or about the passage as a whole. It is a good idea to read through the entire passage before you begin to answer the questions.

Passage I

The Fiddling Emperor

History is filled with stories of dubious origin. One of the <u>most notable stories are</u> the tale of
₁
Nero, Emperor of Rome in the first century A.D., <u>who ostensibly</u> "fiddled while Rome burned."
₂
According to rumor, Nero stood on a hillside overlooking the city of Rome and "fiddled" while the city was destroyed by flames. In fact, some <u>sources crediting</u> Nero with setting the fire so that
₃
<u>they</u> could have a free hand in rebuilding the city to
₄
his liking. While this may be true, historians wonder

1.
  A. NO CHANGE
  B. most notable are
  C. most notable stories is
  D. most is

2. Which of the following alternatives would NOT be acceptable?
  F. who supposedly
  G. who some say
  H. who purportedly
  J. whom they say

3.
  A. NO CHANGE
  B. sources credits
  C. sources credit
  D. would have credited

4.
  F. NO CHANGE
  G. he
  H. them
  J. it

about the "fiddling" image, for violins (or fiddles)

<u>were not invented</u> until the eleventh century.
    5

The writings of the ancient Romans yield some clues to the mystery. Nero was born into a family of Roman nobility. <u>When his father died and his mother</u> Agrippa married Claudius, the emperor of Rome. When his stepfather <u>adopted him; Nero</u> became the official heir to the empire. Upon the death of Claudius, probably by poison administered by Agrippa, Nero, then sixteen years old, became emperor. 8

5.
   A. NO CHANGE
   B. have not been invented
   C. were not being invented
   D. were not inventing

6.
   F. NO CHANGE
   G. Since his father died, and his mother
   H. His father dying, his mother
   J. His father died and his mother

7.
   A. NO CHANGE
   B. adopted him Nero
   C. adopted him: Nero
   D. adopted him, Nero

8. The writer is considering adding the following sentence at this point in the paragraph:

   The first emperor of Rome was Augustus.

   Would this addition be appropriate here?

   F. Yes, because it clarifies Nero's role in the dynasty begun by Augustus.
   G. Yes, because it is a detail that provides information important to the topic.
   H. No, because it is not a relevant detail.
   J. No, because this sentence contradicts a point made earlier in the paragraph.

At first, under the tutelage of his mother and Seneca, Nero <u>originally appeared</u> to be a benign ruler, involved in fostering interest in theater, music, and the arts. He increased <u>trade, supported</u> athletic competitions. As his power and confidence increased, Nero disassociated himself from his mother and engaged in wilder pursuits. <u>Indeed,</u> his behavior became so erratic and characterized by excess indulgences in wicked activities that some thought him mad. He dismissed former advisors, <u>having his mother murdered and becoming</u> a cruel and ruthless dictator. Eventually, he even had his wife assassinated to make way for a new woman with whom he <u>had fallen</u> in love.

9.
   A. NO CHANGE
   B. appeared from the start
   C. appeared
   D. in the beginning appeared

10.
   F. NO CHANGE
   G. trade and supported
   H. trade and he supports
   J. trade, but he supported

11. For the sake of logic and coherence, which would be the best transitional phrase to use?
   A. NO CHANGE
   B. Nevertheless
   C. In contrast
   D. However

12.
   F. NO CHANGE
   G. have his mother murdered and become
   H. to have his mother murdered and to become
   J. had his mother murdered, and became

13.
   A. NO CHANGE
   B. has fell
   C. has fallen
   D. had fell

By 64 A.D., Nero's behavior had become totally outrageous. Then came the great fire in Rome. 14 A rumor started that while the fire burned and the citizens ran for their lives, the emperor climbed up on a distant rooftop and sang. From this apparent disregard for the lives of his people arose the tale that Nero fiddled while Rome burned. We may never know the truth, but we do know that he didn't actually fiddle. 15

14. Suppose the writer wants to add the following detail at this point in the essay:

According to the historian Tacitus, it was " … the most terrible and destructive fire which Rome had ever experienced."

Would this addition be appropriate here?

F. Yes, because the severity of the fire dramatizes the story of Nero's callousness.

G. Yes, because if it had not been a huge fire, the story of Nero would never have been known.

H. No, because the reader does not know if Tacitus is a reliable witness.

J. No, because Nero was not really playing the fiddle anyway.

Question 15 asks about the essay as a whole.

15. Suppose the writer had decided to write a scholarly essay delineating Nero's role in the history of the Roman Empire. Would this essay fulfill the writer's goal?

A. Yes, because the essay is scholarly in tone and provides accurate historical details.

B. Yes, because the essay fully explicates Nero's role in the history of the Roman Empire.

C. No, because so much of the essay is fictional and the tone is sarcastic rather than serious.

D. No, because the essay presents both historical and questionable information with a focus on Nero's reputation.

Passage II

Memories

Memories of my grandparents unravel like a reel of old 8-millimeter film. Some parts <u>are clear, the</u> <u>images intact</u> and decipherable. Others are fuzzy, transparent, and vague. They look like charcoal <u>drawings' that</u> have become smudged and faded with time. Whole sections are <u>missing: gaps appear</u> that account for the years when no memories exist.

The movie begins with impressions <u>due to the</u> <u>fact of a large</u> room with a wildly patterned carpet. My dad tells me <u>they were</u> the apartment my grandparents lived in when I was a young child. I have impressions of noise and laughter, food and

16. All of the following would be acceptable here
EXCEPT:

    F.   are clear: the images are intact
    G.   being clear with images that are intact
    H.   are clear, and the images are intact
    J.   are clear; the images are intact

17.
    A.   NO CHANGE
    B.   drawing's which
    C.   drawings, who
    D.   drawings that

18.
    F.   NO CHANGE
    G.   missing and gaps appear
    H.   missing with gaps that appear
    J.   missing gaps

19.
    A.   NO CHANGE
    B.   coming from a large
    C.   of a large
    D.   largely coming out of a

20.
    F.   NO CHANGE
    G.   they're
    H.   it's
    J.   this was

music. Then I hear a crackling sound as the film breaks, and there is nothing on the screen but white light. 21

I was only four years old when my grandparents retired and moved to Hibiscus Island, Florida, a mystical place of warmth and palm trees that existed in my imagination as a fantasy world of exotic plants and mysterious creatures. It was too costly and expensive to travel to visit them, and they
                    22
rarely ventured up north. I grew up without knowing that special bond between grandparents and the offspring of their offspring. 23

21. If the writer were to delete the preceding sentence, the essay would primarily lose:

   A. a thematic reference that provides a transition from this paragraph to the next one.
   B. a detail that explains why the grandparents moved to the south.
   C. a description of the movie that summarizes the points made previously.
   D. nothing at all since this sentence is not relevant to the rest of the paragraph.

22.
   F. NO CHANGE
   G. extravagant and costly
   H. expensive
   J. costly, so

23. The writer is considering replacing the period at the end of this sentence with a comma and adding the following information to the sentence.

   that unconditional love that never scolded or reprimanded.

   If the writer made this addition, the sentence would:

   A. gain an interesting point that clarifies and explains.
   B. lose a critical transition.
   C. distract the reader with contradictory information.
   D. present an inappropriate opinion.

The images emerge again with a hazy glow of color and sunlight as somehow my parents arranged a trip to Florida. The airplane ride unfolds as a series of crystal clear episodes as <u>my brothers and I</u>
₂₄
board the plane. I can recall the rumbling of the propellers, the sticky feel of the vinyl seats beneath my legs, the faint feeling of nausea as the plane <u>lands, and my</u> unbridled excitement as we walk
₂₅
down the steps off the plane, and I see my first palm tree. The house my grandparents lived in was just as magical as it had been in my mind. <u>Hibiscus flowers</u>
₂₆
<u>are in full bloom, and lemon trees and banana trees</u>
₂₆
<u>grow in the backyard; in a moment of sense memory,</u>
₂₆
<u>I can smell the tang of lemons in the air.</u> The movie
₂₆
speeds up as kaleidoscopic impressions crowd together. My grandparents welcome us, <u>but being</u>
₂₇
<u>that they</u> are just two old people who are strangers
₂₇
to me. I feel that I should know them, but there have been no shared experiences to create a bond. <u>Nevertheless,</u> we have fun as together we stroll on
₂₈
beaches that are white and soft and gather seashells to take home.

24.
- **F.** NO CHANGE
- **G.** my brothers and me
- **H.** myself and my brothers
- **J.** my brothers with myself

25.
- **A.** NO CHANGE
- **B.** lands; my
- **C.** landing and my
- **D.** lands with my

26. Given that all of the choices are true, which BEST conveys the sense of "magical"?
- **F.** NO CHANGE
- **G.** The hibiscus flowers that grow all over the island have given it the name Hibiscus Island.
- **H.** My grandfather was an avid gardener who liked to cultivate fruit trees in his yard.
- **J.** I never knew that bananas grow upside down on a plant and that lemons aren't always yellow.

27.
- **A.** NO CHANGE
- **B.** but they
- **C.** however, they
- **D.** they

28.
- **F.** NO CHANGE
- **G.** Thus,
- **H.** Consequently,
- **J.** Moreover,

From the <u>street vendors stands,</u> we buy strange
                        29
foods, briny clams, and creamy frozen custard.

And then it is over. The film snaps and the movie

ends. [30]

Passage III

A Russian Jewel

Tourists preparing for their first trip to Russia

may imagine dreary, gray cinder-block buildings

<u>with poorly, and badly paved</u> ice-covered streets.
                        31
They may envision a land populated by men wearing

fur hats and women with babushkas <u>(brightly
                                            32
printed head scarves)</u> and peasant dress. True, parts
         32
of Russia do resemble this portrait, but certainly

not the city of St. Petersburg, formerly named

Leningrad. Founded by Tsar Peter I, and the capital

of Russia until 1918, <u>tourists will discover that
                                    33
St. Petersburg</u> is located on Neva Bay in the Gulf of
   33

29.
- **A.** NO CHANGE
- **B.** street's vendor's stands,
- **C.** street vendors stand's
- **D.** street vendors' stands,

30. Which of the following sentences, if included here, would best conclude the essay?
- **F.** It wasn't a real movie, but just a dream that I had.
- **G.** It is so important for a child to have grandparents in his or her life.
- **H.** My brothers have completely different memories of the role my grandparents played in our lives.
- **J.** I don't get the satisfaction of a happy ending, or any ending, for we never get the chance to meet again.

31.
- **A.** NO CHANGE
- **B.** with poorly paved
- **C.** both poorly and badly paved
- **D.** surrounded with poorly, paved

32. The writer is considering deleting the parenthetical information. If this change was made, the paragraph would primarily lose
- **F.** a personal comment
- **G.** an explanatory detail
- **H.** a historical footnote
- **J.** a colorful metaphor

33.
- **A.** NO CHANGE
- **B.** tourists, visiting St. Petersburg, which
- **C.** it is St. Petersburg that
- **D.** St. Petersburg

Finland, this historically and architecturally rich
₃₄

city is reminiscent of a colder, more northern Venice.

First, one is struck by the beauty of the
waterways, the Neva River and its tributaries that
crisscross the city. Bridges that traverse the small
₃₅

rivers and canals and connect the islands that house

some of the oldest buildings in the city. On warm

summer weekends, residents who gather on the
₃₆

shores of some of the nearly one hundred islands to

sunbathe and swim. Because of the city's northern
₃₇

latitude, summer twilight can last until midnight.
₃₇

The beauty of the physical setting is matched by

the magnificence of the baroque and neoclassical

architecture. Perhaps the best known and most
₃₈

famous museum in the world and one of the largest:
₃₈   ₃₉

the Hermitage is the official state museum of
₃₉

34.
- **F.** NO CHANGE
- **G.** Finland; this
- **H.** Finland. For example,
- **J.** Finland, however,

35.
- **A.** NO CHANGE
- **B.** Bridges traverse
- **C.** Bridges, traverse the
- **D.** Bridges that are traversing

36.
- **F.** NO CHANGE
- **G.** Omit underlined part
- **H.** which
- **J.** that

37. Which of the following would NOT be an acceptable replacement for the underlined part?
- **A.** As the city is located in a northern latitude,
- **B.** Being that the city is very far north,
- **C.** Since the city is far north,
- **D.** Just as in other cities in northern latitudes,

38.
- **F.** NO CHANGE
- **G.** most famously known
- **H.** best known
- **J.** most known and famous

39.
- **A.** NO CHANGE
- **B.** largest; the
- **C.** largest. The
- **D.** largest, the

St. Petersburg, its collection, housed in several
40

buildings, numbers over three million masterpieces

including works by Leonardo da Vinci, Michelangelo,

Rembrandt, Renoir, Cezanne, Manet, and

Monet. 41 The most spectacular museum building

and one of the biggest tourist attractions are the
42

Winter Palace, founded by Catherine the Great,

an avid collector of art. The museum's coffers were
43

enriched by wartime acquisitions as the Red Army

marched through Germany and appropriated assets

as they passed. In addition to the Hermitage, the

Stock Exchange, the Summer Garden and Summer

Palace of Peter the Great, and Palace Square are

breathtaking examples of opulent edifices.

40.
  F. NO CHANGE
  G. St. Petersburg; whose
  H. St. Petersburg's collection
  J. St. Petersburg. Its

41. At this point, the writer wants to add a
    sentence that indicates the extraordinary
    nature of the museum's collection. Which
    alternative would best fulfill the writer's goal?

  A. Claude Monet was the founder of the
      French Impressionist movement.
  B. The collection contains exquisite
      examples of art that encompass the
      entire history of mankind, from ancient
      treasures to contemporary works.
  C. Located on the banks of the River Neva,
      the museum fills ten buildings with
      works of art.
  D. Tourists wait in line, sometimes for
      hours, to visit the museum's collections
      of fine artwork.

42.
  F. NO CHANGE
  G. attractions is
  H. attractions were
  J. attractions being

43. Which choice best shows that Catherine the
    Great was passionate about collecting art?

  A. NO CHANGE
  B. a collector of art
  C. a strong and materialistic queen
  D. who loved to decorate her palaces

The center of St. Petersburg also holds attractions for tourists. Visitors and natives alike love to shop on the most famous street in the city, Nevsky Prospekt. 44

This truly magnificent Russian city, with exquisite churches, impressive monuments, and breathtaking physical beauty, will remain an indelible memory to all who visit this vibrant metropolis. 45

44. Given that all of the following are true, which would be the most appropriate to add on to the preceding sentence to fulfill the writer's goal of highlighting the importance of this street? (Change the period to a comma first.)

F. St. Petersburg's main avenue and one of the best-known streets in Russia.

G. known at the beginning of the twentieth century as Avenue of the 25th of October.

H. prospekt being the Russian equivalent of avenue.

J. extending from the Admiralty to the railway station.

Question 45 asks about the essay as a whole.

45. Suppose the writer's goal had been to write an essay about those cities in Russia that exemplify baroque architecture. Does this essay fulfill that goal?

A. Yes, because the writer discusses the specific characteristics of the baroque style.

B. Yes, because the writer describes St. Petersburg as a uniquely baroque city.

C. No, because the essay is an overview of the attractions of a single city.

D. No, because the writer never fully discusses the architecture of this particular city.

Passage IV

The Artist

Rosa Bonheur was the best pupil of her father, Raymond B. Bonheur. In Bordeaux, France, they lived together the peaceful life of artists. <u>Her father being already</u> a well-known painter when his daugh-
46
ter was born. After a time, the Bonheurs moved to Paris where young Rosa could have better <u>opportunities; it was there</u> that she put on men's
47
clothing, which she wore for the rest of her life. She wore a workingman's blouse and trousers and tramped about looking more like a man than a woman with her short hair. This made everybody stare at her <u>and think her very odd</u>. It was then that
48
her enemies, <u>mostly those who were both jealous or</u>
49
<u>envious</u> of her work, said that she dressed in this
49
manner in order to attract attention. Today, most people <u>now believe</u> she dressed so because it was the
50
most comfortable and convenient costume for her.

46.
F. NO CHANGE
G. Her father was
H. Her father was being
J. Her father, being

47.
A. NO CHANGE
B. opportunities, it was there
C. opportunities which she had; it was there
D. opportunities; there

48.
F. NO CHANGE
G. and they had thought she was odd
H. to think her very odd
J. which made them think she was very odd

49.
A. NO CHANGE
B. most of them who were jealous
C. those whom were jealous and envious
D. mostly those who were jealous

50.
F. NO CHANGE
G. believe now
H. believe
J. have believed

She went to all sorts of places; the stockyards, slaughter houses, and all around the streets of Paris—to learn of things and people, especially of animals, which she wished most to paint. She could hardly have traveled so free had she worn women's clothing.

Rosa Bonheur exhibited her first painting in 1841, twelve years before her beloved father died; thus, he would have had the happiness of knowing that the daughter whom he had taught so lovingly was on the road to success and fortune. That year she painted only two little pictures—one of rabbits, the other of sheep and goats—but they were so splendidly done that all the critics knew a great female artist had arrived.

Soon her work began to be bought by the French Government, which was a sure sign of her power. She was already much beloved by the people. In the meantime, art lovers in America and others in England had heard of Mademoiselle Bonheur, but heard far less about her painting as about her

51.
A. NO CHANGE
B. places—the stockyards,
C. places; the stockyards;
D. places, she went to the stockyards,

52.
F. NO CHANGE
G. traveled with the freedom
H. traveled so freely
J. been traveling so free

53.
A. NO CHANGE
B. had
C. would of had
D. had to have

54. Which of the following alternatives to the underlined portion would NOT be acceptable?
F. pictures (one of rabbits, the other of sheep and goats), but
G. pictures, one of rabbits and the other of sheep and goats, but
H. pictures one of rabbits and the other of sheep and goats but
J. pictures: one of rabbits and one of sheep and goats. However,

55.
A. NO CHANGE
B. rather than
C. as than
D. than

masculine garb. She was considered mostly an

eccentric <u>woman, however</u> once the art world saw
₅₆

her great painting, "The Horse Fair," the artist was

no longer judged by the clothes she wore but by her

art. [57] Finally, she received the cross of the Legion

of Honour and was made a member of the Institute

of Antwerp.

Rosa Bonheur lived near Fontainebleau until the

Franco-Prussian War broke out. Then she and

others <u>began to fear</u> that her studio and pictures
₅₈

would be destroyed, <u>and</u> the artist stopped her work
₅₉

and prepared to go elsewhere. But the Crown Prince

of Prussia himself ordered that Mademoiselle

Bonheur should not even be disturbed. Her work

had made her belong to all the world, and <u>all the</u>
₆₀

<u>world would protect her</u> if need be.
₆₀

56.
F. NO CHANGE
G. woman: however
H. woman however,
J. woman; however,

57. In the preceding sentence, the writer would like to underscore the change in the public's attitude toward Rosa Bonheur. Which of the following choices would best accomplish that goal?

A. Leave the sentence as it is now.

OR replace the sentence with one of the choices below:
B. When the people saw "The Horse Fair," they knew Rosa Bonheur was a great painter of animals.
C. Rosa Bonheur did not enjoy a good reputation as an artist because many people thought her weird.
D. In public, Rosa Bonheur's behavior caused a scandal, but in private, she was a serious artist.

58.
F. NO CHANGE
G. have begun to fear
H. begin fearing
J. are beginning to fear

59.
A. NO CHANGE
B. omit this word
C. because
D. so

60.
F. NO CHANGE
G. the entire population of the people of the world were willing to protect her
H. all the other people would protect her
J. protecting her would be done by all the world

Passage V

A Divine Dessert

[1]

Chocolate—just the word ignites cravings that cannot be satisfied until one consumes a piece of the smooth, silky confection. What is it about chocolate that ignites such passion in the hearts of self-confessed "chocoholics"? Some researchers say the response is purely physical: It is the caffeine that is present in chocolate that <u>provide</u> the feeling of
₆₁
pleasure that is <u>associated to</u> indulging in a rich
₆₂
piece of chocolate. Others attribute the sense of well-being to the presence of chemicals like theobromine, a mild stimulant. Whatever it is, for many, chocolate is undeniably addicting.

[2]

Chocolate has a fascinating history. It begins with the Maya <u>who are people who live</u> in the
₆₃
rainforests of South America. <u>No one know</u> exactly
₆₄
when, but about 2,000 years ago, these ancient people discovered that when they harvested the fruit

61.
- **A.** NO CHANGE
- **B.** providing
- **C.** provides
- **D.** provided

62.
- **F.** NO CHANGE
- **G.** associated for
- **H.** associated in
- **J.** associated with

63.
- **A.** NO CHANGE
- **B.** Omit underlined portion
- **C.** whom lived
- **D.** the name of the people who lived

64.
- **F.** NO CHANGE
- **G.** No one knows
- **H.** No one who knows
- **J.** Not knowing

of the cacao tree, roasted the seeds, <u>and they ground</u>
⁶⁵
the seeds to a paste, and mixed this paste with water

and spices, they would have a frothy and spicy

beverage. This drink played an important role in

their social activities and in <u>the religious rituals</u>
⁶⁶
<u>performed by them</u>.
⁶⁶

[3]

Like any other novelty, chocolate inspired

invention and creativity. Using their culinary skills,

<u>chocolate began to be used by chefs</u> to flavor pastries
⁶⁷
and desserts. A dramatic change came about <u>in 1828</u>
⁶⁸
when the Dutch chocolate maker van Houten

developed a machine that reduced the cocoa butter

in the cacao bean and pressed it into a disc shape.

This led to the evolution of the chocolate <u>bar, and,</u>
⁶⁹
<u>as they say,</u> "the rest is history."
⁶⁹

65.
   A. NO CHANGE
   B. and grinding
   C. they ground
   D. ground

66.
   F. NO CHANGE
   G. their religious rituals
   H. those religious rituals that were performed by them
   J. performing religious rituals

67.
   A. NO CHANGE
   B. chocolate was used by chefs
   C. chefs began the use of chocolate
   D. chefs began to use chocolate

68. Which of the following would NOT be an acceptable placement for the underlined phrase?

   F. where it is now
   G. at the beginning of the sentence (before *A dramatic change*).
   H. after *van Houten*
   J. after *butter*

69.
   A. NO CHANGE
   B. bar; and as they say;
   C. bar and, as, they say,
   D. bar, and as they say

[4]

Credit for bringing chocolate to Europe is usually given to Christopher Columbus. <u>Moreover,</u> 70 chocolate did not become an overnight sensation. It was not until Spanish chefs replaced the chili pepper used by the Maya with sugar that chocolate beverages became popular. At first, this <u>drink was a</u> 71 <u>luxury,</u> for only the wealthy elite could afford to 71 purchase it from Spanish merchants. Spain's exclusive hold on chocolate, however, did not last. Other European countries <u>began cultivating</u> the 72 cacao tree in their colonies, and soon the common people were able to enjoy the taste of chocolate.

[5]

Although chocolate has been accused of every "health crime" under the sun including causing acne, tooth decay, and obesity, recent studies have <u>touted the benefits</u> of consuming chocolate. 73 Scientists have discovered that chocolate can reduce

70.
F. NO CHANGE
G. However,
H. Clearly,
J. Despite this,

71.
A. NO CHANGE
B. drink was a high-priced item
C. drink was luxurious
D. drink was over the top

72.
F. NO CHANGE
G. began to cultivate
H. began the cultivation for
J. began in the cultivation of

73. Which of the following would NOT be an acceptable replacement for the underlined portion?

A. publicized the positive qualities
B. laid on thick the good points
C. promoted the advantages
D. announced the healthful nature

high blood pressure and <u>is contributing</u> to overall
74

heart health. For true chocolate-lovers, however, the

most important benefit is how chocolate makes

them feel when they indulge. A piece of good dark

chocolate or rich milk chocolate melting on the

tongue is one of life's simple pleasures. 75

74.
- **F.** NO CHANGE
- **G.** contribute
- **H.** be a contributor
- **J.** make a contribution

Question 75 asks about the essay as a whole.

75. For the sake of the logic and coherence of
this essay, paragraph 4 would be best placed:

- **A.** where it is now.
- **B.** after paragraph 5.
- **C.** before paragraph 2.
- **D.** before paragraph 3.

IF YOU FINISH BEFORE TIME IS CALLED, CHECK YOUR WORK ON THIS
SECTION ONLY. DO NOT WORK ON ANY OTHER SECTION IN THE TEST.

Section 2: Mathematics Test

60 Minutes—60 Questions

Directions: Solve each problem and fill in the corresponding circle on the answer sheet. Figures are not necessarily drawn to scale. You may use a permitted graphing calculator.

1. For all values of x, which of the following is equivalent to $(x^2 - 3) - (4x^2 - 5x + 1)$?

   A. $-3x^2 - 5x - 2$
   B. $-3x^2 - 5x + 4$
   C. $-3x^2 + 5x - 4$
   D. $3x^2 - 5x - 2$
   E. $3x^2 - 5x + 4$

2. In the accompanying diagram, what is the value of x?

   F. 15
   G. 30
   H. 45
   J. 60
   K. 90

3. If $\dfrac{3}{ab} = 6$, then $ab =$

   A. $\dfrac{1}{18}$

   B. $\dfrac{1}{6}$

   C. $\dfrac{1}{2}$

   D. 2
   E. 18

4. In the accompanying figure, $\overline{BD}$ and $\overline{AE}$ intersect at point C, and $AB = AC$. If $m\angle DCE = 40$, what is the measure of $\angle A$?

   F. 40
   G. 60
   H. 80
   J. 100
   K. 120

5. If $2(4^k) = 2^5$, what is the value of k?

   A. 0
   B. 1
   C. 2
   D. 3
   E. 4

6. Two similar triangles have perimeters 16 and 36, respectively. If the shortest side of the smaller triangle is 4, what is the length of the shortest side of the larger triangle?

   F. 3
   G. 6
   H. 9
   J. 12
   K. 18

7. Given the sequence 7, 11, 15, 19, ... , what is the 8th term of the sequence?

   A. 31
   B. 35
   C. 39
   D. 56
   E. 60

8. Karen took 4 math tests and her scores were 96, 85, 92, and 99. What is the sum of the mean and median scores of the 4 tests?

   F. 183
   G. 185
   H. 186
   J. 187
   K. 189

9. For all values of $x \neq 0$, which of the following is equivalent to $\dfrac{2x^4 + 6x^2 - 4x}{2x}$?

   A. $x^3 + 6x^2 - 4x$
   B. $x^3 + 6x - 4$
   C. $x^3 - 3x + 2$
   D. $x^3 + 3x - 2$
   E. 48

10. What is the largest 3-digit integer that is divisible by 11?

    F. 911
    G. 979
    H. 990
    J. 993
    K. 999

11. If a square and an equilateral triangle have the same perimeter, and the area of the square is 36, what is the length of a side of the triangle?

    A. 4
    B. 6
    C. 8
    D. 10
    E. 12

12. In the xy-plane, the point $(-12,k)$ lies on the line $2x - 3y = 6$. What is the value of k?

    F. -10
    G. -6
    H. 6
    J. 10
    K. 15

13. If 50% of k is 20, what is $\dfrac{1}{4}$ of k?

    A. $\dfrac{5}{2}$
    B. 5
    C. 10
    D. 40
    E. 160

14. On a coordinate plane, two lines l and m are parallel. If an equation of line l is $y = 2x - 4$, which of the following could be an equation of line m?

    F. $y + 2x = 4$
    G. $y + 2x = -4$
    H. $y - 2x = 0$
    J. $y = \dfrac{1}{2}x - 4$
    K. $y = -\dfrac{1}{2}x - 4$

15. For all real values of x, which of the following is equivalent to $(2x - 3)(x + 1)$?

    A. $2x^2 - 3$
    B. $2x^2 - 5x - 3$
    C. $2x^2 - x + 3$
    D. $2x^2 - x - 3$
    E. $2x^2 + x - 3$

16. On a coordinate plane diagram, the vertices of $\triangle ABC$ are $A(-1,-1)$, $B(3,-1)$, and $C(3,3)$. What is the measure of $\angle ACB$?

    F. 15
    G. 30
    H. 45
    J. 60
    K. 75

17. If $abc = 0$ and $bcd = 1$, which of the following must be true?

    I. $a = 0$
    II. $bc > 0$
    III. $d = 1$

    A. I only
    B. II only
    C. III only
    D. I and II only
    E. I, II, and III

18. The function $p(x)$ is defined as $p(x) = \sqrt{x}$. If $p(4k) = 8$, what is the value of k?

    F. 2
    G. 4
    H. 8
    J. 16
    K. 32

19. If the sum of three consecutive even integers is 138, what is the numerical value of the middle integer?

    A. 40
    B. 42
    C. 44
    D. 46
    E. 48

20. What is the slope of the line whose x-intercept is -3 and whose y-intercept is 4?

    F. $\dfrac{-4}{3}$

    G. $\dfrac{-3}{4}$

    H. $\dfrac{3}{4}$

    J. $\dfrac{4}{3}$

    K. cannot be determined

21. Set $A = \{-4, -2, 0, 2, 4\}$ and Set $B = \{1, 3, 5, 7\}$. What is the sum of the medians of Set A and Set B?

    A. 1
    B. 2
    C. 3
    D. 4
    E. 5

22. What positive integer has the property such that six more than twice the number is the same as four times the number?

    F. -3
    G. -1
    H. 1
    J. 3
    K. 6

23. Which of the following is equivalent to $x^2 - 8x + 12$ for all values of x?

    A. $(x - 2)(x - 4)$
    B. $(x - 2)(x - 6)$
    C. $(x - 10)(x + 2)$
    D. $(x - 2)(x + 10)$
    E. $-(x + 2)(x + 6)$

24. Mary bought two kinds of pens. One kind cost $2 each, and the other cost $3 each. If Mary spent a total of $48 on the pens, and she bought twice as many of the more expensive pens than of the cheaper pens, how many of the $2 pens did Mary buy?

    F.   2
    G. 4
    H. 5
    J. 6
    K. 8

25. Which of the following is a solution to the equation $x^2 + 9 = 6x$?

    A. −6
    B. −3
    C. 0
    D. 3
    E. 9

26. In the accompanying diagram, $y = g(x)$. How many values of x is $g(x) = 3$?

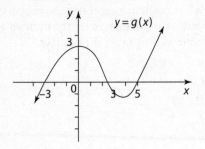

    F. 0
    G. 1
    H. 2
    J. 3
    K. 4

27. Karen has 3 quarters, 4 dimes, 6 nickels, and 2 pennies in her bag. If she takes a coin at random from her bag, what is the probability that the coin is NOT a quarter?

    A. $\dfrac{1}{15}$

    B. $\dfrac{1}{5}$

    C. $\dfrac{3}{5}$

    D. $\dfrac{11}{15}$

    E. $\dfrac{4}{5}$

28. If the point $M(2,-4)$ is the midpoint of a line segment whose endpoints are $A(6,2)$ and $B(h,k)$, what is the value of k?

    F. −12
    G. −10
    H. −2
    J. −1
    K. 10

29. If a and b are positive integers such that $0 < a \le 3$ and $0 < b \le 3$, how many different numerical values are possible for the fraction $\dfrac{a}{b}$?

    A. 5
    B. 6
    C. 7
    D. 8
    E. 9

30. Which of the following is an even function?

    F. $y = 2x - 1$
    G. $y = 4x + 2$
    H. $y = (x - 2)^4$
    J. $y = x^2 - 3$
    K. $y = x^2 - 4x - 12$

31. In the accompanying diagram, the figure is a rectangular prism. If $HG = 8$, $FG = 4$, $CG = 2$, and n is the midpoint of HG, what is the length of $\overline{AN}$?

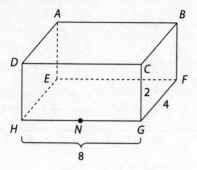

A. 4
B. 6
C. 12
D. 18
E. 36

32. If the distance between $A(-2,5)$ and $B(6,k)$ is 8, what is the value of k?

F. −5
G. 2
H. 5
J. 10
K. 25

33. If $\dfrac{m}{n} = -2$, what is the value of $2\left(\dfrac{m}{n}\right)^2$?

A. −16
B. −8
C. 6
D. 8
E. 16

34. If $3k - 2$ is divided by 4, the remainder is 2. Which of the following could be the value of k?

F. 1
G. 2
H. 3
J. 4
K. 5

35. In the complex numbers, where $i = \sqrt{-1}$, which of the following is equivalent to $(1 + 3i)(1 - i)$?

A. −3
B. 5
C. −2 + 4i
D. 4 + 2i
E. −4 + 2i

36. In the accompanying diagram, the equation of the circle is $x^2 + y^2 = 9$ and the equation of the line is $y = 2x$. Which of the following sets of inequalities define the shaded region?

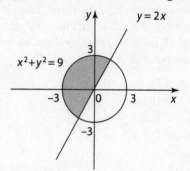

F. $y = 2x$ and $x^2 + y^2 = 9$
G. $y < 2x$ and $x^2 + y^2 > 9$
H. $y < 2x$ and $x^2 + y^2 < 9$
J. $y > 2x$ and $x^2 + y^2 < 9$
K. $y > 2x$ and $x^2 + y^2 > 9$

37. Set $A = \{-3, -1, 0\}$ and Set $B = \{-1, 0, 1, 3\}$. If a number is randomly picked from Set A, what is the probability that the number picked is NOT a number of Set B?

A. $\dfrac{1}{7}$

B. $\dfrac{3}{7}$

C. $\dfrac{1}{3}$

D. $\dfrac{1}{2}$

E. $\dfrac{3}{4}$

275

38. If $(2x)^2 < 2x$, then which of the following could be a value of x?

   F. $\dfrac{1}{4}$

   G. $\dfrac{1}{2}$

   H. $\dfrac{3}{4}$

   J.   1

   K.   2

39. The average height of Janet, Karen, and Mary is 5 ft 4 in. Karen is 5 ft 6 in tall, and she is the tallest of the three. Janet is the shortest. If no two girls have the same height and all heights are integral inches, what is the least possible height for Janet?

   A.   5 ft
   B.   5 ft 1 in
   C.   5 ft 2 in
   D.   5 ft 3 in
   E.   5 ft 6 in

40. If y is a positive integer, $y = x^2$ and $x = -y^2$, what is the value of y?

   F. -2
   G. -1
   H.   0
   J.   1
   K.   2

Use the following information to answer questions 41–43.

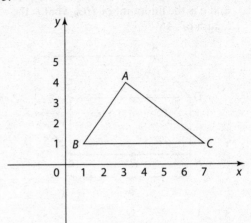

In the accompanying figure, $\triangle ABC$ is shown with vertices $A(3,4)$, $B(1,1)$, and $C(7,1)$.

41. If line l (not shown) is perpendicular to $\overline{AB}$, what is the slope of line l?

   A. $\dfrac{-3}{2}$

   B. $\dfrac{-2}{3}$

   C. $\dfrac{-1}{5}$

   D. $\dfrac{2}{3}$

   E. $\dfrac{3}{2}$

42. If $\triangle A'B'C'$ is the image of $\triangle ABC$ reflected in the x-axis, which of the following are the coordinates of A'?

   F. $(-3,-4)$
   G. $(-3,4)$
   H. $(-4,3)$
   J. $(3,-4)$
   K. $(4,-3)$

43. If $\Delta A''B''C''$ is the image of ΔABC under a dilation of 2 about the origin, what is the area of $\Delta A''B''C''$ in square units?

   A. $4\dfrac{1}{2}$
   B. 9
   C. 18
   D. 36
   E. 72

44. The vertices of a triangle are $M(-1,-2)$, $N(-1,4)$, and $P(3,4)$. What is the area of ΔMNP?

   F. 5
   G. 10
   H. 12
   J. 20
   K. 24

45. If $\cos\theta = \dfrac{-12}{13}$ and $\pi < \theta < \dfrac{3\pi}{2}$, what is the value of $\sin\theta$?

   A. $\dfrac{-13}{5}$
   B. $\dfrac{-5}{13}$
   C. $\dfrac{5}{13}$
   D. $\dfrac{5}{12}$
   E. $\dfrac{12}{13}$

46. In the accompanying diagram, $AB = 14$, $m\angle ABC = 30°$, and $m\angle C = 90°$. What is the length of $\overline{AC}$?

   F. 7
   G. $7\sqrt{2}$
   H. $7\sqrt{3}$
   J. $14\sqrt{2}$
   K. $14\sqrt{3}$

47. If every student in Mrs. Smith's class is on the honor roll, which of the following statements must be true?

   A. If John is on the honor roll, he is in Mrs. Smith's class.
   B. If Mary is not on the honor roll, she is not in Mrs. Smith's class.
   C. If George is not in Mrs. Smith's class, he is not on the honor roll.
   D. If Nancy is in Mrs. Smith's class, she is not on the honor roll.
   E. If Jean is not in Mrs. Smith's class, she is on the honor roll.

48. What is the surface area of a sphere, in square inches, if the volume of the sphere is 288π cubic inches?

   F. 36π
   G. 144π
   H. 288π
   J. 384π
   K. 845π

49. The graph of a function $y = f(x)$ is shown in the accompanying figure. Which of the following could be the function f?

A. $y = \cos 4x$
B. $y = -4 \cos x$
C. $y = 2 \cos 4x$
D. $y = 4\cos\dfrac{x}{2}$
E. $y = 4 \cos 2x$

50. In an xy-coordinate plane, point C with coordinates $(4,0)$ is the center of a circle and point A with coordinates $(4,5)$ is on the circle. Which of the following could be the coordinates of point B, if B is also a point on the circle?

F. $(-3,4)$
G. $(0,0)$
H. $(1,4)$
J. $(4,3)$
K. $(4,10)$

51. If $-3 \le p \le -1$ and $-2 \le q \le 2$, which of the following represents all possible values of pq?

A. $-6 \le pq \le -2$
B. $-5 \le pq \le 1$
C. $-2 \le pq \le 6$
D. $-2 \le pq \le 2$
E. $-6 \le pq \le 6$

52. In the accompanying diagram, $DE = 6$, $EF = 10$, and $m\angle E = 40$. The length of $\overline{DF}$ is given by which of the following expressions?

F. 8
G. $6 \sin 40°$
H. $10 \tan 40°$
J. $6^2 + 10^2 - 2(6)(10) \cos 40°$
K. $\sqrt{36 + 100 - 120 \cos 40°}$

53. In the accompanying diagram, two concentric circles have O as their centers, $\overline{OA}$ is a radius of the larger circle, and $AB = 2$. If the circumference of the larger circle is 16π, what is the circumference of the smaller circle?

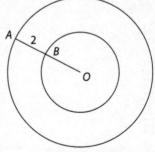

Not drawn to scale

A. 4π
B. 8π
C. 10π
D. 12π
E. 14π

54. A recreational fishing boat charges $20 per adult and $10 per child for a 4-hour fishing trip, plus $2 per fish caught during the trip. If a family of two adults and three children went fishing on the boat, and at the end of the trip paid a total charge of $82, how many fish did the family catch?

   F.   1
   G.   4
   H.   6
   J.   8
   K.   21

55. If $\log A = h$ and $\log B = k$, what is the value of $\log\left(\dfrac{A^2}{B}\right)$ in terms of h and k?

   A. $h^2 - k$
   B. $2h - k$
   C. $2h + k$
   D. $\dfrac{h^2}{k}$
   E. $h^2 + k$

56. What is the matrix product $\begin{bmatrix} -2 & 1 \end{bmatrix}\begin{bmatrix} 3 \\ -4 \end{bmatrix}$?

   F. $\begin{bmatrix} -6 & -4 \end{bmatrix}$
   G. $[-2]$
   H. $[-10]$
   J. $[2]$
   K. $\begin{bmatrix} -6 \\ -4 \end{bmatrix}$

57. In the accompanying diagram, $ACDE$ is a rectangle and the region above the rectangle is a semicircle. If the area of the rectangle is 32 and the length of $\overline{CD}$ is twice the length of $\overline{ED}$, what is the perimeter of the figure $ABCDE$?

   A.   20
   B.   24
   C. $20 + 2\pi$
   D. $20 + 4\pi$
   E. $24 + 4\pi$

58. In the accompanying figure, $ABCD$ is a rhombus with diagonals $\overline{BD}$ and $\overline{AC}$ intersecting at E. If $BC = 8$ and $AC = 8$, what is the $m\angle ADE$?

   F.   20
   G.   30
   H.   40
   J.   50
   K.   60

59. What positive integer has the property such that the square of the number is the same as twice the number?

    A.   −2
    B.   0
    C.   2
    D.   4
    E.   6

60. The accompanying graph summarizes the sales of a company over 6 years. Between which 2 years is the increase in sales the greatest?

    F.   '08–'09
    G.   '09–'10
    H.   '10–'11
    J.   '11–'12
    K.   '12–'13

IF YOU FINISH BEFORE TIME IS CALLED, CHECK YOUR WORK ON THIS SECTION ONLY. DO NOT WORK ON ANY OTHER SECTION IN THE TEST.

Section 3: Reading Test

35 Minutes—40 Questions

Directions: The Reading Test consists of four passages, each followed by 10 questions. After reading a passage, select the best answer and fill in the corresponding circle on the answer sheet. You may look back in the passages as you answer the questions.

Passage I

Prose Fiction

The following is an excerpt from the novel *A Room with a View* written by E.M. Forster in 1908. Lucy Honeychurch and Miss Bartlett are traveling through Italy together.

"The Signora had no business to do it," said Miss Bartlett, "no business at all. She promised us south rooms with a view close together, instead of which here are north (5) rooms, looking into a courtyard, and a long way apart. Oh, Lucy!"

"And a Cockney, besides!" said Lucy, who had been further saddened by the Signora's unexpected accent. "It might be London." She (10) looked at the two rows of English people who were sitting at the table; at the row of white bottles of water and red bottles of wine that ran between the English people; at the portraits of the late Queen and the late Poet (15) Laureate that hung behind the English people, heavily framed; at the notice of the English church (Rev. Cuthbert Eager, M. A. Oxon.), that was the only other decoration of the wall. "Charlotte, don't you feel, too, that we might (20) be in London? I can hardly believe that all kinds of other things are just outside. I suppose it is one's being so tired."

"This meat has surely been used for soup," said Miss Bartlett, laying down her fork.

(25) "I want so to see the Arno. The rooms the Signora promised us in her letter would have looked over the Arno. The Signora had no business to do it at all. Oh, it is a shame!"

"Any nook does for me," Miss Bartlett con-(30) tinued; "but it does seem hard that you shouldn't have a view."

Lucy felt that she had been selfish. "Charlotte, you mustn't spoil me: of course, you must look over the Arno, too. I meant (35) that. The first vacant room in the front—"

"You must have it," said Miss Bartlett, part of whose travelling expenses were paid by Lucy's mother—a piece of generosity to which she made many a tactful allusion.

(40) "No, no. You must have it."

"I insist on it. Your mother would never forgive me, Lucy."

"She would never forgive me."

The ladies' voices grew animated, and—if (45) the sad truth be owned—a little peevish. They were tired, and under the guise of unselfishness they wrangled. Some of their neighbours interchanged glances, and one of them—one of the ill-bred people whom one does meet (50) abroad—leant forward over the table and actually intruded into their argument. He said:

"I have a view, I have a view."

Miss Bartlett was startled. Generally at a pension people looked them over for a day or (55) two before speaking, and often did not find out that they would "do" till they had gone. She knew that the intruder was ill-bred, even before she glanced at him. He was an old man, of heavy build, with a fair, shaven face and (60) large eyes. There was something childish in those eyes, though it was not the childishness of senility. What exactly it was Miss Bartlett did not stop to consider, for her glance passed on to his clothes. These did not attract her. He

(65) was probably trying to become acquainted with them before they got into the swim. So she assumed a dazed expression when he spoke to her, and then said: "A view? Oh, a view! How delightful a view is!"

(70) "This is my son," said the old man; "his name's George. He has a view too."

"Ah," said Miss Bartlett, repressing Lucy, who was about to speak.

"What I mean," he continued, "is that you (75) can have our rooms, and we'll have yours. We'll change."

The better class of tourist was shocked at this, and sympathized with the new-comers. Miss Bartlett, in reply, opened her mouth as (80) little as possible, and said "Thank you very much indeed; that is out of the question."

"Why?" said the old man, with both fists on the table.

"Because it is quite out of the question, (85) thank you."

"You see, we don't like to take—" began Lucy. Her cousin again repressed her.

"But why?" he persisted. "Women like looking at a view; men don't." And he (90) thumped with his fists like a naughty child, and turned to his son, saying, "George, persuade them!"

"It's so obvious they should have the rooms," said the son. "There's nothing else to (95) say."

He did not look at the ladies as he spoke, but his voice was perplexed and sorrowful. Lucy, too, was perplexed; but she saw that they were in for what is known as "quite a (100) scene," and she had an odd feeling that whenever these ill-bred tourists spoke the contest widened and deepened till it dealt, not with rooms and views, but with—well, with something quite different, whose existence she had (105) not realized before. Now the old man attacked Miss Bartlett almost violently: Why should she not change? What possible objection had she? They would clear out in half an hour.

Miss Bartlett, though skilled in the delica- (110) cies of conversation, was powerless in the presence of brutality. It was impossible to snub any one so gross. Her face reddened with displeasure. She looked around as much as to say, "Are you all like this?" And two little old (115) ladies, who were sitting further up the table, with shawls hanging over the backs of the chairs, looked back, clearly indicating "We are not; we are genteel."

"Eat your dinner, dear," she said to Lucy, (120) and began to toy again with the meat that she had once censured.

Lucy mumbled that those seemed very odd people opposite.

"Eat your dinner, dear. This pension is a (125) failure. To-morrow we will make a change."

1. The main purpose of the passage is to:

   A. expose the hazards of traveling to foreign countries.
   B. defend the British subjects who transport their culture as they immigrate.
   C. reveal the class-consciousness of two women.
   D. confirm the snobbish pre-conceptions of British travelers toward their Italian hosts.

2. The effect of the repetition of the phrase "English people" in the second paragraph (lines 10–13) is to:

   F. suggest the Signora's belief that most tourists prefer the similar to the exotic.
   G. underscore the pervasive imperialism of the British Empire.
   H. contrast with the authenticity of the Signora's Italian accent.
   J. allude to the close cultural ties between Britain and Italy.

3. The relationship between Miss Bartlett and Lucy Honeychurch suggests:

   A. they are social equals on an educational mission.

   B. Miss Bartlett is a wealthy woman who has employed Lucy Honeychurch as a companion.

   C. the two women share a mutual dislike but are forced together by circumstances.

   D. Miss Bartlett acts as a chaperone and companion to Lucy Honeychurch.

4. The description of the "two little old ladies" (lines 114–118) implies that they:

   F. try to ignore and remain aloof from the scene erupting around them.

   G. sympathize with Lucy Honeychurch and Miss Bartlett as they cope with the embarrassment of ill-mannered companions.

   H. believe the kindness of George and his father should be rewarded.

   J. are perplexed by the many-layered social dimensions of the drama unfolding before them.

5. The attitudes of Lucy Honeychurch and Miss Bartlett toward the offer of a room exchange is best described as:

   A. suspicion toward the surprisingly forward outburst of the old man.

   B. warm appreciation of a generous suggestion.

   C. amusement at the chivalrous and gentlemanly offer.

   D. admiration for the courage of the old man to assert himself in such lofty company.

6. The author's use of the words "attacked" (line 105), "violently" (line 106), and "brutality" (line 111) suggests:

   F. the encounter in the pension epitomizes a clash of social values.

   G. the arrival of the new-comers is marred by a physical assault.

   H. the old man, a former soldier, is unable to cast off his propensity for violence.

   J. a foreshadowing of the impending hostility between those who have just arrived and those who have been in residence for some time.

7. Which of the following best describes Lucy Honeychurch's response to the old man as opposed to Miss Bartlett's?

   A. Lucy is confused while Miss Bartlett is affronted.

   B. Lucy is angry while Miss Bartlett is conciliatory.

   C. Lucy is amenable while Miss Bartlett is confused.

   D. Lucy is exhilarated while Miss Bartlett is indifferent.

8. All of the following contrasts are present in the passage EXCEPT:

   F. subtlety versus brutality

   G. politeness versus impropriety

   H. senility versus mental sharpness

   J. peevishness versus decorum

9. The author implies the "something quite different" (lines 103–104) refers to:

   A. social strata.

   B. nationalistic feeling.

   C. gender distinctions.

   D. imperialism.

10. The tone of the phrase "a piece of generosity to which she made many a tactful allusion" (lines 38–39) is best described as:

    F. didactic.
    G. sorrowful.
    H. strident.
    J. ironic.

Passage II

Social Science

The following passage is an excerpt from *Politics*, an essay written by Ralph Waldo Emerson in 1844.

The theory of politics which has possessed the mind of men, and which they have expressed the best they could in their laws and in their revolutions, considers persons
(5) and property as the two objects for whose protection government exists. Of persons, all have equal rights, in virtue of being identical in nature. This interest of course with its whole power demands a democracy. Whilst the rights
(10) of all as persons are equal, in virtue of their access to reason, their rights in property are very unequal. One man owns his clothes, and another owns a county. This accident, depending primarily on the skill and virtue of
(15) the parties, of which there is every degree, and secondarily on patrimony, falls unequally, and its rights of course are unequal. Personal rights, universally the same, demand a government framed on the ratio of the census;
(20) property demands a government framed on the ratio of owners and of owning. Laban,* who has flocks and herds, wishes them looked after by an officer on the frontiers … and pays a tax to that end. Jacob has no flocks or herds …
(25) and pays no tax to the officer. It seemed fit that

Laban: a biblical figure, brother-in-law to Isaac. Laban owns many sheep which are tended by his son-in-law, Jacob.

Laban and Jacob should have equal rights to elect the officer who is to defend their persons, but that Laban and not Jacob should elect the officer who is to guard the sheep and cattle.
(30) And if questions arise whether additional officers or watch-towers should be provided, must not Laban and Isaac, and those who must sell part of their herds to buy protection for the rest, judge better of this, and with more right,
(35) than Jacob, who, because he is a youth and a traveller, eats their bread and not his own?

In the earliest society the proprietors made their own wealth, and so long as it comes to the owners in the direct way, no other opinion
(40) would arise in any equitable community than that property should make the law for property, and persons the law for persons.

But property passes through donation or inheritance to those who do not create it. Gift,
(45) in one case, makes it as really the new owner's, as labor made it the first owner's: in the other case, of patrimony, the law makes an ownership which will be valid in each man's view according to the estimate which he sets on the
(50) public tranquillity.

It was not however found easy to embody the readily admitted principle that property should make law for property, and persons for persons; since persons and property mixed
(55) themselves in every transaction. At last it seemed settled that the rightful distinction was that the proprietors should have more elective franchise than non-proprietors, on the Spartan principle of "calling that which is just, equal;
(60) not that which is equal, just."

That principle no longer looks so self-evident as it appeared in former times, partly, because doubts have arisen whether too much weight had not been allowed in the laws to
(65) property, and such a structure given to our usages as allowed the rich to encroach on the poor, and to keep them poor; but mainly because there is an instinctive sense, however obscure and yet inarticulate, that the whole

(70) constitution of property, on its present tenures, is injurious, and its influence on persons deteriorating and degrading; that truly the only interest for the consideration of the State is persons; that property will always follow
(75) persons; that the highest end of government is the culture of men; and if men can be educated, the institutions will share their improvement and the moral sentiment will write the law of the land.

(80)   If it be not easy to settle the equity of this question, the peril is less when we take note of our natural defences. We are kept by better guards than the vigilance of such magistrates as we commonly elect. Society always consists
(85) in greatest part of young and foolish persons. The old, who have seen through the hypocrisy of courts and statesmen, die and leave no wisdom to their sons. They believe their own newspaper, as their fathers did at their age.
(90) With such an ignorant and deceivable majority, States would soon run to ruin, but that there are limitations beyond which the folly and ambition of governors cannot go. Things have their laws, as well as men; and things
(95) refuse to be trifled with. Property will be protected. Corn will not grow unless it is planted and manured; but the farmer will not plant or hoe it unless the chances are a hundred to one that he will cut and harvest it.
(100) Under any forms, persons and property must and will have their just sway. They exert their power, as steadily as matter its attraction. Cover up a pound of earth never so cunningly, divide and subdivide it; melt it to liquid, con-
(105) vert it to gas; it will always weigh a pound; it will always attract and resist other matter by the full virtue of one pound weight:—and the attributes of a person, his wit and his moral energy, will exercise, under any law or
(110) extinguishing tyranny, their proper force,—if not overtly, then covertly; if not for the law, then against it; if not wholesomely, then poisonously; with right, or by might.

11. According to the author, what is "the Spartan principle" (lines 58–60)?

   A. A decision becomes just by being unequal.
   B. A decision that is just is automatically equal.
   C. Any decision that accepts the superiority of wealth is just.
   D. An elected person is automatically a just person.

12. According to the passage, what should be the primary interest of the state?

   F. guarding the borders of a nation
   G. defending property ownership
   H. protecting the rights of its citizens
   J. securing political power based on ownership of land

13. The word "sway" (line 101) most nearly means:

   A. move from side to side.
   B. indecisiveness.
   C. wavering.
   D. influence.

14. The author believes that the "deceivable majority" (lines 90–91) is:

   F. those who are young and naïve.
   G. the old and foolish people.
   H. those who believe that democracy is inevitable.
   J. the hypocritical politicians.

15. The passage contains all of the following EXCEPT:

   A. a biblical allusion.
   B. a farming analogy.
   C. a rhetorical question.
   D. a startling statistic.

16. The main argument of the passage is that:

    F. a truly democratic government is impossible because of the acquisitive nature of human beings.
    G. for the good of the economic health of the nation, property must receive primary consideration from a responsible government.
    H. if a democratic government fulfills its responsibility to protect and educate its citizens, economic prosperity will naturally follow.
    J. those who gain wealth by acquiring property are morally indebted to those who have less.

17. The "accident" (line 13) to which the author refers is the:

    A. naturally occurring inequality in wealth.
    B. protection of the government.
    C. clash between the interests of the state and the rights of individuals.
    D. failure of a system of government to provide protections to its citizens.

18. According to the passage, one may gain wealth through all of the following EXCEPT:

    F. a gift.
    G. an inheritance.
    H. skill.
    J. vigilance.

19. The purpose of the example of the corn (lines 96–99) is to:

    A. elucidate an economic principle.
    B. clarify an agricultural disagreement.
    C. present a humorous example.
    D. compare inherited wealth to acquired wealth.

20. It can be inferred from the example of Laban and Jacob (lines 21–29) that the author believes:

    F. workers are entitled to share in the profits of a business enterprise.
    G. the owners of a business must incur the expense of protecting it.
    H. employees must expect their employer to charge them for the costs of their food and safety.
    J. a worker has the right to bear arms to defend the products of his labor.

Passage III

Humanities

The following is the Preface to *The House of the Seven Gables* written by Nathaniel Hawthorne in 1851.

When a writer calls his work a Romance, it need hardly be observed that he wishes to claim a certain latitude, both as to its fashion and material, which he would not have felt
(5) himself entitled to assume had he professed to be writing a Novel. The latter form of composition is presumed to aim at a very minute fidelity, not merely to the possible, but to the probable and ordinary course of man's
(10) experience. The former—while, as a work of art, it must rigidly subject itself to laws, and while it sins unpardonably so far as it may swerve aside from the truth of the human heart—has fairly a right to present that truth
(15) under circumstances, to a great extent, of the writer's own choosing or creation. If he think fit, also, he may so manage his atmospherical medium as to bring out or mellow the lights and deepen and enrich the shadows of the pic-
(20) ture. He will be wise, no doubt, to make a very moderate use of the privileges here stated, and, especially, to mingle the Marvelous rather as a slight, delicate, and evanescent flavor, than as any portion of the actual substance of
(25) the dish offered to the public. He can hardly

be said, however, to commit a literary crime even if he disregard this caution.

(30) In the present work, the author has proposed to himself—but with what success, fortunately, it is not for him to judge—to keep undeviatingly within his immunities. The point of view in which this tale comes under the Romantic definition lies in the attempt to connect a bygone time with the very present

(35) that is flitting away from us. It is a legend prolonging itself, from an epoch now gray in the distance, down into our own broad daylight, and bringing along with it some of its legendary mist, which the reader, according

(40) to his pleasure, may either disregard, or allow it to float almost imperceptibly about the characters and events for the sake of a picturesque effect. The narrative, it may be, is woven of so humble a texture as to require this

(45) advantage, and, at the same time, to render it the more difficult of attainment.

Many writers lay very great stress upon some definite moral purpose, at which they profess to aim their works. Not to be deficient

(50) in this particular, the author has provided himself with a moral,—the truth, namely, that the wrong-doing of one generation lives into the successive ones, and, divesting itself of every temporary advantage, becomes a pure

(55) and uncontrollable mischief; and he would feel it a singular gratification if this romance might effectually convince mankind—or, indeed, any one man—of the folly of tumbling down an avalanche of ill-gotten gold, or real estate, on

(60) the heads of an unfortunate posterity, thereby to maim and crush them, until the accumulated mass shall be scattered abroad in its original atoms. In good faith, however, he is not sufficiently imaginative to flatter himself

(65) with the slightest hope of this kind. When romances do really teach anything, or produce any effective operation, it is usually through a far more subtle process than the ostensible one. The author has considered it hardly

(70) worth his while, therefore, relentlessly to

impale the story with its moral as with an iron rod,—or, rather, as by sticking a pin through a butterfly,—thus at once depriving it of life, and causing it to stiffen in an ungainly and

(75) unnatural attitude. A high truth, indeed, fairly, finely, and skillfully wrought out, brightening at every step, and crowning the final development of a work of fiction, may add an artistic glory, but is never any truer, and seldom any

(80) more evident, at the last page than at the first.

The reader may perhaps choose to assign an actual locality to the imaginary events of this narrative. If permitted by the historical connection,—which, though slight, was essen-

(85) tial to his plan,—the author would very willingly have avoided anything of this nature. Not to speak of other objections, it exposes the romance to an inflexible and exceedingly dangerous species of criticism, by bringing his

(90) fancy-pictures almost into positive contact with the realities of the moment. It has been no part of his object, however, to describe local manners, nor in any way to meddle with the characteristics of a community for whom

(95) he cherishes a proper respect and a natural regard. He trusts not to be considered as unpardonably offending by laying out a street that infringes upon nobody's private rights, and appropriating a lot of land which had no

(100) visible owner, and building a house of materials long in use for constructing castles in the air. The personages of the tale—though they give themselves out to be of ancient stability and considerable prominence—are really of

(105) the author's own making, or at all events, of his own mixing; their virtues can shed no luster, nor their defects redound, in the remotest degree, to the discredit of the venerable town of which they profess to be inhabit-

(110) ants. He would be glad, therefore, if—especially in the quarter to which he alludes—the book may be read strictly as a Romance, having a great deal more to do with the clouds overhead than with any portion of the actual soil

(115) of the County of Essex.

21. The purpose of the first paragraph of the passage is to:

    A. distinguish between two literary genres.
    B. contrast the purpose of Romantic literature with that of non-fiction.
    C. explain why the author has chosen a particular setting for his work.
    D. argue that an author should not commit the literary sin of embellishment.

22. It may be inferred that the author believes that:

    F. non-fiction is the genre best suited to teaching morals.
    G. romantic literature should tell a love story with a happy ending.
    H. an author has an obligation to be as realistic as possible, even in a work of fiction.
    J. a work of fiction should have a moral purpose.

23. The author uses the contrast between "gray in the distance" (lines 36–37) and "our own broad daylight" (lines 37–38) to:

    A. suggest that it is far better to place characters in recognizable times and places than to build imaginary kingdoms.
    B. connect bygone times with contemporary settings.
    C. stress the importance of color and clarity in storytelling.
    D. contrast the romantic nature of historical fiction with fanciful descriptions of New England towns.

24. The author would most likely define a Romance as:

    F. a relationship in which the most tender affections are engaged.
    G. a tale of legendary heroes who have powers beyond those of mortal men and women.
    H. a literary form in which a writer may take liberties with style and content.
    J. a historical chronology with accurate details.

25. The phrase "minute fidelity" (lines 7–8) most likely means:

    A. minor particulars.
    B. close faithfulness.
    C. trivial occurrences.
    D. ordinary events.

26. In lines 63–65 ("In good faith … of this kind") the author reveals himself to be:

    F. boastful.
    G. secure.
    H. imaginative.
    J. modest.

27. It can be inferred that the author feels that a reader who wishes "to assign an actual locality to the imaginary events" (lines 81–82) is:

    A. making a regrettable mistake.
    B. coming to a wise decision.
    C. committing an unpardonable sin.
    D. doing a favor to the author.

28. According to the author, "to impale the story with its moral" (lines 70–71) is similar to "sticking a pin through a butterfly" (lines 72–73) in that both:

    F. are acts of cruelty and violence.

    G. create a disharmony between the perpetrator and the witness.

    H. cause an unnatural stiffness and awkwardness.

    J. add artistic glory to a literary work.

29. It can be inferred that the moral of *The House of the Seven Gables* concerns:

    A. the error of thinking one is above moral laws.

    B. the inflexibility of those who judge others by harsh standards.

    C. the passing of wrong-doing from one generation to those that follow.

    D. the nature of good versus evil.

30. The author uses all of the following as contrasts in the passage EXCEPT:

    F. clouds overhead versus actual soil.

    G. evanescent flavor versus actual substance.

    H. a subtle process versus an ostensible one.

    J. mellow lights versus enriched shadows.

Passage IV

Natural Science

The following passage (written in 2013) is a discussion of the ongoing investigation into the presence of water on the planet Mars.

    The mystery of how Mars changed from a warm, wet world to a cold, dry, bleak planet has intrigued scientists for decades. The absence of water on Mars today poses a per-
(5) plexing dilemma—how to explain all the surface features that were apparently produced by flowing water. While most scientists embrace the idea that water once flowed across the Martian surface, how long it flowed, the
(10) amounts that flowed, and the climatic conditions under which it flowed are still being debated. For now, images of channels, meanders, and eroded landforms on Mars strongly tantalize as ghosts of flowing water.

(15)   With information retrieved from the Mars rover Opportunity—still going strong after almost a decade of cruising the Martian landscape—researchers hope to add to their growing store of evidence. With the additional
(20) inflow of information from the newest Mars rover, Curiosity, which landed in August 2012, researchers have accumulated support for the theory that water, essential for the formation of life as we know it, once streamed on the red
(25) planet.

    To try to account for this water, the scientific community is debating whether the climate of Mars has slowly changed over time or whether it has remained the same for the
(30) last several billion years. The two positions lead to two very different views of the planet and of life and water on Mars: If Mars has always had the climate we find today, huge quantities of water must have been released
(35) over a short period of time to create the water-related landforms found on the surface, many of which require significant amounts of water to form. These great quantities of water would have to have shaped the
(40) surface quickly, before evaporating or boiling away. Also, life would not have had a chance to evolve in such short-lived bodies of water. Alternately, if Mars once had a warmer, wetter climate, water could have existed over a
(45) long period of time, altered the surface gradually, and allowed for the possible formation of life. These different water scenarios give rise to different views of the planet's evolution. Regardless of whether water existed for
(50) long or short periods of time, it probably escaped into space and/or sank into the ground to become permafrost.

    Supporting evidence of the presence of water is mostly gathered from the chemical
(55) composition of the rocks examined by the

rovers. To date, many of the rocks analyzed by scientists indicate signs of water, but water with a very high level of acidity. Some scientists even conjecture that the ancient
(60) water was more like sulfuric acid than H_2O. With the newest information, however, NASA researchers' hopes for proof of the possibility that Mars was hospitable to life-formation have been lifted. The minerals in the newest
(65) finding, a large rock given the name Esperance by geologists, point to the presence of less acidic water that is much more like Earth's water. Esperance contains aluminum, calcium, and magnesium, elements that might be
(70) deposits left by water flowing over volcanic rocks. It is hoped that the chemical laboratory aboard Curiosity will send back more detailed data on rock strata that will allow researchers to uncover the history of the changing pH of
(75) the water on Mars.

The necessity of water to the evolution of life-forms is the trigger that keeps researchers seeking confirmation of its presence on Mars. The first clues that water once flowed on
(80) Mars appeared in the photographs sent back to Earth in 1971 by the orbiting Mariner 9 spacecraft. Images of riverbeds and canyons led scientists to the tentative hypothesis that running water had formed these topographi-
(85) cal features. What appeared to be ice caps on the north and south poles of the plane also pointed to the presence of water. It is also possible that the red dust that covers the surface of the planet may conceal a layer of ice.
(90) Studying water on Mars gives scientists insights into how planets evolve, how water accumulates, how climates develop, and, possibly, how life begins. For these reasons, understanding the story of water is central to
(95) most of NASA's planetary missions.

31. According to the passage, what is the current thinking about the presence of water on Mars?

   A. Scientists have found irrefutable evidence that water is currently present on Mars.

   B. Scientists doubt they will ever find evidence that water flowed on Mars.

   C. The ice caps indicate that any water found on Mars today is frozen.

   D. Geologic evidence indicates that some form of water was once present on Mars.

32. Which of the following are elements that support the hypothesis that water once flowed over volcanic rocks?

   F. aluminum, sulfuric acid, calcium

   G. magnesium, clay, aluminum

   H. aluminum, magnesium, calcium

   J. calcium, magnesium, sulfuric acid

33. In context, the word "embrace" (line 7) most nearly means:

   A. hug.

   B. accept.

   C. encircle.

   D. grip.

34. The first clues that Mars had water resources came from:

   F. the chemistry lab aboard the Mars rover Opportunity.

   G. images taken by video cameras aboard Curiosity.

   H. photographs sent by Mariner 9 spacecraft.

   J. astronauts who landed on the surface of Mars.

35. The primary purpose of the second paragraph (lines 15–25) is to:

   A. present the most current information on the search for water on Mars.
   B. challenge the original hypothesis about the waterless surface of Mars.
   C. provide historical context to the NASA rover program.
   D. specify the source of the debate over the presence of water on Mars.

36. According to the speculation of some scientists, ancient water on Mars was:

   F. less acidic than water on Earth.
   G. more basic than water on Earth.
   H. more acidic than water on Earth.
   J. the same pH as water on Earth.

37. All of the following questions are answered by the passage EXCEPT:

   A. Who named the large rock Esperance?
   B. What landforms lead scientists to suspect that water once flowed on Mars?
   C. What scenario would support the theory that life once existed on Mars?
   D. What is the chemical composition of the red dust that has given Mars the name "the red planet"?

38. It can be inferred from the passage that scientists are MOST certain that:

   F. the climate of Mars has been constant for billions of years.
   G. at some point in time, life-forms flourished on Mars.
   H. like Earth, Mars has two ice caps.
   J. the Martian landscape contains water-related landforms.

39. According to the passage, investigations into the possibility of the presence of water on Mars will yield insights into all of the following EXCEPT:

   A. how climates develop.
   B. how life begins.
   C. how planets evolve.
   D. how volcanoes are formed.

40. According to the passage, all the following are possible explanations for the current absence of water on Mars EXCEPT:

   F. It evaporated.
   G. It boiled away.
   H. It escaped into space.
   J. It was consumed.

IF YOU FINISH BEFORE TIME IS CALLED, CHECK YOUR WORK ON THIS SECTION ONLY. DO NOT WORK ON ANY OTHER SECTION IN THE TEST.

Section 4: Science Test

35 Minutes—40 Questions

Directions: The Science Test consists of seven passages; each passage is followed by several questions. After reading each passage, select the best answer to each question and fill in the corresponding circle on the answer sheet. Refer to the information in the passages as often as necessary to respond to the questions. Use of a calculator is NOT permitted on this test.

Passage I

The most common type of light bulb still employed worldwide today is the incandescent bulb popularized by Thomas Edison in the late 1800s. In recent years, new types of light bulbs have been introduced to consumers, including the halogen and compact fluorescent light (CFL). Although each type of bulb employs electricity as the initial energy source, each bulb utilizes a different mechanism of energy transfer to emit light. Incandescent bulbs use heat to produce light from a filament; halogen bulbs improve on this mechanism by sealing the filament in an envelope filled with inert gas. CFLs involve the emission of UV light from a gas contained within a tube; this UV light in turn excites a phosphor coating such that it emits visible light.

Various light bulb types were tested for the character and quality of light produced. The data are shown in Table 1. (*Note:* W = watts, a unit of power; lm = lumens, a measure of output from a light source.)

Table 1				
Bulb type	Power (W)	Light output (lm)	Light efficiency (lm/W)	Operating temperature (°K)
Incandescent	40	500	12.5	2800
	60	850	14.2	3100
	100	1700	17.0	3300
Halogen	60	1150	19.2	3200
	100	2400	24.0	3500
CFL	20	1200	60.0	2700

The industry-standard equivalencies between the color temperature of the bulb (used to indicate light quality to the consumer) and the actual maximum operating temperature of the bulb are shown in Table 2.

Table 2	
Color temperature	Maximum temperature (°K)
Soft white	3000
Bright white	3500
Cool white	4000
Daylight	5000

Many consumers are concerned not only with the quality of the light their bulbs can provide, but also with the electricity used to power such bulbs and any pollution associated with the production of the bulbs. Relevant information regarding the energy use and costs for various bulb types is summarized in Table 3. (*Note:* kWh = kilowatt hour, the typical unit of measurement used by electric companies.) The levels of mercury, a known environmental toxin and health hazard, associated with incandescent and CFL bulbs are shown in Figure 1. No mercury is associated with halogen bulbs.

Table 3	
Consumer concern	**Formula**
Electricity used (kWh)	$\dfrac{\text{Power (W)} \times \text{time used (hours)}}{1000 \text{ (W/kW)}}$
Greenhouse gas emissions (pounds of pollution)	Electricity used (kWh) × (1.58 pounds/kWh)

Figure 1

1. If an incandescent bulb with a power of 80 W were tested, which of the following is a likely value for its light efficiency?

   A. 10.5 lm/W
   B. 15.8 lm/W
   C. 18.2 lm/W
   D. 22.1 lm/W

2. Which of the following graphs correctly summarizes the relationship between power of bulb and light output for all light bulb types according to the data in Table 1?

3. If a 100 W halogen bulb were being marketed to consumers, what color temperature is likely to be claimed on the packaging?

A. soft white
B. bright white
C. cool white
D. daylight

4. Which of the following statements is supported by the data in Table 1 regarding bulb type, power, and light efficiency?

F. A higher-powered bulb is always more efficient in producing light, regardless of bulb type.
G. Within incandescent bulbs, the lower the power, the higher the efficiency.
H. Bulb type is more significant than power in predicting light efficiency.
J. High-powered halogen bulbs have the best efficiency overall.

5. In order to estimate the electricity used to power a CFL bulb for 24 hours, which mathematical model should be used?

A. $\dfrac{60 \text{ W} \times 24 \text{ h}}{1000 \text{ W/kW}}$

B. $\dfrac{20 \text{ W} \times 24 \text{ h}}{100 \text{ W/kW}}$

C. $\dfrac{60 \text{ W} \times 12 \text{ h}}{1000 \text{ W/kW}}$

D. $\dfrac{20 \text{ W} \times 24 \text{ h}}{1000 \text{ W/kW}}$

6. If consumers are interested in reducing the amount of greenhouse gases and potential mercury contamination, which of the following bulbs is most appropriate?

F. 40 W incandescent
G. 60 W incandescent
H. 100 W incandescent
J. 20 W CFL

Passage II

Bacteria represent most of the organisms on Earth that are limited to asexual modes of reproduction. Since they are unable to introduce genetic diversity into their offspring during reproduction as do sexually reproducing organisms, and since genetic diversity enhances not only offspring but also species survival, bacteria have evolved different, non-reproductive mechanisms for achieving the same goals. One of these is called transformation and involves a bacterium picking up and expressing short segments of DNA from its surroundings.

Experiment 1

Bacteria can be encouraged to transform in a laboratory setting for biotechnological research purposes. (For example, the *E. coli* bacterium can transform such that it takes up and expresses the human insulin gene for diabetic therapy.) Before they can be artificially transformed in the lab, they have to be encouraged to take up foreign DNA through one of two means.

During electroporation, short bursts of a high-voltage current are passed through a solution containing bacteria. The bacterial cell membranes become leaky in response, and the cells become more likely to pick up free DNA molecules present in the solution and become transformants.

A research group uses the electroporation method to transform *E. coli* bacteria in different environments (Petri dishes, or *plates*). The gene they insert provides the trait of ampicillin-resistance; transformed bacteria will not be affected by the presence of the ampicillin antibiotic. The presence of ampicillin (or other antibiotics, like penicillin) is fatal in bacteria that lack the specific resistance gene. The total numbers of bacterial colonies present in each Petri dish after a 24-hour incubation period are displayed in Table 1. (***Note:*** NM = the standard nutrient medium for growing bacteria; lawn = many indistinguishable colonies; amp = ampicillin; pen = penicillin.)

Table 1		
	Untreated _E. coli_	**Transformed _E. coli_**
NM	Lawn	Lawn
NM/amp	0	13
NM/pen	0	0

Experiment 2

During chemical transformation, bacteria are exposed to solutions that chemically or thermally alter their cell membranes enough to make the DNA molecules pass through the membrane and into the cell. The research group follows the same procedure as described in Experiment 1 except that chemical transformation by means of heat-shock is employed instead to encourage the uptake of the ampicillin-resistance gene. The data are shown in Table 2.

Table 2		
	Untreated _E. coli_	**Transformed _E. coli_**
NM	Lawn	Lawn
NM/amp	0	18
NM/pen	1	0

To compare the results from Experiments 1 and 2, the research group calculates the transformation efficiency. Transformation efficiency is a measure of the number of cells within the colonies of a bacterial culture that take up the DNA of interest; it is described by the number of transformants per given mass of plated DNA and is calculated according to the following formula:

$$\text{Transformation efficiency} = \frac{\text{Number of transformed cells}}{\text{Quantity of DNA plated (µg)}}$$

7. From the data presented in Table 1, _E. coli_ colonies grew in what type of environments?

   A. NM only
   B. NM/amp only
   C. NM/pen only
   D. NM/amp or NM

8. Which of the statements below is supported by the data in Tables 1 and 2?

   F. There is evidence that the bacteria in the plates containing penicillin experienced transformation while those in the ampicillin-containing plates did not.
   G. The untreated _E. coli_ produced more colonies in both experiments than did the transformed _E. coli_.
   H. Both mechanisms of transformation were effective in growing colonies, but chemical transformation produced more colonies than electroporation.
   J. The presence of a bacterial lawn in the NM plates indicates inefficient transformation.

9. What is the purpose of the NM plate in Experiments 1 and 2?

   A. It shows the set of conditions that prevent bacterial growth.
   B. It acts as a control group to demonstrate the plate conditions in which both untreated and transformed bacteria will grow.
   C. It demonstrates the conditions necessary for growing the antibiotics used in the experiments.
   D. It acts as an experimental group and can be used to calculate the transformation efficiency of the experiment.

10. Which of the following statements might provide an explanation for the one colony observed in the NM/pen plate in Table 2?

   F. A researcher must have transformed a bacterium with the ampicillin-resistance gene by mistake.
   G. A bacterium must have had a natural resistance to the penicillin antibiotic, so that bacterium was unaffected and produced a visible colony.
   H. A researcher must have transformed a bacterium with the penicillin-resistance gene by mistake.
   J. The penicillin used in the experiments must have been ineffective.

11. In Experiment 1, 0.01 μg of DNA was plated. What is the corresponding transformation efficiency?

   A. 1300 transformants/μg DNA
   B. 2600 transformants/μg DNA
   C. 13,000 transformants/μg DNA
   D. 15,000 transformants/μg DNA

12. If twice as much DNA were plated in the transformation conducted in Experiment 2 than in Experiment 1, which of the following statements would be supported?

   F. The chemical method of transformation demonstrated higher transformation efficiency than that using electroporation.
   G. The transformation efficiency is not dependent upon the quantity of DNA plated, so there would be no difference in transformation efficiency between the two methods.
   H. The chemical method of transformation is concluded to be the most effective method under any conditions.
   J. The electroporation method of transformation demonstrated higher transformation efficiency than that using chemical transformation.

Passage III

Burning of hydrocarbon fuels occurs in the typical internal combustion engine to produce heat and (eventually) kinetic energy according to the following reaction:

$$C_xH_y + O_2 \rightarrow CO_2 + H_2O + heat$$

Complete combustion data (including the relative number of CO_2 molecules produced per fuel molecule and the heat of combustion of the fuel in kJ/mol) for specific hydrocarbon fuels were collected using a bomb calorimeter and are shown in Table 1.

Table 1			
Hydrocarbon fuel	**Chemical formula**	**CO_2 molecules produced**	**Heat (kJ/mol)**
Methane	CH_4	1	890
Ethane	C_2H_6	2	1555
Propane	C_3H_8	3	2208
Butane	C_4H_{10}	4	2861
Octane	C_8H_{18}	8	5472

More recently, alternative fuel sources have become more readily available and are often considered to be more environmentally friendly and/or easier to transport and store than some of the more traditional hydrocarbon fuels. Some data on the combustion of two alternative fuels are shown in Table 2.

Table 2			
Alternative fuel	**Chemical formula**	**CO_2 molecules produced**	**Heat (kJ/mol)**
Methanol	CH_3OH	1	726
Ethanol	CH_3CH_2OH	2	1300

13. According to the data presented in Table 1:

    A. propane produces more heat per molecule than does butane.
    B. methane produces more heat per molecule than does ethane.
    C. butane produces more heat per molecule than does octane.
    D. butane produces more heat per molecule than does propane.

14. If hexane, C_6H_{14}, were analyzed and the data placed in Table 1, which of the following heat values is a logical measurement?

    F. 1580 kJ/mol
    G. 2600 kJ/mol
    H. 4160 kJ/mol
    J. 5750 kJ/mol

15. A hydrocarbon can be converted into an alcohol by replacing a hydrogen atom with an alcohol ($-OH$) functional group. Which of the following statements is then consistent with the information presented in Tables 1 and 2?

    A. A hydrocarbon fuel has a higher heat of combustion than an alcohol molecule with the same number of carbon atoms.
    B. An alcohol molecule releases relatively more CO_2 molecules than a hydrocarbon fuel with the same number of carbon atoms.
    C. A hydrocarbon fuel has a lower heat of combustion than an alcohol molecule with the same number of carbons.
    D. An alcohol molecule releases relatively fewer CO_2 molecules than a hydrocarbon fuel with the same number of carbon atoms.

16. The production of CO_2 has been linked to global warming because CO_2 acts as a greenhouse gas, trapping radiation in Earth's atmosphere. If a goal then is to limit CO_2 production while reaching a minimum heat of combustion of 3000 kJ/mol, which of the following is the worst option for a fuel choice according to the data in Tables 1 and 2?

    F.   using 3 molecules of ethanol
    G.   using 4 molecules of methane
    H.   using 2 molecules of ethane
    J.   using 1 molecule of octane

17. Instead of pure oxygen, engines are primarily supplied air, a mixture of approximately 78% nitrogen gas (N_2), 21% oxygen gas (O_2), and 1% other trace gases. The air-fuel ratio (AFR) describes the proportion of air to fuel that is necessary for the complete combustion of the fuel with no production of excess exhaust gases. Calculating the AFR is important when analyzing engine efficiency and performance. If an AFR is too low, then complete combustion of the gas cannot occur and undesirable CO (carbon monoxide) will be present after combustion. Alternatively, an AFR that is too high results in a lower heat transfer from the combustion products than desired. A graph demonstrating the relationship between the AFR and CO production is shown in the following figure:

Which of the following options is the optimal AFR for a gasoline fuel?

    A.   14
    B.   16
    C.   19
    D.   20

Passage IV

The theory of evolution is central to understanding the history of life on Earth and the planet's current levels of biodiversity. Still being debated, however, is the rate at which evolution occurs. Researchers and professors of evolutionary biology regularly examine the fossil record, which provides strong structural evidence for evolution. This evidence is contained in the remains of organisms that had been preserved over geologic time in layers of sedimentary rock called strata. The distribution of fossils within the strata provides a relative date for the fossils, while radioactive dating can provide an absolute date of the fossils' age.

Several students of evolutionary biology were presented with the scenario illustrated in Figure 1 and asked to explain how Species 2 and 3 present in stratum 2 evolved given the ancestral species present in stratum 1. Everyone agreed that stratum 1, the lowest layer containing any fossils, provides evidence that Species 1 was in abundance in that time period and showed diversity in size. The students were divided into two groups and asked to use the data in Figure 1 to defend one of two hypotheses regarding the rate at which evolution occurs.

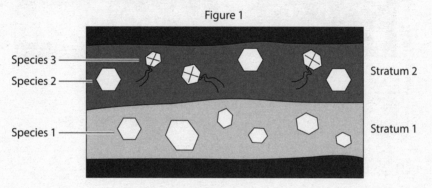

Figure 1

Hypothesis 1

The concept of phyletic gradualism can explain the "sudden" appearance of Species 3 in stratum 2. Most large-scale evolutionary changes are actually the result of the summation of many small changes over geologic time. Because the fossil record is incomplete, not all transitional forms are preserved in any stratum. Although Species 3 possesses several different characters than Species 1, those traits actually accumulated slowly over millions of years within many transitional species that existed that were not preserved in the fossil record. This is demonstrated in Figure 2:

Figure 2

301

Hypothesis 2

The concept of punctuated equilibrium can explain the sudden appearance of Species 3 in stratum 2. The most important factor affecting the rate of evolution is the rate of environmental change. Most of the time the environment is not changing, but periodically there are large-scale, drastic changes in the environment that influence evolution to act quickly. Adaptation by a population happens relatively quickly, and then the population reaches equilibrium and stasis resumes. This explains how Species 3 very quickly accumulated new traits from Species 1 while Species 2 continued to exist in much the same form as did Species 1. This is demonstrated in Figure 3:

Figure 3

18. According to Hypothesis 1:

    F. the gradual change in form that occurs is not always well-preserved in the fossil record.
    G. the gradual change in form is not influenced by environmental change.
    H. there is no evidence to support punctuated equilibrium.
    J. the fossil record shows that the rate of evolution never changes.

19. The major difference between Hypotheses 1 and 2 concerns:

    A. whether evolution occurs.
    B. the rate at which evolution occurs.
    C. if mutation contributes to evolution.
    D. if natural selection leads to evolution.

20. The following figure demonstrates the evolution of foraminiferans (forams), a type of protist, as preserved in the fossil record over three epochs:

Which of the following conclusions is illogical?

F. The evolution of protists in the Pliocene supports gradualism.
G. The evolution of protists in the Miocene supports gradualism.
H. The evolution of protists between the Miocene and the Pliocene supports punctuated equilibrium.
J. The evolution of protists between the Pliocene and the Pleistocene supports punctuated equilibrium.

21. Which of the following is true regarding the two hypotheses presented?

A. Hypothesis 1 involves a short generation time between strata; Hypothesis 2 involves a longer time.
B. The entire fossil record provides more support for Hypothesis 1 than Hypothesis 2.
C. Both hypotheses involve the notion of transitional forms, although they differ in number of transitional forms that occur.
D. Both hypotheses attempt to explain gaps in the fossil record as periods of very little environmental change.

22. Data were collected regarding the evolution of trilobites, an early arthropod present in the Cambrian Period. An evolutionary lineage was established based on the number of "ribs" possessed by a trilobite species. The results are shown in the following figure:

Which of the following is a logical conclusion?

F. Trilobite evolution provides strong evidence for the support of punctuated equilibrium because rapid change happened quickly.

G. Trilobite evolution provides strong evidence for the support of phyletic gradualism because the gaps in the fossil record of trilobites can be explained by missing transitional forms.

H. Trilobite evolution provides strong evidence for the support of phyetic equilibrium because change accumulated relatively slowly over time.

J. Trilobite evolution provides inconclusive evidence; neither hypothesis is strongly supported.

23. A third idea regarding evolutionary rates, called punctuated gradualism, has also been proposed. Punctuated gradualism suggests that a species remains in stasis (a period of virtually no change) until it experiences short bursts of change that may or may not result in speciation (the production of a new species from its ancestor). This third hypothesis is:

A. in conflict with both Hypotheses 1 and 2.

B. more closely aligned with Hypothesis 2 because of the inclusion of rapid change in a short amount of time.

C. in conflict with Hypothesis 2 because of the lack of an intermediate form.

D. more closely aligned with Hypothesis 1 because of the inclusion of rapid change that does not necessarily result in speciation.

24. Which of the following conclusions is most consistent with the entirety of the data presented in Passage IV?

F. Evolution most typically occurs at a very slow and steady pace.

G. The rate of evolution can be gradual or can occur in short, quick bursts depending on the specific situation present.

H. Evolution is most predictable when examined over a very short time frame.

J. The rate of evolution is dependent solely on the rate of environmental change experienced by the population over time.

Passage V

Ozone (O_3) is an important component of Earth's atmosphere with both positive and negative associations. Ozone is found at its highest levels in the stratosphere, also called the ozone layer. Here, the ozone serves a helpful function in filtering out the smaller wavelengths of UV light from the sun that would otherwise pose serious health threats to all forms of life on Earth. Ozone is typically generated in the stratosphere according to the following sequential reactions:

$$(1)\ O_2 \xrightarrow{\text{UV light}} 2O_2$$
$$(2)\ O + O_2 \longrightarrow O_3$$

Ozone found in the lower troposphere, also called low-level ozone, is considered a major pollutant by environmental advocates and is recognized as such by governmental agencies. Although not directly produced from automobiles, fossil fuel power plants, or oil refineries, ozone is produced when UV light acts on their nitrous oxide emissions. At this level of the atmosphere, different wavelengths of UV light are present that can break N_2O molecules down into NO (nitric oxide) and O (free oxygen). Once the O atoms are formed, reaction number 2 (above) proceeds to form ozone.

Typical ozone concentrations at increasing altitudes in Earth's atmosphere are shown in Figure 1.

Figure 1

The low-level ozone levels in a major metropolitan city were collected over a decade. Average daily levels of ozone for each month in year 6 of the study are presented in Figure 2 (where month 1 = January, etc.), while a summary of the average daily levels of ozone (in parts per billion, or ppb) for each year in the study are listed in Table 1.

Figure 2

Table 1	
Year	Average ozone level (ppb)
1	34
2	35
3	38
4	39
5	33
6	43
7	39
8	39
9	41
10	42

25. Using the data presented in Figure 1, which statement correctly represents the relationship between altitude and ozone concentrations?

   A. As altitude increases, ozone concentration increases, peaks, then decreases.
   B. As altitude decreases, ozone concentration increases, peaks, then decreases.
   C. As altitude increases, ozone concentration decreases then increases.
   D. As altitude decreases, ozone concentration decreases then increases.

26. According to the data in Figure 2, a month in which this city experienced low-level ozone levels averaging approximately 50 ppb is:

    F.   January

    G.   May

    H.   July

    J.   November

27. According to the passage, both stratospheric and tropospheric ozones are directly produced from:

    A.   UV light reacting with N_2O.

    B.   free O atoms reacting with O_2 in the air.

    C. O_2 atoms combining with each other.

    D.   UV light reacting with O_2.

28. Considering the information in Table 1 and Figure 2, which of the following conclusions is logical?

    F.   Ozone levels will reach hazardous levels in the next decade unless drastic measures are taken.

    G.   Ozone levels will fall in the next year; beyond that it becomes unpredictable.

    H.   Ozone levels will remain relatively stable throughout the next decade.

    J.   Ozone levels will continue to rise in the next 5 years, although levels will continue to fluctuate throughout any given year.

29. Guidelines for issuing smog alerts are summarized in the following table.

Category	Air quality index	Low-level ozone (ppb)
Green/safe	0–50	0–59
Yellow/moderate	51–100	60–75
Orange/potentially unhealthy	101–150	76–95
Red/unhealthy	151–200	96–115
Purple/very unhealthy	201–300	116–374
Maroon/hazardous	301–500	375 and above

Using this and the data in Figure 2, the corresponding air quality index for the city in August would be:

    A.   green.

    B.   yellow.

    C.   orange.

    D.   red.

Passage VI

Hooke's Law describes the behavior of springs when a force is applied that results in an extension, the difference between the initial length (X_0) and the stretched length (X) of the spring (see Figure 1). Hooke's Law states that the extension of the spring is directly proportional to the magnitude of the force applied. It also states that, due to the elastic nature of the spring, the spring will return to its original length once the force is removed.

Figure 1

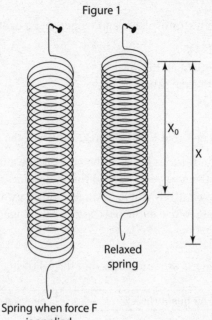

X_0

X

Relaxed
spring

Spring when force F
is applied

Both aspects of Hooke's Law apply up until the spring is stretched to its elastic limit; beyond this position the spring will have a permanent extension and will behave differently when new forces are applied. Students in a physics class measure the extension of three different springs as increasing force is applied. Their data are shown in Table 1. (*Note:* N = Newtons, a unit of force.)

Table 1			
	Extension (mm)		
Force applied (N)	Spring A	Spring B	Spring C
1	0.5	2.2	1.4
2	1	4.4	2.8
5	2.5	11	7
10	5	22	14
12	6	26.4	16.8

30. If Spring C is retested using a force of 8 N, what approximate extension is likely to be measured?

    F. 7 mm
    G. 11 mm
    H. 15 mm
    J. 18 mm

31. An unknown force is applied to Spring A and results in an extension of 0.25 mm. What magnitude of force was applied?

    A. 0.5 N
    B. 0.75 N
    C. 1.5 N
    D. 2.0 N

32. The spring constant (k) is a measure of the rigidity or strength of a spring. The higher the k value, the more resistant a spring is to an extension. According to the data in Table 1, which is true regarding the tested springs?

    F. The spring constant for Spring B is greater than that for Spring A.
    G. Spring A has the highest k value of all springs tested.
    H. The spring constant for Spring C is greater than that for Spring A.
    J. Spring B has the highest k value of all springs tested.

33. The restoring force (F_r) is the force exerted by a spring that returns it to its original conformation after a stretch. It is equal to the opposite of the product of the spring constant (k in Newtons per meter) and the resultant extension of the spring (x in mm) according to the following formula:

$$F_r = -kx$$

The negative product indicates that the restoring force from the spring is applied in the opposite direction as the initial force applied to the spring that caused the extension.

If a student is told that the spring constant of an unknown spring is 2.2 N/mm and that a force had been applied to the spring such that it was extended by 11 mm, then the restoring force exerted by the spring is:

    A. −24.2 N
    B. −1.1 N
    C. −0.2 N
    D. 24.2 N

34. A curious student disassembles his retractable pen. He compresses the small spring against his desk a few times and re-assembles the pen; the pen remains functional. He takes it apart again, but this time pulls on each end of the spring simultaneously before reinserting it. This time, the pen does not work properly. Which statement correctly explains what has happened?

F. The summation of the forces exerted by the student during the compression and the stretch is greater than the potential energy of the spring.

G. The spring exerted a force on the student that was stronger than the force exerted by the student on the spring.

H. The force exerted by the student when he stretched the spring extended it beyond its elastic limit, so it remains permanently extended.

J. The elastic limit of the spring exceeded the maximum force applied by the student, so the spring bent.

Passage VII

Environmental engineers worked with public health researchers to compare methods of freshwater filtration. Primary concerns were the removal of both *Cryptosporidium* and *Giardia,* two water-borne protozoans that can cause mild to severe gastrointestinal disease in humans.

Information about four municipal water treatment plants was gathered by the engineers. Main features of the treatment plants and the effectiveness of the removal of *Cryptosporidium* oocysts and *Giardia* cysts are reported in Table 1.

Table 1					
Plant	Primary treatment	Secondary treatment	Disinfection	% removal of *Cryptosporidium* oocysts	% removal of *Giardia* cysts
1	Screening, grit separation	Oxidation, sedimentation	None	92.7	93.5
2	Screening, grit separation, sedimentation	Activated sludge	Chlorination	87.0	85.1
3	Screening, grit separation, sedimentation	Activated sludge	Chlorination	96.6	97.0
4	Screening, grit separation, sedimentation	Activated sludge	Filtration	97.9	98.6

A variety of water purification means were then tested in the lab. The removal efficiency was calculated and the data recorded in Table 2. (*Note:* The units for removal efficiency are in $\log_{10}$ form; an efficiency of 1-log translates to 90%, 2-log to 99%, log-3 to 99.9%, etc.)

Table 2		
Purification process	*Cryptosporidium*	*Giardia*
Chlorine	0	0–2
Chlorine dioxide	0	0–2
UV light	0–4	0–4
Slow sand filtration	1.2–3.7	1.2–3.5
Membrane filtration	2–3	2–2.7

One final concern to be addressed by the research team was the relationship between the removal of turbidity (cloudiness) of the water and the removal of protozoans. Specifically, it was hypothesized that the clarity of the water is an indicator of the successful removal of protozoans. The removal efficiencies for turbidity and for *Cryptosporidium* are related in Figure 1.

Figure 1

35. According to the data in Table 1, which treatment plant was most successful at removing *Giardia* cysts?

    A.   Plant 1
    B.   Plant 2
    C.   Plant 3
    D.   Plant 4

36. Which of the following statements regarding the type of treatment methods employed is supported by the data presented in Table 1?

 F. Plant 1 was more successful removing *Cryptosporidium* than *Giardia*.
 G. Plants 2, 3, and 4 all employed the same primary and secondary treatment methods yet varied in the ability to remove protozoan cysts and oocysts.
 H. Plants that did not use a disinfectant method were the least successful with removing *Giardia* cysts.
 J. Plants that used chlorination experienced the most success with removing protozoan cysts and oocysts.

37. According to the data in Table 2, the maximum removal efficiency of *Giardia* by UV light is:

 A. 90%
 B. 99%
 C. 99.9%
 D. 99.99%

38. The most reliable and effective purification method for both protozoan types according to the laboratory data is:

 F. UV light.
 G. chlorination.
 H. membrane filtration.
 J. slow sand filtration.

39. According to the data in Figure 1, which of the following is true?

 A. As the efficiency of the turbidity removal increases, the efficiency of the *Cryptosporidium* removal also increases.
 B. As the efficiency of the turbidity removal increases, the efficiency of the *Cryptosporidium* removal decreases.
 C. When low levels of turbidity are removed, high levels of *Cryptosporidium* are removed.
 D. When high levels of turbidity are removed, low levels of *Cryptosporidium* are removed.

40. According to the data in Tables 1 and 2, which of the following methods is LEAST effective overall in removing protozoans like *Cryptosporidium* and *Giardia* from water?

 F. Filtration
 G. Oxidation
 H. Chlorination
 J. UV light

IF YOU FINISH BEFORE TIME IS CALLED, CHECK YOUR WORK ON THIS SECTION ONLY. DO NOT WORK ON ANY OTHER SECTION IN THE TEST.

Section 5: Writing Test

30 Minutes

Directions: Think about the issue presented below. Then plan and write an essay in which you support your position with specific reasons and examples. You may choose to support one of the positions stated in the prompt or you may create an original perspective. Be sure to support your position with specific reasons and examples.

Increasingly, teachers are attempting to make education learning-based rather than simply a process of retention and recall. To this end, some are discarding traditional in-class testing in favor of take-home exams that allow students to process all they have learned about a topic. Critics of the take-home exams assert that outside the classroom, the teacher has no control over testing conditions: Students can use the Internet, ask parents or friends for help, or refer to other resources. Proponents argue these conditions are ideal for learning. In fact, they believe this process is exactly what learning should be: a system of utilizing all available resources to create a solution. In your opinion, should teachers assign take-home tests or should all testing be done in a controlled environment?

IF YOU FINISH BEFORE TIME IS CALLED, CHECK YOUR WORK ON THIS SECTION ONLY. DO NOT WORK ON ANY OTHER SECTION IN THE TEST.

Scoring the Practice Test

Answer Key

Section 1: English Test

1. C (UM)	17. D (UM)	33. D (UM)	49. D (RH)	65. D (UM)
2. J (UM)	18. F (UM)	34. G (UM)	50. H (RH)	66. G (UM)
3. C (UM)	19. C (RH)	35. B (UM)	51. B (UM)	67. D (RH)
4. G (UM)	20. J (UM)	36. G (UM)	52. H (UM)	68. J (RH)
5. A (UM)	21. A (RH)	37. B (RH)	53. B (UM)	69. A (UM)
6. J (UM)	22. H (RH)	38. H (RH)	54. H (RH)	70. G (RH)
7. D (UM)	23. A (RH)	39. D (UM)	55. D (RH)	71. A (RH)
8. H (RH)	24. F (UM)	40. J (UM)	56. J (UM)	72. G (UM)
9. C (RH)	25. A (UM)	41. B (RH)	57. A (RH)	73. B (RH)
10. G (UM)	26. F (RH)	42. G (UM)	58. F (UM)	74. G (UM)
11. A (RH)	27. B (UM)	43. A (RH)	59. D (RH)	75. D (RH)
12. J (UM)	28. F (RH)	44. F (RH)	60. F (RH)	UM = Usage/
13. A (UM)	29. D (UM)	45. C (RH)	61. C (UM)	Mechanics
14. F (RH)	30. J (RH)	46. G (UM)	62. J (UM)	
15. D (RH)	31. B (RH)	47. A (UM)	63. B (RH)	RH = Rhetorical
16. G (UM)	32. G (RH)	48. F (RH)	64. G (UM)	Skills

Section 2: Mathematics Test

1. C (EA)	11. C (GT)	21. D (EA)	31. B (GT)	41. B (AG)
2. G (GT)	12. F (AG)	22. J (EA)	32. H (AG)	42. J (GT)
3. C (EA)	13. C (EA)	23. B (EA)	33. D (EA)	43. D (GT)
4. J (GT)	14. H (AG)	24. J (AG)	34. J (EA)	44. H (GT)
5. C (EA)	15. D (EA)	25. D (EA)	35. D (AG)	45. B (GT)
6. H (GT)	16. H (GT)	26. H (AG)	36. J (GT)	46. F (GT)
7. B (AG)	17. A (EA)	27. E (EA)	37. C (EA)	47. B (GT)
8. J (EA)	18. J (AG)	28. G (AG)	38. F (EA)	48. G (GT)
9. D (EA)	19. D (EA)	29. C (EA)	39. B (EA)	49. D (GT)
10. H (EA)	20. J (AG)	30. J (AG)	40. J (AG)	50. H (AG)

51. E (AG)
52. K (GT)
53. D (GT)
54. H (EA)

55. B (AG)
56. H (AG)
57. C (GT)
58. G (GT)

59. C (EA)
60. K (EA)

GT = Plane Geometry/ Trigonometry

EA = Pre-Algebra/ Elementary Algebra

AG = Intermediate Algebra/Coordinate Geometry

Section 3: Reading Test

1. C (AL)
2. G (AL)
3. D (AL)
4. G (AL)
5. A (AL)
6. F (AL)
7. A (AL)
8. H (AL)
9. A (AL)

10. J (AL)
11. B (SS)
12. H (SS)
13. D (SS)
14. F (SS)
15. D (SS)
16. H (SS)
17. A (SS)
18. J (SS)

19. A (SS)
20. G (SS)
21. A (AL)
22. J (AL)
23. B (AL)
24. H (AL)
25. B (AL)
26. J (AL)
27. A (AL)

28. H (AL)
29. C (AL)
30. J (AL)
31. D (SS)
32. H (SS)
33. B (SS)
34. H (SS)
35. C (SS)
36. H (SS)

37. D (SS)
38. J (SS)
39. D (SS)
40. J (SS)

AL = Arts/ Literature

SS = Social Studies/ Sciences

Section 4: Science Test

1. B (RS)
2. H (RS)
3. B (RS)
4. H (RS)
5. D (RS)
6. J (RS)
7. D (RS)
8. H (RS)
9. B (RS)
10. G (RS)

11. A (RS)
12. J (RS)
13. D (DR)
14. H (DR)
15. A (DR)
16. J (DR)
17. B (DR)
18. F (CV)
19. B (CV)
20. J (CV)

21. C (CV)
22. G (CV)
23. B (CV)
24. G (CV)
25. A (DR)
26. G (DR)
27. B (DR)
28. J (DR)
29. C (DR)
30. G (DR)

31. A (DR)
32. G (DR)
33. A (DR)
34. H (DR)
35. D (RS)
36. G (RS)
37. D (RS)
38. H (RS)
39. A (RS)
40. H (RS)

DR = Data Representation

RS = Research Summaries

CV = Conflicting Viewpoints

Answer Explanations

Section 1: English Test

Passage I

1. **C.** Subject/verb agreement: The singular subject **one** needs the singular form of the verb **is.**

2. **J.** Pronoun case: The objective pronoun **whom** is incorrect because **who** is the subject of the verb **fiddled.** All other answer choices create a grammatically correct sentence.

3. **C.** Verb formation: The plural subject **sources** needs the present tense (plural) of the verb **credit.**

4. **G.** Pronoun/antecedent agreement: The singular (masculine) pronoun **he** is needed to refer to the singular antecedent **Nero.**

5. **A.** Verb tense: The verb phrase is correct because the past tense is needed.

6. **J.** Sentence structure: The sentence is not complete; it is a fragment and requires a main clause.

7. **D.** Punctuation: An introductory adverb clause must be followed by a comma.

8. **H.** Rhetorical strategy: The suggested sentence is not relevant to the paragraph and should be omitted.

9. **C.** Redundancy: The sentence begins with **At first**, so **originally** is redundant.

10. **G.** Punctuation: The sentence needs the conjunction **and** instead of a comma between the verbs.

11. **A.** Logic and Coherence: **Indeed** is the correct transitional word to use for emphasis.

12. **J.** Parallelism: The verbs **had** and **became** are needed to be parallel with the verb **dismissed.**

13. **A.** Verb tense: The past perfect tense is correct in this sentence.

14. **F.** Rhetorical strategy: The additional sentence adds specific details that heighten the effect of the description.

15. **D.** Purpose: This essay would not qualify as a scholarly essay. It is an informal investigation of the history behind a common saying.

Passage II

16. **G.** Verb tense/Punctuation: The -ing form of a verb cannot be used without a helping verb. All the other choices are punctuated correctly.

17. **D.** Punctuation: No apostrophe is needed because there is no possession in this sentence.

18. **F.** Punctuation: The sentence correctly uses the colon before an explanation.

19. **C.** Wordiness: The phrase **due to the fact** is a wordy expression.

20. **J.** Pronoun/antecedent agreement: The singular antecedent **room** needs the singular pronoun reference **this.**

21. **A.** Organization: The sentence provides a transition into the next paragraph.

22. **H.** Redundancy: The words **costly, extravagant,** and **expensive** mean the same thing; only one is necessary.

23. **A.** Rhetorical strategy: The phrase clarifies **that special bond.**

24. **F.** Pronoun case: **I** is the correct nominative pronoun because it is the subject of the verb **board.**

25. **A.** Punctuation: The comma is used correctly before a conjunction that connects items in a series.

26. **F.** Style: The sentence as it is written best conveys the **magical** quality of the garden.

27. **B.** Verb formation: The -ing form of the verb cannot be used without a helping verb.

28. **F.** Coherence: The sentence contrasts with the preceding sentence, so **nevertheless** is the correct transitional word to use here.

29. **D.** Punctuation: The apostrophe is needed to indicate the plural possessive **vendors'.**

30. **J.** Organization: This choice is the most effective and relevant conclusion to the essay.

Passage III

31. **B.** Redundancy: **poorly** and **badly** denote the same condition, so it is redundant to use both words.

32. **G.** Rhetorical strategy: The parenthetical information provides an explanatory detail.

33. **D.** Modification: The introductory participial phrase **Founded by Tsar Peter I, and the capital of Russia until 1918,** modifies **St. Petersburg,** which must follow the comma.

34. **G.** Sentence structure: This sentence has a comma splice error. The semicolon is needed to join two main clauses.

35. **B.** Sentence structure: The word **that** must be omitted so **Bridges** can be the subject of the verb **traverse.**

36. **G.** Sentence structure: The word **who** must be omitted so **residents** can be the subject of the verb **gather.**

37. **B.** Style: **Being that** is considered a stylistically inappropriate expression when used to mean **because.**

38. **H.** Redundancy: **best known** and **famous** denote the same thing; only one is needed.

39. **D.** Punctuation: The comma rather than the colon is used after an introductory participial phrase.

40. **J.** Sentence structure: This is a run-on sentence that needs to be separated into two sentences.

41. **B.** Rhetorical strategy: The details in Choice B best reflect the extraordinary quality of the collection.

42. **G.** Subject/verb agreement: The **Winter Palace** is the singular subject of the verb **is.**

43. **A.** Style: The phrase **an avid collector of art** best conveys Catherine's passion.

44. **F.** Rhetorical strategy: Choice F is the most relevant to the importance of the street.

45. **C.** Rhetorical strategy: The essay does not focus on baroque architecture; it is an overview of the highlights of a city.

Passage IV

46. **G.** Verb formation: The -ing form of the verb cannot be used without a helping verb.

47. **A.** Punctuation: The semicolon is appropriately used to join two main clauses.

48. **F.** Rhetorical strategy: The sentence is correct; all the other choices are wordy or use awkward phrasing.

49. **D.** Redundancy/awkwardness: **Jealous** and **envious** have essentially the same meaning and **both** needs **and** rather than **or. Whom** cannot be used as a subject.

50. **H.** Redundancy: The sentence begins with the word **Today,** so **now** is redundant.

51. **B.** Punctuation: The dash is used to set off a list that functions as an appositive for **all sorts of places.** Notice that a dash is used later in the sentence at the end of the list (a clue because the list is set off by dashes).

52. **H.** Adjective/adverb confusion: The adverb **freely** (not the adjective **free**) is needed to modify the verb **traveled.**

53. **B.** Verb tense: The past tense **had** is needed rather than the present perfect conditional.

54. **H.** Rhetorical strategy/punctuation: All of the constructions are acceptable except Choice H, which has no appropriate punctuation.

55. **D.** Diction: The appropriate word to use in comparisons using **less** is **than.**

56. **J.** Punctuation: When **however** is used to join two main clauses, it must be preceded by a semicolon and followed by a comma.

57. **A.** Rhetorical strategy: The original sentence best accomplishes the goal of emphasizing the change in attitude toward Rosa Bonheur.

58. **F.** Verb tense: The past tense is correct in this sentence.

59. **D.** Style: The word **so** best conveys the logical relationship of the ideas in the sentence.

60. **F.** Style: The sentence is stylistically effective as it is.

Passage V

61. **C.** Subject/verb agreement: The singular form of the verb **provides** is needed because the subject, **that,** refers to a singular antecedent, **caffeine.**

62. **J.** Idiom: The correct idiom is **associated with.**

63. **B.** Wordiness: The underlined portion is wordy and unnecessary to the meaning of the sentence.

64. **G.** Verb tense: The correct verb form is **No one knows.**

65. **D.** Parallelism: The verb **ground** is needed to be parallel with the verbs **harvested** and **roasted.**

66. **G.** Parallelism: The phrase **their religious rituals** parallels the phrase **their social activities.**

67. **D.** Misplaced modification and Style: Whenever possible, avoid the use of the passive voice (**chocolate began to be used by chefs**). In this sentence, the use of the passive voice creates a modification error: The phrase **Using their culinary skills** modifies **chocolate** rather than **chefs.**

68. **J.** Logic and coherence: Putting the phrase **in 1828** after **butter** is not a logical placement.

69. **A.** Punctuation: The sentence is correctly punctuated.

70. **G.** Logic and coherence: **However** is needed to convey the contrasting ideas between this sentence and the preceding sentence.

71. **A.** Style: The sentence contains the most appropriate wording for the style of the passage.

72. **G.** Idiom: The correct idiom is **began to cultivate.**

73. **B.** Style: Choice B uses an inappropriately slangy tone.

74. **G.** Parallelism: The verb **contribute** parallels the verb **reduce.**

75. **D.** Logic and coherence: To follow the chronological order of the essay, the most logical placement for paragraph 4 is before paragraph 3.

Section 2: Mathematics Test

1. **C.** Applying the distributive property, you have $x^2 - 3 - 4x^2 + 5x - 1$, which is equivalent to $-3x^2 + 5x - 4$.

2. **G.** The sum of the measures of all the angles is 360. Thus, $2x + 2x + 4x + x + 3x = 360$ or $12x = 360$ or $x = 30$.

3. **C.** Since $\dfrac{3}{ab} = 6$, you have $3 = 6ab$ by cross-multiplying. Thus, $ab = \dfrac{3}{6}$ or $\dfrac{1}{2}$.

4. **J.** Since $m\angle DCE = 40$, $m\angle ACB = 40$ because $\angle ACB$ and $\angle DCE$ are vertical angles. Since $AB = AC$, $m\angle B = m\angle ACB = 40$. In $\triangle ABC$, $m\angle A + \angle B + m\angle ACB = 180$. Thus, $m\angle A + 40 + 40 = 180$ or $m\angle A = 100$.

5. **C.** Rewrite $2(4^k) = 2^5$ as $2(2^2)^k = 2^5$, then as $2(2^{2k}) = 2^5$, and then as $(2^1)(2^{2k}) = 2^5$, and finally as $2^{(1 + 2k)} = 2^5$. Set $1 + 2k = 5$, and you have $k = 2$.

6. **H.** Set up a proportion, $\dfrac{4}{16} = \dfrac{x}{36}$, with x being the shortest side of the larger triangle. Cross-multiply and you have $16x = 4(36)$ or $x = 9$.

7. **B.** This is an arithmetic sequence with a common difference of 4. The nth term of an arithmetic sequence is $a_0 + (n - 1)d$, where a_0 is the first term. In this case, the 8th term is $7 + (8 - 1)(4)$ or 35.

8. **J.** The mean of the 4 tests is $\dfrac{96 + 85 + 92 + 99}{4}$ or 93. The median is $\dfrac{96 + 92}{2}$ or 94. Thus, the sum of the mean and median is $94 + 93$ or 187.

9. **D.** The expression is equivalent to dividing each term in the numerator by the denominator $2x$. Therefore, $\dfrac{2x^4}{2x} + \dfrac{6x^2}{2x} - \dfrac{4x}{2x} = x^3 + 3x - 2$. Remember, when dividing monomials with the same base, you subtract the exponents.

10. **H.** Only two of the numbers, 979 and 990, among the five choices are divisible by 11. But 990 is the larger number.

11. **C.** Since the area of the square is 36, a side of the square is 6. The perimeter of the square is 4(6) or 24, which is the same as the perimeter of the equilateral triangle. Thus, a side of the triangle is $\dfrac{24}{3}$ or 8.

12. **F.** Since $(-12, k)$ lies on the line $2x - 3y = 6$, the coordinates of $(-12, k)$ satisfy the equation of the line. Therefore, $2(-12) - 3k = 6$ or $-24 - 3k = 6$, which is equivalent to $-3k = 30$ or $k = -10$.

13. **C.** Since 50% is equivalent to $\dfrac{1}{2}$, you have $\left(\dfrac{1}{2}\right)k = 20$. Multiply both sides by $\dfrac{1}{2}$ and you have $\dfrac{1}{4}k = 10$.

14. **H.** If two lines are parallel, then their slopes are equal. The slope-intercept form of a line is $y = mx + b$. The slope of the line $y = 2x - 4$ is 2. The equation $y - 2x = 0$ is equivalent to $y = 2x$, and thus its slope is 2.

15. **D.** Applying the distributive property, you have $(2x - 3)(x + 1) = 2x^2 + 2x - 3x - 3$, which is equivalent to $2x^2 - x - 3$.

16. **H.** Note that $AB = 4$, $BC = 4$, and $\triangle ABC$ is a right triangle. Since $AB = BC$, $\triangle ABC$ is an isosceles right triangle. Thus, $m\angle ACB = 45$.

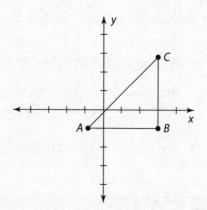

17. **A.** Since $bcd = 1$, you know that all three variables, b, c, and d, cannot be 0. Since $abc = 0$ and $b \neq 0$ and $c \neq 0$, you have $a = 0$. The product bc could be either positive or negative. And $bcd = 1$ does not require $d = 1$.

18. **J.** If $p(4k) = 8$, then $\sqrt{4k} = 8$. Squaring both sides, you have $4k = 64$, or $k = 16$.

19. **D.** Begin with $x + (x + 2) + (x + 4) = 138$. You have $3x + 6 = 138$ or $3x = 132$ or $x = 44$. Thus, the middle integer $x + 2$ is 46.

20. **J.** Since the x-intercept is -3 and the y-intercept is 4, the line passes through the points $(-3, 0)$ and $(0, 4)$. The slope of the line is $m = \dfrac{4 - 0}{0 - (-3)} = \dfrac{4}{3}$.

21. **D.** The median of Set A is the middle number, and in this case, 0. The median of Set B is $\dfrac{3 + 5}{2}$ or 4. Thus, the sum is $(0 + 4)$ or 4.

22. **J.** Begin with $2x + 6 = 4x$. You have $6 = 2x$ or $x = 3$. Thus, the number is 3.

23. **B.** The factors of 12 are ±1, ±2, ±3, ±4, ±6, and ±12. Since the sum of (−2) and (−6) is (−8) and the product of (−2) and (−6) is 12, the expression $x^2 - 8x + 12 = (x - 2)(x - 6)$. Another approach to this problem is to multiply the two binomials in each of the five choices and check the results.

24. **J.** Let x represent the number of $2 pens and $2x$ represent the number of $3 pens. Then $2(x) + 3(2x) = 48$ or $8x = 48$ or $x = 6$. Mary bought 6 $2 pens.

25. **D.** Rewrite $x^2 + 9 = 6x$ in standard form and obtain $x^2 - 6x + 9 = 0$. Factor $x^2 - 6x + 9 = 0$, and you have $(x - 3)(x - 3) = 0$. Set $x - 3 = 0$ and $x = 3$.

26. **H.** Draw the line $y = 3$, which is horizontal and parallel to the x-axis, crossing the y-axis at $y = 3$. This line intersects $g(x)$ at 2 points. Thus, there are 2 x-values.

27. **E.** There are a total of 15 coins and 12 of the 15 are not quarters. Thus, the probability of getting a coin that is not a quarter is $\dfrac{12}{15}$ or $\dfrac{4}{5}$.

28. **G.** Since $M(2,-4)$ is the midpoint of $\overline{AB}$ with $A(6,2)$ and $B(h,k)$, you have the equations $\dfrac{6+h}{2} = 2$ and $\dfrac{2+k}{2} = -4$. Solve $\dfrac{2+k}{2} = -4$ and obtain $2 + k = -8$ or $k = -10$.

29. **C.** The integer a could be 1, 2, 3 and b could be 1, 2, 3. The fraction $\dfrac{a}{b}$ could be $\dfrac{1}{1}, \dfrac{1}{2}, \dfrac{1}{3}, \dfrac{2}{1}, \dfrac{2}{2}, \dfrac{2}{3}, \dfrac{3}{1}, \dfrac{3}{2}$, and $\dfrac{3}{3}$. However, $\dfrac{1}{1}, \dfrac{2}{2}$, and $\dfrac{3}{3}$ are all equivalent to 1. Thus, there are 7 different numerical values.

30. **J.** If a function, f, is an even function, then $f(x) = f(-x)$. In Choice J, let $y = f(x)$ and compare $f(x)$ and $f(-x)$. Since $f(x) = x^2 - 3$ and $f(-x) = (-x)^2 - 3 = x^2 - 3$, they are equal. Thus, $y = x^2 - 3$ is an even function. Another approach to the problem is to look at the graph of the function. The graph of an even function is symmetrical with respect to the y-axis. The graph of $y = x^2 - 3$ is symmetrical with respect to the y-axis as shown in the accompanying diagram.

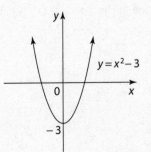

31. **B.** Note that ΔHEN is a right triangle with $EH = 4$ and $HN = 4$. Using the Pythagorean theorem or 45°-45° right-triangle relationship, $EN = 4\sqrt{2}$. Now, look at the right triangle AEN. Note that $AE = 2$ and $EN = 4\sqrt{2}$. Using the Pythagorean theorem, you have $(AN)^2 = (2)^2 + (4\sqrt{2})^2$ or $(AN)^2 = 4 + 32 = 36$ or $AN = 6$.

32. **H.** Using the distance formula, you have $\sqrt{(6-(-2))^2 + (k-5)^2} = 8$ or $\sqrt{8^2 + (k-5)^2} = 8$. Squaring both sides, you have $64 + (k-5)^2 = 64$ or $(k-5)^2 = 0$ or $k = 5$.

33. **D.** Since $\dfrac{m}{n} = -2$, then $2\left(\dfrac{m}{n}\right)^2 = 2(-2)^2 = 2(4) = 8$.

34. **J.** Substituting $k = 4$ in the expression $3k - 2$, you have $3(4) - 2$ or 10. Then divide 10 by 4, and you have a remainder of 2.

35. **D.** Apply the distributive property and obtain $(1 + 3i)(1 - i) = 1 - i + 3i - 3i^2 = 1 + 2i - 3i^2$. Since $i^2 = -1$, $1 + 2i - 3i^2 = 1 + 2i - 3(-1) = 1 + 2i + 3$ or $4 + 2i$. Also, you could have entered $(1 + 3i)(1 - i)$ into your calculator and obtained the same answer.

36. **J.** Since the shaded region is inside the circle, the inequality is $x^2 + y^2 < 9$. The region is also above the line $y = 2x$. Therefore, the inequality is $y > 2x$. The points in the shaded region must satisfy both inequalities. Thus, the shaded region are points satisfying both $y > 2x$ and $x^2 + y^2 < 9$.

37. **C.** Note that -3 is the only number in Set A but not in Set B. Thus, the probability of picking a number from Set A not in Set B is $\dfrac{1}{3}$.

38. **F.** Substituting $x = \dfrac{1}{4}$ into the inequality, you have $\left(2\left(\dfrac{1}{4}\right)\right)^2 < 2\left(\dfrac{1}{4}\right)$ or $\left(\dfrac{1}{2}\right)^2 < \dfrac{1}{2}$ or $\dfrac{1}{4} < \dfrac{1}{2}$. The inequality holds.

39. **B.** Since the average height is 5 ft 4 in, the sum of their heights is 3 times 5 ft 4 in or 16 ft. Since Karen is the tallest and Karen is 5 ft 6 in tall, the maximum possible height for Mary is 5 ft 5 in. Thus, the least possible height for Janet is as follows: 16 ft − (5 ft 6 in + 5 ft 5 in) = 5 ft 1 in.

40. **J.** If $y = x^2$ and $x = -y^2$, then $y = (-y^2)^2$ or $y = y^4$. Rewriting the equation, you get $y^4 - y = 0$ or $y(y^3 - 1) = 0$. So $y = 0$ or $y^3 = 1$ or $y = 1$. Since y is a positive integer, $y = 1$.

41. **B.** Since line l is perpendicular to $\overline{AB}$, the slopes of line l and $\overline{AB}$ are negative reciprocals. The slope of $\overline{AB}$ is $\dfrac{4-1}{3-1} = \dfrac{3}{2}$. Thus, the slope of line l is $\dfrac{-2}{3}$.

42. **J.** The image of a point (x,y) reflected in the x-axis is $(x,-y)$. Therefore, the image of $A(3,4)$ reflected in the x-axis is $A'(3,-4)$.

43. **D.** The area of a triangle is $\frac{1}{2}$(base)(height). For $\triangle ABC$, let $BC = 6$ and be the base. The height is the altitude from point A to $\overline{BC}$, and the altitude is 3. Therefore, the area of $\triangle ABC$ is $\frac{1}{2}(6)(3) = 9$. Since $\triangle A''B''C''$ is the image of $\triangle ABC$ under a dilation of 2, $\triangle ABC$ is similar to $\triangle A''B''C''$. Thus, $\left(\frac{1}{2}\right)^2 = \frac{\text{area } \triangle ABC}{\text{area } \triangle A''B''C''}$, or $\frac{1}{4} = \frac{9}{\text{area } \triangle A''B''C''}$, and the area of $\triangle A''B''C''$ is $(4)(9)$ or 36.

44. **H.** Note that $MN = 6$, $NP = 4$, and $\triangle MNP$ is a right triangle. Thus, the area of $\triangle MNP = \frac{1}{2}(6)(4)$ or 12.

45. **B.**

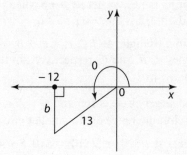

Using the Pythagorean theorem, you have $b^2 + 12^2 = 13^2$, which is equivalent to $b^2 + 144^2 = 169$ or $b = \pm 5$. Since θ is in the third quadrant and the sine function is negative in the third quadrant, you have $\sin \theta = \frac{-5}{13}$.

46. **F.** Since $\sin B = \dfrac{AC}{AB}$, you have $\sin 30° = \dfrac{AC}{14}$ or $AC = 14 \sin 30°$. Since $\sin 30° = \dfrac{1}{2}$, $AC = 14\left(\dfrac{1}{2}\right) = 7$.

Another approach to the problem is to note that $\triangle ABC$ is a 30°-60° right triangle. Thus, the length of the side opposite the 30° angle is equal to $\dfrac{1}{2}$ the length of the hypotenuse.

47. **B.** The statement "Every student in Mrs. Smith's class is on the honor roll" is equivalent to "If a student is in Mrs. Smith's class, the student is on the honor roll." A statement and its contrapositive always have the same truth value. The contrapositive in this case is "If a student is not on the honor roll, the student is not in Mrs. Smith class." Thus, the statement in Choice B is true.

48. **G.** Since the volume of a sphere is $\dfrac{4}{3}\pi r^3$, set $288\pi = \dfrac{4}{3}\pi r^3$ and obtain $r = 6$. Thus, the surface area of $4\pi r^2$ is $4\pi(6)^2$ or 144π.

49. **D.** Since all five choices involve the cosine function, you can assume that the given graph is that of a cosine function. The given graph completes one cycle of the cosine curve from $x = 0$ to $x = 4\pi$, which implies that the period of the function is 4π. Using the formula period $= \dfrac{2\pi}{\text{frequency}}$, you have $4\pi = \dfrac{2\pi}{\text{frequency}}$ or the frequency is $\dfrac{1}{2}$. The graph also indicates that the range of the f is $-4 \le y \le 4$, which means the amplitude of f is 4. Thus, the cosine function is $y = 4\cos\dfrac{x}{2}$, where the amplitude is 4 and the frequency is $\dfrac{1}{2}$.

50. **H.** Since $\overline{CA}$ is a radius of the circle, the length of the radius of the circle is $\sqrt{(4-4)^2 + (5-0)^2} = 5$. Because B is a point on the circle, $\overline{CB}$ must also be a radius with length 5. Using the distance formula with each choice, only when the coordinates of B are (1,4) does the length equal $\sqrt{(4-1)^2 + (0-4)^2} = \sqrt{3^2 + 4^2} = 5$.

51. **E.** The smallest possible value for pq is -6. We get $pq = -6$ when $p = -3$ and $q = 2$. The largest possible value for pq is 6 when $p = -3$ and $q = -2$. Thus, $-6 \le pq \le 6$.

52. **K.** The law of cosine states that in a triangle, $\triangle ABC$, $c^2 = a^2 + b^2 - 2ab \cos C$, where a, b, and c are lengths of the sides opposite angles A, B, and C, respectively. In this case, $(DF)^2 = 6^2 + 10^2 - 2(6)(10) \cos 40°$ or $DF = \sqrt{36 + 100 - 120 \cos 40°}$.

53. **D.** Since the circumference of the larger circle is 16π and $C = 2\pi r$, the radius $OA = 8$. Thus, $OB = 8 - (2) = 6$, and the circumference of the smaller circle is $2\pi(6)$ or 12π.

54. **H.** Two adults and three children cost $2(\$20) + 3(\$10) = \$70$. So $\$82 - \$70 = \$12$ for the fish caught. Thus, $\dfrac{\$12}{\$2} = 6$ fish.

55. **B.** Applying the properties of the logarithmic functions, you have $\log\dfrac{A^2}{B} = \log A^2 - \log B = 2\log A - \log B$. Since $\log A = h$ and $\log = k$, the expression $2\log A - \log B$ is equivalent to $2h - k$.

56. **H.** Since $\begin{bmatrix} -2 & 1 \end{bmatrix}$ is a 1×2 matrix and $\begin{bmatrix} 3 \\ -4 \end{bmatrix}$ is a 2×1 matrix, the product $\begin{bmatrix} -2 & 1 \end{bmatrix}\begin{bmatrix} 3 \\ -4 \end{bmatrix}$ is a 1×1 matrix. Carrying out the matrix multiplication, you have $[(-2)(3) + (1)(-4)]$ or $[-10]$.

57. **C.** Let $x = ED$ and $2x = CD$. Then $x(2x) = 32$ or $2x^2 = 32$ or $x^2 = 16$ or $x = 4$. Thus, $ED = 4$, $CD = 8$, $AE = 8$, and the diameter $AC = 4$. The circumference of the semicircle is $\frac{1}{2}(2\pi r) = \frac{1}{2}(2\pi(2)) = 2\pi$. Therefore, the perimeter of $ABCDE$ is $8 + 8 + 4 + 2\pi$ or $20 + 2\pi$.

58. **G.** A rhombus has 4 congruent sides, diagonals bisecting each other and diagonals perpendicular to each other. In this case, $BC = AD = 8$, $AE = 4$, and $\triangle AED$ is a right triangle. Note that $\overline{AD}$ is the hypotenuse and that AD is twice AE. Thus, $\triangle AED$ is a 30°-60° right triangle and $m\angle ADE$ is 30.

59. **C.** Begin with $x^2 = 2x$. Thus, you have $x^2 - 2x = 0$ or $x(x - 2) = 0$. Thus, $x = 0$ or $x = 2$. Since x is a positive number, $x = 2$.

60. **K.** Between '12–'13, the increase is 2 million, the greatest increase.

Section 3: Reading Test

Passage I

1. **C.** The main purpose of the passage is to introduce the characters and their positions in society. The interactions reveal how two upper-class women respond to an offer they consider as "vulgar" as the man making the offer. As the incident erupts into a "scene," (line 100) the awareness of class differences becomes paramount.

2. **G.** The passage is set in Italy, yet the English tourists are surrounded by portraits of English monarchs and served by an Italian host with a British accent. As Lucy says, "It might be London." The author establishes the pervasive influence of England.

3. **D.** The clues scattered throughout the passage reveal that Miss Bartlett is the companion to a younger woman, Lucy. Miss Bartlett says, "Eat your dinner, dear," and we know Lucy's mother is paying Miss Bartlett's expenses.

4. **G.** Miss Bartlett makes eye contact with the two women, and they exchange a look of understanding and shared experience.

5. **A.** The offer is clearly unexpected and obtrusive. Miss Bartlett is "startled," (line 53) and the others are shocked by the familiarity and forwardness of the old man.

6. **F.** The words connote violence, not physical but social. The women are shocked, and the aggressiveness of the old man is like a verbal assault.

7. **A.** Lucy is "perplexed" and has "an odd feeling" about the situation (lines 98–100). Miss Bartlett is obviously insulted by the offer of a room exchange.

8. **H.** There is no evidence of senility; in fact, according to the passage, "it was not the childishness of senility" (lines 61–62).

9. **A.** The passage implies that the "something" goes beyond the rooms and the views into larger realms. The emphasis on the men being "ill-bred" suggests class differences.

10. **J.** The irony arises from Lucy's mother making **many** references to her paying Miss Bartlett's expenses, which is NOT a tactful thing to do.

Passage II

11. **B.** According to the passage, when something is just (fair) we automatically say it is equal.

12. **H.** The passage states (lines 72–79) the government should be most concerned with the welfare of its people.

13. **D.** In context, the word most nearly means *influence*.

14. **F.** The deceivable majority refers to "young and foolish persons" (line 85).

15. **D.** There are no startling statistics in the passage. The biblical allusion (Choice A) is the story of Laban. The farming analogy (Choice B) is the example of corn (lines 96–99), and the rhetorical question (Choice C) occurs on lines 30–36.

16. **H.** The author states the main idea clearly in lines 74–79: " … that property will always follow persons; that the highest end of government is the culture of men; and if men can be educated, the institutions will share their improvement and the moral sentiment will write the law of the land."

17. **A.** The "accident" to which the author refers is the "rights in property" (line 11) or the amount of wealth a person accumulates.

18. **J.** The author mentions all of the choices except "vigilance" as a way to accumulate wealth (skill: line 14, gift: line 44, inheritance or patrimony: lines 44–50).

19. **A.** The corn example (lines 96–99) elucidates the economic principle of profit. A farmer will not plant corn unless he expects to make money from this endeavor.

20. **G.** The author states that Laban, the employer, should select and pay those who guard his flock (lines 21–29).

Passage III

21. **A.** The author makes it clear at the beginning of the passage that he is writing a Romance, which he wants to distinguish from a Novel.

22. **J.** The only choice that can be supported by the passage is Choice J. The author states that he does not want to be "deficient" (line 49) in providing himself and the reader with a moral.

23. **B.** In the sentence before these phrases, the author states that he wants "to connect a bygone time with the very present" (lines 33–34).

24. **H.** In the first sentence, the author says that a Romance gives the writer "latitude" or leeway in presenting his tale. The rest of the paragraph explains his view that a writer of Romance may take liberties with reality, unlike the writer of a Novel.

25. **B.** The phrase "minute fidelity" refers to the close faithfulness to reality to which the writer of a Novel must adhere.

26. **J.** The author modestly states that he doesn't flatter himself by thinking his work will have a great impact on the reader.

27. **A.** When the author says, "The reader may perhaps choose to assign an actual locality to the imaginary events of this narrative … the author would very willingly have avoided anything of this nature" (lines 81–86), he suggests the reader would be making a regrettable mistake.

28. **H.** The author describes the effect of being heavy-handed with a moral as the same as that of sticking a pin in a butterfly: "at once depriving it of life, and causing it to stiffen in an ungainly and unnatural attitude" (lines 73–75).

29. **C.** The author states his moral on lines 52–53: "the wrong-doing of one generation lives into the successive ones."

30. **J.** The author uses all of the choices as contrasts except Choice J; he uses both phrases in Choice J to refer to the way he plans to "manage his atmospherical medium" (lines 17–18).

Passage IV

31. **D.** The passage states that " … most scientists embrace the idea that water once flowed across the Martian surface" (lines 7–9), but they haven't found irrefutable evidence (Choice A). They aren't doubtful, so Choice B is incorrect. No physical evidence of frozen water has been found on the ice caps (Choice C); its existence there is speculative.

32. **H.** According to the passage (lines 68–71), "Esperance contains aluminum, calcium, and magnesium, elements that might be deposits left by water flowing over volcanic rocks." The other choices are inaccurate based on the information in the passage.

33. **B.** The context suggests that scientists **accept** the idea rather than hug (Choice A), encircle (Choice C), or grip (Choice D).

34. **H.** While the passage refers to the chemistry lab on Opportunity (Choice F) and video cameras aboard Curiosity (Choice G), the photographs from Mariner 9 (1971) are credited with the first clues to the existence of water. Astronauts (Choice J) are not mentioned in the passage.

35. **C.** By referring to the Mars rover Opportunity (operating for the past ten years) and the latest rover, Curiosity, the paragraph provides a brief historical context. The second paragraph doesn't present the most current information (Choice A), challenge a hypothesis (Choice B), or specify the source of a debate (Choice D).

36. **H.** Some scientists "conjecture that the ancient water was more like sulfuric acid than H_2O" (lines 59–60). Choices F and G are essentially the same answer choice: "less acidic" is the same as "more basic," but this scientific knowledge is not necessary to eliminate the two choices; the passage offers no evidence for either choice. Choice J is incorrect because the ancient water was more like sulfuric acid, not the same pH as Earth's water.

37. **D.** While the "red dust" is mentioned in line 88, its chemical composition is never explained. All the other choices are discussed—Choice A, "a large rock given the name Esperance by geologists" (lines 65–66); Choice B, "huge quantities of water must have been released over a short period of time to create the water-related landforms" (lines 33–36); and Choice C, "The necessity of water to the evolution of life-forms is the trigger that keeps researchers seeking confirmation of its presence on Mars" (lines 76–78).

38. **J.** The rovers have sent back photographs of water-related landforms. Choice F is contradicted by the passage (lines 26–30): "the scientific community is debating whether the climate of Mars has slowly changed over time or whether it has remained the same for the last several billion years." Choice G is the subject of speculation (lines 76–78): "The necessity of water to the evolution of life-forms is the trigger that keeps researchers seeking confirmation of its presence on Mars." Choice H is not confirmed; there "appeared" to be ice caps (line 85).

39. **D.** The passage specifically states, "Studying water on Mars gives scientists insights into how planets evolve, how water accumulates, how climates develop, and, possibly, how life begins" (lines 90–93). The formation of volcanoes is not mentioned.

40. **J.** The passage offers Choices F (line 40), G, (lines 40–41) and H (line 51) as possible explanations for the absence of water, but not Choice J, which is an unreasonable option in any case.

Section 4: Science Test

Passage I

1. **B.** According to Table 1, an incandescent bulb with a power of 80 W should fall between the values shown for the 60 and 100 W values (14.2 and 17.0 lm/W, respectively). This is supported by a gradual increase in light efficiency values for incandescent bulbs over the range of 40–100 W. The only appropriate option is 15.8 lm/W.

2. **H.** This chart correctly shows the wattage of each bulb and its corresponding light output (e.g., the only 20 W bulb tested was a CFL that gave a light output of 1200 lm). Note that three incandescent bulbs were tested, two halogens, and only one CFL; there are different numbers of columns present for each wattage displayed.

3. **B.** The 100 W halogen bulb is associated with an operating temperature of 3500°K and a light output of 2400 lm according to Table 1. Using the index in Table 2, this corresponds most closely with a rating of bright white.

4. **H.** The CFL light output data are most convincing in the support of the notion that bulb type is a more significant predictor of light output than is power of the bulb. The CFL bulb demonstrated the lowest power rating of any bulb tested (20 W), yet produced more light than a 60 W halogen bulb that uses three times the power (1200 lm versus 1150 lm).

5. **D.** Substituting the values "20 W" for the power and "24 hours" for the time used into the equation $\frac{\text{Power (W)} \times \text{time used (hours)}}{1000 \text{ (W/kW)}}$ provides the correct model for determining the electricity used to power the CFL bulb.

6. **J.** The CFL bulb has a significantly lower power (20 W) than any of the incandescent bulbs (40, 60, and 100 W), so the greenhouse gas emissions for the CFL bulb will be a fraction (between 50% and 80% less) of the emissions associated with the incandescent bulbs. According to the information in Figure 1, more mercury is associated with the use of any incandescent bulb than with any CFL bulb; this is true even though no mercury is used to produce an incandescent bulb, while almost 4 mg are used to manufacture a CFL bulb.

Passage II

7. **D.** Both types of *E. coli* grew significantly in the NM plates (i.e., bacterial lawns were present), while 13 colonies were observed in the NM/amp plate. No colonies were observed in the NM/pen plate. Only the NM and NM/amp plates seemed to support the growth of *E. coli*.

8. **H.** Both methods of transformation were successful in producing colonies, but the chemical transformation associated with Experiment 2 produced more colonies (18) than did the electroporation used in Experiment 1 (13 colonies). The bacteria in the NM/pen plates generally did not survive

because they had no antibiotic resistance to penicillin, which is unrelated to whether they were transformants. The presence of the bacterial lawn in the NM plates indicates that bacteria grew very easily under those conditions; this too is unrelated to whether they are transformants. The bacteria that did transform grew in the NM/amp plates, while the non-transformants did not.

9. **B.** The NM plate demonstrates the control conditions under which any type of *E. coli* can easily grow and reproduce. It represents a point of comparison for the experimental groups represented by the NM/amp and NM/pen plates.

10. **G.** The growth of one colony in the NM/pen plate in Experiment 2 is unexpected, as no bacteria used in the experiments were observed to tolerate the presence of the penicillin antibiotic in its environment. Either one original *E. coli* bacterium utilized possessed the penicillin-resistance trait and created a colony in the plate where no other bacteria could survive, or a bacterium experienced a mutation in its DNA providing for penicillin-resistance when the trait was not previously present in the gene pool.

11. **A.** To calculate the transformation efficiency, substitute the quantity of DNA plated (0.01 μg) and the number of colonies observed (13) into the following equation:

$$\text{Transformation efficiency} = \frac{\text{Number of transformed cells}}{\text{Quantity of DNA plated (μg)}}$$

The resultant quotient is 1300 transformants/μg DNA.

12. **J.** If twice as much DNA were used in Experiment 2 than in Experiment 1, then the denominator in the equation above will change to 0.02 μg. Since the number of observed colonies in Experiment 2 was 18, the resultant quotient is 900 transformants per μg of DNA plated. Experiment 2 is then less efficient than Experiment 1 even though more total colonies were observed in Experiment 2 plates.

Passage III

13. **D.** According to the data presented in Table 1, butane produces 2861 kJ of heat per mole of fuel, while propane produces only 2208 kJ of heat. In fact, the more carbon atoms present in the hydrocarbon fuel, the more kJ of heat are associated.

14. **H.** A molecule of hexane has 6 carbon atoms present, so the quantity of heat produced through its combustion should fall somewhere between the values for the burning of butane with 4 carbon atoms and the burning of octane with 8 carbon atoms. Thus, it should fall between 2861 kJ/mol and 5472 kJ/mol, and the only appropriate value provided is 4160 kJ/mol.

15. **A.** When comparing three carbon-based fuels, methane (890 kJ/mol) has a higher heat of combustion than methanol (726 kJ/mol). Similarly, ethane (1555 kJ/mol) has a higher heat of combustion than ethanol (1300 kJ/mol). Thus, a hydrocarbon with a given number of carbon atoms is associated with a higher heat of combustion than an alcohol with the same number of carbon atoms.

16. **J.** According to the data, combusting 1 molecule of octane would produce enough heat (5472 kJ/mol) to satisfy the given set of conditions, and would also produce 8 molecules of CO_2. If one uses 4 molecules of methane or 2 molecules of ethane, sufficient heat would be generated, but only 4 CO_2 molecules would be produced. If 3 molecules of ethanol were combusted, 6 CO_2 molecules would be produced.

17. **B.** According to the graph, at an AFR of 16, the CO level is relatively low, as is the hydrocarbon level. At an AFR of 14, both levels are slightly higher than at an AFR of 16. Additionally, at AFRs of 19 and 20 the hydrocarbon levels increase significantly.

Passage IV

18. **F.** Hypothesis 1 clearly states that evolution happens gradually over time. It also argues that the fossil record is incomplete, and thus all change is not preserved. Although Choice H might also seem consistent with this hypothesis, there is no direct statement of this position, and change might happen gradually while not always at the same pace.

19. **B.** The main difference between the two hypotheses concerns the rate at which evolution occurs. Hypothesis 1 holds that evolution happens gradually over time, while Hypothesis 2 argues that evolution happens in short bursts of rapid change followed by long periods of relatively no change.

20. **J.** According to the figure, the time between the Pliocene and the Pleistocene demonstrates a period of relatively gradual change over time, similar to that observed within the Pliocene and within the Miocene. Between the Miocene and the Pliocene, forams demonstrated a period of very rapid change in shell shape, thus punctuated equilibrium is supported.

21. **C.** Hypothesis 1 argues that many transitional forms are often not well preserved in the fossil record; Figure 2 demonstrates these many forms as occurring gradually over time. Hypothesis 2 states that change happens very quickly; this is demonstrated in the single transitional form presented in Figure 3. Thus, the number of transitional forms is a point of conflict between the two hypotheses.

22. **G.** The figure demonstrates that trilobite evolution included the relatively slow accumulation of "ribs" (increased segmentation) over time. Thus, the concept of phyletic gradualism and Hypothesis 1 are supported by this example.

23. **B.** This third notion of punctuated gradualism includes the notion of quick bursts of change in a short period of time; it simply expands on the concept by including the idea that a new species may or may not be formed even when rapid change does occur.

24. **G.** When summarizing all of the data presented, it becomes clear that evolution happens very gradually in some instances (e.g., trilobites), and then in other cases happens very suddenly and then not at all again for a very long time (e.g., forams between the Miocene and the Pliocene).

Passage V

25. **A.** As the value for altitude increases from 20 km to 40 km, the corresponding ozone concentrations increase from 0.0025 ppb to over 0.006 ppb. The curve peaked just before this point (0.008 ppb, 35 km) and then, as altitude continued to increase to 60 km, the corresponding ozone concentration decreased to 0.002 ppb.

26. **G.** According to Figure 2, May (month 5) demonstrated an average ozone concentration of 50 ppb. April was slightly lower and June slightly higher.

27. **B.** The passage explains that an ozone molecule is created as a free oxygen atom collides with an oxygen gas molecule. This reaction produces O_3, ozone. UV light is involved in the production of free oxygen atoms through the splitting of oxygen gas molecules, and is thus indirectly involved.

28. **J.** Table 1 shows that, although there have been slight variations in this trend from one year to the next, overall the average annual ozone concentrations are gradually increasing. Figure 2 demonstrates that, within one year, average monthly ozone concentrations increased during the summer months, peaked in August, and then decreased to the initial values during the fall and winter months.

29. **C.** According to Figure 2, the average ozone concentration in August was 80 ppb. Since 80 ppb falls within the 76–95 ppb range, then August would require an orange alert to indicate that the air quality is potentially unhealthy.

Passage VI

30. **G.** Table 1 indicates that when Spring C was tested with a force of 5 N, the spring was extended by 7 mm. When tested with 10 N, it was extended by 14 mm. Thus, if an 8 N force were applied, Spring C would be extended by a distance between 7 mm and 14 mm. The 11 mm value meets this criterion.

31. **A.** When the unknown force was applied to Spring A, it was stretched by a distance of 0.25 mm, a shorter distance than observed in any of the initial trials. This indicates that the force is less than the 1 N force that resulted in a 0.5 mm extension. Additionally, the effect of the force on the spring is proportional to the force applied, so because the new stretch was half of the stretch at 1 N, then the force applied must be half of that value. The 0.5 N value meets these criteria.

32. **G.** The spring constant k is defined as a measure of a spring's rigidity: The higher the value of k, the more rigid the spring (i.e., the less it will extend). According to the data in Table 1, when the heaviest force was applied (12 N), Spring B extended the most (26.4 mm) and Spring A the least (6 mm). Thus, Spring A has the highest k value and Spring B the lowest.

33. **A.** Applying the values of $k = 2.2$ N/mm and $x = 11$ mm to the equation, $F_r = -kx$, the value of $F_r = -24.2$ N (the opposite product of 2.2 and 11).

34. **H.** The initial compression of the spring did not affect its functioning when replaced into the pen, but the extension that resulted from the stretching must have exceeded the elastic limit of the spring, the distance beyond which any extension will be permanent and will produce a different result when new forces are applied. That is why it no longer allowed the pen to function properly when the spring was reinserted into the pen the second time.

Passage VII

35. **D.** According to Table 1, Plant 4 recorded the highest efficiency of *Giardia* cyst removal at 98.6%. All other plants recorded values lower than 98.6%.

36. **G.** According to Table 1, Plants 2, 3, and 4 all employed the same primary and secondary methods of purification, yet the results ranged from 87% to 97.9% for *Cryptosporidium* and from 85.1% to 98.6% for *Giardia*. None of the other descriptions is consistent with the data provided.

37. **D.** According to Table 2, the maximum value for the removal of *Giardia* using UV light is 4-log. This is equivalent to a 99.99% removal.

38. **H.** According to the data in Table 2, chlorine, chlorine dioxide, and UV light have either no or unreliable effectiveness in removing *Cryptosporidium* and *Giardia* from water. Of the remaining methods, slow sand filtration and membrane filtration, the latter method demonstrated the highest and most reliable efficiency values for the removal of both types of protozoans (a minimum of 2-log for both *Cryptosporidium* and *Giardia*).

39. **A.** According to Figure 1, a clear and direct positive relationship is demonstrated between the efficiency of the turbidity removal and the efficiency of the *Cryptosporidium* oocyst (i.e., as the efficiency of the turbidity removal increases steadily, the efficiency of the removal of *Cryptosporidium* also increases steadily).

40. **H.** When summarizing the data presented in Tables 1 and 2, it becomes clear that the least effective method of purification of both types of protozoans is chlorination. The lab results in Table 2 indicate that chlorination was not at all effective in removing *Cryptosporidium* and was unreliably effective in removing *Giardia*, and the data in Table 1 demonstrate the lowest removal rates of both *Cryptosporidium* and *Giardia* in Plant 2, where chlorination was used.

Section 5: Writing Test

Sample Scored Essays

Essay receiving a score of 3:

Alot of teachers try to make education learning-based rather than simply a process of retention and recall. In order to do this some are discarding traditional in-class testing in favor of take-home exams that allow students to process all they have learned about a topic. But on the other side, critics of the take-home exams assert that outside the classroom, the teacher has no control over testing conditions: students can use the Internet, ask parents or friends for help, or refer to other resources. Some people argue these conditions are ideal for learning. In fact, they believe this process is exactly what learning should be: a system of utilizing all available resources to create a solution. Both sides of this problem make a good case but I agree with the people who say that kids shouldn't be allowed to take tests home.

Kids can cheat if they take tests home. They can look up all the answers on the Internet. You can find everything online at some website. Sometimes when I do my homework, I can look up the answers, Then the teacher doesn't know if I know the work or if the Internet knows it. I can get 100 on a test and I still won't know the work.

I feel that teachers are not doing their jobs if they give me a take-home test. They are not checking to see that I learn what they are supposed to be teaching. How do they know if I studied? Maybe if I copied all my answers from a friend or the computer? The only way for the teacher to know for sure is if they watch me and the other students take the test in the class. They can mark the test and see if I studied enough to pass.

A test belongs in school. Teachers need to do their job and give the tests so they can watch the class take it. Take home tests are just a way to make it easy for kids to cheat. They can't be a good way to give grades to kids.

Explanation of score of 3:

This essay shows some understanding of the task, but lacks the development characteristic of higher-scoring essays. The first paragraph is almost entirely copied from the prompt, but the writer does take a position at the end of the paragraph (*I agree with the people who say that kids shouldn't be allowed to take tests home*). The writer then presents some supporting evidence, but it is repetitious and somewhat general (*Kids can cheat if they take tests home. They can look up all the answers on the Internet*). The supporting detail is a brief personal note (*Sometimes when I do my homework, I can look up the answers*) without any acknowledgment of a counter-argument. Transitions, when used, are very simple (*Then the teacher doesn't know …*). The writer's language shows a basic control with little sentence variety, occasional spelling errors (*alot*) and sentence structure errors (*Maybe if I copied all my answers from a friend or the computer?*). While this essay is weak, it does demonstrate developing skill in responding to the prompt.

Essay receiving a score of 5:

Nobody likes tests, but they are a factor in every student's education. Sometimes starting as early as first grade, testing is a big part of school life. Kids have to take quizzes, mid-terms, and finals every year of their schooling. Some educators are advocating take-home tests to save class time and to give kids a chance to spend more time working out problems. This might sound like a reliable plan, but testing is as much a part of life as reading and writing. People face some kind of tests throughout their lives, driver's tests, certification tests, civil service tests. I think take-home tests are unreliable and give students a license to use help to find answers. Testing should be done in the classroom where the teacher has control over the conditions.

It may be less stressful to take a test at home, but are you really preparing kids for real life if you let them work at a slow place and take breaks whenever they want? Let's face it, that's what kids do on take-home tests. More importantly, a teacher has no way of knowing how much the student actually knows and how much he looked up or asked other people. Some people may argue that a teacher can write a test so that kids can't look up answers, but there is nothing that you can't find on the Internet. There are even whole essays on almost every topic from Shakespeare to the Causes of the Civil War available online. Teachers won't even know if the work is the students or something he bought online.

It is also not fair to kids to take away the experience of taking a test under testing conditions. Life is filled with tests of every kind. The more experience you have with performing under stressful conditions, the more you will be able to handle pressure. If a high school kid never faces the pressure of a final exam, how will they be ready to face the pressure of a high-powered job? Would you want a surgeon to operate on you who had taken all his medical tests at home? This may be an exaggeration, but it still is a valid example. Handling stressful challenges is a big part of life and testing is good practice.

I am not saying that teachers should never give students assignments to take home and complete. Essays and papers should be done at home (with teachers checking for plagerism), but students should be required to perform in a controlled situation. It is important for teachers to know for sure what each student has learned. Only then can they move on knowing that students have mastered the material.

Explanation of score of 5:

This effective essay shows a clear understanding of the prompt, takes a position (*Testing should be done in the classroom where the teacher has control over the conditions*) and provides context for discussion (*People face some kind of tests throughout their lives, driver's tests, certification tests, civil service tests*). The writer acknowledges the counter-argument (*It may be less stressful to take a test at home*) but doesn't fully discuss it. The development of ideas is logical with examples given to support generalizations (*there is nothing that you can't find on the Internet. There are even whole essays on almost every topic from Shakespeare to the Causes of the Civil War available online*). The writing is competent with a few errors (misspelling of *plagiarism,* pronoun agreement: *a high school kid … they*). This essay fulfills the requirements of the task, just not as insightfully or as eloquently as the essays that receive a score of 6.

Essay receiving a score of 6:

Educators are always attempting to make learning more meaningful to students. To evaluate the success of these attempts, students are often tested to death. In fact, so much valuable class instruction time is taken up by testing that teachers are hard-pressed to complete the curriculum. One solution to this academic dilemma is to have students evaluated by "take-home" tests. These tests would allow teachers to assess student progress without utilizing irreplaceable class time.

Of course, some will argue that "take-home" tests are not accurate measures, for with no supervision, students will have access to the Internet, can ask for help from their older siblings or their parents, and can work with their fellow students to complete the tasks. But, if the test is constructed carefully, are these aids actually detrimental to learning? In the real world—whether in the workplace or in academia—people often work in teams to complete projects. Thus, a group effort to complete an assignment could be an authentic assessment.

Another advantage to take-home tests is that they reduce the stress and anxiety that plague many students. Poor test-takers may experience "brain-freeze," a situation that occurs when the brain suddenly refuses to recall all the information that the student had studied for hours. At home the previous night, the studier had the Krebs Cycle down pat; the day of the test, his brain refuses to function. Furthermore, some students just need more time than one class period to complete a test. Not everyone's brain processes at the same pace.

Yet another consideration is that so much of the work students do is research-based. In our information-loaded society, students can't know everything; they mostly need to know where to look to find answers. Testing using questions that require evidence for support would provide teachers with a way of evaluating their students' abilities to find acceptable evidence and to use that evidence to support their conclusions. In addition, at home test-takers have the time to develop their arguments and polish their responses.

Clearly, teachers have to design tests to be done at home very carefully: they have to go beyond simple recall of facts and require thoughtful responses. But, education is moving toward developing more critical thinking skills, more evidence-based answers, and more reading and writing. What better way to encourage this movement than to have students spend more time researching subjects and preparing logical arguments in support of their positions rather than memorizing facts to spew back on multiple-choice tests.

Explanation of score of 6:

This outstanding essay takes a clear position on the issue (*These tests would allow teachers to assess student progress without utilizing irreplaceable class time*) and provides context for the issue (*so much valuable class instruction time is taken up by testing that teachers are hard-pressed to complete the curriculum*). The writer anticipates several of the counter-arguments (*some will argue that "take-home" tests are not accurate measures, for with no supervision, students will have access to the Internet, can ask for help from their older siblings or their parents, and can work with their fellow students to complete the tasks*) and addresses them with a logical question (*if the test is constructed carefully, are these aids actually detrimental to learning?*) that demonstrates understanding of the larger issues at stake here, namely good educational practices. Development is thorough and logical, providing effective support for the writer's position. The essay is well organized with effectively placed transitions (*another, furthermore, yet another, in addition*). The writing shows an excellent command of language (*In the real world—whether in the workplace or in academia—people often work in teams to complete projects*) and thoughtful understanding of both the practical issues (*teachers are hard-pressed to complete the curriculum*) and the philosophical issues (*education is moving toward developing more critical thinking skills, more evidence-based answers, and more reading and writing*). This insightful essay fits the criteria for a grade of 6.

Scoring Worksheets

Sections 1–4

English Test

Number Correct (Raw Score)

Usage/Mechanics (UM) Subscore Area _____ (40)

Rhetorical Skills (RH) Subscore Area _____ (35)

Total Number Correct for English Test (UM + RH) _____ (75)

Mathematics Test

Number Correct (Raw Score)

Pre-Algebra/Elementary Algebra (EA) Subscore Area _____ (24)

Intermediate Algebra/Coordinate Geometry (AG) Subscore Area _____ (17)

Plane Geometry/Trigonometry (GT) Subscore Area _____ (19)

Total Number Correct for Math Test (EA + AG + GT) _____ (60)

Reading Test

Number Correct (Raw Score)

Social Studies/Sciences (SS) Subscore Area _____ (20)

Arts/Literature (AL) Subscore Area _____ (20)

Total Number Correct for Reading Test (SS + AL) _____ (40)

Science Test

Number Correct (Raw Score)

Data Representation (DR) Subscore Area _____ (15)

Research Summaries (RS) Subscore Area _____ (18)

Conflicting Viewpoints (CV) Subscore Area _____ (7)

Total Number Correct for Science Test (DR + RS + CV) _____ (40)

Test	Raw Score	Scale Score
English		
Mathematics		
Reading		
Science		
Sum of Scale Scores (English + Math + Reading + Science)		
Composite Score (sum ÷ 4)		

		Raw Score Conversions			
		Raw Scores			
Scale score	Section 1: English Test	Section 2: Mathematics Test	Section 3: Reading Test	Section 4: Science Test	Scale score
36	75	60	40	40	36
35	74	59	38–39	—	35
34	73	58	37	39	34
33	70–72	55–57	36	—	33
32	69	54	35	38	32
31	68	53	34	—	31
30	67	50–52	33	37	30
29	66	49	32	36	29
28	64–65	48	31	35	28
27	63	44–47	29–30	33–34	27
26	62	41–43	28	32	26
25	57–61	39–40	27	31	25
24	55–56	37–38	26	29–30	24
23	53–54	35–36	25	28	23
22	50–52	34	24	25–27	22
21	49	33	23	23–24	21
20	47–48	30–32	22	21–22	20
19	43–46	27–29	21	18–20	19
18	39–42	25–26	20	17	18
17	37–38	22–24	19	16	17
16	34–36	19–21	18	14–15	16
15	30–33	15–18	16–17	12–13	15
14	29	12–14	14–15	10–11	14
13	26–28	09–11	12–13	09	13
12	24–25	08	10–11	08	12
11	22–23	06–07	09	07	11
10	20–21	05	07–08	06	10
9	19	04	06	05	9
8	15–18	—	05	04	8
7	13–14	03	—	03	7
6	10–12	02	04	—	6
5	09	—	03	02	5
4	06–08	—	02	–	4
3	04–05	01	—	01	3
2	02–03	—	01	—	2
1	00–01	00	00	00	1

Refer to the sample essays on pages 332–334 and to the rubric given at the end of the diagnostic test (pages 67–68) to score your essay.

A. Using a Graphing Calculator

All the problems in the ACT Math Section can be done without a calculator. There are some problems, however, that can be solved easily by using a graphing calculator. Below are several illustrations of how to use a graphing calculator (TI-83 Plus) to solve some of the math questions on the Diagnostic Test.

Evaluating an Expression Involving the Imaginary Number *i* (From Diagnostic Test, Problem 30):

1. Given $i = \sqrt{-1}$, which of the following is equivalent to $2i(i^3 - 4i)$?

   A. -6
   B. $-6i^2$
   C. 6
   D. 7
   E. 10

TI-83 Plus Solution:

(Please note that the imaginary number *i* can be found as the second function of the decimal point key located at the bottom of the calculator.)

Correct Answer: **E**

Simplifying a Trigonometric Expression (From Diagnostic Test, Problem 29):

2. If $0 < \theta < \dfrac{\pi}{2}$, which of the following is equivalent to $\dfrac{\cos\theta}{\sqrt{1-\sin^2\theta}}$?

    F. -1

    G. $-2 - \cos 2x$

    H. $2 - \sin x$

    J. $1 + \cos\theta$

    K. 1

TI-83 Plus Solution:

Set the calculator in radian mode.

Press: Y =

Enter: COS   X,T,θ,n   )   ÷   2ND   √ 1   –

(SIN   X,T,θ,n   )   )   ^ 2   )

Press: ZOOM 7

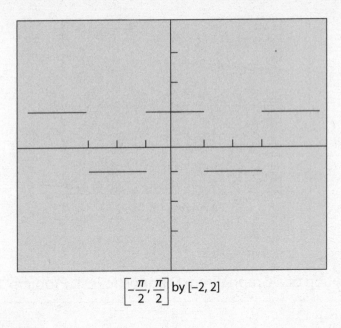

$$\left[-\frac{\pi}{2}, \frac{\pi}{2}\right] \text{ by } [-2, 2]$$

Remember that $y = \dfrac{\cos\theta}{\sqrt{1-\sin^2\theta}}$. Notice that $0 < \theta < \dfrac{\pi}{2}$, $y = 1$.

Correct Answer: **K**

Identifying an Odd or Even Function (From Diagnostic Test, Problem 22):

3. Which of the following is an odd function?

    A. $h(x) = 3x - 5$
    B. $k(x) = x^2 - 7x + 9$
    C. $p(x) = x^3 - 3$
    D. $q(x) = x^3 + 1$
    E. $f(x) = x^5 - 2x^3$

TI-83 Plus Solution:

Use the calculator to produce the graph of each equation in the five choices. The equation with a graph that has symmetry with respect to the *origin* is an odd function.

[−4.7, 4.7] by [−3.1, 3.1]

Correct Answer: **E**

Identifying an Equation of a Graph (From Diagnostic Test, Problem 10):

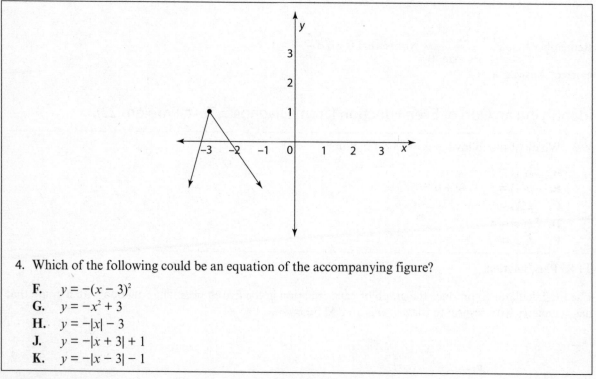

4. Which of the following could be an equation of the accompanying figure?

   F. $y = -(x - 3)^2$

   G. $y = -x^2 + 3$

   H. $y = -|x| - 3$

   J. $y = -|x + 3| + 1$

   K. $y = -|x - 3| - 1$

TI-83 Plus Solution:

Look at the graph of each equation by using the calculator. The equation whose graph matches the one in the given figure is the correct answer.

Press: | Y =

Enter: | (−) | 2ND | CATALOG

Select: ▷ abs (| ENTER

Enter: | X,T,θ,n | + | 3 |) | + | 1 | ENTER

Press: | ZOOM | 6

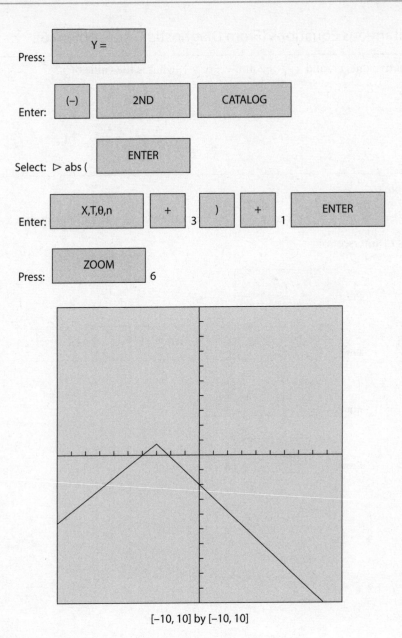

[−10, 10] by [−10, 10]

Correct Answer: **J**

Solving Simultaneous Equations (From Diagnostic Test, Problem 6):

5. If x is a negative integer, and $xy = -2$ and $y + x = 1$, what is the value of x?

   A. -2
   B. -1
   C. 0
   D. 1
   E. 2

TI-83 Plus Solution:

Write $xy = -2$ as $y = \dfrac{-2}{x}$ and $y + x = 1$ as $y = 1 - x$. Enter the two new equations into the calculator and look at the points of intersection.

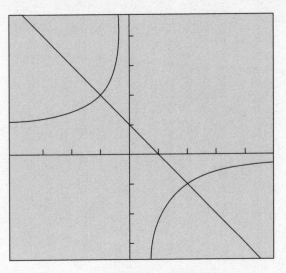

[−4.7, 4.7] by [−3.1, 3.1]

Notice that there are two intersection points $(-1,2)$ and $(2,-1)$. Since x is a negative integer, $x = -1$.

Correct Answer: **B**

B. Common Math Formulas and Theorems for the ACT

Real Numbers

- Primes
  - Prime numbers are 2, 3, 5, 7, 11, 13, ...
  - 1 is not a prime number.
  - 2 is the only even prime number.
- Zero
  - 0 is the only number that is neither positive nor negative.
  - 0 is an even number.
  - If $ab = 0$, then either $a = 0$ or $b = 0$ or both equal 0.
- Even/Odd
  - even + even = even and (even)(even) = even
  - odd + odd = even and (odd)(odd) = odd
  - even + odd = odd and (even)(odd) = even

Use substitution to determine if an algebraic expression is even or odd.

Sequences

	nth term	Sum of the first *n* terms
Arithmetic sequences	$a_n = a_1 + (n-1)d$ a_1 = first term d = common difference	$s_n = (a_1 + a_n)\left(\dfrac{n}{2}\right)$ or $s_n = \left(\dfrac{n}{2}\right)\left[2a_1 + (n-1)d\right]$
Geometric sequences	$a_n = a_1 r^{n-1}$ a_1 = first term r = common ratio	$s_n = \dfrac{a_1 - a_1(r)^n}{1-r}$

Absolute Values

The absolute value of a number is never negative. It's either positive or zero.

For example: $|-3| = 3$, $|3| = 3$, and $|0| = 0$.

- The definition of the absolute value of a number is $|x| = \begin{cases} x, & \text{if } x \geq 0 \\ -x, & \text{if } x < 0 \end{cases}$.

- There are three common types of questions involving absolute value:
  - If $|x| = a$, $a > 0$, then solve the two equations $x = a$ or $x = -a$.
  - If $|x| > a$, $a > 0$, then solve the two inequalities $x < -a$ or $x > a$.
  - If $|x| < a$, $a > 0$, then either solve the two inequalities $x > -a$ and $x < a$ or solve $-a < x < a$.

Exponents

1. $(x^a)(x^b) = x^{a+b}$ e.g., $(x^3)(x^4) = x^7$

2. $\dfrac{x^a}{x^b} = x^{a-b}$, $x \neq 0$ e.g., $\dfrac{x^{10}}{x^4} = x^6$

3. $(ax^b)^c = (a^c)(x^{bc})$ e.g., $(2x^5)^3 = (2)^3(x^5)^3 = 8x^{15}$

4. $x^0 = 1$, $x \neq 0$ e.g., $(-4)^0 = 1$ but $-4^0 = -1$

5. $x^{-n} = \dfrac{1}{x^n}$, $x \neq 0$ e.g., $3^{-2} = \dfrac{1}{3^2}$

6. $x^{\frac{a}{b}} = \left(\sqrt[b]{x}\right)^a$ or $\sqrt[b]{x^a}$ e.g., $8^{\frac{2}{3}} = \left(\sqrt[3]{8}\right)^2$ or $\sqrt[3]{8^2}$ or $= 4$
   if $\sqrt[b]{x}$ exists

Direct and Inverse Variation

- When two non-zero quantities x and y are directly proportional, then:
  - $y = kx$ or $\dfrac{y}{x} = k$ for some constant k.
  - The graph is a line whose slope is k and the y-intercept is 0.
  - If (x_1, y_1) and (x_2, y_2) are points on the graph, then $\dfrac{x_1}{y_1} = \dfrac{x_2}{y_2}$.
- When two non-zero quantities x and y are inversely proportional, then:
  - $y = \dfrac{k}{x}$ or $xy = k$ for some constant k.
  - The graph is a hyperbola.
  - If (x_1, y_1) and (x_2, y_2) are points on the graph, then $(x_1)(y_1) = (x_2)(y_2)$.

Measurement of Angles

- The sum of the measures of the three angles of a triangle is $180°$.
- The measure of an exterior angle of a triangle is equal to the sum of the measures of the two nonadjacent interior angles.
- The measure of an exterior angle of a regular polygon with n sides is $\dfrac{360}{n}$. The measure of an interior angle of a regular polygon with n sides is $\dfrac{(n-2)180}{n}$.
- If two parallel lines are cut by a transversal, then the alternate interior angles are congruent.
- If two parallel lines are cut by a transversal, then the corresponding angles are congruent.
- If two lines intersect, then the vertical angles are congruent.

Properties of Triangles

- The Triangle Inequality: $c + d > e$

  The sum of the lengths of any two sides of a triangle is always greater than the length of the third side.
- If the lengths of two sides of a triangle are unequal, the measures of the angles opposite these sides are unequal and the greater angle lies opposite the greater side. Example: $\overline{BC} > \overline{BA} \Leftrightarrow m\angle A > m\angle C$

- The Pythagorean theorem: $a^2 + b^2 = c^2$

- Special Right Triangle: 30°-60° right triangle

- Special Right Triangle: 45°-45° right triangle

Similarity

If two triangles are similar, then:

- The ratio of the *perimeters* is equal to the ratio of the lengths of any pair of corresponding line segments.
- The ratio of the *areas* is equal to the square of the ratio of the lengths of any pair of corresponding line segments.

Solids, Volumes, and Surface Areas

Shape	Volume	Surface Area
Cube	s^3	$6s^2$
Rectangular box	lwh	$2(lh + hw + lw)$
Right circular cylinder	$\pi r^2 h$	Total surface area: $2\pi r^2 + 2\pi rh$ Lateral surface area: $2\pi rh$
Sphere	$\dfrac{4}{3}\pi r^3$	$4\pi r^2$

Properties of Circles

Given a circle O with radius r and diameter d:

- Circumference: $C = 2\pi r$ or $C = \pi d$
- Area: $A = \pi r^2$

- The length of an arc: $\dfrac{m\overset{\frown}{AB}}{2\pi r} = \dfrac{m\angle AOB}{360}$

- The area of a sector: $\dfrac{\text{area of sector } AOB}{\pi r^2} = \dfrac{m\angle AOB}{360}$

Coordinate Geometry

Given $A(x_1, y_1)$ and $B(x_2, y_2)$:

- The midpoint of $\overline{AB}$: $\left(\dfrac{x_1 + x_2}{2}, \dfrac{y_1 + y_2}{2}\right)$. Think of a midpoint as the "average."
- The distance between A and B (the length of $\overline{AB}$): $d_{\overline{AB}} = \sqrt{(x_2 - x_1)^2 + (y_2 - y_1)^2}$.
- The slope of $\overline{AB}$: $m_{\overline{AB}} = \dfrac{y_2 - y_1}{x_2 - x_1}$.

Slopes and Lines

- The slope of the line through the points (x_1, y_1) and (x_2, y_2) is $\dfrac{y_2 - y_1}{x_2 - x_1}$. The slope of a line written in $y = mx + b$ form is m, e.g., the slope of the line $y = 3x - 2$ is 3.
- If two lines are parallel, their slopes are equal.
- If two lines are perpendicular, their slopes are negative reciprocals and the product of their slopes is -1.

Counting Principle

- If one activity can occur in m ways, and then following that a second activity can occur in n ways, then the number of ways both activities can occur in that order is mn.
- **Permutations**
  The number of permutations of n things taken r at a time is $_nP_r = \dfrac{n!}{(n-r!)}$. (Order matters.)
- **Combinations**
  The number of combinations of n things taken r at a time is $_nC_r = \dfrac{_nP_r}{r!}$. (Order *does not* matter.)

Probability

- Probability that an event A will occur is $P(A) = \dfrac{\text{number of ways event } A \text{ can occur}}{\text{total number of possible ways}}$.
- Probability that event A will occur is $0 \le P(A) \le 1$.
- Probability that event A will not occur is $P(\text{not } A) = 1 - P(A)$.

The probability that event A or event B will occur is $P(A \cup B) = P(A) + P(B) - P(A \cap B)$.

Mean, Median, and Mode

- The **mean** of a set of numbers or algebraic expressions is the average of the set. For example:
  - The average of 5, 6, and 10 is $\dfrac{5+6+10}{3}$ or 7.
  - The average of $x + 8$ and $5x - 4$ is $\dfrac{x+8+5x-4}{2}$ or $3x + 2$.
- The **median** of an ordered list of numbers is the middle value. For example:
  - The median of 2, 6, 10, 11, 14 is 10.
  - The median of 2, 6, 8, 20 is $\dfrac{6+8}{2}$ or 7.
- The **mode** of a list of numbers is the number that appears most often. For example:
  - The mode of 2, 3, 5, 5, 5, 6, 6, 8 is 5.
  - The mode of 2, 3, 6, 6, 8, 8, 12, 15 is 6 and 8.

Quadratic Formula

- $ax^2 + bx + c = 0$, $a \ne 0$: $x = \dfrac{-b \pm \sqrt{b^2 - 4ac}}{2a}$

Equation of a Parabola

- $y = ax^2 + bx + c$, $a \ne 0$: axis of symmetry $x = \dfrac{-b}{2a}$

Equation of a Circle

- $(x - h)^2 + (y - k)^2 = r^2$ with center of circle (h,k), radius r

Trigonometric Functions

The mnemonic SOHCAHTOA, written as $S\dfrac{o}{h}C\dfrac{a}{h}T\dfrac{o}{a}$, may be helpful in remembering some of the trigonometric ratios.

$\sin A = \dfrac{\text{opp}}{\text{hyp}}$ 　　　 $\cos A = \dfrac{\text{adj}}{\text{hyp}}$ 　　　 $\tan A = \dfrac{\text{opp}}{\text{adj}}$

$\csc A = \dfrac{\text{hyp}}{\text{opp}}$ 　　　 $\sec A = \dfrac{\text{hyp}}{\text{adj}}$ 　　　 $\cot A = \dfrac{\text{adj}}{\text{opp}}$

Pythagorean Identities

- $\cos^2\theta + \sin^2\theta = 1$
- $1 + \tan^2\theta = \sec^2\theta$
- $\cot^2\theta + 1 = \csc^2\theta$

Quotient Identities

- $\tan\theta = \dfrac{\sin\theta}{\cos\theta}, \ \cot\theta = \dfrac{\cos\theta}{\sin\theta}$

Reciprocal Identities

- $\csc\theta = \dfrac{1}{\sin\theta}, \ \sec\theta = \dfrac{1}{\cos\theta}, \ \cot\theta = \dfrac{1}{\tan\theta}$

Functions of the Sum of Two Angles

- $\sin(A + B) = \sin A\cos B + \cos A\sin B$
- $\cos(A + B) = \cos A\cos B - \sin A\sin B$

Functions of the Double Angle

- $\sin 2A = 2\sin A\cos A$
- $\cos 2A = \cos^2 A - \sin^2 A$
- $\cos 2A = 2\cos^2 A - 1$
- $\cos 2A = 1 - 2\sin^2 A$

Law of Sines

- $\dfrac{a}{\sin A} = \dfrac{b}{\sin B} = \dfrac{c}{\sin C}$

Law of Cosines

- $c^2 = a^2 + b^2 - 2ab\cos C$
- $b^2 = a^2 + c^2 - 2ac\cos B$
- $a^2 = b^2 + c^2 - 2bc\cos A$

Properties of Logarithms

- $\log_a b = c \Leftrightarrow a^c = b$ with a and $b > 0$
- $\log_c(ab) = \log_c a + \log_c b$ with a, b, and $c > 0$
- $\log_c \dfrac{a}{b} = \log_c a - \log_c b$ with a, b, and $c > 0$
- $\log_c(a^b) = b\log_c a$ with a and $c > 0$
- $\log_c b = \dfrac{\log_a b}{\log_a c}$ Change of Base Formula with a, b, and $c > 0$

Graphs of Sine and Cosine

- $y = a\sin(bx - c) + d$ and $y = a\cos(bx - c) + d$
- Amplitude $= |a|$
- Frequency $= b$
- Period $= \dfrac{2\pi}{b}$
- Midline $y = d$
- Phase shift $= \dfrac{c}{b}$
- Left endpoint $x = \dfrac{c}{b}$
- Right endpoint $x = \dfrac{c}{b} + \dfrac{2\pi}{b}$